NEW BABYLONIANS

NEW BABYLONIANS
A History of Jews in Modern Iraq

Orit Bashkin

STANFORD UNIVERSITY PRESS
STANFORD, CALIFORNIA

Stanford University Press
Stanford, California

©2012 by the Board of Trustees of the Leland Stanford Junior University. All rights reserved.

No part of this book may be reproduced or transmitted in any form or by any means, electronic or mechanical, including photocopying and recording, or in any information storage or retrieval system without the prior written permission of Stanford University Press.

Printed in the United States of America on acid-free, archival-quality paper

Library of Congress Cataloging-in-Publication Data

Bashkin, Orit, 1974- author.
 New Babylonians : a history of Jews in modern Iraq / Orit Bashkin.
       pages cm
 Includes bibliographical references and index.
 ISBN 978-0-8047-7874-9 (cloth : alk. paper)--ISBN 978-0-8047-7875-6 (pbk. : alk. paper)
 1. Jews--Iraq--History--20th century. 2. Jews--Iraq--Identity. 3. Jews--Iraq--Intellectual life. 4. Iraq--Ethnic relations--History--20th century. 5. Iraq--History--Hashemite Kingdom, 1921-1958. I. Title.
      DS135.I7B3745 2012

305.892'4056709041--dc23   2012007609

Typeset by Bruce Lundquist in 11/15 Bembo

In memory of Mina and Ze'ev [Velvel] Bashkin

Contents

Acknowledgments ix

Abbreviations xi

1. Brothers and Others: Iraqi Identity and Arab Jewishness   1

2. Nationalism and Patriotism: Visions of the Nation   15

3. The Effendia: Questions of Secularism and Judaism   58

4. Friends, Neighbors, and Enemies:
Fascism, Anti-Semitism, and the Farhud   100

5. Red Baghdad: Iraqi Jews and the ICP, 1941–51   141

6. An End? Iraqi Jews and the Iraqi State, 1946–51   183

Conclusions   229

Notes   241

Bibliography   283

Index   297

Acknowledgments

Man 'alamani harfan . . .

I wish to thank friends, colleagues, and family members who helped me while writing this book. I am grateful, and extremely proud, that four prominent scholars read this book: Sasson Somekh, Dina Rizk Khoury, Peter Wien, and Rashid I. Khalidi. Their thoughtful works informed the ways in which I think about nationalism and modernity, and I feel truly privileged to have them comment on my work. I also wish to express my gratitude to my friend and mentor, Israel Gershoni, a constant source of inspiration and support.

I deeply thank my friends and colleagues at the University of Chicago: Tahera Qutbuddin, Holly Shissler, Cornell Fleischer, McGuire Gibson, Kay Heikkinen, Theo van Den Hout, Wadad Kadi, Farouk Mustafa, Waiel Hindo, Leora Auslander, Noha Forster, Rusty Rook, Basil Salem, Tolga Cora, Cihangir Gundogdu, Rana Barakat, Erol Ulker, Joe Yackley, and Basima Bazargan. In particular, I am grateful to Frank Lewis and Fred Donner, for their advice, for their innovative ideas, and for being such fantastic colleagues over the past years. Parts of this book were written at the Franke Institute for the Humanities at the University of Chicago. The leadership of Jim Chandler, the perceptive commentary by my fellows, Rebecca Hasselbach in particular, and the kind assistance of Margot Browning and Harriette Moody helped making this a better a work. I also wish to express my thanks to the Dean of Humanities, Martha Roth.

I am grateful to dear friends and colleagues whose insightful commentary I very much appreciated over the years: Didier Monciaud, Hanan Hammad, Marilyn Booth, Hala Fattah, Leyla Dakhli, Sami Zubaida, Eve Troutt Powell,

Joel Beinin, Geraldine Chatelard, Keith Watenpaugh, and Ami Ayalon. I also wish to express my deepest gratitude to Daniel McNaughton, Andrew Frisardi, Mariana Raykov, and to Kate Wahl, the best editor an author could wish for.

I was privileged to work with the dedicated staff in the library of the Babylonian Jewry Heritage Center in Or Yehuda (Israel). A special word of appreciation is due to the late Yerahmiel Assa, as well as to Menashe Somekh and Moshe Hakham who were gracious enough to converse with me at length about their experiences in Iraq of the 1940s and shaped many directions which this book has taken.

Ovadia Ezra was always there for me, as were Youval Rotman and Kobi Auslander. I have no idea what I would have done without my dear friends Arnika Fuhrmann, Lucy Pick, and Persis Berlekamp whose understanding, talents, humor, and brilliance were so encouraging, at every step of the way.

Finally, I thank my wonderful parents, Yossi and Rachel Bashkin, for their love, support, guidance, and their many meaningful contributions to this book, and to my life.

It is a source of great remorse that my friend Oded Pilavsky could not see this book; it now seems as if the chapter on the communists was written especially for him. I dedicate this book to the memory of my beloved grandparents, Mina and Ze'ev Bashkin. I do miss them very much and am grateful for the many invaluable lessons they have taught me.

Abbreviations

AIR Records created or inherited by the Air Ministry, the Royal Air Force, and related bodies.

CO Records of the Colonial Office, Commonwealth and Foreign and Commonwealth Offices, Empire Marketing Board, and related bodies, National Archives, London.

FO Records created and inherited by the Foreign Office, National Archives, London.

MS Al-Shurta al-'amma, *Mawsu'a siriyya khassa bi'l hizb al-shuyu'i al-'iraqi*. 3 vols. Baghdad: Matba'at mudiriyyat al-tahqiqat al-jina'iyya, 1949. Numbers after abbreviations indicate volume numbers: *MS*, 1 for volume 1, *MS*, 2 for volume 2, and *MS*, 3 for volume 3.

MZH Mordechai Bibi, *Ha-Mahteret ha-zionit ha-haluzit be-'iraq*. 4 vols. Jerusalem: Yad Ben-Tzvi, 1988. An edited and annotated collection of documents.

OYA Or Yehuda Archive, Merkaz Moreshet Yahadut Bavel, Museum for the History of Babylonian Jewry, Or Yehuda.

S Jewish Agency, Central Zionist Archive, Jerusalem.

WO War Office. Record created or inherited by the War Office, Armed Forces, Judge Advocate General, and related bodies.

YS Yad Va-Shem, Oriental, Holocaust Museum, Jerusalem.

NEW BABYLONIANS

I

BROTHERS AND OTHERS
Iraqi Identity and Arab Jewishness

Though I take my faith from the religion of Moses,
I live under the protection of Muhammad's religion,
I take refuge in the tolerance of Islam,
And my inspiration is the sublime language of the Qur'an,
I love of the nation of Muhammad,
Although I worship Moses,
I shall remain as loyal as al-Samaw'al,
Whether miserable or blissful in my beloved Baghdad.[1]

This poem, written in Arabic by Jewish Iraqi poet Anwar Sha'ul (b. 1904), references al-Samaw'al ibn 'Adiya, a celebrated pre-Islamic Jewish poet. The modern Jewish poet evoked the memory of the medieval Arab Jewish bard in order to highlight his own loyalty to Arab culture, his admiration of the Arabic language, and his desire to be part of this culture. This poem, I believe, reflects many of the cultural and political choices adopted by Iraqi Jews in the twentieth century. Following Sha'ul's contemplations on the nature of Arab, Iraqi, and Jewish identities, I explore the writings of modern Iraqi Jews, including their perceptions of patriotism, secularism, and communism. The story I shall tell ends with the tragic departure of some 100,000 Jews from Iraq in the years 1949–51, a country they had considered a homeland for many years. This story, however, will also focus on Jewish hopes for a democratic Iraqi state and a pluralistic Arab Jewish culture.

. . .

Iraq, the political entity we know today, was officially formed as a state in 1921. Its king, Faysal I, played a dominant role in the formation of a constitutional monarchy, as Great Britain, based on a mandate from the League of Nations, oversaw Iraq's process toward independence. After gaining official independence in 1932, Iraq witnessed a wave of radicalization, marked by intense anticolonial and nationalist activities in the public sphere, and two military coups, in 1936 and 1941. During the 1940s, a new, radical intelligentsia emerged that was more accepting toward socialist and communist organizations. All these processes—namely, state building, the anticolonial struggle, and the opposition to the state—shaped the ways in which Iraqi Jews defined their identities and their approaches to the Iraqi state and the Arab nation.

During the monarchic period, some Iraqi Jewish intellectuals began calling themselves Arab Jews. This is a rather extraordinary case, as Jews not only considered themselves citizens of the new nation of Iraq, but also adopted a new Arab ethnicity. This term, however, could be employed to describe many Jews who spoke Arabic, lived in an Arab country (Iraq), and saw this country as their homeland. Thus, when using the term *Arab Jews* in this book I mean not only the writers who referred to themselves as such, but also the Jews who, while not identifying themselves as Arab Jews, practiced what I call Arab Jewishness, in that they wrote in Arabic, read Arabic texts, interacted with fellow Muslim and Christian Arabs, and enjoyed Arab cinema, music, and theater.

Rogers Brubaker, who has studied the processes by which heterogeneous individuals come to think of themselves as ethnic groups and nations, argues that these categories are relational and dynamic. To Brubaker, *nation* and *ethnicity* are practical categories, cultural idioms, institutional forms, and political projects which are understood within social, political, cultural, and psychological contexts. He thus suggests that scholars consider the process of ethnicization rather than utilize the fixed category of ethnicity.[2] In the Jewish

Iraqi context, a minority community sought to forge a relationship with the cultural and historical framework of the Arab majority community by claiming Arab ethnicity as its own. In fact, three interrelated processes of ethnicization were at work. The first form took place at the level of the state, as Arab Muslim elites debated the categories of Arabness and Iraqiness; the second involved Iraqi Jews themselves and their conceptualizations of the Arab nation and the Iraqi homeland; and the third was the ethnicization of Iraqi Jews by Iraqi national elites (Sunnis, Shi'is, and Christians). Iraqi Jews were thus represented as "Iraqis," "citizens," "Iraqis of the Jewish faith," "Arab Jews," "Zionists," and "people of the book," depending on the sociopolitical and sociocultural orientation of those who described them.

The appropriation of Arab nationalism by Iraqi Jewish intellectuals meant that Jews were orienting themselves to new spatial forms (the nation), and that Iraqi Jews came to think differently about time, since Jewish writers were affected by Arab national periodizations and narratives of decline and revival. They hailed, for example, the religious harmony between Jews and Muslims under the golden ages of the Abbasid and the Ottoman empires, and bemoaned the decline of Iraq after the Mongol conquest (1258). Jewish intellectuals, moreover, were fascinated by Arab history and Arab culture and advanced the thesis that Arab and Islamic history testified to their cultural affiliations with the Arab community. Subsequently, Iraqi Jews sought to affect Arab national discourses from within by accepting certain key components of Arab nationalism, imbuing them with tolerant and inclusive meanings, and working in tandem with other Iraqis who held similar views. Furthermore, when Jewish intellectuals addressed matters such as the status of Jewish women and the need to reform Jewish tradition as well as to alter the structure of the Iraq's rabbinical leadership, they turned to Arab Muslim reformers who were grappling with similar dilemmas in their own communities. Jewish intellectuals thus stimulated an ongoing dialogue between Muslims and Jews and bolstered the understanding that they had shared concerns in the face of Western modernity, as both Muslims and Jews wondered what it meant to be modern and non-European and tried to come to terms with European Christian dominance.

The Arab component in Iraqi Jewish identity encompassed linguistic and literary elements. In her essay "Nationalism and the Imagination," literary critic Gayatri Spivak attempts to locate the moment when love of the mother tongue becomes integrated into exclusionist nationalism. She asks:

> Why is the first learned language so important? Because it teaches every human infant to negotiate the public and the private outside of the public-private divide as we have inherited it from the legacy of European history. Language has a history; it is public before our births and will continue so after our deaths. Yet every infant invents it and makes it the most private thing, touching the very interiority of the heart. On a more superficial level it is this underived private that nationalism appropriates.[3]

To Spivak, the promotion of multilingualism ("recognizing that there are many first languages") democracy, comparative criticism, and pluralism means undoing this nationalist appropriation. Similarly, Iraqi Jews grew up speaking and reading in Arabic. Iraqi Jewish nationalists have certainly appropriated the Arabic language in order to show that they were an integral part of the Arab nation. But their love of Arabic should not be conceptualized only within a historical moment when their Arabic mother tongue became the business of the nation-state; it should be reconstructed in relation to daily speech, reading practices, neighborly relations, and friendships with Arab Muslims and Christians, which have shaped the lives of many of Jews and affected their hopes and dreams.

Arab Jewishness was not the only relevant form of identity for Iraqi Jews. During the nineteenth century, they had come to identify themselves as Ottoman subjects; their elites were eager to learn Turkish, and some Iraqi Jews were tapped for high-ranking posts created in the new imperial order.[4] With the establishment of the state, many Jewish writers identified themselves as Iraqi patriots, underlining the fact that Iraq, and not the entire Arab nation, was their homeland. Iraq, a land whose history dated back to the glorious days of ancient Babylon, and whose unique culture and geography molded a specific form of nationalism, was therefore at the core of many Jewish national narratives. The recognition that Iraqi Jewry belonged to the East was likewise of extreme importance. On the one hand, the tensions that Iraqi Jewish intellectuals grappled with regarding the need to modernize the community within the framework of the nation-state, the genres with which they expressed their concerns (the newspaper article, the short story, the modernist poem), and the places in which they discussed such concerns (the café, the literary salon, the communist cell, and the school), all constitute profound parallels between European Jews and Iraqi Jews.[5] The Jews of Iraq themselves attempted to accommodate their histories, and their ideas about nationhood, subjectivity, and selfhood, into a universal narrative that evoked the concepts of civilization, progress, and sovereignty, modeled after European ideals. On the other hand, Iraqi Jewish intellectuals emphasized the differences between themselves and Western Jewry. They contended that Iraqi Jews and Iraqi Muslims and Christians shared an internal domain of Eastern authenticity which included motifs from Semitic, Islamic, and Arab cultures.[6] This shared Eastern domain was located outside, and often constructed in opposition to, European colonialism.

Iraqi Jews debated not only their identities as Iraqis and Arabs, but also the very meaning of being Jewish within an increasingly secularizing milieu. They saw the shift from a religious to a nonreligious society as a step toward the goal of achieving modernity, which Talal Asad defined as the undertaking of projects aimed at institutionalizing several principles (constitutionalism, democracy, human rights, and civil equality), and the employing of technologies of production, warfare, travel, entertainment, and medicine to generate new experiences of space and time.[7] Partha Chatterjee has shown that secularization was not simply the onward march of rationality, untainted of coercion and power struggles, but rather an effort carried out unilaterally by national elites in order to define and classify the identity of religious minorities.[8] Similarly, in Iraq, secularism was often seen by the state's Arab Sunni elites as a means to combat sectarianism. Secularism was tied to political stability, national unity, and Westernization, although the very same elites that promoted secularization took great care not to upend the political hegemony of the Arab Sunnis and their supporters (landed and tribal elites in particular). In Iraq, then, liberty was practiced without equality, as the state permitted freedom of consciousness and religious practice (the idea of liberty), yet rejected the idea of equality in that it privileged one ethnoreligious group over all others. For Jewish intellectuals, moreover, the discussions about secularism related not only to a vision of a secular democratic state but to the community's internal concerns regarding gender and family relationships, communal worship, morality, and privacy.

Zionism did not play a major role in the debates about Iraqi Jewish identity before 1947. What determined the differences between the many kinds of Arab Jews who lived in Iraq was not how they felt about Zionism—most rejected it—but rather how they defined their relationship to the Iraqi state. In the early 1920s a generation of educated Jews hoped that the newly established Iraqi state would materialize their hopes for integration and citizenship rights. Because of their excellent bilingual education, Jewish urban elites were able to gain employment in the bureaucracy, while others benefited from the economy that emerged in the interwar period, working as lawyers, administrators, bankers, and merchants. These Jews very much supported the state, and felt that citizenship and democratic rights could, and should, be achieved by working within the state apparatus. In the 1940s, with the radicalization of the entire Iraqi public sphere, many young Jews turned toward the left. They critiqued the state for failing to provide social justice to most of its subjects and championed socialist, Marxist, and communist visions. They were also willing to take risks that the previous generation had shunned, namely, to join prohibited radical cells and engage in illegal activities. Significantly, liberal and capitalist Iraqi Jews, as well as radical Jewish leftists, all employed the term *Arab Jew* in their writings, yet each group excoriated the actions of the other faction as detrimental to the Iraqi Jewish community and the possibility of its integration into Iraqi Arab society. To understand these Jewish groups and the historical narratives they proposed, we should, to paraphrase Dipesh Chakrabarty's famous title, provincialize Zionism, and look into the many meanings the term Arab Jew entailed.[9]

The central approach accorded to Zionism in Jewish Iraqi history, however, colored much of its historiography. Some Arab nationalist historians identified Jewish cultural phenomena such as educational activities in Jewish schools and synagogues as a mere veneer for Zionist propaganda. Zionist historians, for their part, underlined the longing of Iraqi Jews to return to their Jewish homeland and dwelt on the violence perpetrated against the Jews, and on the subsequent activities of the Iraqi Zionist underground in the 1940s. Both types of analysis, however, decontextualized the realities of the Jewish community by projecting the realities created during and after 1948 onto the previous years.[10] Historian Nissim Kazzaz advanced the discussion of Arab Jewish relations in Iraq, arguing that Iraqi Jews had indeed desired to be fully integrated into Iraqi society, and yet the Arab nationalism of the 1930s, which integrated chauvinist and militant elements, could not countenance their vision of Iraq. The combination of support for totalitarian European regimes, sympathy for the Palestinian cause, and a nationalist discourse that privileged Arab ethnicity over a shared Arab culture, fanned the flames of anti-Jewish sentiments. In June 1941 a wave of urban riots against Baghdadi Jews, known as the Farhud, left over 170 Jews dead and turned the attention of young Iraqi Jews to Zionism. Kazzaz thus labeled the attempts at creating new modes of Iraqi Jewish nationalism as "the failure of the Iraqi orientation."[11] Nonetheless, in recent years, historians, sociologists, and literary critics have highlighted the degree of acceptance of Iraqi Jews in Iraqi society, as evidenced by their involvement in the political, cultural, and economic life of modern Iraq, and rejected the notion of "failure," which was central to Kazzaz's analysis.[12] Reuven Snir in particular has perceptively illustrated the degree to which Iraqi Jewish culture shaped, and was shaped by, literary and cultural discourses current in the Arab public sphere.[13]

New scholarly evaluation of Iraqi Arab nationalism has likewise affected the ways in which Arab Jewish nationalism is conceptualized. Iraqi Arab nationalism was typically described as being Pan-Arab and Sunni-centered, and aimed at stifling Shi'i and Kurdish protests of the political hegemony of the Sunni Arab elites (although the participation of Shi'is in Arab nationalist discourses was also recognized).[14] More recent scholarship on Iraqi nationalism, however, while acknowledging militaristic and ultranationalist elements in Iraqi political culture, has argued that liberal, democratic, and leftist voices were not drowned out. Intellectuals in the monarchic period included actors who collaborated with the state as well as artists, writers, poets, and painters who worked more independently in what was a lively public realm. Most significantly, as established by Sami Zubaida and Eric Davis, at any given moment of the period, there was not a single national narrative or a single memory of the nation, but rather competing visions advanced by the state and opposition forces. Furthermore, despite Iraq's sectarian and ethnically diverse makeup, a unique Iraqi, nonsectarian nationalism marked a sense of nationalism that differentiated the denizens of Iraq from their Arab brethren.[15] Finally, scholars of the Levant, Syria in particular, have noted the function of the urban middle classes, the effendia, in transmitting and popularizing national ideology. These Western-educated middle-class professionals have not only defined the nature of the national discourse and the anticolonial struggle, but also, and more crucially, they have delineated the meaning of Middle Eastern modernity itself.[16] However, the creation of this national civil order was not simply the outcome of their efforts; it also originated from the endeavors of subaltern and semi-subaltern groups, such as women and popular nationalists, to appropriate the national discourse and to alter its exclusionist nature.[17] In Iraq, the effendia negotiated the significations of nationalism, urbanism, and modernity and shaped the nation's historical memory by the development of memory sites and commemoration ceremonies.[18]

This new historiography on Iraqi state and society bears immense relevance to Iraqi Jewish history. While ultranationalist Iraqi elements identified Judaism with Zionism, or evoked antidemocratic and exclusionary views, the democratic elements in Iraqi society were receptive to a public Jewish presence. The vision of Iraq as a territorial unit whose history, geography, and culture united Jews and Muslims (much as it brought together Arabs and Kurds) was very attractive to Jews, and thus Jews were active in social democratic and communist circles that embraced this Iraqi ideology. The Iraqi Jews who propagated these national visions belonged mostly to the educated middle classes. By the 1920s a network of Jewish schools had substantially increased the number of educated individuals in the community. In the 1940s, with the expansion of the Iraqi educational system, Jews from the lower middle classes were able to obtain primary and secondary educations, often in schools in which the majority of the students were Muslim.[19] These processes created what might be termed as "a Jewish effendia," that is, an urban middle class that identified with, and actively propagated, the goals of Iraqi Arab nationalism.

Another important historiographical discourse concerns the responses of Arab nationalists to Nazism and fascism. A great deal of scholarly attention has been devoted to the military and intellectual elites who supported the Nazi and fascist regimes. These Arab elites saw the fascist and Nazi modernization efforts as acceptable and even worth-emulating, and felt that a strategic alliance with Germany, Italy, and Japan might help challenge the dominance of British colonialism in the region. However, as Israel Gershoni, James Jankowski, Götz Nordbruch, and Gilbert Achcar have illustrated, major segments within the Arab intelligentsia challenged their peers who espoused fascist views. Be they Egyptian liberals educated in France and bemoaning its fall in 1941; Arab nationalists troubled by the potential threat of Italian colonialism, particularly after the occupation of Ethiopia; social democrats; or communists, the profascist and pro-Nazi camp, albeit very significant, was met with meaningful resistance.[20]

In Iraq, militarist and ultranationalist groups affiliated with the state did look into cooperation with Germany and some of their voices were heard loudly and clearly in the 1941 coup.[21] However, revisionist scholarship has recently shown that the profascist contingent was sharply criticized by pro-British politicians, and by social democrats, the nascent communist party, and religious intellectuals who objected to what they saw as the deification of the state under fascism. Although the latter groups were small, they were influential in the public sphere.[22] The Jews, then, were not an isolated minority with nothing in common with their fellow Iraqis, politically speaking, and potential alliances between anti-Nazi Jews and anti-Nazi Iraqis could be formed. The media is key here, since BBC radio, the newspapers of the social-democrats, communist pamphlets, the Jewish press, and the larger Arab print market, especially in Egypt, helped to reassure Iraqi Jews that they were not alone in their abhorrence of Nazism and fascism, despite the popularity of these systems in nationalist circles.[23]

The historiography of Iraqi Jews also relates to ways in which the history of Jews in Muslim lands has been written and analyzed. This history is typically told in one of two ways: either as a model of a harmonious of coexistence, or, conversely, as a tale of perpetual persecution. Nonetheless, many scholars of Jewish Islamic history have concurred that writing the histories of Jewish communities in Muslim societies requires looking into particular contexts and unique historical circumstances. These scholars have also acknowledged that Islamic law protected Jews from the kinds of persecutions to which they were subjected in medieval Europe, and that Jewish culture—namely, theology, grammar, philosophy, and literature—thrived and was transformed in the medieval and early modern periods, as a result of its fruitful interactions with Muslim and Arab cultures. Yet alongside these ideas, an orientalist interpretation emerged, asserting that while in the premodern era Jews and Muslims enjoyed a coexistence marked by cultural reciprocity, this tradition ceased to exist in the modern period because of the inability of Arab societies to absorb democratic principles and grant citizenship rights to ethnic and religious minorities.[24]

While there is no doubt that the toxic mixture of colonialism and ethnic nationalism had devastating consequences for the Middle East's ethnic and religious minorities, it is important to note that during the first half of the twentieth century, for Iraqi Jews, as well as other non-Jewish Iraqis, the modern world symbolized a promising new beginning, and not a fatal end, to the Arab Jewish cultures of their ancestors. Thus, liberal Iraqi Jews hailed the universal significance of democracy and human rights, and praised the great achievements of the Enlightenment and the French Revolution, while radical Jewish communists argued that a class-based revolution would unavoidably integrate Jews into the state. More broadly, Jews in the modern Arab societies did not necessarily consider their religious and cultural identity to be problematic. In the Ottoman world, Jews were only one minority among many, in a multiethnic and multireligious empire. The national narratives that emerged in the newly established Arab states spoke of the emancipation of the Arab peoples from Ottoman rule and expressed their hopes for liberation from colonialism. There was therefore no point in talking about separate Jewish emancipation because the perception implicit in the dominant national narrative was that the entire Arab community was to be liberated from the bonds of the Ottoman past and the colonial present, and that Arab statehood, independence, and sovereignty would emancipate all former subjects of the empire.[25]

Furthermore, Jews in Arab lands expressed great excitement concerning the process of the Arab revival, and wished to be active participants in this process. Starting in the second half of the nineteenth century and the early years of the twentieth century, the Arabic literary and cultural renewal, or the *Nahda* (a term usually translated as "renaissance" or "revival"), was typified by the attempts of Muslim and Christian Arabs to reassess the relationship between Europe and the Arab world, to redefine the place of Islam within modern society, and to consider Western genres as vehicles of literary and cultural expression.[26] Jews internalized the modernist discourses typical of the *nahdawi* print culture.[27] Concurrently, Muslim and Christian Arab intellectuals had come to treat Jews not as "others" but rather as "brothers."[28] The pioneers of the Arab Nahda were attentive to Jewish affairs and defended the rights of European Jews. Leading Arab journals protested the persecution of Jews in Europe; they reported on pogroms and anti-Jewish activities, especially in Russia and the Balkans, and evoked the image of the Jew as an individual forced to exist under perpetual persecution. Arab intellectuals, moreover, supported Jewish emancipation in Europe, and noted favorably that Jews were granted certain citizenship rights in Britain and Germany. Yet they also recognized the domains in which this emancipation had fallen well short. In addition, many journals celebrated the harmony between Muslims, Jews, and Christians under Islamic rule, while cultural magazines like *Al-Hilal* and *Al-Muqtataf* published essays on Jewish history ancient and modern, the Jewish religion, and Hebrew and Semitic linguistics.[29]

These egalitarian positions should be seen as an attempt to expose European doublespeak, since such Arab intellectuals underlined the fact that Europe, seeking to represent itself as the beacon of justice, democracy, and modernity, was treating its own minorities in an appalling fashion. During the nineteenth century portions of the Balkans were gaining independence from Ottoman rule, and it was therefore important to position a just Ottoman-Muslim polity in pointed contrast to the case in Europe. Some of these accounts were responding to a Pan-Islamic discourse of which one element was a concern for the welfare of Muslims throughout the world, and in Europe (most notably, Russia) in particular. Calling attention to discrimination against Jews, in the very same lands where Muslims were persecuted, fitted well into this general critique of Europe. In addition, the interest in Semitic cultures, especially in the philological realm, was important to prominent Arab intellectuals. To deepen their understanding of their own cultural heritage, Arabs needed to know more about Hebrew, ancient Israel, and the connections between Semitic cultures and languages. Finally, many of the Christian intellectuals writing in these journals favored citizenship rights which were not based on religion. The critique of the mistreatment of the Jews outside the Ottoman empire thus dovetailed with the campaign to promote secularism, equality, and new notions of empire and state within the Ottoman realm.[30]

This interest in Semitic cultures was certainly not limited to the late nineteenth century. The identification of Arabs as Semites served Arab nationalism during the interwar period, and colored the writings of many nationalists. Arab nationalists took to heart the European binary opposition of Aryans and Semites, and turned it on its head. The Semites—that is, the Arabs as well as many ancient nations of the Near East—came to represent an ethnic group whose cultures formed the foundation for civilization, whose glorious leaders had ruled great empires, like Assyria and Babylon, and whose spirituality had given rise to Judaism, Christianity, and Islam.[31] This narrative counted many adherents in the Levant and in Iraq. Importantly, it allowed Jews to claim a role in the formation of the new national language, as having a great deal in common with their non-Jewish Arab brethren. Iraqi Jewish intellectuals thus made use of the Aryan-Semite dichotomy as a difference between a model of cultural integration (in the world of the Semites and the Arabs) and a one of persecution and victimization (in the non-Semitic world).

Tragically, these shared Jewish Arab and Iraq visions were silenced in the years 1948–52, when Zionism, Arab nationalism, and communism each played their part in making Iraqi Jewish identity into a "question" or a "problem." Zionist activities in Iraq had commenced in the early 1920s, but did not receive a great deal of support until the late 1940s. A minor phenomenon, Zionism attracted some adherents from among the Iraqi Jewish youth; the majority of intellectuals did not become partisans, viewing it with great suspicion. In fact, Zionist emissaries sent to Iraq in the wake of the Farhud complained bitterly that their movement received little in the way of support. After 1948, however, Zionism became a meaningful force in Jewish Iraqi life. There were more Zionist emissaries and local activists in Iraq who were able to organize small groups of young people, and became bolder in their illegal operations.[32]

In the 1920s, some bourgeois Jews had thought that Jewish settlement in Palestine could actually lead to Jewish Arab cooperation, and projected their hopes for coexistence in Iraq onto the Palestinian situation. By 1929, when it became clear that the Zionist and Palestinian national movements were headed for a drawn-out bloody conflict, Iraqi Jews were forced to choose a side. The intellectual elites came down in favor of the Palestinians, a position made crystal clear by their petitions in support of the Arab national revolt in Palestine (1936–39). The anti-Zionist outlook persisted into the 1940s.

An influential political organization, the 'Usbat mukafahat al-Sahayuniyya (League for Combating Zionism), led by Iraqi communists and made up primarily of Jewish activists, enjoyed a fair measure of popular support at the time. Combating Zionism, however, meant grappling with its key terms— "the Jewish question," "exile," and "anti-Semitism"—and forced Iraqi Jews to position themselves vis-à-vis Jewish communities in other countries. For the communists, it also meant addressing the Jewish question with respect to the proletariat, and refuting labor-Zionism's claim that it resolved both the Jewish question and the question of the Jewish proletariat.[33]

Zionism, however, did more than complicate the relationships between Iraqi Jews of various political inclinations. It also complicated the relationships between Jews and Iraqi Muslims and Christians, as Iraqi ultranationalist elements and the Iraqi state itself were unable or unwilling to draw a distinction between Judaism and Zionism. No matter how adamant Jews were in emphasizing their Iraqi identity or how vigorously their fellow Iraqis defended them in this regard, radical elements within the Iraqi nationalist elite dismissed their claims. Moreover, influential nationalist bureaucrats and intellectuals often spoke of "perilous" minority communities, ones not fully integrated into the nation, as "problems." These included, for example, Kurdish identity and tribalism, Shi'i tribalism, or independent Shi'i leaders.[34] Beginning in 1948 Jews were also singled out as a major problem, because of their suspected disloyalty to the state. To preserve national harmony and homogeneity, they had to leave. The creation of Israel as an internationally recognized, sovereign body that could negotiate with the Iraqi government about the departure of Iraqi Jews facilitated their emigration from Iraq.

The appeal of communism to Jews was the final reason that they came to be considered problematic from the standpoint of the state's elites. Prior to the end of World War II, the national elites affiliated with the state had rarely doubted the loyalty of Iraqi Jews. Even the most fanatic anti-Semites in the mid-1920s were forced to recognize that Iraqi Jews were different from their "devious" Russian and Eastern European brethren. Sherifian officers (officers who participated in the Arab Revolt) turned Iraqi politicians and other members of the political and cultural elites had welcomed Jewish involvement in the state's institutions and its nascent cultural revival. The authorities, with British encouragement, were willing to patrol Jewish neighborhoods during the Arab revolt in Palestine in order to protect Jewish citizens. The turn of some radical Jews to communism in the 1940s had the effect of turning the state against the Jewish community as a whole. In 1948, many young Jews, including Jewish communists, participated in the Wathba, a name given to a series of demonstrations against the state's pro-British policies and Iraq's failure to provide social justice to its subjects. The Wathba demonstrated to the state's elites that the communists had become a force to be reckoned with, and the state reacted in a brutal fashion by arresting communists (actual or suspected), leftists, and other radicals. Communist Jews suffered as well, although this persecution was directed against all radical, antistate voices in Iraq. Thus, in 1948–49, under the banner of the fight against Zionism and communism, the long-serving Iraqi prime minister, Nuri al-Sa'id, and other Iraqi officials moved to enact laws that discriminated against Jews. Persecutions now became the lot of the not only the radical elements within the Jewish effendia but of the Jewish community as a whole.[35] Its members began to feel that they were strongly encouraged to leave.

The following pages, however, will detail neither the interactions between the Zionist movement (and later Israel) with the Iraqi state nor the involvement of Jews in the Iraqi economy and the effects of their departure on it. This is a book about intellectual, social, and cultural histories. It seeks to analyze texts produced by Iraqi Jews and reflect on their meanings and the historical contexts that shaped the world of their authors. It likewise reflects on the many types of Arab Jews who saw Iraq as their homeland, Arabic as their language, and a shared coexistence between Iraq's various communities as their political vision. It focuses on those Jews who both rejected and feared Zionism. It tries to respect the visions of Iraqi Arab Jews and situate them in an Iraqi and Arab context, rather than labeling them as mere "failures." Reading such texts without taking into account the contexts of Arab and Iraqi nationalism and the problems with which Iraqi intellectuals of all sects and ethnicities were grappling dehistoricizes Iraqi Jewish history and does a great injustice to its rich cultural productivity and creativity.

2

NATIONALISM AND PATRIOTISM
Visions of the Nation

The noted Egyptian literary critic Zaki Mubarak taught at Baghdad's Teachers Training College (Dar al-mu'allimin al-'aliya) during the 1930s. An interested observer of Iraqi life, Mubarak was especially struck by the Arabization of Iraqi Jews and their integration into Iraqi society. A Pan-Arabist, Mubarak understood Jewish life in Iraq as emblematic of a society whose Islamic and Arab heritage had managed to Arabize its Jews to an unimaginable degree.[1] Mubarak had correctly identified what was significant and exceptional about the Jewish community in Iraq: in no other Arab country did Jews figure so prominently in the greater cultural arena. In part, this was because Iraqi Jews felt they belonged to an Arab Jewish culture, whose origins were located in a long historical process beginning in the pre-Islamic era. Yet this Arabization was also a relatively new phenomenon, which was achieved through the apparatus of the modern nation-state: the educational system, the urban public sphere, and the Iraqi and wider Arab press and literary scenes.

The stories, newspaper articles, and collections of poetry by Iraqi Jews suggest that they were aware of the fluid and constructed nature of the national culture. They could see this culture being shaped before their eyes and wished to have a hand in its creation. Yet the terminology they used, like many of their Iraqi peers, and like many other nationalists across the globe, did not involve such terms as *creation* and *construction*, but rather *discovery*, *revival*, and *renewal*. Iraqi Jews, moreover, endeavored to weave distinctly Jewish traditions into the Iraqi Arab national realm. If Iraqis imagined the period of pre-Islamic antiquity as the foundation of modern Iraq's history, Jewish intellectuals noted that Jewish prophets (who were regarded as holy Muslims as well) had lived and prophesied in Iraq and that their shrines were to be found in Iraqi territory; if Iraqis imagined Arabic as the cultural marker of their identity, Iraqi Jews began writing in Arabic in order to contribute to the new literary canon. The constructed and temporal nature of the national discourse thus assisted them in claiming a stake in the nation's history, cultural values, and sacred traditions.

The fact that Iraqi Arab nationalism was understood and practiced differently among various sectors in Iraqi society created a space in which Jews could participate as well. One broad distinction between the various visions of Iraqi Arab nationalism(s) turned on two forms of national identity: Pan-Arab (*qawmiyya*), which considered Arab culture, history, and language as markers of one's national identity, and often strove for political unity with other Arab states; and territorial-patriotic (*wataniyya*), which considered Iraqi (rather than Arab) geography, archeology, and history the key features of national identity. Neither the Pan-Arab version of Iraqi Arab nationalism nor the territorial-patriotic version were monolithic, however, as there were many variations of both.[2] This multiplicity of national narratives, moreover, rendered any consensus as to the definition of an "ethnically pure" Iraqi nation impossible. Ethnically, Iraq was divided between an Arab majority and Kurdish and Turkmen minorities, the latter groups living primarily in the north. Religiously, the country was roughly divided between a Shi'i majority (inhabiting southern and central Iraq); a substantial Sunni minority comprised of Arabs, the Kurds, and Turkmen; the Christian (of various dominations) portion of the country's population; and varied smaller religious groups. The Jews, then, were only *one* minority among many.[3] This ethno-religious makeup engendered various perceptions of Iraqi national identity. Emphasizing Arabic as the basis of nationalism meant that Jews, Christians, as well as anyone else who cared to make Arabic his speaking and writing language, could become members of the larger Arab nation. The emphasis on loyalty to the Iraqi nation-state and its landscape meant that the Kurds, the Jews, and the Turkmen, among others, could be part of the nation-state. These national narratives offered alluring cultural opportunities, and Jews made careful use of them.

The Rise of the State and Iraqi Jewish Identity

The Iraqi state was formed from three former Ottoman provinces—Baghdad, Basra, and Mosul. While the leadership of newly independent Iraq emphasized its central role in the creation of a *modern* Iraqi entity, the process of modernization and state-building was already underway. Beginning in 1831, with the reestablishment of Ottoman authority over Iraq, the reform and modernization efforts of the empire left their mark on the region, especially during Midhat Pasha's time as governor of the province of Baghdad (1869–72). During the nineteenth century, Iraq's economy, especially that of Basra, became integrated into the global market, while Baghdad emerged as the administrative, social, and cultural hub for the three provinces. Many Iraqi intellectuals, Sunnis and Shi'is alike, supported the Ottoman constitutional revolution of 1908, believing that this movement might curb the autocratic power of sovereigns and allow for greater political participation by the Arab subjects of the empire.[4]

When World War I broke out, Iraqis generally supported the Ottomans as fellow Muslims engaged in an anticolonial struggle. But as the war continued, with Iraq itself becoming an actual battlefield, and with large segments of the population suffering from hunger and especially from the burden of conscription, anti-Ottoman voices began to be heard. Consequently, some Iraqi officers in the Ottoman army defected and joined the British-sponsored Arab Revolt, which originated in the Arabian Peninsula. The Arab Revolt did not bring about Arab independence, however, as the British and the French assumed control of the Middle East following the end of the war and the defeat of the Ottomans. British rule in Iraq was challenged in 1920, when a Shi'i revolt in the southern and central regions exploded into full-fledged armed resistance that united both Shi'is and Sunnis. The British responded by implementing a form of indirect control: Iraq's government was established as a constitutional monarchy with Faysal ibn 'Abdallah as king. Faysal, one of the leaders of the Arab Revolt, was of the house of Hashim, who traced their lineage to the Prophet Muhammad—and a staunch British ally. Iraq was placed under a British mandate, accorded by the League of Nations, with the Arab Sunnis as the politically dominant group, as had been the case in the Ottoman era. King Faysal I ruled Iraq with the support of the Sherrifians, yet he did cooperate with tribal leaders, mostly Shi'is, who recognized his authority in return for their control over vast tracts of land. Under Faysal, the 1920s saw Iraq's government engaged in state-building processes: the parliament, senate, and court system were established and, most importantly, the Iraqi constitution was drawn up and ratified (1924). In addition, the state cultivated Iraqi education as a means of instilling a sense of Iraqi Arab nationalism in the youth. An independent Iraqi public sphere, represented by a modest yet significant number of newspapers, books, and journals, came into being and decreased Iraq's dependency on the print medias of Cairo, Beirut, Damascus, or Istanbul.[5]

Iraq officially gained its independence in 1932, though a treaty signed with Britain in 1930 cemented that country's political and socioeconomic influence in Iraq. Anger at this compromised independence led to the radicalization of both state and society in the 1930s. The need for the Arabs to unite in order to throw off the yoke of oppression, a slogan from the Arab Revolt, was taken up by those opposed to the British presence in Iraq and by those Iraqis who supported the Palestinian cause. With Faysal's death in 1933 and the rise to power of King Ghazi, the army became more involved in national politics. Although the 1930s witnessed the formation of the first Iraqi social-democratic party, the People (al-Ahali), and the illegal Iraqi Communist Party (ICP; al-Hizb al-shuyu'i al-'iraqi), nationalist intellectuals and bureaucrats, critical of democracy and championing a more powerful and centralized leadership, became influential in the public sphere and in political circles. Finally, in this decade the educated middle classes, the effendia, became much more active in politics, the culmination of a trend that went back to the late nineteenth century.

The low-level unrest of the 1930s did not dissipate in the following decade. On the contrary, the 1940s were marked by great instability and heightened social tensions. The mysterious death of King Ghazi in a car accident in 1939 brought to power Ghazi's son, Faysal II, a young boy who ruled under the guardianship of his uncle (who was the true representative of the monarchy at the time), Regent 'Abd al-Ilah. In April 1941, a military coup orchestrated by Rashid 'Ali al-Kaylani and his military supporters was viewed unfavorably by the British, which led to the reoccupation of Iraq, followed by a wave of mass arrests of Pan-Arab nationalists and the deportations of Palestinian, Syrian, and Egyptian Pan-Arab intellectuals and politicians from Iraq. The British allowed leftist parties, including the outlawed ICP, more freedom and thus by the end of the Second World War, the left emerged as a vital force both in politics and in intellectual circles. The left was divided into two factions, the ICP and the newly formed National Democratic Party (the NDP; al-Hizb al-watani al-dimukrati), which superseded al-Ahali.[6] By 1945, however, the radical Pan-Arab faction was able to regroup under the leadership of a party called al-Istiqlal. Despite having at its disposal revenue from the oil industry, which it used to expand Iraq's education system, increase rates of literacy, and support projects of urban development, the state suffered from an ongoing political crisis. Sherrifian power declined, strikes shut down oil refineries and factories, and the effendia grew more vocal in their demands. The radical Pan-Arab nationalists and the leftists competed for primacy in the cultural and political realms, on the one hand, yet both camps were united in their critique of the Hashemite monarchy and demands for greater civil liberties, electoral and legal reform, women's suffrage, nationalization of lands, and curbs on the power of tribal leaders. These tensions burst into flame in 1948, when the Wathba, a series of demonstrations against a proposed treaty with Britain, quickly turned into a nationwide protest against the state's unjust social policies. The demonstrations were led by the left but won the support of many progressive elements of the society. The authorities reacted to this threat with a bloody crackdown, as between one hundred and four hundred demonstrators were killed by police fire.[7]

The factors and forces that shaped the character of modern Iraq left their mark on Iraqi Jews as well. To begin with, the country's geographical divisions mirrored distinctions between three Jewish communities. The Jews of central and southern Iraq, most of whom lived in Baghdad, Basra, and Hilla, had a more cosmopolitan outlook than the isolated Jews of Kurdistan. Mosul's Jews, on the other hand, exhibited a mixture of northern and central cultural elements, as their level of education and involvement in trade were similar to that of Baghdadi and Basran Jews. The central and southern Jews, especially those who lived in Baghdad, were more educated and were directly affected by Ottoman reform efforts. During the nineteenth century, Iraqi Jewish elites spoke a local dialect of Arabic, wrote in Hebrew, Arabic, and Ottoman Turkish, and used both Hebrew and Aramaic as liturgical languages. The Jews of Kurdistan by contrast were far less educated, and among themselves spoke an Aramaic dialect containing some Arabic, Kurdish, and Turkish words, although most of them could speak some Kurdish, Turkish, and Arabic as well. This mountainous community was more agricultural in nature, with its members working as sheep shearers, shopkeepers, weavers, and goldsmiths. Their existence depended at times on collaboration with local tribal elites.[8]

The integration of Iraq into the modern economy in the nineteenth century brought new opportunities for Iraqi Jews—the Baghdadis and Basrans in particular. British trade provided the network through which they subsequently established satellite communities in Bombay, Calcutta, Shanghai, Rangoon, and Hong Kong. Affluent families from these Indian communities made financial contributions to support various synagogues and schools in Baghdad. The Indian Iraqi community also established a print industry that published books and journals in Judeo-Arabic (Arabic written in Hebrew characters) for a Baghdadi Jewish readership. In addition, Jews benefited from the constitutional, administrative, and legal reforms undertaken by the Ottomans. They were appointed to new administrative councils in the province of Baghdad and represented Iraq in the Ottoman parliament. The substantial domestic migration of Iraqis to Baghdad included Jews, whose numbers increased from 3 percent of the city's population in the beginning of the century to 35 percent at its end. The comfortable socioeconomic conditions of the city encouraged the rise of a rich rabbinical literature, as articulated in the writings of Rabbis Yosef Haim (1834–1903), 'Abdallah Somekh (1813–89), and Shelomo Bekhor Hotzin (1843–92), who promoted the adoption of modern technologies and scientific innovations by Iraqi Jews.[9] As a result of these broad historical and cultural processes, Hebrew ceased to be a solely liturgical and religious language. It took on a new role as a transregional medium for communication that allowed Baghdadi Jews to read journals published by European Jews in Berlin, Warsaw, Odessa, Mainz, and Jerusalem. Concurrently, Arabic and Ottoman Turkish were taught in Jewish schools. Rabbi Hotzin, for example, called upon members of the community to learn both Arabic and Turkish so that they can get positions in the newly founded Ottoman administration.[10] The 1908 constitutional revolution brought about further changes in the cultural practices of Iraqi Jews, in the sense that it accelerated the processes of Arabization and Turkification. In 1908, Sasun Hesqel was elected (as one of six representatives) to represent Iraq in the Ottoman parliament; he was reelected in 1912 and again in 1914. Linguistically, the revolution marks the adoption of Arabic and Turkish as the written languages of choice and the abandonment of Judeo-Arabic, as Jews began publishing newspapers in Arabic and Ottoman Turkish. Iraqi Jews, like their Muslim and Christian peers, would later on split on whether to support the revolution; for example, Sulayman 'Inbar, the editor of the prorevolutionary journal *Al-Tafakkur*, attended the Arab National Congress held in Paris in 1913.[11]

The British occupation received a mixed reaction from the Jewish community. Some demanded British citizenship in 1918 and supported British direct rule. Others supported the Ottomans until the collapse of the empire: for example, Sasun Hesqel retained his seat in the Ottoman parliament during the entire period of British direct occupation. When Iraq was formed as a constitutional monarchy, Jewish elites came to support the Hashemite option. The Iraqi constitution enshrined the principle of religious equality, and according to the new electoral law, Jews were granted a fixed number of seats in parliament. In the first Iraqi parliament, which convened in 1925, four representatives out of the total of eighty-eight were Jews, and in the second (1928–30), five representatives were Jews: two from Baghdad, two from Basra, and one from Mosul. This number rose to six in 1946. The community had one representative in the Senate during the first thirty years of its existence: from 1925 to 1932 Menahem Salih Daniel served in that capacity, followed by his son, Ezra Menahem Daniel. Sasun Hesqel became the nation's first minister of finance, while Ibrahim al-Kabir was the director general of the ministry of finance for almost twenty years. A large number of Jews gained positions in the new bureaucracy, such as the Ministries of the Treasury, Legal Affairs, and Public Works, thanks to their Western education, while merchants grew wealthy through the sale of supplies and food to the British army, banking, and the general expansion of commerce.[12]

This new Iraqi Jewish prosperity manifested itself demographically. In 1919 Iraqi Jews numbered 87,488 in a population of 2.8 million: 50,000 lived in Baghdad and 14,000 in the north. As mentioned above, Iraqi Jews joined the general migration within Iraq from provincial towns and villages to the cities. By the end of 1949, a British account estimated the number of Jews at 180,000: 90,000 lived in Baghdad, 30,000 lived in other towns, and 60,000 were listed as rural Jews.[13]

In the 1930s the Iraqi Jewish community's sense of optimism, based on the progress that had been made in the previous decade, gave way to a feeling of concern. Greater competition from educated Muslims and Christians, the prominence of the Palestinian cause in Iraqi politics and culture, and the antidemocratic voices among the state's elites alarmed the community's leaders. In response they sought to draw attention to their loyalty to the Iraqi nation and Arab nationalism and to underline their contribution to the Iraqi state. Living under a pro-German regime during the days of Rashid 'Ali al-Kaylani's coup and the subsequent Farhud profoundly altered their perceptions of Iraqi Arab nationalism. Nonetheless, during the years 1942–45, the community's socioeconomic conditions had actually improved. At end of the World War II, the community's intellectuals and middle classes were divided into three camps, one of which was the established politicians, bureaucrats, and intellectuals who still very much believed in the vitality of the state and the monarchy; the second was comprised mostly of young Jews who were radical and communist but did, like the first group, consider Iraq their homeland. Notwithstanding their belief that religious categories were of no importance in the formation of the community, they felt, like many Jewish communists before and after them, that Jewish participation in a class-based, anticolonial struggle would benefit all Iraqi Jews. The third and smallest group, the Zionists, counted its adherents primarily among the youth.

Language, Time, and the Question of Islam

The distinction between a Pan-Arab and a territorial-patriotic identity mentioned above was collapsed in the Jewish print media. Some Iraqi Jews had shown a keen interest in a unique Iraqi culture and had heeded the call to cultivate it in terms of literature and a spatialized awareness of the country as a unified whole. The Jewish intelligentsia, however, were in general eager to display their markers of Arab identity by emphasizing their fascination with and mastery of the Arabic language and underlining the correspondence between Jewish and Islamic and Arab history.

Indeed, the autobiographies written by Iraqi Jews testify to their great interest in the Islamic past of Iraq, and especially the formation of the first Arab Islamic state, and the Umayyad and Abbasid caliphates. Most commonly, however, such autobiographies convey romanticized notions about medieval Arabic literature, as writers describe their love for the rhythm and magical wording of both the Qur'an and Arabic poetry (many reference the famed poetry of Abu al-Tayyib al-Mutanabbi and Abu al-'Ala al-Ma'arri).[14] In his youth, Jewish writer Mir Basri (b. 1911) loved anything written in Arabic, "from the time of the pre-Islamic era [al-Jahiliyya] to the period of modern revival ['asr al-nahda al-haditha]. . . . What spiritual pleasure was [embodied] in the recitation of [Arabic] poetry and the reading of books of wisdom and stories! To my mind, these were not immortal writers—I saw in them teachers and friends. I imagined them alive, as if I heard their words, talked to them, gained knowledge from them, and walked with them in imaginary tours across history."[15] Interestingly, the poets whose works Basri cherished included both medieval bards and twentieth-century authors, such as the Egyptians Ahmad Shawqi and Hafiz Ibrahim and the Iraqis Jamil Sidqi al-Zahawi and Ma'ruf al-Rusafi.[16] Salman Darwish (b. 1910) summed this process: "Arabic language and culture were mixed in our blood."[17]

The Arabic publishing industry of the time helped feed this love of Arab culture. Children who could read Arabic were exposed to a world of fantasy as depicted in children's books printed in Egypt and Lebanon. These included original works in Arabic, such as those by the Egyptian writer Kamil Kilani, as well as translations of European novels such as *Arsène Lupin*, *The Three Musketeers*, *Sherlock Holmes*, and *Tarzan*. Older Jewish students were mesmerized by works of philosophy, social theory, and autobiographies: they were especially taken with the works of Taha Husayn, which reflected on what it meant to be a modern Arab intellectual. The ability to read Arabic, then, opened the gates of a new modern culture.[18] During the 1940s and early 1950s the modernist free verse movement, pioneered by Iraqi poets, found an enthusiastic audience in the Arab world. Aspiring Jewish writers, like Sasson Somekh (b. 1933), read these works and were able to attend readings, and sometimes converse with the Iraqi poets associated with this movement in cafés in Baghdad.[19]

The keen interest in Arabic is further evidenced by the fact that many Jews were active in Iraqi literary circles as journalists, poets, and short story writers. Murad Mikha'il, Anwar Sha'ul, Mir Basri, Ya'qub Balbul, Shalom Darwish, and Maliha Sehayek, were some of the Iraqi Jewish authors who wrote short stories and poems in Arabic. In the 1930s the journal *Al-Hatif* (published in al-Najaf and read mostly by Shi'is) discussed the role of Balbul (b. 1919) as a pioneer of new Iraqi prose fiction.[20] By the 1950s, the place of Sha'ul and Darwish in the first generation of Iraqi writers who had created new literary genres was generally acknowledged.[21] In addition to their literary contributions, Jews were prominent in Iraqi journalism, as writers, editors, and publishers.[22]

The first Iraqi Jewish newspaper to be published in the Arabic language, *Al-Misbah* (The Lamp), printed its inaugural edition in April 1924, beginning what would be a run of nearly five years. *Al-Misbah* published Arabic poems; it printed the works of Egyptian and Lebanese poets such as Iliya Abu Madi and Jubran Khalil Jubran as well as that of young Jewish writers, such as Murad Mikha'il, who challenged conventional neoclassical norms in their romantic poetry. *Al-Misbah* also published short stories, again a new addition to the Iraqi literary canon of the 1920s. The paper made mention of medieval Arabic writers like al-Jahiz or Ibn al-Muqaffa' and devoted much space to discussions of the features of modern Iraqi and Arab cultures. The literary talents of the paper's young writers were recognized by the noted Muslim Iraqi poet Ma'ruf al-Rusafi, who wrote to the paper to thank its writers for their contribution to the modernization of Arabic poetry.[23]

The first editor of *Al-Misbah* was the Jewish intellectual Anwar Sha'ul. The second paper that he edited was not directed at a Jewish audience, but rather at a Muslim Iraqi one. The paper, *Al-Hasid* (The Reaper), appeared for almost a decade, beginning in 1929. Although many of its writers and readers were Jews, the paper's contributors constituted the backbone of Iraq's cultural elite. Initially, *Al-Hasid* printed articles by a relatively small number of Muslim authors (albeit famous and respected ones); over time more and more Muslim writers contributed work to the paper. These Arab intellectuals included the historian 'Abbas 'Azzawi; 'Abd al-Razzak al-Sanhuri, the Egyptian legal theorist who lived in Iraq; the educator Sati' al-Husri; the short story writer Mahmud Ahmad al-Sayyid; the poets Muhammad Rida al-Shabibi, Ma'ruf al-Rusafi, and Jamil Sidqi al-Zahawi; journalists such as Rafa'il Butti; and Iraqi politicians and professors at the Teachers Training College. Upon momentous events, such as the death of a great Iraqi literary figure, *Al-Hasid* featured articles by such Egyptian luminaries as Ahmad Hasan al-Zayyat, Taha Husayn, or 'Abd al-Qadir al-Mazini.[24]

As Arab writers, Iraqi Jews followed the lead of their Iraqi peers. It was important for them to win the approval of their Arab colleagues in the Middle East and to have their works read throughout the Arab world. Sha'ul, for example, was very proud of the contacts he maintained with the Egyptian intellectuals Zaki Mubarak and Ahmad Hasan al-Zayyat and with the Lebanese poet Bishara al-Khuri.[25] Testifying to the activity of Iraqi Jewish authors in the wider Arab print media are the varied locations where their works were published. Sha'ul contributed to the Egyptian journal *Al-Risala*; Maliha Sehayek's collections of short stories were published in Cairo as well as Baghdad; Mir Basri wrote for the Egyptian journals *Al-Adib* and *Al-Katib al-Misri*; and Ibrahim Obadiah published in the Lebanese journal *Al-'Irfan*, the Tunisian journal *Al-Tharaya*, and the Egyptian journals *Al-Katib al-Misri* and *Al-Thaqaqfa*, while his poems were printed by Egyptian publishing houses. Iraqi Jewish intellectuals, as readers and writers, were thus active participants in the wider Arab universe of discourse.

With the Jewish appropriation of Arabic language as a marker of their national identity came new notions of time and space. Iraqi Jews saw themselves as Jews of the East, and correspondingly accepted the idea that the decline and rise of the Arab and Eastern nations had affected them as well. Unlike European Jews, they did not feel that the society around them progressed while they somehow remained behind. On the contrary, they argued that their culture had gone into decline with the waning of the East, and that its revival would go hand in hand with that of the East. The Arab national narrative, the Hashemite in particular, contended that the Arab world was going through a period of revival or an awakening, signified by the word *al-nahda*. This word signified not only the Arab cultural revival of the late nineteenth century, but also the great achievements of Arab nationalism and the Arab Revolt (often called "the great Arabic *nahda*," *al-nahda al-'arabiyya al-kubra*). An articulation of this politicized understanding of the Arab revival is found in the 1946 poem "In the Memory of the Great Arab Revival" ("Fi dikrat al-nahda al-'arabiyya al-kubra"), written by the Jewish court poet Ibrahim Obadiah (b. 1924). Dedicated to the Hashemite monarchy, the poem describes how the sons of Arabism (*banu al-'uruba*) were oppressed until King Faysal's father, Sherif Husayn, rescued the East and led the Arabs in a heroic battle against the Ottomans. Husayn, the father of Arabism (*abu al-'uruba*), thus deserved the credit for Iraq's new and glorious revival.[26]

Other Jewish intellectuals tried to embed Jewish and Iraqi histories within these narratives of rise and decline and, looking forward, contemplated the state of Iraq's culture following this social and political revival. Essays published in *Al-Misbah* called upon Iraqis to wake from the state of stagnation (*jumud*) that characterized the East and to adopt bilingual education and expansion of educational missions abroad.[27] *Al-Hasid* espoused this line of thinking as well. Patriotism, Sha'ul argued in one of his editorials, was the best manifestation of the Arab Nahda.[28] In an article published in honor of *'id al-fitr*, Sha'ul contended that the people of Iraq were eager for a revival (*nahda*) and that the whole world expected Iraq to recover its former glory. Though there was little evidence that Iraqis were willing to expand any effort toward this revival, the journal urged them to work toward its realization.[29] Other articles in *Al-Hasid* specified what was meant by revival: emphasis on education, a stronger sense of Iraqi patriotism, women's rights, democracy, and a revived Arab culture and literature invigorated through experimentation with old and new genres. A wide range of cultural activities were understood as serving the Arab nationalist revival. Ya'qub Balbul dedicated his first collection of short stories to all those interested in the revival of this genre in Iraqi literature and stated that his new work served the Nahda.[30]

Another Jewish journal that saw its first edition in 1929 was the short-lived *Al-Burhan*, edited by Sha'ul Haddad (b. 1909), a journalist and author of short stories. One of the newspaper's first editorials marveled at the achievements of the Nahda. The editorial dealt with the worldwide economic crisis, declaring that the people of Iraq suffer from the changing global circumstances. It went on to acknowledge that, following World War I, Iraq had experienced a great political and social revolution (*inqilab*), as that country's way of life had undergone a dramatic transformation. Iraq was now open to the light of modern civilization, and its citizens, who had once privileged the old, now asked for all that was new and modern.[31] Other editorials, however, in tune with *Al-Hasid*, expressed the concern that the Nahda marked only a superficial change in Iraqi social norms and did not indicate a true revolution. One editorial contended that the manifestations of the Nahda in Iraq were only to be found in the leisure activities of the youth: the playing of billiard, the frequenting of cafés and hotels, the consumption of alcoholic beverages, and the enjoyment of music. It went on to state that all nations were bound to progress, but that voluntary progress should be distinguished from ignited progress. A natural progress which was involuntary was destined to be much slower than a progress driven by human will. Iraqis, accordingly, should ignite their own process of awakening. Such a rapid revival (*nahda sari'a*) should be modeled after the Kemalist movement in Turkey or what was occurring in other parts of the Eastern world. This very social-Darwinist editorial ended by expressing the hope that Iraqi youth, the most crucial sector in the life of the nation (*umma*), would not remain stationary and static, since the key element of any *nahda* is motion.[32]

The views these editorials expressed were hardly revolutionary; dozens of essays published in the Iraqi and Arab press from the late nineteenth century onward had made the same points. Nevertheless, the adoption of the concept of the Nahda as central to the intellectual life of Iraqi Jews demonstrates that they had come to view their history in nonreligious terms. Thus the Iraqi Jewish revival of the modern period was not ushered in by specific events in the history of their own community. Rather, Jews saw themselves as part of the Arab community in whose cultural revival they shared and whose achievements they appreciated. While it is true Iraqi Jewish writers had been celebrating the triumph of reason and science over stagnation and conservatism since the nineteenth century,[33] it was only in the twentieth century that the use of the word *nahda* became widespread in Iraqi Jewish intellectual circles.

A significant aspect of Arab Iraqi nationalism, which made it palatable to Iraqi Jews, was its secularization of the Islamic past. Early Arab nationalists were in fact Islamic reformers, whose writings interwove Islamic and Arabist motifs. In the 1930s, Arab nationalists labored to transform Islamic historical figures into nationalist heroes, whose bravery and glorious victories exemplified modern patriotism and nationalism.[34] This made it possible for Iraqi Jews to claim Islam for themselves as a national and cultural belief system. If Islam was to be nationalized, Iraqi Jews felt they should have a hand in that process and make Islamic culture their own. They thus intertwined their history with Islamic history, arguing that the two were inseparable. Articles in *Al-Misbah*, for example, praised the Abbasid empire and Islam more generally for having granted freedom to the peoples of the book. Another narrative hailed the Ottoman empire for having provided refuge to Jews expelled from Spain in 1492.[35] Proponents of these views were appropriating a position articulated by many a Muslim reformer: that the modern concepts of tolerance and equality did not originate in modern Europe but, rather, in Islamic thought. While Europe was in the darkness of the Middle Ages, Islamic empires were cultivating religious coexistence. These narratives, however, were now imbued with a particular Jewish meaning, as it was suggested that this tolerance enabled medieval Jewish communities to flourish.[36]

The unified whole which Islam and Judaism formed, in the eyes of the Arab Jews, served as the basis for the argument that Iraqi Jews should mimic the efforts of Islamic reformers in their attempt to modernize. The latter blamed Islam's long decline into cultural rigidity on the disinterest in scientific inquiry and the refusal to recognize that Islamic sacred texts were open to reinterpretation, an analysis which Arab Jews accepted as correct. Reform-minded Islamic scholars further contended that the path to revival lay in the reinterpretation of Islamic traditions according to modern needs and the harmonization of scientific and religious knowledge.[37] This agenda was taken up by Iraqi Jews, who made references to it in their writings: the words of the Muslim reformer Muhammad 'Abduh decorated the pages of *Al-Misbah* as early as 1924. In July of the same year, articles calling for the liberation of Jewish women referenced the writings of Egyptian Muslim reformer Qasim Amin by way of conceptualizing the reform of the Arab tradition in the context of gender relations.[38]

The ways in which Islamic terminology was evoked in a Jewish context are evident in one of Anwar Sha'ul's very first essays in *Al-Hasid*, "In the name of religion," which was written at a time of intense debate in Baghdad with respect to the position of the chief rabbi. Sha'ul admitted that he was not "a religious leader" (*ra'is ruhani*), but rather a man who wished to speak truthfully and freely to those who supposedly permitted what was wrong (*munkar*) and forbade what was right (*ma'ruf*); and to those who said that they spoke in the name of religion, yet in truth were only concerned with satisfying their personal desires by utilizing the name of religion in vain. We do respect, Sha'ul asserted, men of religion who dealt with spiritual affairs, cared for humanity, and taught true religious principles. However, those individuals who made religion nothing more than a vehicle for self-satisfaction, to become wealthy, and spread discord, and those who carried holy books in their hands but had no interest in their meanings, merited only contempt and disrespect.[39] In the following issue, Sha'ul confirmed that his goal was to raise objections to the conduct of the misguided group (*al-fi'a al-dalla*) within the Jewish community, who hailed what was false (*batil*), rejected reason, and upheld blind extremism.[40]

Although Sha'ul's critique was pertinent to questions relating to the chief rabbi, his articles exposed the flaws and contradictions in religious practice on a general level. Conspicuously, the terminology used by Sha'ul is highly Islamized, as the words *misguided* (*dall*) and *false* (*batil*) reference concepts with important Qur'anic connotations. Moreover, the article's argumentation appropriated discourses from Muslim Iraqi reformers, such as the Sunni Muhammad al-Hashimi, who bemoaned the fact that the Sunni religious leadership witnessed what was wrong (*munkar*) and did nothing to prevent it.[41] Sha'ul cited the Qur'anic notion which called upon the believers to order what is good and condemn what is bad (*al-amr bi'l ma'ruf wa'l nahi 'an al-munkar*) in making his argument, while using the exact vocabulary of his reformist Muslim peers. Furthermore, following their readings of the writings of the Egyptian reformer Muhammad 'Abduh, Iraqi Muslim reformers avowed that the religious establishment understood only the literal meaning of the Qur'an and the prophetic tradition, an understanding that was devoid of true spirituality.[42] Sha'ul repeated these very same ideas in his article, and, moreover, referenced the famous poem of Ma'ruf al-Rusafi, in which the poet expresses his contempt for imams, rabbis, and priests. Thus even very local debates about the rabbinical leadership of the Jewish community were framed by Islamic terms.

As Iraqi Jews felt they were members of Islamic Iraqi society, some even dared to offer judgments concerning certain aspects of Islamic history and culture. They sensed that as insiders—that is, as Iraqi Arab citizens—they could evaluate certain traditions which they felt had corrupted the true Islamic faith. This type of critique was put forth with a great deal of sensitivity, and it is found in just a few texts, mostly in works of literature. Reuven Snir has shown how Sufi motifs as well as metaphors borrowed from religious texts colored the works of Jewish writers and poets such as Ibrahim Obadiah, Murad Mikha'il, and Anwar Sha'ul.[43] The examples put forward here, however, relate to a new genre, parody and satire, in which the two best-known writers were Ya'qub Balbul and Shalom Darwish.

Balbul's collection of short stories, *The First Ember* (*Al-Jamra al-ula*; Baghdad, 1938), reflects his interests in religiosity and culture and his willingness to tackle Islamic traditions. It received positive reviews in Iraqi, Egyptian, and Lebanese literary journals.[44] One story, "The Revolt of Ignorance" ("Thawrat al-jahl"), discusses the anxieties instigated by modern technology in traditional Iraqi society. The protagonist, Wa'il, is a simple-hearted, ignorant Bedouin who has recently settled in a village where he frequents the local coffee shop. There he is utterly mesmerized by a mysterious speaking box. As he has never seen a radio in his life, he is incapable of understanding the functions of the machine. At first he thinks that demons (*jin*) are inside, but he quickly dismisses this explanation. Strangely, the box can predict events: it announces that the government has decided to build a particular road, and this actually comes to pass within a short span of time. He wonders what the nature of the box was: "It could be magic [*sihr*], but then again, it could not. Is magic capable of composing poetry, relating the news, and reciting the Qur'an? Can magic deliver speeches about religious, ethical, and health-related issues? Not at all! . . . Could it be a Divine miracle [*mu'jiza ilahiyya*]? Perhaps it is a miracle, for it produces the Qur'an from this voiceless piece of wood and makes it speak and sing!"[45] A married man (with two wives) and father of eight children, Wa'il is unable to stop thinking about the box; he therefore decides sneak into the café at night. He is astonished by the strange sounds coming from it, to the point that he becomes convinced he is in the kingdom of demons and that actual devils (*shayatin*) are before him. Determined to fight them, he smashes the box. The story ends with Wa'il being taken by the police to the central jail for having damaged someone else's property.

Although narrated in the third person, the encounter with the radio is mediated through the tribesman's consciousness. Significantly, the word *radio* is not mentioned in the text at all. In Iraq, the migration of tribal people to Baghdad, tribal revolts in the countryside, and debates among the Baghdadi intelligentsia as to how to discipline the tribes assumed immense importance. Balbul's story conveys a point of view held by many intellectuals, that tribal violence was inextricably bound up with their ignorance. However, once disciplined and educated by urban elites, these tribesmen could be successfully integrated into society.[46] In the story, the settled Bedouin is unfamiliar with life in the village, and especially with modern technology, an unfamiliarity that leads to destruction and punishment at the hands of the state. Yet had he been properly introduced to the radio, there would have been no need to jail poor Wa'il. Noticeably, the word *revolution* signifies the potential peril of the encounter between the nation's uneducated tribal population and the state's modes of instruction. The radio does provide vital information: it gives advice regarding health and moral behavior, as well as information about government decisions. Wa'il's inability to absorb such instructions, his superstitions, and his misguided notions of religiosity, then, prevent him from enjoying the benefits of modern technology.

Most significant is the evocation of an Islamic vocabulary in order to show how Islamic religious texts are understood by the naïve Bedouin. The story focuses on the question of the origins of the mysterious voices: they might come from either a satanic-demonic source or a divine source, in which case they must be considered a religious miracle (*mu'jiza*). Qur'anic verses and Islamic traditions about the Prophet's first mission in Mecca underscore the disbelief of Muhammad's tribe in the divine source of his revelation. The Meccans, according to tradition, tended to believe that Muhammad's words were inspired by demons. The Qur'an, however, emphasizes on a number of occasions that Muhammad was neither a soothsayer nor a poet (and thus a man whose speech was inspired by demonic voices), but rather a prophet. The Qur'an, then, is not a work of magic but rather a miracle—its linguistic and thematic achievements place it above any creation by a human or demon.[47] Balbul's text makes uses of this very same language in its account of Wa'il's encounter with modern technology. Like the Prophet's tribe, Wa'il is unable to determine whether the voices of modern technology are a miracle or the deeds of demons. Moreover, the story illustrates how Wail's popular perceptions of religion adapt Qur'anic verses to modern-day reality. Balbul was familiar enough with this vocabulary to use it with parodic intent. Significantly, he felt that the literary circles in which he moved and the wider Iraqi public would tolerate his parody, and he was not afraid to publish it (unlike, say, Salman Rushdie). It was thus possible, in the monarchic Iraq of the late 1930s, for a Jew to participate in a discourse about religion and technology since he was accepted as a member of the nation-state. Balbul's familiarity with modernist and secular tendencies in Iraq and his knowledge of Arab culture thus enabled him to contribute to the debate about the nation's cultural values.

A decade later, Shalom Darwish's short story "The Liberation of a Slave" ("Tahrir 'abd") treated a theme similar to that of Balbul's story. The short story focuses on a servant, Fayruz, and his infatuation with his master's daughter, who had recently come back from Europe. To describe the total submission of "the slave" to his master, the vengeful Pasha, the narrator observes: "Whereas I am the slave of my God [*'abd rabbi*] and you are the slave of Allah[,] . . . Fayruz is better than us all, for he is also the slave of the Pasha." The master (*sayyid*) is extremely cruel to Fayruz, physically and verbally abusing him. Fayruz, however, endures this horrendous treatment calmly, finding refuge in religiosity and devotion (*taqwa*). He prays; he is immersed in the worship (*'ibada*) of his noble God (*rabbihi al-karim*), "mentioning His name in every moment."[48] What seems to present a much more formidable torment for Fayruz, causing him to plead for divine protection constantly and persistently, is the presence of women. In his encounters with women Fayruz asks his God to defend him from "the evil He had created" since, in Fayruz's mind, women, in particular the beautiful ones, belonged to hell (*al-jahim*).[49] Luckily, Fayruz's views of women change later on as he falls in love and comes to learn that women might have some redeeming qualities as well.

Of particular interest is the use by Darwish of the word *slave* (*'abd*) in the text, and the connections he makes between servant/slave, master, and the lord. Darwish applies the vocabulary used in the Islamic tradition, which compares the relationship between God and the believer to the relationship between master and slave (*'abd*), in order to ridicule the interactions between a rich and abusive man and his poor obedient servant. Moreover, Fayruz's inability to rebel against his master parallels his inability to rebel against his God. His religiosity is shown to have walled him off from human interaction and emotional relationships with fellow human beings. In satirizing this religious vocabulary Darwish takes a rather radical position, since the text represents Fayruz's religiosity as synonymous with misogyny, fanaticism, and intolerance.

The two stories, by Balbul and Darwish, have much in common. While they do not attack the Islamic faith, they do offer criticisms about the ways in which the Islamic religion was practiced and understood by the poor, whose misinterpretation of Islam, ignorance, and lack of rationality are grounded in a societal context in which they receive no education and guidance and are cast to the margins of society. In both stories, the authors' knowledge of Islamic religious vocabulary is employed in order to confirm their relationship with the greater Iraqi society. Simply put, these Jewish authors possessed the ability to communicate in the secularized Islamic idiom of other Muslim Iraqi writers. As Islam became a cultural, rather than religious, marker of Arab identity, it was permissible, even desirable, to comment on the religiosity of the underclass and the ways to reform it.

Not all aspects of Iraqi life were open to discussion by Iraqi Jewish writers, however. When Balbul submitted a short story condemning the practice of honor killings, his publishers forced him to change the distinctly Muslim names of the killers to ones that could be Jewish, Muslim, or Christian, arguing that Jews in Iraq also practiced honor killings.[50] Despite this alteration, it was not difficult to guess that the protagonists of the story were Muslims. Before the girl is murdered, she is ordered to say her last prayer: "There is no God but Allah."[51] A midwife who tries to save her life appeals to the girl's relations by saying: "Have mercy on her. I plead to you in the name of Allah and the prophets. Have mercy on her. . . . Allah does not condone such a thing."[52] The identification of the characters in Balbul's story as Muslim was crucial, as his contention was that honor killings were contrary to Islamic law as well as to human reason. Given the sensitivity of the issue and his being a Jew, Balbul was forced to walk a fine line in his critique of Iraqi society.

A Jewish *qawmiyya* was not only articulated linguistically (the adoption of the Arabic language) and culturally (the appropriation of Arab and Islamic narratives into Jewish print culture), but also in terms of politics, economics, and the common anticolonial interests of the Arab world. That Iraq was not yet politically independent troubled all Iraqi writers, Jews and non-Jews alike. In his introduction to his translation of Richard Sheridan's *Wilhelm Tell* (1932), Anwar Sha'ul wrote: "In every Arab state, there is a longing for freedom and a desire for independence. For every wandering Arab, who is seeking the right path, I hereby present *Wilhelm Tell*, as a good lesson of true nationalism and bravery."[53] The most significant Pan-Arab issue was the question of Palestine, in regard to which Iraqi Jewish intellectuals from the mid-1930s on made a point of voicing their support for the Palestinians. *Al-Misbah* staked out a unique position in this area, as it printed articles recounting the activities of the Zionist movement and reported on the lives of Jews who lived in mandatory Palestine. In fact, its publisher and second editor, Salamn Shina, asked for financial support from several Zionist organizations. At the same time articles in *Al-Misbah* called for coexistence between Jews and Arabs in Palestine and for cooperation between "the children of Abraham," in the building of a just society.[54] As naïve and unrealistic as this vision might seem today, the writers shared their own hopes for a society founded upon equality between Jews and Muslims in Iraq with their Palestinian and Jewish brethren.

Since 1929, however, most Iraqi Jewish intellectuals had sided with the Arab Palestinians. In this year, a full-fledged national rebellion against both the British and the Zionists broke out in mandatory Palestine. In August, representatives of the Jewish community in Baghdad expressed the hope that "no animosity is to be directed against their community . . . as a result of the Moslem-Jewish outbreak in Palestine." Taking heed of the public outcry in Baghdad against the events in Palestine, these Jews wanted to point out that "they in Baghdad were not connected with the Zionist movement, or in the British efforts to oust the Moslems from their holdings in Palestine in favor of Jews from abroad."[55] On the 30th of August 1929, a mass meeting was held at the Haydarkhane Mosque in Baghdad to pray for Arabs killed in Palestine, during which a petition from the Young Jews Association was read to show their solidarity of its authors with the rebels in Palestine. In protesting against the British colonizers, the petition writers called on their fellow participants to dispel "the erroneous impression that the Baghdadi Jews were in sympathy with those in Palestine," and argued that the Muslims of Iraq "were dearer to them than their brothers."[56]

Following the same line of thinking, Nissim Susa (a Jew who would later convert to Islam) attacked Zionism in articles published in the Lebanese press during 1931. He deemed any sympathy of Iraqi Jews for Zionists a sign of dangerous religious sectarianism. In an article that appeared in the Lebanese daily *Al-Ahrar*, Susa explores the ways in which the Palestinian national struggle was presented to Western audiences. He argues that when Europeans came to the new world, they enslaved the Native Americans, took their lands, and averred that "the Indian was barbaric and rights belonged only to the civilized [*mutammadiyun*] [?] Westerner [*sic*]." This story was being repeated anew, as the British were ill-treating the Palestinians in a similar manner. Susa provides examples from American newspapers that portray the war in Palestine as a battle between the barbarians (the Arabs) and the civilized peoples (the Zionists and the British).[57] Susa, however, makes it clear that he considered himself one of the "barbarians." As an educated Iraqi Jew, who had studied at American educational institutions, Susa felt he was especially capable of explaining to fellow Iraqi and Arab readers the mentality of contemporary American audiences. This was necessary in order to debunk these stereotypes and combat what he perceived to be the Zionist peril to the Arab world.

During the Arab Revolt in Palestine (1936–39), Iraqi Jews, including Chief Rabbi Sasun Khaduri (b. 1880), signed petitions against Zionism that were sent to local newspapers and the League of Nations. In October 1936, a letter by Khaduri was printed in the nationalist daily *Al-Istiqlal* in which he claimed that his community had no connection to Zionism, since the Jews of Iraq were Iraqis and shared the concerns of their countrymen.[58] In August 1938 a petition published in the daily *Al-Mustaqbal* in the name of Arab Jewish young people working on behalf of Palestine, "our Arab sisternation," underscored the commitment of Iraqi Jews "to the Arab nature of Palestine and the rights of her Arab sons." The authors swore to support with their hearts and souls "those who defend a strong Arab Palestine."[59] On Palestine Day (Yawm Falistin: August 26, 1938) journalists Ezra Haddad and Menashe Za'rur published articles expressing their support for the Palestinians. Iraqi Jews continued to make declarations of solidarity after the revolt ended: in 1946 the poet Ibrahim Obadiah composed a long ode, "Palestine and Colonialism" ("Falastin wa'l istim'ar"), in support of Palestine and against colonialism.[60] In the late 1940s, communist Jews frequently criticized the Zionist movement as a colonial, Western enterprise.

On certain occasions Iraqi Jews joined their voices with those of radical Pan-Arabists. Salman Darwish, for example, published articles in the radical Pan-Arab daily *Al-Istiqlal*. Darwish relates the following anecdote about his experiences with the newspaper:

> I used to write for the newspaper *Al-Istiqlal* published by 'Abd al-Ghafur al-Badri, who was known for his patriotism and his blind zealotry in his attacks against the British colonizers. I used to sign my articles with the name Sayyid . . . , and I used to attack the British in my writings, calling them wolves and foxes, [to such a degree] that Badri asked me one day: "Baba, when will you became a *sayyid* in the full sense of the word?" He meant by that, naturally: "When would you become a Muslim?" I answered him immediately: "When the majority believes that religion is a matter of God, and the homeland is for all the people [*al-din li-llahi, wa'l watan li'l-jami'*]."

Badri apologized immediately.[61]

Needless to say, Darwish's condemnation of British imperialism was consistent with the views expressed throughout the pages of *Al-Istiqlal*. However, his pen name, Sayyid, has as one of its meanings "a man who is a descendent of the Prophet," namely, a Muslim. Darwish felt that the content of his essays was enough to make him a *sayyid* of a sort, thinking that his anticolonial stance was sufficient evidence of his patriotism. For Badri, the ultimate form of belonging to the nation entailed conversion to Islam. Consequently, Darwish felt the need to remind Badri that loyalty to the homeland stood above religion. A Pan-Arabist, Badri accepted this position. The anticolonial outlook of young Iraqi Jews prevailed in the 1940s, as leftist Jews became staunch critics of Britain, although it backed that country in its struggle against Nazism and fascism. Iraqi-Jewish advocacy of anticolonial politics did not escape the notice of the British: in 1943, for example, the journalist Salim al-Basun was arrested and jailed along with Arab nationalists for his anti-British activities.[62]

Baghdadi Jewish intellectuals did not come by their identity as Arab Jews by virtue of having been born in an Arab country. Their Arab Jewishness was created in a national context, in which new forms of expression, the short story in particular, were of great importance. It was mediated in a print market that made available books, newspaper articles, and essays both written and to be read by Iraqi Jews. Importantly, this Arab Jewish vision was embraced by the rise of educated elites of the Jewish effendia and upper classes, who expressed support for Arab concerns as well as a great love of Arab culture, both medieval and modern. Arab Jewishness involved the appropriation of narratives of time and space as relevant to Iraqi Jews, who came to speak of themselves as individuals whose lot was intimately bound up with the revival of the Arab East. Finally, Jews internalized discourses related to Islam. They incorporated Islamic ideas into their thinking, and their perceptions of religiosity and religious reform reflected the influence of debates in Arab and Muslim intellectual circles. To be an Arab Jew, then, was a reflection of where one was educated, the printed materials one read, and the ways in which one framed the approach to Islamic reform and Arab nationalism.

Modern Babylon

On July 20, 1921, a British colonial official, Gertrude Bell, described a ceremony she had attended two days prior:

> On Monday the Jewish community gave a great reception to Faisal in the Grand Rabbi's official residence. . . . It was filled with rows of seats, with rows of notables sitting in them, the Jewish rabbis in their turbans of twisted shawls, the leading Christians, all the Arab ministers and practically all the leading Moslems, with a sprinkling of white robed, black cloaked 'ulama. The court was roofed over with an awning, the gallery hung with flags and streamers of the Arab colours. The Jewish school children filled it and the women looked out from the upper windows. . . . Faisal was clapped to the echo when we came and we all sat down to a programme of 13 speeches and songs. . . . The most interesting speeches were those of the Jews (Moslems spoke too). The Rabbi is too old, luckily, to say anything, but he is a wonderful figure, stepped straight out of a picture by Gentile Bellini. . . . They [the Jews] brought the Rolls of the Law in three gold cylinders which were kissed by the Grand Rabbi and then by Faisal, and they presented him

with a small gold facsimile of the tables of the Law and a beautifully bound Talmud. I whispered to him that I hoped he would make a speech.... Towards the end he got up and spoke really beautifully; it was straight and good and eloquent.... The Jews were delighted at his insistence on their being of one race with the Arabs.[63]

Bell's report conveys much information about the ways in which an *Iraqi* national event was orchestrated: it discloses that Muslim *'ulama*, Jews and Christians were all sitting in a room which was decorated by symbols of the Hashemite monarchy and that Faysal saw Jews and Arabs as "being of one race." Faysal, moreover, was presented with a Babylonian Talmud, a powerful symbol as it was one of the greatest masterpieces of Jewish thought and was compiled in Iraq. Faysal's speech on this occasion was extremely important. He stated that: "I do not wish to hear that this country has Muslim, Christian, or Jewish elements, since this is the land of nationalism, the land of the grand Arabs. Nationalism does not have anything to do with Muslims, Christians, or Jews, but with an entity called Iraq."[64] Jews, the king continued, lived in Babylon and shared with Arabs their trials and triumphs. "We are all branches in a large tree called Iraq."[65] Faysal's speech employed a rhetoric emblematic of the Arab Revolt that hailed the great achievements of the Arabs. Yet at the same time he spoke of a commonality that overcame religious differences and had come into being in a nation called Iraq. This Iraqi nation, furthermore, functioned as a grand family, in which members of all religions had a common interest. Noticeably, the roots of this Iraqi nation were to be found in not only its Arab-Islamic past[s], but also in its grandeur during antiquity, at the time when the Talmud was composed.

Iraqi Jewish intellectuals took Faysal's appeal to heart. They became absorbed with the Iraqi nation-state, its unique territorial and historical features, geography, archeology, and culture. The nation-state of Iraq seemed an appropriate and even desirable vehicle for attaining equality and citizenship rights. That Jews could serve in the new state apparatus demonstrated that secular considerations were now driving the appraisal of their loyalty to their country; *Al-Misbah* noted with great pride those Iraqi Jews who had achieved prominence in Iraq's political and legal establishment, such as Ibrahim al-Kabir and the judge Da'ud Samara.[66] In addition, contributors to the paper expressed their appreciation for the new constitution, which granted equal rights to all Iraqis, regardless of their religion or ethnicity. This new sense of national belonging impelled Iraqi Jewish commentators to call for additional measures as reinforcement: Shalom Darwish, for example, bemoaned the lack of Iraqi national holidays in which all members of the community could participate.[67] Any and all manifestations of the new state were taken seriously. Essayists in the pages of *Al-Misbah* discussed the Iraqi flag and national anthem as concerns relevant to Iraqi Jews who identified themselves as Iraqis first and foremost.

Former Jewish-Iraqi students recall their identification with symbols relating to the Hashemite monarchy and their excitement in the presence of individuals who represented the royal family. In 1925, students in Rachel Shahmon were greatly impressed when King Faysal visited their school.[68] A year earlier, King Faysal had visited the Alliance school in Baghdad, along with Ja'far al-'Askrai and other ministers. The school prepared to welcome the king: children memorized speeches in honor of the monarchy, while one, Mir Basri, was selected to recite a poem by the famous Shi'i poet Safi al-Din al-Hilli in honor of the king.[69] In 1925, Prince Ghazi, the minister of education, and other dignitaries attended the graduation of the al-Wataniyya, a school which aimed at enhancing Arab culture and Arab nationalism among Iraqi Jews.[70] After Faysal's death, Jewish schools encouraged their students to participate in ceremonies of national importance, in order to underscore their loyalty to the Iraqi nation and the Hashemite monarchy. In 1945, in honor of Regent 'Abd al-Ilah's visit to Basra, the Alliance high school participated in the celebrations organized by al-'Ashshar public high school. Jewish students performed songs of the Egyptian singers 'Abd al-Wahhab and Umm Kalthum, and preparations for the ceremony occupied the students for many days.[71] Notably, the idea that a representative of the monarchy would visit was enough to excite students and teachers long before Faysal, Ghazi, or the regent actually set foot in the school.

Novelist Ishaq Bar-Moshe (b. 1927) describes the deep sorrow felt by his family upon the death of King Faysal: "All the men in the household went out to see the grand funeral. It was an unforgettable day." Uncertain as to the inclinations of the new king, Ghazi, Jews remembered the late king very fondly. The remarks of Bar-Moshe's family were typical: "Faysal

I loved the Jews, and made them close to him"; "Fasyal I knew all the notables of the community and welcomed them during the holidays. He consulted the Jews on political and other matters"; "The king did not confuse events in Palestine with events in Iraq. Iraqi Jews were Iraqis to him, because they [had] lived here over two thousand years"; "He visited Jewish schools and community centers and even took pictures with the notables of the community"; and, "Too bad he passed away, now when independence is stronger and Iraqi currency is no longer dependent on the Indian currency."[72] The king, as reflected in these short conversations, is a national symbol. The admiration of the members of this household for the king grew out of his favorable treatment of Iraqi Jews, and the rise of Iraq as an independent state, whose history, from antiquity to the present, included that of the Jews. The king's speech at the grand rabbi's residence in 1921, confirming that Jews, Muslims, and Christians were all sons of the same motherland, is thus echoed in the statements of these family members.

Iraqi Jewish fiction writers in the monarchic period translated the focus on the new Iraqi polity into a concern with Iraqi social issues. As Shemu'el Moreh has noted, many of the characters who populated the fictional universes of Iraqi Jewish writers belonged to the Iraqi middle classes and grappled with issues faced by the nascent Iraqi bourgeoisie: social mobility, urban life, education, and the condition of Iraqi women. Jewish writers Anwar Sha'ul, Shalom Darwish, Ya'qub Balbul, and Estherina Ibrahim wrote about gender relationships, and Darwish, Balbul, and Sha'ul focused on the lives of the urban poor and their relationships to other classes, with Balbul even using the colloquial Iraqi dialect in dialogue as a measure of authenticity. Although some of the characters of this fiction were clearly identified as Christian, Muslim, or Jewish, in general these authors tried to create "Iraqi" characters who were defined as Arabic-speaking and as belonging to a specific social strata (urban poor, middle or upper class). Many of these stories place particular people and objects in an Iraqi space and time; they mention Baghdad, its neighborhoods, the state's institutions, and the country's northern and southern halves. This aesthetic became ever more pronounced during the 1940s. In this period the Iraqi public sphere began to look inward rather than to Pan-Arab ideology, as the politically dominant left attempt to cultivate Iraqi patriotism among the intelligentsia.

The aims of these stories, as their authors declared, were to bring into being a unique Iraqi literary scene.[73]

A 1937 short story by Ya'qub Balbul exemplifies this literary current. Its protagonist is Yusuf Adham, a man who has left Baghdad for Athens, changed his name to Joseph Adam, and was trapped in a miserable marriage to a sexually promiscuous Christian wife:

> He recalled his beautiful country and its features. He remembered what he had heard and had read about his country; that it had progressed greatly; that it had revolted against the yoke of colonialism and had driven the colonizers out; that it had become an independent kingdom whose rulers are pure Arabs; and that its capital had become a momentous center in the world of politics and commerce. He felt a longing for his country and yearned to return to it.[74]

Yusuf's religious identity is not mentioned. His national (Iraqi) and ethnic (Arab) identities, by contrast, are evoked as he considers his failed marriage. Moreover, the basis of the bond between the exiled Yusuf/Joseph and his motherland is made clear: his love of his family and kin in Baghdad, his childhood memories, and his Arabic language.

Iraqi Jewish poetry of this era also commonly took the nation of Iraq as its subject.[75] Perhaps the most noted patriot was Ibrahim Obadiah, whose poetry praised the beauty of his homeland. While Obadiah did view Iraq through the lens of a broader Arab nationalism, referring to his country as the lighthouse of Arabism (*manar al-'uruba*),[76] he reserved his greatest enthusiasm for celebrating the unique characteristics of Iraq. In his 1944 poem "My Country" ("Biladi"), the speaker pledges his allegiance to his motherland in the name of the Tigris and Euphrates. The nation's history, embodied in the country's various archeological sites, encompasses the progressive culture of Sumer, the wonders of Babylon, and the might of Assyria. This history of prosperity and progress continued in the golden days of the Abbasids, "Days when the West lived in Darkness // and when Iraq was the guiding lighthouse."[77] At times, his Iraqi patriotism turned from a vision of his country as a whole to particular spaces. For example, in a poem dedicated to Baghdad, the speaker depicts himself as a man in love with the city. His love for Baghdad is an article of faith (*din wa-iman*), yet such love also emanates from his love for the city's youth, its river, and beautiful gardens.[78] Poems professing love for the *watan* or the *bilad* were common throughout the Arab world; what makes these examples significant is Obadiah's articulation of patriotism as local. Moreover, his sense of patriotism incorporates important elements: the beautiful scenery of the country, its archeological sites, and its glorious history in antiquity.

Local patriotism was a common theme of stories in *Al-Misbah* that discussed the youth in the land of the two rivers, Iraq's future, and its constitutional regime. The journal *Al-Hasid* was another venue for the expression of this idea. In an essay, "The National Sentiment" ("Al-hiss al-watani"), Sha'ul declared that patriotism (*wataniyya*) burned in the souls of his readers, motivating them to serve their country. Unfortunately, the spread of patriotism in Iraq was not rapid enough. The education of young people was seen as key, in order to introduce them to the principles of freedom and imbue them with patriotic ideals. Sha'ul, however, identified a major problem with the available educational materials: "The Arab textbooks, small and large, are Egyptian. You cannot find in them even *a mere mention of the name of Iraq or its special features*. . . . Did our honorable Ministry of Education think about addressing this shortcoming by publishing a series of Iraqi textbooks that are written in a modern fashion?" (emphasis mine). The production of Iraq-focused textbooks, argued the editorial, would be the only way to ensure that students would become loyal Iraqis.[79] The patriotic argument here was in keeping with a point of view commonly voiced in the Iraqi press, which called for the privileging of Iraqi intellectual production over that of Egypt and Syria.[80]

Al-Hasid did much to cultivate the Iraqi literary scene by nurturing talented Iraqis of all faiths through publication of their writing. As mentioned above, many of the nation's thinkers and writers found the journal a receptive venue for their ideas. To further the development of Iraqi intellectualism, the journal hosted essay-writing competitions; in one such competition, it invited readers to answer the question, "How do I imagine Iraq after a hundred years?"[81] *Al-Hasid* also made ample mention of the different societies which emerged in Iraq, and especially in Baghdad, that were dedicated to art, music, literature, and education. Among these were the Society for the Protection of the Child (Jam'iyyat himayat al-atfal), the Education Club (Muntada al-tahdhib), the Teachers Club (Nadi al-mu'allimin), and the Society for the Revival of Art (Jam'iyyat ihya' al-fann). The journal listed important events coordinated by these organizations, such as lectures by Sati' al-Husri; gatherings attended by the leading lights of the Iraqi literary scene, such as the poet Ma'ruf al-Rusafi and short story writer Mahmud Ahmad al-Sayyid; or funerals of great Iraqi men. The names of these intellectuals and organizations were usually unfamiliar outside of Iraq, but were very meaningful to a Baghdadi local audience. The journal also referenced poems dedicated to the sons and daughters of Iraq or to locations within Iraq. Readers were signified by such expressions as "the Iraqi brothers," "the sons of the Tigris and the Euphrates," and "brothers in patriotism." In a report about the meeting of the "family of the Baghdadi press," Sha'ul expressed his hope that a sense of solidarity would come into being between writers that would provide a model to an Iraqi society seeking unity.[82]

Another Jewish journal, *Al-Burhan*, also focused on patriotism and issues particular to Iraq during the year 1929. One essay published in the journal decried "the thieves in governmental departments": it suggested that the people (sha'b)—"and I mean here, of course, the Iraqi people"—suffered from great difficulties because taxes supposed to go toward public health, defense, and education were instead supporting a huge bureaucracy that did nothing for the people.[83] Another editorial proposed that economic projects in Iraq were not conducted for the interests of the nation (watan): there were no major industrialization projects planned for, while the Westerners profited from an Iraqi market flooded with foreign goods. The sons of the nation (abna' hadha al-watan) could not resist this merchandise, which was cheap because foreign manufacturers paid low duties on their goods. The answer was the development of local Iraqi industries, and the protection of local goods via tariffs. These steps, the editorial concluded, would lead Iraqis out of the present nightmare in which they were living.[84] An anonymous letter to the editor revealed similar anxieties. The country, its author admitted, was in a peculiar situation (wad' shad). It was in a state of poverty and ignorance, as one major consequence of the global economic crisis was severe unemployment. Worse yet, existing jobs in the country were not the prerogative of the citizens (wataniyun), but of the English and the Indians who worked for them. The author satirized the process by which clerks were appointed in Iraq. First, an order came from Downing Street, requesting the appointment of British citizens to certain posts in Iraq, an order that was accepted with no questions or hesitation. Second, these British officials appointed Indian employees, again with no questions asked. The poor Iraqi citizens, in contrast, were required to take exams in order to demonstrate their knowledge of all the sciences (like engineering, math, and biology), and their mastery of Arabic, English, and French, and possibly of Greek, Spanish, and Sanskrit.[85]

Clearly, an Iraqi-focused agenda influenced the content of *Al-Burhan*. Its editorials conceptualized the community as being Iraqi, rather than as Pan-Arab, with their call for protection of the Iraq economy. *Al-Burhan* was not alone in voicing this concern, as others in the Arab-Iraqi press of the time protested the inflated number of Indian and British workers in the country's administration. The phrase "the peculiar situation," was common as a characterization of an Iraq that appeared to be independent, democratic, and sovereign, yet that in reality was controlled by British interests.[86] Further underscoring that the journal imagined its audience as broader than the Jewish community, the advertisements in *Al-Burhan* were often addressed to the sons of the country (*ahl al-watan*).

In addition to concrete national and economic concerns, Jewish identity itself was intertwined with Iraqi identity. Iraq was a land whose roots stretched back to the days of Babylon, a history in which Jews had participated as well. Mir Basri explained: "The land of the two rivers has also a share in the development of the Jewish religion and monotheism [*tawhid*]. From it, Abraham, the father of all prophets, went to the holy land [*al-bilad al-muqaddasa*]."[87] A number of sites in Iraq were connected to Judaism: in Nineveh, Jonah warned the people against evil and the prophet Ezekiel experienced his visions about the chariots of fire while in Iraq: "In Babylon, after a while, the Jewish rabbis wrote the Talmud, the lighthouse of Moses' law [*al-shari'a al- musawiyya*].... And we, those who lived in Iraq, in ancient and modern times, in the times of the Chaldeans and the Babylonians, the Persians and the Abbasids, and then in the eras of the Turks, the British, and the Arabs, carried in our minds and on our tongues, their lofty mission [*risala*]."[88] Central to Basri's view of Iraqi history is the conception of the motherland as an entity whose features had been shaped in different periods of time. Similarly, the intellectuals Anwar Sha'ul and Na'im Kattan spoke of Jews as denizens of Iraq, who had dwelled in the country for two thousand years, since the time when Abraham left Ur.[89] Jonah Cohen, who attended high school in Hilla, reported that he and his primarily Shi'i classmates "took great joy in studying the golden days of the kingdoms of Assyria and Babylon, which controlled all the lands of the East."[90]

In the 1940s, Iraq turned leftward, with one result being an intensification of patriotic sentiment. Most leftist organizations, such as the social-democratic NDP or the outlawed ICP, hewed to a policy of "Iraq first" and privileged local concerns over Pan-Arab nationalism. One reason for this was that the left associated this ideology with the profascist stance of some of their Iraqi Pan-Arab rivals. Moreover, these parties hoped that the new vision of the nation would enable the Kurds, Turkmen, and other ethnic and religious minorities to feel that they were all Iraqis. In the Jewish community, radical Pan-Arabism was not only perceived as being sympathetic to fascism but was also associated with the Farhud; the appeal of the left, especially to the younger generation, grew much stronger as a result. Nonradical Jewish elements gravitated toward the social-democratic camp. An early incarnation of the NDP, the Ahali group, which already promoted a patriotic Iraqi option, included Jewish members Ya'qub Cohen and Yusuf Mukmal. Na'im Tweig was affiliated with *Al-Mabda'*, a journal published by Ja'far Abu Timman, a member of al-Ahali. In the 1940s, the NDP became an important vehicle for Jewish political activity. The Jewish journalist Murad al-'Umari edited its publications, while Shalom Darwish became a member.[91] The ICP, by contrast, attracted many students, members of the effendia, former social democrats, as well as the urban poor, groups that sought more radical solutions to the nation's problems.

This new generation of leftist Jews was willing to confront the state directly and many participated in the demonstration that engulfed Baghdad during the Wathba. Consequently, the more established leaders of the Jewish community found themselves in a precarious position. On the one hand, if they did not join the demonstrations or condemn the killings of innocent demonstrators, many would see this as a sign of their conservativism and antipatriotism. On the other hand, too harsh a criticism of the state and identification with the Wathba's victims would possibly jeopardize the community in the eyes of the authorities. The leaders of the community thus attempted to resolve these tensions; prominent leaders in the Jewish community marched with the protesters and attended the major funerals of those killed in the riots.

The funerals of the victims of the Wathba became important ceremonies in which Jewish leaders accentuated their loyalty to Iraq. Rabbi Khaduri declared in one of these funerals that the Iraqi people had lost its sons for the sake of patriotism (*wataniyya*), and blessed the Wathba, which he saw as an expression of unity when all Iraqis, regardless of ethnicity or religion wanted to serve the homeland (*watan*). He ended his eulogy with a hope for an Iraq under the protection of the king and the regent.[92] Shalom Darwish delivered a passionate speech while bringing flowers in the name of the community to the graves of the martyrs. All of Iraq, he proclaimed, mourned those who died for the sake of freedom. If Allah willed, their death would not be in vain. The people (*sha'b*) and future generations had gained much, thanks the efforts of these heroes, who had marched into the line of fire so that their pure blood would bring together the different groups that formed the homeland, regardless of religion.[93]

Jewish journalist and educator Ezra Haddad (b. 1900) addressed the Muslim audience at the Hadyarkhana Mosque as brothers and cousins, greeting them in the name of "fellow Jewish citizens, who are honored to belong to this blessed valley."[94] Jews, Haddad told his listeners, have lived under the Iraqi sun and on Iraqi soil for centuries, and have benefited from the *shari'a* and from the lofty principles of Islam, namely, the principles of justice and equality, of tolerance and freedom—the principles that the great Prophet, Muhammad bin 'Abdallah, called for in Mecca (*umm al-qura*). Jews and Iraqi Muslims are brothers because they share the same ethics and culture and speak the Arabic language, the language of the honorable Qur'an. We come to the funerals, Haddad continued, to bless the souls of the innocent *shahid*s who battled so that the nation could satisfy its just demands for complete sovereignty and freedom, untouched by the hands of the colonizers. In this holy site of worship, Haddad said, we pledge to fight sectarianism, the enemy of the people. The speech ended with praises to the king and the regent and the words, "Long live the Arab nation! Long live Iraq, united, proud of its sons! Long live the memory of the innocent *shahid*s. Peace be upon you."[95]

The speeches delivered in the funerals referenced some of the touchstones of Pan-Arabism, notably the Arab motherland, the Qur'an, and the Arabic language, but on the whole their subject was Iraq. Each speaker took pains to articulate the idea that Jews were as patriotic as their fellow Iraqis, the result of a common history and struggle against colonial powers. Iraqi Jews, Christians, and Muslims alike cherished the martyrs who had died for the sake of Iraqi freedom and independence. For Jewish intellectuals, these funerals were opportunities to articulate an antisectarian position which cautioned against the perils of religious separatism, as well as one of nationalism which evoked the metaphor of a motherland whose soil was watered with the blood of its innocent sons. The funerals, then, became important sites to commemorate Iraqi patriotism on the part of Iraqi Jews, although the speakers were prudent and absolved the regent and the royal household of responsibility for the violence on the part of the authorities. In 1948, when these speeches were made, events in Palestine loomed in the background. It was critical for Iraqi Jews to underscore that their concern was for their fellow Iraqis, not their religious brethren in Palestine. Anyone who disputed this was consequently jeopardizing Iraqi unity.

The Arab Jews whose works have been the subject of the foregoing discussions saw themselves as loyal Iraqi citizens, and identified Iraq's historical, sociocultural, and sociopolitical concerns as their own. The Jewish experience illustrates that the idea of the Iraqi nation, as an entity with unique history and territorial identity, was accepted very early on by Iraqi Jews, who hoped that an independent Iraqi state would be able to grant them full citizenship rights. The very same Jewish intellectuals who professed their allegiance to a Pan-Arab culture also self-identified as Iraqis and did their utmost to emphasize their contributions to their country. In their opinion, Jews had played a vital part in the formation of Iraqi history, literature, and culture, while Iraqi culture had shaped Jewish life from the days of Babylon to the present.

Arabizing Benjamin

A superb example of the appropriation by Iraqi Jews of Islamic, Iraqi, and national narratives, and of the incorporation of both *qawmi* and *watani* elements into Iraqi Jewish nationalism, is the partial translation into Arabic of the travels of Benjamin of Tudela, *Rihlat Binyamin* (Hebrew: *Masa'ot Binyamin*, *Sefer ha-masa'ot*), by Ezra Haddad. A Navarrese medieval explorer who traveled from northern Spain in 1165 to Europe, Asia, and Africa, Benjamin's accounts of life in Palestine and Baghdad had important ramifications for Arab Jewish nationalists.[96] Haddad dedicated his translation to all Arabs (*al-natiqun bi'l dad*), and proclaimed that it would be of particular interest to his "brothers, the intellectuals of Iraq and its historians," because of the information it contained concerning the world and especially the Islamic East in a formative period in the history of both East and West.[97]

Haddad's introduction began with a brief survey of Muslim travelers and geographers, including al-Ya'qubi (d. 897), Ibn Hawqal (tenth century), Nasir Khusraw (d. 1088), and Ibn Jubayr (d. 1217), and the importance of travel literature to the understanding of the Arab and Islamic empires. This led into a discussion of the place of Jews in the Muslim world during the Middle Ages, in which Haddad contended that "the Jews in Spain and in the East mixed with the Arabs in their golden ages, and were influenced by their thinking."[98] Haddad maintained that Jews of this era were greatly interested in Arabic and Arab literature and thought; the parallel with contemporary Iraqi Jews was hard to miss.

Haddad then moved to an elaboration of the motivations of European Jews to travel and document their travels, drawing attention to the fact that they always journeyed from West to East. The reason, he maintained, was to be found in the differences between Europe and the East. First, Jews in medieval Europe lived in a constant state of fear, as they frequently had to flee to where they could observe their faith in peace. This created the historical figure of the wandering Jew (*al-yahudi al-ta'ih*). Second, the desire of European Jews to make the pilgrimage (*hajj*) to the Temple Mount and to receive blessings at the shrines of Jewish prophets and saints (*salihun*), as well as to see the places depicted in Torah, caused them to travel to the Middle East. Third, since European Jews were unable to engage in agriculture (as they did not own land in many cases), they turned to trade, which naturally entailed a great deal of travel. In contrast, Jews of the East lived in comfort and stability since the caliphs and the sultans permitted them freedom of religion in return for the payment of a small tax (*jizya basita*). These Jews suffered only when the political order eroded or a particularly extreme ruler came to power. Generally, however, Eastern Jews were not impelled to travel because of difficult living conditions. They did feel the need to travel to Jerusalem and see the graves of Jewish saints, yet this was relatively easy as it did not oblige them to travel by sea, which was dangerous because of pirates and other threats. Moreover, a Jew who lived in Egypt, Iraq, or Syria, when traveling throughout the Middle East, did not feel that he was encountering an environment that was alien and thus worthy of note. Finally, an Arab Jewish merchant could acquire most of his merchandise within the boundaries of the Muslim empires without traveling great distances—unlike his European counterpart. Due to these various factors, travel literature did not become a significant component in Eastern Jewish culture, as it did in Europe.[99]

Haddad's introduction highlighted the differences between East and West, or more precisely it used the East-West binary to construct two images, one of the tolerant Muslim empires characterized by religious pluralism and the other of the fanatical Western Christian empires, in which Jews were persecuted. Haddad drew on the work of a variety of Jewish historians, some of them Zionist, manipulating the negative accounts of Jews in exile not to extol a return to the land of Israel but to glorify the achievements of the Muslim and Arab empires. His accounts call into question the universality of Jewish history by showing that such terms as *the wandering Jew* had their genesis in a particular sociohistorical European context. Moreover, Haddad saw Palestine, Egypt, Iraq, and Syria as belonging to the same historical and geographical setting. Although he recognized the immense importance of Jerusalem, Haddad contended that for Jews who lived in Arab lands there was no difference between Palestine and other regions, since the people of Palestine spoke languages with which Eastern Jews were familiar and lived under the same imperial regime. Intentionally minimizing instances of persecution in Jewish Arab history, Haddad celebrated coexistence and religious tolerance in presenting the East-West binary as pertinent to the Mizrahi-Ashkenazi binary. In so doing, he intended to offer his contemporaries not simply a Jewish Arab model from bygone days, but also, and more significantly, a model for the modern Iraqi state.

Let us now turn to the translation itself. I will not evaluate its quality; instead I will focus on how the text became accessible to Arab readers, and on the textual strategies Haddad utilized to underline the connectivities between Jewish and Arab cultures. In other words, I will explore the processes of the Arabization of Benjamin's text, as expressed through the translation of Hebrew terms into Arabic, the intertwining of information provided by Muslim geographers, travelers, and historians into the text, and the citations from the Qur'an and the prophetic tradition (*hadith*) Haddad inserted into his work.

The names of each city described by Benjamin were given in Hebrew, Arabic, and Latin. Haddad's annotations were often much longer than the text itself and usually covered half or more of the written page. The entry on Acre serves as a good example of Haddad's Arabizing techniques. Benjamin's account related that Acre was mentioned in the Torah as having been built by the tribes of Asher, and described its port and its Jewish inhabitants. Haddad added (in a much longer footnote) that the city was mentioned in the Book of Judges and in the New Testament. He then provided following information:

> The Commander of the Faithful [*amir al-mu'minin*], 'Umar ibn al-Kattab, conquered [*fatah*] the city in the year 663. Later the crusaders took the city, in the year 1104. Then Salah al-Din returned it back (to the Muslims) in 1187. Richard the Lionheart retook the city in 1191 after a siege that lasted for two years. Al-Malik al-ashraf reconquered Acre in the year 1291 and it came under Ottoman Turkish rule in 1517. In recent years, Acre achieved a degree of fame due to the siege of Napoleon and its failure in the year 1799. The famous Rabbi Ishaq al-Akawai, the famed kabbalah Sufi scholar, lived there in the Middle Ages.[100]

Haddad constantly referenced dates that were of interest to Muslim and Arab readers: the period of the Islamic conquest (when the city became a part of the Arab empire) and the period of the crusaders (thus evoking the memory of the heroism of Saladin, a key figure in the Arab national pantheon). The city was constructed as a perpetual site of battle between West and East, between occupiers who invaded and laid siege, and authentic Arabs who managed to "return the city back" to the Muslims. Framed as such, Napoleon's siege is only one in a long series of failed attempts to wrest the city away from its rightful owners. The silences that Haddad perceived in the Hebrew text were addressed by adding historical details about the city under Muslim rule. This was done in order to underline Haddad's own mastery of the Arab national narrative, and, more importantly, to make the text comprehensible to Arab readers. To this end, major terms and concepts were Arabized and Islamized. Jewish mysticism was denoted by the words

Sufi and *kabbalah*. Haddad also used Islamo-Arabic names like *al-malik al-ashraf*, assuming that the readers would know their meanings. The intended readership of the text was thus not only Arabic speaking, but also conversant in Islamic history and culture.

Benjamin's long entry on Jerusalem was accompanied by twenty-two footnotes, which were much longer than the text itself. The first footnote addressed the city's name and described the city named al-Quds or Bayt al-maqdas as the site of prophets and the location of prophecy (*mahall al-anbiya', mahbat al-wahy*). Haddad commented that documents found in the Egyptian city of Tel al-Amarna gave Jerusalem's original name as having been Uruashlim, which he translated as *dar al-salam*, "city of peace" (which was also Baghdad's name in the Abbasid period). Relying on the Book of Genesis, Haddad mentioned the city's name in the days of Abraham the Patriarch (Ibrahim al-Khalil), and then discussed the Assyrian and Babylonian meanings of the city's name. The city, Haddad asserted, boasted a history of five thousand years. His short history recalled how King David occupied the site and established it as his capital. Haddad then recounted the Babylonian and the Roman occupations, the city's history under Byzantine rule, followed by accounts of the Islamic conquest of Jerusalem, the building of the mosques on the Temple Mount, and finally the crusaders. The fact that Haddad continued narrating the city's history *after* the destruction of the Second Temple by the Romans marks a clear difference between his text and modern Zionist historiography. The Zionist notion of Jewish miserable existence in exile after the Romans had destroyed Jerusalem was difficult to maintain, since Haddad's annotations accentuated the continuity of Jewish life in Palestine itself and the prosperity of the Jewish people under Islamic rule. He was careful, at the same time, to acknowledge the city's importance for Muslims and Christians. The latter were mentioned in discussions of the crusaders, naturally, but also when Benjamin described Palestine's Christian populations and their holy sites. The annotation on Benjamin's entry for Bethlehem, for example, noted that "our Lord the Messiah [*sayyiduna al-masih*] was born there," and then recounted the history of that city under Constantine and offered portraits of its many churches.

Haddad's descriptions made extensive use of Islamic terms. When Haddad annotated Benjamin's narration of the story of Lot's wife, who turned into a pillar of salt when escaping with her family from the city of Sodom, he added that Sodom was destroyed because of the evil of its people "as mentioned in the Torah (Genesis 13:13)": "The reference to Lot and his people appears in the Noble Qur'an in a few suras, namely, al-I'raf 80–84; al-Nahl 54–58; and Hud 77–83. The Arab geographers mention it [the city of Sodom] as "the dwelling of Lot" [*diyar lut*]. . . . The Torah says that Lot's wife was transformed [*masakhat*] into a pillar of salt. Consult also the Holy Qur'an, sura Hud, 81."[101] Haddad used both the Qur'an and the Bible as historical sources. He did not weigh in on the truth of the story about Lot's wife, though he did describe the geological features of Sodom, and related that some travelers claimed to have seen the pillar, while others denied that it existed. His commentary, nonetheless, indicated that the Qur'an and the Torah narrated similar stories from which one could reconstruct factual history. Accounts drawn from Judaism and Islam did not always agree, however, and for that matter Benjamin's claims were occasionally at odds with how Iraqi Jews saw their history. Benjamin's discussion of Sepphoris, the important city of the Sanhedrin (*al-majma' al-'ilmi al-yahudi al-a'la*), mentioned his belief that the city contained the tomb of the prophet Jonah. This was contrary to the prevailing view among Iraqi Jews: Haddad commented in the footnote that "it is known that the tomb of Nabbi Yunus, as the Arabs name him, is found in Mosul."[102]

Haddad's analysis of Benjamin's visit to the land of Israel can be understood as an attempt to create a shared Judeo-Islamic tradition. With his commentary on Benjamin's travels to Iraq, Haddad endeavored to construct a history of an Iraqi nation from the days of Babylon to the present that had always known a prominent Jewish presence. The sites in Iraq associated with the religion and history of all Jews were a source of great pride for Haddad. This was reflected in his long footnotes on Benjamin's account of the Shrine of Ezekiel, which Haddad characterized as one of the most important and sacred sites for the Jewish community in Iraq, and as being famed for its beauty (as noted by various travelers).[103] Haddad's commentary also drew on the work of Muslim and Arab scholars in order to underline Iraq's significant place in Islamic history. The first footnote on Baghdad (out of a total of twenty-four) began with the statement that Baghdad was *dar al-salam*, the city of peace, the dwelling of the caliphs, and a place of the

Qurayshi imams. Haddad then analyzed the city's names over the course of its history: the geographer Yaqut al-Hamawi (d. 1229) had identified the city's name as Persian; others had understood it as being Aramaic (*Beit dad*); the Talmud had mentioned the city of Bagdata, and later on the city had been named *al-zawra'* by the Arabs and *'adina* by the Jews. A short aside discussing the contemporary archeological excavations around Baghdad was followed by a brief history of the city from the days of the second Abbasid caliph Abu Ja'far al-Mansur (r. 754–75) until its destruction by the Mongols in 1258. The remaining footnotes incorporated a large number of Muslim historians, Ya'qubi and Ibn 'Abd Rabbihi (d. 940), among others, as well as studies on the history of the Jewish community in Babylon.

Building on Benjamin's observations, Haddad tried to establish that the Jewish presence in Iraq dates back to the nation's earliest days. A case in point is his description of Kufa. Haddad depicted the construction of the garrison town and its importance during the caliphate of 'Ali ibn Abi Talib, adding that not only Muslims, but also Jewish exiles from Hijaz and Khaybar, settled in it. Jewish scholars and doctors, moreover, had relations with the Kufan Muslims, especially in the eleventh century.[104] Haddad's point here was that when the city had flourished, the Jewish community had done so as well. Haddad did call attention to some inaccuracies in Benjamin's accounts about the mosque in Kufa, and argued that the historical accounts by the Shi'is (*shi'at al-imam 'Ali*) must be privileged over Benjamin's reports when it came to such sites. More generally, as a Jew writing on Iraq, Haddad had to be extremely careful not to insult any of the nation's religious communities. He therefore omitted historical details concerning Kufa that were the source of Sunni-Shi'i tension (such as the fact that 'Ali ibn Abi Talib was murdered there). In addition, Haddad followed each of the names of 'Ali and second caliph 'Umar ibn al-Khattab with the expression "May God have mercy upon him" (*rahimahullah*). As an Arab and an Iraqi, Haddad felt the need to illustrate that Shi'i, Sunni, Jewish, and Christian historical accounts all provided precious information about his homeland, its histories, geographies, and places of communal worship. At times, however, Haddad's pride regarding the history of Iraq overcame his Jewish identity. When commenting on Benjamin's depiction of the ruins of Babylon, Haddad opened with the words: "This is Great Babylon, the capital of

Hammurabi, the seat of Nebuchadnezzar's empire, the ruler [*sayyida*] of the ancient East."[105] This, despite the fact that (as Haddad mentioned later in the text) the Babylonians had exiled the people of Judea and destroyed the First Temple.

The text ended with four appendixes related to the history of Samaritans, Karaites, the institution of the head of the Jewish exile (Ra's al-Jalut, a Jewish official whose interaction with the Caliph was beautifully described by Benjamin himself), and the revolt (*fitna*) of Da'ud ibn al-Ruhi. These sections supported Haddad's contention that Jews living under Islamic rule had fared much better than Jews living under Western, European, Christian rule. In the chapter on the Samaritans, Haddad suggested that in the seventh century, the oppressive Byzantine occupation of Palestine had ended "by the grace of the Islamic conquest," and that both the Jews and the Samaritans were treated with tolerance by the Muslims, being entitled to protection under Islam. These communities likewise flourished during the days of Fatimid rule. Strangely (although, it seems, unintentionally), the Samaritans were characterized, in the Arabic translation, as to suggest a comparison with the Wahhabis: "The Samaritans are monotheists [*muwahiddun*], and there is no doubt about their monotheism ... but they only recognize the five books of Musa from the Holy Book, and follow their text literally."[106] Jewish-Islamic intellectual exchange was celebrated further in the chapter on the Karaites, a group that had coalesced under the leadership of 'Anan bin Da'ud (d. ca. 790–800). Haddad drew attention to the fact that Muslim intellectual life had thrived during this period, benefiting from interchange with a diverse range of cultures, most notably Greek and Persian. This intellectual ferment was not limited to the Muslim community: "Some Jews were influenced by the opinions of the *mu'tazilla* and the people of *kalam* among the Muslims, and began criticizing the teachings of the rabbis."[107] Haddad, however, noted that the ruling caliph, Abu Ja'far al-Mansur, feared all intellectual innovations, seeing them as a source of possible political opposition and had 'Anan jailed for this reason. According to the historians of the Karaite community, this was how 'Anan met the great scholar of Islamic law, Abu Hanifa (699–767), who was also incarcerated at the time. The proceeding chapter on Ra's al-Jalut emphasized that Jews had suffered under Sassanid rule and therefore hailed the Arab conquerors of Iraq as liberators (*muharrirun*). What followed were many years of prosperity for Iraqi Jews, which came to an end, for all Iraqis including Jews, in the days of the Buyhids and the Selcuks, a period depicted in the text as the era of decline (*inhitat*).[108]

The analysis presented in Haddad's annotation is not always profound or original. In many instances Haddad merely inserted material from Arabic dictionaries, books of medieval Arab geography, and Arab chronicles. The significance of the text lies in its "performance" of the Arabism of its author. His commentary sought to address what Haddad saw as the silences in Benjamin's original text with respect to the history of Arabs and Muslims. These gaps were easily filled with citations from Arab and Muslim sources. Furthermore, the mere act of translation imposed a new vocabulary on the text, which was not only Arab but also Islamic. Haddad's imagined readership might have been Arabic-speaking Jews; the inclusion of an opening page in Hebrew and the dedication of the text to Senator Ezra Menahem Daniel corroborate this assumption. However, the text was also addressed to non-Jews. The commentary on matters relating to Islamic and Arab history (regardless of their bearing on the actual text, such as referencing Napoleon's siege of Acre while discussing the city as it was in the twelfth century), the clarification of certain Jewish practices, the references to Muslim historians, and above all, the constant emphasis on the connections between Islam and Judaism indicate that Haddad also had a non-Jewish readership in mind. It seems that Haddad wished to demonstrate to this readership that Islamic history and thought were highly relevant to Jewish culture.[109]

Ultimately, Haddad's goal was to produce a national text that conveyed the continuity of Iraqi history, from the ancient Mesopotamian empires to the present day. He employed the sophisticated device of the outsider, the foreign traveler, who looked at an unknown space, in order to celebrate the features of this space. It is the role of the translator, the insider, to transcend the strangeness of Benjamin of Tudela and provide the correct information about Iraq. Another nationalist assumption that informed Haddad's thinking was that all the peoples of the region had contributed to the culture of Iraq, and should be able to access the religio-cultural texts of other communities in order to fathom the nation's history. Thus, a Jew could look into Shi'i biographical dictionaries or Sunni chronicles in order to glean information on Iraq, just as a Muslim could turn to Jewish sources to do likewise.

Finally, the text is a challenge to the attempt to universalize Jewish history. Crucial to Haddad's point of view in this regard is the contention that Jewish life under Islamic rule was characterized by tolerance and coexistence. The Jews welcomed the Muslims as their liberators from Byzantine and Sassanid oppression; and their optimism was justified. Not only did they not suffer, as did their European brethren, but they and their cultures thrived. Even when a Jew such as 'Anan bin Da'ud was thrown into jail, he encountered the Muslim legal genius Abu Hanifa, who was a fellow prisoner. Thus, the images of the "wandering Jew" or the "persecuted Jew" were European in nature and had no relevance for the Middle Eastern context. When we remember that Haddad's translation of Benjamin was completed in 1945, his historical statements made much sense for contemporary Jewish readers. Iraqi Jews were keenly aware the lot of their brethren in Europe. No matter how horrible the experience of 1941 was, the context of the Holocaust made Iraqi Jews realize how fortunate they were compared to fellows Jews in Europe. As we shall see, Iraqi Jews prayed on behalf of their European brethren, and participated in anti-Nazi propaganda efforts. Haddad's treatment of Benjamin may very well reflect the (ultimately Zionist but quite reasonable) assumption that what happened to European Jewry during the Holocaust was the tragic culmination of many years of persecution and anti-Semitism. This historical narrative was contrasted with another which stressed cooperation between peoples of different religions. Ironically, it was the fate of European Jews in the postwar years that would determine the lot of Iraqi Jews as well, and endanger the coexistence so celebrated by Haddad.

Conclusions

Scholars of Iraqi-Arab nationalism have tended to highlight the tensions between local Iraqi patriotism, on the one hand, and Pan-Arabism, on the other. Indeed, such tensions figured prominently in the Hashemite period, especially in the political realm, as Pan-Arabists and leftist patriots competed for power, especially from the 1940s on. For the Iraqi Jewish intellectuals of the period, these identities coexisted with one another. Iraqi Jews, as subjects educated in Arabic and living in an Arab country, came to think of Arabic as a marker of their national identity and of Islam a signifier of their cultural affiliations with the nation. This orientation toward wider Arab culture at the same time accommodated a local Iraqi patriotism that saw Judaism as a part of Iraq's historical and cultural heritage. The emphasis on Iraqi patriotism took on greater urgency in the 1940s. As Pan-Arabism became increasingly identified with nationalists whom Jews considered partially responsible for the Farhud, the attractiveness of an Iraq-centered ideology became more pronounced. Nonetheless, Jewish expressions of Iraqi patriotism dated back to the early 1920s and appeared in the Jewish press long before 1941. Iraqi-Jewish intellectuals, in other words, had come to view the nation-state of Iraq as the political construct most able to meet their demands for citizenship rights and equality. Significantly, most of these intellectuals, especially those active in the interwar period, saw no contradiction between embracing Pan-Arabism and maintaining their sense of Iraqi patriotism. In the final analysis, their love of Arabic medieval and modernist poetry, their fascination with the tonality and magic of the Qur'an, and their choice of Arabic as a writing language enabled Iraqi Jews to communicate with their fellow Iraqis more effectively, thus consolidating the basis of the modern Iraqi state.

Iraqi Jews employed the same narratives and tropes used by Muslims and Christians in this period. While some Iraqi Jews chose to emphasize the links between Judaism and Islam, between Iraqi and Jewish history, and between Arabic and Hebrew, others focused on Arab and Iraqi affairs in works that could have been written by any Iraqi. Their symbols, metaphors, and historical narratives could easily "pass" as written by Iraqi nationalists who were Muslims or Christians. Jews, as citizens in the new state, wanted a place in the nascent Iraqi public spheres and therefore sought to illustrate, by writing in Arabic, that their contribution to the new institutions of the Iraqi Arab nation-state and its culture was equal to that of any other religious or ethnic community.

3

THE EFFENDIA

Questions of Secularism and Judaism

Sasson Somekh recalled his skeptical reaction to the story of Hannah and her seven sons, which he heard at his high school in the late 1940s:

> Deeply engraved in my consciousness is the story of Hannah and her seven sons, which the rabbi would tell on the eve of the Ninth of Av in a tearful voice. The plot of the story was impressive, but the concept of "martyrdom" sounded a bit silly to me, as I had no clear grasp of the principles of the religion for which the martyrs gave their lives. The belief in one God—fine. But what about all those science-fiction stories that abounded in the pages of the Scripture? What about the creation of the world in six days, the parting of the Red Sea, the sun standing still[,] . . . and the rest of the stories of wonders?[1]

Somekh was clearly unmoved by the martyrdom of Hannah and her sons, who refused to eat nonkosher meat and thus sacrificed their lives for their faith. Although his upper-middle-class family celebrated Jewish holidays and went to a synagogue during the High Holidays, a belief in the absolute truth of the sacred Jewish texts appeared to him rather unscientific.

Somekh was hardly alone in his views, as many of his fellow Iraqi Jews regarded their faith with a critical eye. In their writings, Iraqi Jewish intellectuals supported a secular nation-state, which they linked to the creation of a nonreligious belief system that would guarantee equality to all the members of the nation. Their deliberations about secularity and modernity were conducted in a transregional Arabic print market, which discussed concepts related to religion, rationality, and law, as well as the theories of the major proponents of secularism, like Auguste Comte, Herbert Spencer, Karl Marx, and locally, Salama Musa and Taha Husayn. In this intellectual milieu the adherence of empirical standards of evidence and the celebration of the powers of reason and scientific knowledge were the dominant themes.[2] Being part of this universe of discourse, the Iraqi print media was very much concerned with questions relating to religion as well.[3]

Several articles of the Iraqi constitution taken together guaranteed freedom of religion to all Iraqis citizens. Article 13 specified that Islam was the official religion of the state, but asserted that "complete freedom of conscience and freedom to practice the various forms of worship in conformity with accepted customs are guaranteed to all inhabitants of the country, provided that such forms of worship do not conflict with the maintenance of order and discipline or public morality." The status of religious education was confirmed in Article 16, which stated that "the various communities shall have the right of establishing and maintaining schools for the instruction of their members in their own tongues, provided that such instruction is carried out in conformity with such general programmes as may be prescribed by law." Finally, Article 18 affirmed that government appointments shall be bestowed to each citizen "without discrimination, in accordance with his capacity and fitness."[4]

These articles inspired much hope among Jewish intellectuals. They were aware of the tensions between the nationalist opposition to sectarianism on the one hand, and the need to maintain political hierarchy based on religion and ethnicity on the other, yet the ideal of a secular democratic state remained firm in their minds. Furthermore, modernity and secularism were discussed, not with regard to the macrolevel, but rather as pertinent to practices and behavior within the Jewish community itself. The state had intervened (at times, at the request of Jews themselves) in certain cases, such as the appointment of a chief rabbi, regulations pertaining to his position, or the accreditation of Jewish schools. Nonetheless, certain discourses about worship, hermeneutics, gender, and public morality did not involve consideration of the state. This cultural dynamic was not unique to the Jewish community. Rafa'il Butti, a Christian, and 'Ali al-Wardi, a Shi'i, recalled clashes within their respective communities between young, rebellious intellectuals (in which faction these writers counted themselves) and the more conservative religious leadership. While Iraqi intellectuals of all faiths worked together in nonsectarian settings, such as publishing houses, schools, and political parties, they remained closely tied to their own communities. Consequently, the discussions about what it meant to be a Jew (and for that matter, a Sunni, a Shi'i, and a Christian) was not simply the prerogative of the state, but was also very much in the hands of agents within each religious community.[5]

Whereas the degree of secularization among the poorer classes of Jewish Iraqi society has been debated,[6] there is no doubt that conceptualizations regarding secularism and reform are related to the rise of the Jewish upper and middle classes. The Jewish economic elites, comprised of bankers and merchants, expanded their ranks during the monarchic period, and played an important role in the state's financial and economic life.[7] Hashemite Iraq was also engaged in state and nation building. Integral to these processes was the expansion of the state's bureaucracy and its administration, its education systems, and its ties to the global economy. Because the community's urban members, especially in Baghdad, were able to get a Westernized education in schools such as the Alliance, they were better positioned to capitalize on the new opportunities in the 1920s. The bilingual and often trilingual nature of their education qualified Jews for positions in the state's ministries and private companies as administrators, bureaucrats, teachers, lawyers, and doctors. A British account noted: "After the British occupied Iraq and the new administration was formed, the number of government officials required was large. The only educated and capable elements in the country being the Jews, a great number of the officials were drawn from their ranks."[8] During the years 1921–48, young Jewish men who were graduates of high schools, middle schools, and universities became part of the Iraqi effendia. Religion aside, they had much in common with other members of the urban middle classes by virtue of their education, their interests in Arab and global politics, and the social norms they upheld. The more secularized character of the Jewish effendia manifested itself in its leisure practices, as young Jewish men came to spend more and more time outside the boundaries of their religious community. Cafés, especially the more luxurious ones opened in Baghdad in the 1940s, movie houses, concert halls, and nightclubs were very attractive options for those with time on their hands. *Al-Misbah* would occasionally grumble about the younger generation who preferred to spend their time in casinos and billiard halls rather than in libraries and scientific institutions. This collective bemoaning of the state of the youth, it should be pointed out, went on in the Muslim and Christian communities as well. During this period participation in sports grew in popularity among Jews. A Baghdadi Jewish fitness club (*mahall tanshit al-abdan*) opened in 1923 and others soon followed. For wealthier members of the community, the club (*nadi*), a private institution which offered space for socializing with individuals from the upper classes, became an important hub.[9]

Iraqi Jews interested in spiritual and cultural matters turned to libraries, reading salons, and cultural clubs. In the years 1920–31 societies such as the Cultural Jewish Society (Al-Jam'iyya al-adabiyya al-isra'iliyya; 1920–21), the alumni societies of the Alliance graduates in Baghdad and Basra, and the Society of Jewish Youth (Jam'iyyat al-shuban al-isra'iliyyin; 1930–31) met periodically to discuss sociocultural issues and to produce plays. The Jewish Cultural Society, for instance, mounted a production of *Salah al-Din al-Ayyubi*, and the Society of Jewish Youth performed plays by Shakespeare and Molière (in Arabic renditions). Other important venues were libraries, located either in schools or in small shops. In the 1920s, many libraries held lectures, and members would come to converse on the given topics: examples of these libraries include Progress Library (al-Taqaddum) and the Economic Class (Saff al-iqtisadi), active in 1926. From the 1930s on Jews spent more time in the Iraqi (rather than a Jewish Iraqi) cultural realm, intermingling with their Muslim and Christian peers. By the 1940s Baghdad boasted a network of cafés and literary salons as well as a public library, and young Jews seemed to have been mesmerized by the city's thriving cultural scene.[10]

The prestige of the rabbinical leadership of the Jewish community declined, as Iraqi Jews who held positions of significance in the public and private sectors became prominent players in the community's life. Among these new leaders were senators, such as Ezra Menahem Daniel, parliament representatives, such as Abraham (Ibrahim) Haim, successful lawyers such as Yusuf al-Kabir and Reuben Battat, as well as officials in the government's ministries and rich merchants. The value of secular education, in the form of a law degree or simply the ability to read and write in a foreign language, increased since education could help Jews secure a position in the state bureaucracy and thus a stable livelihood. The waning of the prominence of the rabbinical leadership was underway in the late nineteenth century, but became more pronounced during the monarchic period.[11]

These social and cultural shifts played out in the print media. Some secular leaders of the community, and especially the younger Jewish effendia, used the press to criticize the Jewish religious leadership as conservative and behind the times. The former's concerns—secularism, women's emancipation, and educational and religious reform—also occupied Iraqi Muslim and Christian intellectuals as being germane to Iraqi society as a whole. Transregionally, Turkey, Iran, and to a lesser degree Egypt, were undergoing varying degrees of secularization (unveiling, secularizing the education system, and legal reforms), and educated Jews, Christians, and Muslims wanted to see such changes in Iraq as well.[12]

Debating the Secular

Iraqi Jews did not view integration into the majority society as requiring them to discard aspects of their identity. Iraqi Jewish intellectuals had shown a keen interest in the lives of fellow Jews, in Iraq and across the globe. However, the comparisons the former made between their status, and that of their brethren across the diaspora, often served to highlight the success of their own community.

Al-Misbah paid great heed to Jewish affairs beyond Iraq's borders. It reported on the activities of Jewish organizations such as Hadassa and Beney Berith; and on the anti-Semitism to which Jews were exposed all over the world, from the pogroms in Russia to the Ku Klux Klan in the United States (aptly described as *al-jam'iyya al-sharira*, "the evil society").[13] Furthermore, articles about Jews in Italy and Russia, for example, suggested that these authors believed that European Jews were worse off than Iraqi Jews, who enjoyed a certain measure of security, prosperity, and emancipation. The wider Jewish community was a matter of great interest to the editors of *Al-Burhan* as well. This journal reported on issues affecting Jews in Czechoslovakia, the United States, Poland, England, Australia, the Soviet Union,

China, and India. It boasted of Albert Einstein's great achievements, yet also took notice of anti-Semitic incidents in Europe. Moreover, *Al-Burhan* brought news of other non-European Jewish communities that it viewed as being progressive to the attention of its readership. One article detailed the efforts by the Jews of Ethiopia in the direction of reform: study in Europe, the learning of Hebrew, and abandonment of archaic religious practices.[14] Notably, the steps taken by this community were those recommended by *Al-Burhan* for Iraqi Jews, namely, Westernization, education, and secularism.

In secularizing Jewish circles the position that a citizen's religion was a private matter became prevalent and responded to a national discourse which viewed sectarianism as dangerous. The expectation that nationalism would obliterate sectarian differences was voiced on numerous occasions. *Al-Misbah*, for example, called on the Jewish educational system to provide an education that was not narrow and sectarian in nature.[15] Authors such as Nissim Susa (before his conversion to Islam) urged the community to downplay its uniqueness and take into account all the communities in the nation.[16] Anwar Sha'ul made the demand to secularize not only Jews but all Iraqis: "Why do we judge the faults of a man according to his religion or ethnicity [*qawmiyyatuhu*]? Why do we not trace any faults (in a man's character) to his nature, but rather to his being a Jew, Christian, or Muslim?"[17] An anonymous letter sent to *Al-Burhan*, however, doubted that Iraqis would be able to shed their sectarian identity. The letter writer argued that while he respected the editor's efforts to guide the people (*al-sha'b*), they were still bound by old traditions, which neither the editor nor twenty like him would be able to dislodge. The people tended to cling to the past, seeing the future as dangerous. They refused to believe in scientific theories or in anything that challenged religious beliefs, mainly because they were still enslaved to their imaginations. While the contemporary era was one of technological innovation, the people recited medieval love poetry. Worse yet, the people worshiped priests, and invested their utmost efforts to satisfy the desires of their priests. These misguided individuals did not understand the importance of capital and considered a poor man to be closer to Allah, who, naturally, would provide for him. This nation was thus content with its poverty and its reliance on God's assistance. My brother, the author of the letter concluded his plea, I am critical of religion in the East, of the Eastern priests and clerics (*kahana, qusus*), and wish you success in your mission."[18]

The defining characteristic of the people of Iraq, according to the letter writer, was their belief in God. The writer did not specify whether the people of whom he spoke were of the Jewish or Muslim faith; in using a Christian term, *priest*, his intent was apparently to be as vague as possible. Nonetheless, the essay conveyed an unambiguous message: in order for Iraqis to progress, they needed to turn away from men of religion and religion itself, to modern science, technology, and capitalism. The author, however, remained skeptical as to the chances for such a dramatic shift in mentality. An editorial column in *Al-Burhan*, titled "The Reflections of a Madman," summed up the problem as follows: "Allah—if I were a reasonable man I would deny His existence, but as long as I am crazy, I believe in Him."[19]

The intellectual tools by which Iraqi Jews reoriented themselves to their religion also changed. They kept up with debates in the Arab press and reprinted articles about science, technology, and secularism in their own journals and newspapers. Articles in *Al-Hasid*, for instance, tackled the myth of creation, the writings of Friedrich Nietzsche, and the need to curb the powers of the religious establishment. One writer who greatly influenced how spirituality and reform were conceptualized in the Arab world was Henry Bergson (1859–1941). Egyptian intellectuals were particularly taken with his work, many having become familiar with it during study in France. Ya'qub Balbul had been introduced to Bergson's thinking through his education at the Alliance school and the secular cultural milieu he moved in, as well as through Arabic newspapers and journals. Analyzing his collection of poetry published in 1942, Balbul confessed that "these poems were written under the influence of the modern French philosopher, Henry Bergson, and in particular his book *L'Evolution créatrice*."[20] In Balbul's poetry, Bergson's notion of *force vital* (or *élan vital*), a concept that rejected causality and privileged the coincidental and the unintentional, played a considerable role.[21]

Reflections on religious authority, however, were not always expressed as broad statements about the nature of human beings and the universe. At times, writers named names, pointed a finger at those whom they considered to be conservative and treacherous. Yet the tensions between Jewish religious institutions and the new secularized Jewish elites were not as grave as one might think. During the nineteenth century, Iraqi Jewish rabbis had expressed progressive views regarding science and modernity: Rabbi 'Abdallah Somekh, for example, allowed traveling in trains and trams within the city boundaries on the Sabbath, and supported the adoption of technology and Western education.[22]

The community's religious leadership changed under the monarchy. The Ottoman regulations, which stipulated that the Iraqi chief rabbi (Hakham-bashi; Hahambaşı) was to take the leading role in all religious matters pertaining to the community (with the help of local committees), remained in force through 1920s.[23] After the collapse of the Ottoman empire, the Hakham-bashi acquired greater power since he was no longer subject to the authority of the rabbis and officials in Istanbul. The years 1928–30 were marked by fierce debates within the community concerning the conduct of the Hakham-bashi. Rabbis accused the community's Hakham-bashi, Rabbi Sasun Khaduri, of not adhering strictly to Jewish dietary law, embezzling communal funds, visiting places of questionable repute, and labeling his opponents as Zionists. Rabbi Khaduri for his part was supported by journalists such as Anwar Sha'ul and Ezra Haddad.[24] To put an end to this strife, the state enacted new regulations concerning the general governance of the Jewish community in June 1931. The new law canceled the previous Hakham-bashi order, but retained a similar structure. The community was divided into three regions, Mosul, Basra, and Baghdad, each overseen by a general council ('umumi), a body elected every four years. The council was in charge of the yearly budget, and supervised the activities of two subcouncils: a secular council (jismani), which dealt with matters pertaining to health, education, and social life; and (only in Baghdad) a spiritual council (ruhani), which was in charge of religious affairs (such as religious courts, marriages, divorces, and synagogues).[25] An equally significant outcome of the debates about Rabbi Khaduri was a discussion in both *Al-Burhan* and *Al-Hasid* about the roles of rabbis in Jewish societies. There was much disagreement, except on one fundamental point: all considered the rule of religious men as being obsolete and thought that presently the Jewish community subscribed to an archaic belief system that allowed ignorant men of religion to govern its affairs.

A close look at Iraqi Jewish journals of the 1920s and 1930s reveals that many aspects of Jewish religious practice were called into question. An important matter was the slaughter of animals for food. This was of great concern because the community benefited from the taxes levied on kosher meat, revenue which was used to support various educational and religious activities. Younger Jewish intellectuals, however, called for a lowering of these taxes; they believed that the poor within the Jewish community were unable to purchase meat because the taxes made the prices too high. This viewpoint was shared by other elements within the general public. In 1937, when the general council decided to raise the tax on kosher meat, Jewish butchers organized demonstrations against Rabbi Khaduri and the community's leaders.[26]

Corruption on the part of religious officials was another matter taken up by the Iraqi Jewish press. *Al-Hasid*, although more moderate than *Al-Burhan*, did not hesitate to levy attacks on those who used religion for personal gain. Anwar Sha'ul criticized rabbis who, he felt, betrayed the interests of the community and used the Jewish faith in order to obtain power and capital.[27] His position on matters related to politics and religion crystallized in an essay of his commemorating the death of Na'im Zilkha. Zilkha (1879–1929), a lawyer and a member of the secular council, was known for the battles he fought in the 1920s in order to modernize Jewish education. A number of Iraqi journals printed obituaries and articles in which Muslim and Christian writers praised Zilkha's progressive views. The journalist Salman al-Sheikh Da'ud lauded Zilkha's efforts toward reform with the aim of attaining a true revival (*nahda*). Zilkha, Sheikh Da'ud maintained, did so out of loyalty to Allah and the homeland. Another writer, Ibrahim Hilmi al-'Umar, hailed Zilkha as a true Arab and Iraqi brother, who had fought for equality and justice for the sons of his community and the sons of his nation.[28] *Al-Hasid* also published pieces by several Jewish authors, including Sha'ul, which were gathered in a book the community published as a memorial to Zilkha. Sha'ul recalled Zilkha's position toward men of religion (*rijal al-din*): Zilkha was the first to stand against those who had made religion a deadly net with which to capture their prey, and to challenge their hegemony in the community's institutions. Some of these men of religion, Sha'ul reported, wanted to visit Zilkha when he was ill. "He had listened to them for about a minute or so and then shouted at them: 'Go away, hypocrites [*munafiqun*], go! I do not want to see you!'"[29]

Zilkha's eulogy testifies to some significant historical processes at work within the community. A man who played a key role in the Jewish community's effort to integrate itself into the Ottoman empire after 1908 and in establishing its legal institutions, Zilkha was commemorated not only by Jews but also by Muslims and Christians. His appeal to equality, which was not based on religious dogma but rather on law, was extolled as one of his contributions to Iraqi society as a whole. Sha'ul, moreover, used the death of Zilkha to celebrate Zilkha as a secular hero, who had shown a great deal of courage in challenging the conservative voices within the Iraqi Jewish community. This resoluteness was seen as a typical character trait of a modern and progressive man.

The debates concerning secularism and reform were not confined to the pages of newspapers and journals. The establishment in 1931 of a theosophical society by Khaduri 'Ayni in Basra, for example, sparked a full-fledged battle between the Iraqi rabbinical leadership and the theosophists. The rabbinical side staged demonstrations against the theosophists and their society, refused to allow them to pray in the community's synagogues, and banned the burial of Jewish theosophists in Jewish cemeteries. The theosophists, for their part, built their own cemetery and sold their own kosher meat for cheaper prices. In 1934, a group of rabbis from Baghdad came to the city but were unable to put an end to the crisis. Only a very generous donation by one of the Jewish community's leading men, on the condition that all conflicts cease immediately, eased these tensions. The debate about theosophy affected the lives of Basran Jews and the Jewish religious leadership in Baghdad. All of a sudden, buying food, praying, being laid to rest in a Jewish cemetery, or simply socializing with Jews and non-Jews alike indicated one's position on secularism and reform. Although the rabbis won this particular battle, it seems that in most cases the younger generation gained the upper hand, the most obvious instance being Jewish education.[30]

Discipline and Education

Avraham Twena, a man active in the community's educational committees in the 1940s, described the fears of the rabbis concerning modern education during the interwar period: "The graduates of high schools registered at the law college. Every high school graduate or whoever knew English and Arabic became a government official and worked on the Sabbath. The rabbis viewed those who went to school as the ones who intended to break all boundaries, violate the Sabbath laws, and consume nonkosher food. The rabbis thought that one boy might lead another to bad culture and they saw heresy in the horizon. In truth, the rabbis were right."[31] Of the factors that caused Iraqi Jews to develop a sense of identity that was not based on religion, the Iraqi education system loomed large. It introduced secular subjects such as science, history, and geography and provided venues in which Jewish students could meet and befriend Muslim and Christian students and teachers. Through school Iraqi Jewish students performed ceremonies of national import (such as trips to historic sites) and came to find their place in Arab (rather than Jewish) history and by extension in Iraqi society as a whole. The process of becoming Arab Jews thus depended in no small measure on the state, which sent teachers to instruct Jewish students in Arab history and culture. At the same time, Jewish students and teachers showed an equal interest in promoting Arab culture. Teachers such as Ezra Haddad believed in the vitality of Arabic as a language and Arab culture, and many parents and students realized that fluency in Arabic would speed their integration into Iraqi society.

During the nineteenth century primary religious education for Iraqi Jews was offered in schools called *kuttab* or *ustaz*, where children learned the Hebrew alphabet and biblical exegesis. More advanced religious instruction was provided at the school Midrash Talmud Torah (established in 1832). In 1840, the first *yeshiva* was established in Baghdad. By the monarchic period, however, Jewish *kuttab*s had come to function as preschools rather than as primary schools. A major event in the life of the community was the opening of the Alliance israélite universelle, on December 10th, 1864. The Alliance's language of instruction was French, though Hebrew, Arabic, Turkish, and English were taught as well. In the late nineteenth century it began to offer classes in math, history, geography, physics, biology, and chemistry. The Alliance opened a school for girls in 1893 and additional schools for boys in Basra, Mosul, Hilla, and 'Amara. Moreover, as the school's reputation grew, Muslims and Christians also sent their children to the Alliance.[32] Other educational options for Iraqi Jews in the nineteenth century included Ottoman institutions. The Jews who assumed leadership roles in the province of Baghdad in 1908 and later held important positions in the Hashemite state had studied in Ottoman schools—some in Baghdad, while others, not unlike their Sunni Iraqi peers, traveled to Istanbul for higher education.[33]

The monarchic era in Iraq saw changes to the country's educational system, from which Iraqi Jews benefited as well. The state ran preschools (*awaliyya*), primary schools (*ibitida'iyya*), middle schools (*mutawasita*), and high schools (*i'adadiyya*). The Iraqi education system introduced into the curriculum classes in science, modern geography, and secularized history.[34] The number of Jews in the education system increased dramatically during the Hashemite period.[35] In the academic year 1949–50, nineteen thousand Jewish students attended schools in Iraq: one-third of these students were female; thirty-five hundred attended high schools; and five hundred perused a higher degree after their high school graduation.[36] The number of Jewish students in the state educational system was considerable, given that Jewish students had the option of attending schools run by the government or by the community. From 1920 on, government schools were by law open to all pupils regardless of religion, and thus both Christians and Jews attended schools with Muslim-majority student bodies. This trend became more pronounced after World War Two, when the state embarked on a campaign of school building. This enabled Jews from a lower socioeconomic background to receive primary and higher education. Since religion formed part of the curriculum, Jewish students were allowed to absent themselves from Islamic religious lessons. Jews also attended missionary schools, especially the American School for Boys in Baghdad.[37]

Denominational schools in Iraq were founded and run by the Jewish, various Christian, and the Shi'i communities. Of these, Jewish schools were the most numerous. The schools were largely funded by the community, but did receive annual grants from the Ministry of Education. These were made according to the needs of the school, its standard of teaching, and the degree of conformity of its curriculum to state educational requirements. The state's goal was that all Iraqi students pass standardized exams at the primary and secondary levels. British reports to the League of Nations noted that the Jewish schools had succeeded in improving their programs along the lines suggested by the Ministry of Education through great effort. The 1927 report observed that Jewish schools deserved more grants: "The Jews have a moral claim to be heard because, by providing so many schools of their own, they relieve ... the pressure on government schools." Regrettably, however, "under present financial stringency it is difficult for the government to maintain a school for a community which already provides, though at its own expense, proportionately more primary schools for its children than the government provides for the Mohammedan children."[38] A 1936 law that exempted anyone possessing a high school diploma from military service expedited the process of integration into the state's curricula, as it required Jewish students to take the nationwide matriculation exams.[39]

The Jewish community itself had formed an education committee which was a subcommittee of the Baghdadi secular council (*al-majlis al-jismani*). The committee worked to bring about various reforms intended to modernize the curriculum, improve the standards of teaching and the teaching methodologies in Jewish schools, and limit the imposition of corporal punishment in schools. In 1948 the committee counted Shalom Darwish and Ya'qub Balbul among its members. Both were not only well-known public figures, but also gifted writers, who believed in the vitality of Iraqi Arab literature and culture and proponents of integration in the Arab cultural milieu.[40]

The Iraqi Jewish education system was diversified, and offered a number of pedagogical and educational opportunities to members of the community. Most of the schools were located in Baghdad. An account provided by the Baghdadi Jewish community for the year 1950 divided the community's main schools into two categories, schools that were not supported by private religious endowments (*waqf*, plural *awqaf*) and schools that were.[41] Basra had two Midrash schools (established in 1880 and in 1907), as well as an Alliance primary school and high school for boys and primary school for girls (established in 1913). Many of the Jews in Basra, however, attended mixed-state schools. Mosul had a Midrash Talmud Torah and two Alliance primary schools, one for boys and one for girls.[42] The education system in the north was not as well developed as it was in central Iraq; girls' education was particularly neglected. Most northern Iraqi Jews attended state schools in which they were the minority. In Sulaimaniya, for instance, Jewish students faced unique linguistic problems: the language of the majority was Kurdish—which teachers, if Arab, had to learn—and the textbooks were often in Arabic. When King Ghazi came to power, the Sulaimaniya Jews asked to build a school for their community to be named after him. This school, which opened in 1933, served the needs of Jewish students (and also offered night classes to their parents); its classes were mainly taught by Arab teachers.[43]

The Jewish community established new schools, or asked the state to do so, for a number of reasons, such as an increase in the Jewish population in a neighborhood or the availability of funding from a rich Jewish donor who would make a donation as way of memorializing a family member. Schools were also founded with an ideological goal as the impetus, such as the promotion of Arab culture (as was the case with the Baghdadi school al-Wataniyya [Patriotism]). More practical considerations were behind school establishment as well: the Shammash high school was intended to specialize in English-language instruction. Denominational schools were funded by students' tuition (although the community gave stipends to students from poor families), allowances earned by the community from taxation, donations, and religious endowments.[44] The education committee tried to modernize the schools, equipping them with laboratories, libraries, and various teaching aids.[45] The teaching staff was mostly Jewish, with Muslim teachers instructing students in Arabic language and literature, civics, geography, and Arab history.[46]

The experience of Iraqi Jews in the educational system was key to the reconceptualization of their Arab and secular identity.[47] Students in modern schools were told they were living in a new age, characterized by scientific innovations and the spread of literacy. Ishaq Bar-Moshe, a student in Rachel Shahmon, reported that their teacher, Shim'on Mu'allim Nissim, explicated the meaning of the new age to his class:

> Children, you are living today in a period with an abundance of comforts and services provided by science. Schools are everywhere. Education has become mandatory and nothing could be done without it. This period is called the modern age. Every period is seen by its sons as being modern, but that is a different topic altogether. We are living in a period where the number of educated people outnumbers that of the illiterate.... There have been, [however,] generations in the history of the human race when ignorance reigned, and superstition prevailed over books of science. Magicians occupied positions now held by the teacher, the doctor, and the ruler.[48]

The teacher's narrative was meant to instill in the students the belief that their education mattered and that it was bound up with a momentous cultural shift, namely, with their living in a modern era. Here modernity is associated with the reign of science ("the doctor"), education ("the teacher"), and new notions of sovereignty ("the ruler"), whereas the past is symbolized by witchcraft, ignorance, and illiteracy.

A central element in the state's educational vision was to reinforce the idea that all Iraqi students were first and foremost Arabs. Language played a major role in the Arabization of Iraqi Jews and in their subsequent secularization. British accounts to the League of Nations noted the improvement in the methods of instruction in Arabic in the Jewish schools in the mid-1920s. The 1925 account to the League of Nations had reported that Jewish schools sorely lacked teachers who could teach Arabic. Those who could teach, according to the report, did not know Arabic, and those who did were poor teachers "and thus much excellent material is wasted." In response, the Ministry of Education set up a program through which Jewish schoolmasters and schoolmistresses received additional training.[49] In the same year, a committee was appointed by the Jewish community to oversee the standardization of teaching methods in all Jewish schools, and it worked with the state to achieve this goal. The joint effort resulted in a two-year course of study, which included classes in pedagogy and psychology taught by the Pan-Arab intellectual Sati' al-Husri and by professors from Iraq, Lebanon, and Egypt.[50] Jewish teachers thus became familiar with instruction methods their Arab Iraqi colleagues utilized. Beginning in 1934, the Jewish education committee forbade to appoint a teacher who did not hold at least a high school diploma at Jewish schools.[51]

Instruction in Arabic and Arab history and culture in Jewish schools had momentous cultural effects, predominantly because Islam was propagated in the education system as a cultural component of Iraqi national identity. Jewish students learned about the rise of Islam, the Islamic conquests, and the great Islamic empires.[52] Jewish students also read the works of Arab thinkers and discussed contemporary issues, such as the struggle across the Arab world for independence from British imperialist rule.[53] Arabization was most successful in government schools where Jews were a minority. Such Jewish students often lived in mixed neighborhood and were curious about the students' religion.[54]

Not always, however, was the introduction of the Qur'an to Jewish children favorably received. In 1923 Ezra Haddad, then a teacher at

Midrash Talmud Torah, was charged with opening a new branch of the school in a Muslim neighborhood into which Jews were moving. He used a book that cited Qur'anic verses in his teaching of Arabic grammar, leading to the rumor that Haddad was attempting to convert Jewish children to Islam. Haddad was publicly condemned in synagogues, and individuals came to Haddad's home to express their personal grievances. The rabbis warned that, based on this scandal, secularization had gone too far. The branch was closed down, leaving its students without a school. Members of the community's education committee who were not religious officials came to Haddad's aid and established a school in the same neighborhood called al-Wataniyya (Patriotism). They retained Haddad as principal of the school, the purpose of which was improving instruction in Arabic and Arab culture and literature. In keeping with the school's goals, students performed plays in Arabic and participated in the Iraqi Boy Scouts.[55] In 1968 Haddad summed up the experience: "I believed that the sons of Israel needed education. I was certain that the God of Israel would not hear the curses of the rabbis [against me], because rabbis were important to me, but the people of my community mattered more."[56] This affair illustrates how an attack motivated by religiosity and separatism inadvertently promoted the growth of Arab nationalism and secular education in the Iraqi Jewish community.

A testimony to the Arabization of Jewish schools was the contents of their libraries, whose holdings included Arabic, English, French, and sometimes Hebrew books. The library of the Alliance schools in Baghdad contained history books by Jurji Zaydan, Butrus al-Bustani's encyclopedia *Da'irat al-Ma'arif*, and journals such as *Al-Muqtataf*, *Lughtat al-'Arab*, and *Al-Masrhiq*, as well as poetry collections by Iraqi, Egyptian, and Syrian poets.[57] A community account from 1950 on the state of the libraries in the Jewish Baghdadi schools shows that the total number of Arabic books in these libraries was 8,170, the number of English books: 4,889, of Hebrew books: 2,261, in addition to children's books (3,157 in number).[58] The number of Arabic books in each library was probably higher, because children books were often written in Arabic.[59]

Jewish newspapers reported about plays preformed in Jewish schools. In the 1920s, *Al-Misbah* reported on the plays presented by Alliance students, which were often Arabic renditions of famous European works.⁶⁰ *Al-Hasid* likewise kept its readers informed as to students' endeavors in the performing arts: one report hailed the production of *Hamlet* at the Alliance. The critic was somewhat displeased, however, that boys played women's roles because (notwithstanding this being in keeping with Shakespearean tradition) a particularly tall and somewhat masculine Gertrude overshadowed poor Hamlet. The Alliance, which had an orchestra, recorded a few songs that were aired on the radio during the late 1940s.⁶¹

The effect of an education informed by Arab nationalism on the minds of Jewish students was reflected in the memorializing by the Alliance students of their friend Eliyahu Khaduri Mu'allim, who died at a young age. Eliyahu had translated some short stories, in particular some by de Maupassant, into Arabic. To honor him, Eliyahu's friends collected these and added a few essays (one was by Eliyahu and the others were written versions of speeches delivered by friends after his death), which they printed as a small booklet in the publishing house Matba'at al-Rashid. Eliyahu had written the essay just before his death, in which he expressed the hope that his works would contribute, in some way, to his nation's revival. The Arab East will not rise again, the young writer said, as long as foreign control denies the Arabs freedom and enforces ignorance upon them. Promises from foreigners, however, will not release the Arab East from its chains, but rather a spirit of rebellion and uprising. Eliyahu was optimistic enough to believe that the nation's innocent souls and the pure blood of its sons would overcome the formidable hurdles that stood in the way of true independence. Eliyahu thus called on his fellow students to struggle relentlessly for freedom and knowledge (*'ilm*). One of Eliyahu's friends recalled that Eliyahu's knowledge of English and French motivated him to translate texts in these languages into Arabic. Eliyahu, his friend added, wished to move beyond literal translation and find new modes to render French and English texts more successfully than previous translators had done. Finally, the friend remarked that Eliyahu himself also composed short narratives in Arabic prose.⁶²

This account of Eliyahu's activity as a translator and writer contains three key details. First, despite his knowledge of French and English, Eliyahu chose to translate into Arabic, thus making a contribution to Arabic literary culture. Second, Eliyahu's own writing (and the many clichés that Eliyahu used) connected his literary activities to the national aspirations of the Arab peoples. Eliyahu's essay, in fact, addressed themes current in the Arab press of the time. Iraq, many editorials argued, needed true independence rather than the false sovereignty it possessed, under which Iraq's interests were subordinated to British imperial interests. Other editorials and speeches by Iraqi officials lionized the heroism of the youth and their willingness to sacrifice their lives for the sake of the nation. Eliyahu's short speech reproduced these discourses. Finally, the importance of the venue of the memorial cannot be overstated. The students of the school gathered publicly to listen to a very anti-British and nationalist text. There was nothing religious about Eliyahu's memorial; in fact it resembled funerals of poets and writers at which mourners hailed the deceased's contribution to the nation. The Jewish school, then, served as the site of a small-scale version of a national commemoration ceremony in which the student's activities were depicted as a form of service to his country.

For Jews who attended public schools in which they were a minority, the schools became microcosms reflecting the classes and religions of Iraqi society. Jewish students recall picking up the Baghdadi Muslim dialect and making friends with Iraqis of various religions and ethnicities.[63] Jonah Cohen, a student from Hilla, recalls that during the first ten days of the month of Muharram, he and the other Jews watched the processions commemorating the death of Husayn, the Prophet's grandson. Jonah attended a high school populated mostly by Shi'i students. He was called by a Shi'i classmate to march with him. These young men marched together not at the prompting of religion or state policies, but because of the bonds formed inside and outside of the classroom.[64]

The link between the Jewish student and the Iraqi nation was strengthened by field trips to various sites around the country. The purpose of these was to encourage students to learn more about Iraq, its geography, and history, as well as to reinforce the very secular notion that Iraq's history was as important as, if not more important than, Jewish history.[65]

Jonah Cohen who grew up in Hilla provides the most detailed descriptions of these trips during his schooling in the latter portion of 1940s. The destination of the first was a village south of the city: "Great joy seized all the students. . . . Some students had never left our hometown! Cars were not yet a common sight, and a great deal of money was needed in order to leave the city and see other places, and the limited means of most of the residents did not allow them to spend so much."⁶⁶ During the trip the teachers pointed out plants and animals and geographical features of the area, as the students sang national songs.⁶⁷ In high school, field trips became even more interesting. For example, Jonah and his fellow students traveled to the mansion of al-Sayyid al-Qazwini, the religious leader of the Shi'i community whose son and nephew attended the high school.⁶⁸ Another memorable tour was of Baghdad. Not all students could go on the trip, because of its cost. One of the students, who remained behind in Hilla, "gave half a dinar to his friend and told him to sleep with a prostitute, and let this be counted as if he had slept with her."⁶⁹ In Baghdad, the students were guided by the history teacher, who showed them the government ministries and the archeological museum. The trip, in Jonah's eyes, flowed directly from what they studied in their history lessons.⁷⁰

The most exhilarating excursion, however, was to the ruins of Babylon, a few kilometers north of Hilla. The students went to the site, carrying flags and marching to the sound of drums: "These are the ruins of Babylon, the city to which our ancestors were exiled. On its banks they cried, remembering Zion."⁷¹ They toured the site, and discussed the importance of the Lion of Babylon, a replica of which stood in a garden in Hilla. The teacher described the city in its heyday, pointing to the location of the city's main buildings. His explanation resonated strongly with Jonah, who felt as if the Babylonian buildings "still exist today." The teacher also repeated to the students what they had read in history books about the first Babylonian kingdom, "which existed in the time of Abraham, our patriarch," and about Hammurabi and his laws. This story reminded Jonah of the drawing in his history textbook depicting King Hammurabi.⁷²

Jonah's account illustrates how the state's national discourse shaped these field trips. The state hoped to strengthen the connections between center and periphery. To this end it was important that the students from Hilla see the capital city—for students from poor families, such trips were their only means to get to know other parts of the nation. On many such field trips, the teacher functioned as a mediator, endowing the trip with nationalized and secularized meaning. Religious distinctions were not entirely erased in these nationalizing excursions; students visited the Qazwini mansion because it belonged to their city's leading religious authority and because many of them were Shi'i themselves. Similarly, the site of Babylon evoked in Jonah's memory not only the Iraqi national tradition, but also his own Jewish tradition, via the biblical verses about Babylon. Nonetheless, the memory of the destruction of the First Temple in Jerusalem was tempered by sentiments of pride concerning Babylon's glorious past.[73] Finally, it is worthwhile noting that despite the state's plans, children and teenagers had their own ideas about the significance of such trips. They saw the trip to the big city as an opportunity to act out their masculinity and their sense of manhood via visiting prostitutes and taking part in illegal activities.

The teachers played an immensely important role as agents of Arab Iraqi nationalism in the Jewish community. As noted, Jewish schools of their own accord began to hire Muslim teachers in the 1920s.[74] This trend accelerated in 1939, when the Ministry of Education announced that it would appoint teachers of Arabic, history, geography, and civics.[75] At Rachel Shahmon, the poet Mahmud al-Mallah taught Arabic, and dedicated a few verses in Arabic to the memory of Rachel Shahmon—verses that were painted on the walls of the school. The school also employed Muslim teachers who were or would soon become prominent intellectuals, such as the famous historian 'Abbas al-'Azzawi.[76] At the Alliance high school in Basra, the Arabic professor was 'Abd al-Rida Sadiq, a Shi'i from Najaf, who encouraged extracurricular activities. Sadiq initiated the building of an Arabic library in the school; assisted students in the writing of poetry and prose and the performance of plays; and supervised the publication of the school's Arabic newspaper. The school's English teacher was an Egyptian and the geography and civics teacher was an Algerian who had been banished from his country by the French.[77] At Shammash high school, the Shi'i teacher and intellectual Muhammad Sharara introduced his students to Arab poets like Muhammad Mahdi al-Jawahiri.[78] The influence of these Arab teachers was enormous. They assumed positions of authority in a Jewish educational setting, reminding their students about the existence of the state and its Arab Islamic culture. Students' autobiographies and reports from the time indicate that some of these teachers (especially those who were poets and writers themselves) were regarded as beloved mentors and friends.

The Jewish teachers themselves, moreover, frequently turned out to be Arab nationalists and carried the mission of Arabization into their schools. Moshe Sofer, a Zionist activist, said of the teachers at Rachel Shahmon during the interwar period: "Some of the teachers, who were Jews deep in their hearts, did not object explicitly to Zionism. But there were others who [had gotten] their diplomas at the Teachers Training College in Baghdad, which belonged to the government. They [had] absorbed Arabism and Arab nationalism and had no inclination at all toward the Jewish and Zionist affair."[79]

Jews also worked as teachers within the Arab school system, and this had consequences for the teachers themselves as well as for the students. Fahima Mu'allim Nissim, who had studied with the Iraqi feminist Sabiha al-Sheikh Da'ud, was one of the first Jewish teachers appointed to teach in a Muslim school for girls in 1925. Fahima was from an influential Jewish family, and this probably influenced her conditions of employment. Fahima did not place her religious commitments and social status before her responsibilities to her students, however, and was willing to reduce her time off for the holiday of Sukkoth. Her students and fellow female teachers continued visiting her even after she married and left the teaching profession.[80] Another example of nonsectarian trends in Iraqi Jewish education is the career of two bothers from a humble socioeconomic background, Victor and Salman Mu'allim, who established a few schools in Baghdad. One of their projects was the night school al-Ahali, which was opened in 1943–44. Victor intended his school to be a night school for students of all religions, being motivated by the desire to demonstrate that a Jew could be a loyal Iraqi patriot. The school's students were divided between Jews, Muslims, and Christians (of various denominations). The school enrolled students from the ages of fifteen to forty-five who were in need of a primary education. The school also had tutorials which were taught voluntarily by its teachers.[81] Both Fahima and Victor, it seems, considered the larger Iraqi community as the space in which they sought to educate the next generation of Muslims, Christians, and Jews.

Iraqi schools also cultivated nonsectarian identities among teachers. Gurji Barshan was appointed as a physical education teacher in a Jewish school and attended a meeting of all physical education teachers in Baghdad. The Ministry of Education sent a Syrian instructor to address the teachers. He was not warmly received: the Iraqi teachers wanted one of their own, an Iraqi, and were not impressed by the Syrian's interests in adopting Iraqi customs. The Syrian instructor then said that he was surprised to see that most shops in Baghdad were owned by Jews. Syria, he assured his listeners, was different. Gurji turned to an old high school friend of his, a Muslim Shi'i who told the Syrian teacher that "there is no difference here between a Jew and a Muslim." The Syrian instructor fell silent and said, "I did not mean to offend the Jews."[82]

The account posits two sorts of Iraqi-ness: one false, that of the Syrian instructor, and one authentic, shared by Iraqi Muslim and Jewish teachers. The Syrian teacher's attempt to mark a difference between Jews and Muslims, as a sign of the superiority of Syrian Arab-ness and nationalism, is rejected by the Iraqis, Jews and Muslims alike. Moreover, they force him to alter his representation of nationalism. Significantly, Barshan's narration conveys a sense of a distinctly Iraqi nationalism, contrasting the Iraqis' vision of coexistence with the divisive nationalism of an outsider who was misguidedly sent by the state. In the historiography of modern Iraq, the Arab teachers from Syria and Palestine recruited by the state are represented as symbols of the nation's commitment to Pan-Arab causes. Their presence inspired criticism, however: they were seen as collaborating with the Hashemite state, and as hostile towards Shi'is and Kurds.[83] Gurji's description captures this point of view.

The cultivation of the students' bodies, especially of healthy masculinity, was a significant part of the school's curriculum and was promoted by the state.[84] *Al-Burhan*'s editor, Sha'ul Haddad, a fervent believer in eugenics, embarked on a campaign, beginning in 1932, to have physical education incorporated into the school curriculum. He was joined by Shalom Darwish and the lawyer Me'ir Zachariah in the attempt to organize sports groups in schools, an effort that was successful despite the objections of conservatives to the inclusion of basketball, volleyball, tennis, and soccer in the schools' programs.[85] Jewish students also participated in extracurricular activities such as the Boy Scouts and the more problematic state-sponsored paramilitary youth group al-Futuwwa (The Youth). Though al-Futuwwa had some ties to the profascist camp, some Jews joined its ranks as part of their school curriculum.[86] After the failure of the Kaylani coup, al-Futuwwa was abolished and

Jewish children again joined the Boy Scouts (an organization which was in competition with the Futuwwa and much closer to the British).[87]

The teaching of foreign languages in schools was seen as crucial to the project of secular modernity in Iraq. The connection between modern education and the Enlightenment was especially relevant to the Alliance school in Baghdad as well as to the students of this institution in other cities in Iraq, who felt that their education imbued them with the values of French culture. This argument was made by students who became leading intellectuals in the interwar period, such as Anwar Sha'ul and Mir Basri, as well as by students who attended the school in the late 1940s. Sha'ul declared that his French lessons enabled him to admire the philosophy of Rousseau and Voltaire, while Basri fondly remembered the library of the Alliance, where he was exposed to the works of Rousseau, Voltaire, and Hugo.[88]

With the arrival of the British, the Alliance was criticized for its choice of French as the language of instruction. Shammash, an English-language high school that prepared its students for the London matriculation exams, soon became the preferred school in British and Jewish circles. Generally speaking, most Jewish schools in this period privileged the teaching of English as a foreign language, in the hope of improving the prospects for students in both Iraq and England.[89] The British report for the League of Nations on the year 1925 noted: "The *Alliance Israelite* still makes their pupils . . . study four languages at once, and this leaves very little time for any other subjects," whereas in "schools outside of the orbit of the *Alliance* a more sensible programme is being introduced, to the great advantage of the pupils."[90] The opening of Shammash, a new school under a British headmaster, won British support.[91] This development was not favorably regarded by some of the officials in the Ministry of Education, however, because it promoted the colonizers' culture.[92]

In the same manner that the Alliance promoted French culture, teachers and students in Shammash saw the school as an emissary of modern English culture. Adolph Brotman, who was appointed supervisor of English instruction in Jewish schools in 1926, and a headmaster of Shammash, stated that "English was the language which was more looked up to."[93] The new relationship between Iraq and Great Britain was the reason: "There were soldiers and commercial enterprises that opened up which brought in English people."[94] Sasson Somekh, a student at Shammash, recalled that the study of English fostered a love of English literature and the desire to translate works in English into Arabic.[95] To supplement the school library's holdings, Brotman brought novels by Dickens as well as Carroll's *Alice in Wonderland* to the school. Jonah Cohen recalls how he went to the British cultural center in Hilla, which possessed the only library in the city, in order to read adventure books such as *Gulliver's Travels*, as well as English newspapers and journals.[96] Testifying to the increasing hegemony of English as the foreign language of choice was the curriculum of Rachel Shahmon. This school, which was established after the Young Turks Revolution, dropped Turkish in favor of English with the British occupation of Iraq. In 1921 Arabic became the language of instruction, while the teaching of French ceased in 1925.[97]

Nonetheless, the Alliance schools continued to attract students. The competition between English and French education meant that in Iraq students were exposed to more than one foreign language. By contrast, in North Africa, where French was adopted by both the colonial state and the schools, a single language was identified with the colonizers, Western culture, and modern education. In Iraq, Arabic was taught in all schools, and was privileged by the state's education ministry. In terms of secularization, English and French, like Arabic, introduced students to a modern world whose values they came to cherish. Iraqi Jews thus gained a sense of the West that was not monolithic. They could see positive as well as negative aspects to Western culture, and therefore did not identify French and English solely with imperialism and colonialism. The competition between the two languages, however, reinforced the position of Arabic, since, regardless of the foreign language to which Jewish students were exposed, the connections between Arabic, Arab culture, and Iraqi Arab nationalism were made abundantly clear to all students by their teachers and by their state.

Finally, not only Arabic, English, and French, but also Hebrew had a significant impact on the mindset of Jewish students. The teaching of Hebrew in Jewish schools was permitted during the 1920s; it was banned only because the state feared that the teaching of Hebrew would aid the spread of Zionism.[98] These teachers were often agents of secularization, as their attitude toward religion tended to be more critical than credulous. Hebrew teacher Moshe Sofer recalled that he had objected to synagogue-goers being allowed during Yom Kippur to light as many candles as they liked in the memory of the deceased, since this practice turned the synagogues into stifling and unpleasant spaces. Sofer also opined that Jewish women not cover their faces as did Muslim women. In response the Baghdadi rabbis, including Chief Rabbi Sasun Khaduri, summed Sofer to a meeting and threatened to excommunicate him. Nonetheless the support Sofer received from the headmaster in the school in which he taught helped him keep his post.[99]

Other Hebrew teachers faced complaints about their misconduct, especially from the rabbinical leadership of the community. Most commonly they were reproached for not keeping the Sabbath and for violating Jewish dietary laws, as was the case in 1927 with Me'ir Ezra and Reuben Goldberg; these charges were refuted by their headmasters. Ezra Haddad, of al-Wataniyya, acted to dispel similar rumors concerning his Hebrew teacher, Isaac Devash.[100] Female kindergarten teachers from Mandatory Palestine experienced a great deal of difficulty, as their employment was not looked upon favorably by local rabbis.[101] In a blunt letter to Zionist organizations in Palestine, Adolph Brotman mentioned Jewish accusations against Hebrew teachers for not being "sufficiently religious for Baghdad" and for failing to be "nationalist propagandists." Brotman commented angrily: "It need[s] only to be said that no Jew of Palestine or any other part of the world *would* be religious [enough] for the local hahamin and . . . [that] it is not desirable that the teachers here should engage in any political activities in the schools. . . . The enlightened elements of the Jewish population are grateful for, and appreciative of, the very fine efforts made by the Palestinian teachers I engage through your department" (emphasis in the original).[102] That Brotman was wary of Zionist activities in Jewish schools is understandable. This letter does make clear, however, that Brotman, one of the leading figures in Iraqi Jewish education in the 1920s, was not on good terms with the local rabbis. Not surprisingly, Brotman noted that his secularizing efforts enjoyed the support of the enlightened Jewish community in Baghdad. The different approaches to secularism were thus not anchored in an East-West binary, but an enlightened-religious binary, with Jews from Baghdad, Palestine, and England falling into the former category.

The relationship between Jewish teachers and students and the majority society worsened considerably in the late 1940s, especially after the establishment of the state of Israel. Ironically, the Arabization of Iraqi Jewish students reached a new height in these years. By then, Jewish schools had excellent teachers of Arabic, while Iraq itself was experiencing a literary and cultural renaissance. Chapters 5 and 6 will treat these trends in further detail, but suffice it to say that being a Jew in Iraq became increasingly difficult at this time because of discriminatory laws, especially regulations that restricted the ability of Jews to enroll and teach at colleges. Interestingly, however, although Iraqi Jews complain in their memoirs about the prejudices they encountered as students, they remember that Muslim and Christian students had stood by them in times of trouble. The integration of Jews, Christians, Shi'is, and Sunnis in the schools thus fostered notions of Iraqi communalism from below even at moments when the patriotism of Iraqi Jews was called into question by the state.

As a result of the state's discriminatory policies, Jewish students were drawn to communist ideology, which was compatible with their ideas of brotherhood and communal solidarity, yet at the same time bolstered their critique of the state for their denial of citizenship rights. Schools became important hubs for communist activities, where Jewish students were convinced by fellow students that the state had wronged them and that only a class-based revolution would end their suffering. In this sense, the schools still acted as a secularizing institution, with communism replacing Arab Iraqi nationalism as the ideology driving the process of secularization. Jonah Cohen testifies that in Hilla the communists "circulated propaganda among the students because they wished to attract as many Jews as possible to their movement."[103] Former students have also portrayed their Muslim teachers as agents who introduced them to communist ideas, although it was forbidden for teachers to conduct political propaganda in the classroom.[104] Muslim teachers convinced the students that Iraq was a colonized state and that its ruling elites were denying people their rights. Sami Zubaida related the following about his teacher Muhammad Hasan al-Suri:

> I was taught by Muhammad Hasan al-Suri, a writer and a journalist, who influenced me greatly in literature, politics, and history. He was a product of the *hawza* (*madrasa*) of Najaf . . . but like many of his generation he had rejected religion in favour of leftist politics. I helped him translate articles and stories from an English-language magazine, *Soviet Literature*, a risky business under the monarchy.[105]

Zubaida attended Shammash, the high school that had been received so warmly by the British community when it was established. By the late 1940s, however, the school had become a venue for discussion not only of secular ideas but also of leftist ones, in part because of a Muslim teacher who had been sent by the state. The relationship between teacher and student, as described by Zubaida, was not based on discipline and authority but rather on mutual dependence and reciprocity. The teacher informed his student's opinions about literature and history, and the student helped his teacher in working against the state that employed him.

The presence of Jewish students in the Iraqi education system led to their attraction to both nationalism (in the interwar period) and communism (in the 1940s), with both having the effect of breaking communal boundaries and secularizing further the Jewish effendia. Though education was a system, it was a system composed of individuals. A charismatic Muslim teacher or the friendship of Christian and Muslim students seem to have done more in fostering intercommunal relationships and notions of Arab Jewishness than the countless fervent nationalist speeches by the state's officials.

The Jewish Women Question and the Iraqi Women Question

Jewish women lived in a society in which the rights of all women—be they Muslim, Arab, or Iraqi—were expanding. The urban Arab Muslim intelligentsia debated such issues as emancipation, women's education, seclusion, veiling, and family law. In the interwar period, the conversation about the roles of women in Iraq was mostly conducted among men who analyzed the relationship between modern male subjects and the liberties they gave their women. Policymakers and bureaucrats were concerned about the lack of national consciousness among Iraqi women and implemented programs in the domains of education and health to better the conditions of Iraqi women nationwide. King Faysal I supported women's emancipation, as did several prominent intellectuals: the neoclassical poets Ma'ruf al-Rusafi and Jamil Sidqi al-Zahawi called for the expansion of women's education and the ending of seclusion. During this period, middle- and upper-class Iraqi women organized clubs and reading societies and published newspapers. In the 1930s, nationalized and militaristic discourses influenced how both genders thought about the role of women: in this context, women were valued as the mothers of the next generation of Iraqi Arab patriots. The social democrats of al-Ahali and the ICP, however, introduced other solutions for the women's question, especially social justice and legal reform. Thus, when Iraqi Jewish intellectuals articulated positions on women of their community and their relationship to men, their children, and their nation-state, these intellectuals were also participating in a very Iraqi and Arab discourse in which one's positions on the "the women question" signified one's political and social affiliations. The issue of gender relations, more than any other, brought progressive intellectuals into conflict with religious and conservative groups in terms of their respective visions of society and education.[106]

Middle- and upper-class Jewish women attained a relatively high degree of education. The first Jewish primary school for girls, a branch of the Alliance named for Laura Kedourie, opened its doors in 1893, largely due to the efforts of young Francophile Jewish men who had graduated from the Alliance. Some Jewish families had already engaged French tutors for their daughters, and hoped the school would provide further instruction. Interestingly, poor parents, who wanted their daughters to work for economic reasons, also supported the establishment of the school though in later years they could not afford the tuition. Initially, Jewish Baghdadi rabbis objected to the school and made their views known through the Hebrew press. They characterized the school as being "objectionable to [the] laws of decency" and threatened to punish girls who attended the school by not writing their marriage contracts. In 1913, Rabbi Shim'on Agasi declared in a sermon that all the troubles that had recently befallen the Jewish community were caused by the school for girls. Luckily, the majority of Baghdadi Jews did not share his opinion. Rabbi Agasi's own daughter and son-in-law, for instance, sent their daughters to the school. In the years 1900–1919, the number of girls attending the school tripled. In the beginning the teaching staff of the Alliance was composed entirely of non-Iraqis, but over time former graduates returned to the school as teachers.

During the interwar period, the curriculum included instruction in four languages (French, English, Arabic, and Hebrew). Girls who finished the primary school could either continue to the Alliance middle school or to other high schools, but few actually did so. Most of the students at

Laura Kedourie came from upper-class families that did not intend for their daughters to enter the workforce. Mrs. Brotman, who taught English at the school, stated that the middle school girls' education was "on a par with what the boys received." "Her girls" spoke French and English well; they were taught a little history and their prayers; some played the piano, and others acted in school plays. She took particular pleasure in introducing her students to athletic activities, especially tennis. Nonetheless, Mrs. Brotman, as well as other teachers during the 1920s, frequently complained that girls left the school at the age of fourteen to fifteen to get married.[107]

During the Hashemite period, the number of schools for Jewish girls increased, as did their opportunities for going on to higher education outside the boundaries of the community. In 1923 the Alliance opened a kindergarten, in which female teachers taught according to the Montessori method.[108] A primary school for girls, named after No'am and Tova Nur'el, was founded in 1927 and the Ministry of Education established a school for girls named after Menashe Salih in 1930. The middle school al-Mutawasita al-ahliyya li'l banat (Public Middle School for Girls) was built in 1941–42 and a high school was built in 1950 to absorb the graduates of the elementary schools in the Jewish community. Very few schools, however, were coed beyond the third grade. The Shammash high school, offering mixed classes, was an exception; as of 1949–50 the school had 20 girls out of 447 students. In part, the lack of coed schools was due to conservative elements in the Jewish community, who expressed their resistance to mixed schools for boys and girls, even those under the age of twelve.[109]

Concern for the occupational options of poor Jewish girls led to the establishment, beginning in 1927, of vocational schools that instructed girls in sewing, knitting, and other gendered professions. Some limited academic instruction was offered, as volunteers among the community took to heart the sentiment current in the public sphere during this period concerning the need to combat illiteracy. A vocational school affiliated with Laura Kedourie School was opened in 1923 so that girls who could not afford to study at either No'am or Laura Kedourie would be trained there, and often prepared dresses for the graduates of the latter. Sixty young women graduated from the school in 1923; the number of graduates per year rose to two hundred in a short time. In 1946–19 Menahem Salih Daniel opened a professional school for girls, the purpose of which was to instruct students with an elementary school diploma who wanted to continue with their professional and academic studies. The school proved to be quite successful. Generally speaking, after the end of World War II women's educational opportunities increased throughout Iraq, and thus Iraqi women became more visible both in the labor market and in Baghdad's colleges.[110]

To compare the educational experiences of Jewish women, let us consider the biographies of Lulu (b. 1931), from a middle-class family, and Amal (b. 1926), from the influential Haim family. Lulu was sent first to a primary school run by Catholic nuns to improve her knowledge of French. She convinced her father to let her transfer to a Jewish school for girls, because a friend of hers attended the school. Lulu graduated from primary school, but her father would not allow her to go on to high school, sending her instead to the vocational unit of the Laura Kedourie School. She found herself in a class where most girls were illiterate or had a third-grade education at best, and consequently refused to attend that school. After making inquiries she learned about Menahem Daniel's school, which had recently opened and was offering classes in Arabic, math, and English, in addition to sewing and knitting. She was in the first graduating class.[111]

Amal was the granddaughter of Abraham (Ibrahim) Haim, an influential parliament member. She began at a primary school named after Menahem Salih Daniel and then moved on to Frank 'Ayni, a middle school for girls. After a short and unsuccessful experience at Shammash (due to her poor achievements in science), she transferred to a high school for girls where she studied with non-Jewish students. Her good grades there enabled her to enter the law faculty and later in her career she worked as a teacher at the No'am school for girls. In the course of her education, Amal was taught not only by Jewish teachers but also by Muslims and Christians from Iraq, Lebanon, and Egypt. In high school many of her classmates were Muslim, as was the case during her university studies. An Arab nationalist and an Iraqi patriot, she loved to salute the flag during school ceremonies and collected popular songs about Arab freedom and independence in her notebooks. Arabic was her favorite subject; in the sixth grade she delivered a speech on the poet al-Mutanabbi, and while at middle school, she read books on Arabic rhetoric and prosody. With the encouragement of her uncle, Anwar

Sha'ul, Amal wrote short essays in Arabic and edited the school paper while at Frank 'Ayni.[112] One issue she edited included some advice for fellow female students, suggesting that girls should be always happy, hopeful, and smiling, as well as closer to nature, as a way of protecting their bodies from diseases. The issue closed with the opinion that a true orphan is not a child who had lost a parent but rather one who lacked knowledge and culture.[113] Amal's literary skill was partially a result of her upbringing. Her grandfather appreciated her talent and read stories about Sayif bin Yazan.[114] One aunt, Esterina Ibrahim, was a writer and a journalist; and another, Fahima Nissim, was the first Jewish teacher to work in a public school in Baghdad.

The two biographies have a theme in common: the agency of each girl as student, and of each family, vis-à-vis the educational system. Lulu's father predetermined, to a degree, Lulu's path in life, as he felt that she should learn French and obtain a profession. Yet her desires to learn and to be with other Jewish girls changed her father's plans. Amal's family predisposed her to a love of Arabic, because many in her family read and wrote in Arabic. Significantly, Amal had female role models who encouraged her to think that she could be successful in whatever career she chose. Both girls transferred frequently from one school to another, which speaks to the fact that in the late 1940s both the Jewish community and the state could offer several educational options for girls, and that female students were quick to take advantage of this range of choices.

Amal's and her Aunt Fahima's employment as teachers was in line with a larger trend dating to the 1930s, when upper- and middle-class Jewish women first entered the workforce as teachers and directors of schools for girls. The range of professions open to women broadened somewhat in the 1940s to include professions like nurses, pharmacists, and clerks in banks and private companies.[115] Coincident with their work outside the home from the mid-1930s, Jewish women began to make their voices heard via the Iraqi print media. Esterina Ibrahim, Maliha Sehayek, and Miriam al-Mulla became known for their short stories with Jewish and Iraqi themes. Esterina Ibrahim worked for *Al-Hasid*, which was edited by her husband, Anwar Sha'ul, and was the journal's correspondent for women's affairs. Rina Tweig wrote for Iraqi journals. Miriam al-Mulla (Basun) saw her stories and essays printed in *Al-Fatat*, *Al-Siyasa*, and *Al-Musawwar* in the years

1945–51. Maliha Sehayek's three collections of short stories were published in Baghdad and Cairo between 1948 and 1952.[116]

For upper-class Jewish women, philanthropy became an important channel of public activities; their projects focused on the education of poor girls and on clothing the poor. In 1924, for example, Rachel Hakham assisted in the establishment of a school for the blind. Rina al-Kabir, the wife of Ibrahim al-Kabir, aided Jews and Muslims alike through her volunteering, and received the Red Crescent Award in recognition for her work. Elite women also established clubs and literary societies. The first was organized in the 1930s for the purposes of assisting poor women who had recently given birth and soliciting donations for a new hospital. After the Farhud, women collected money and clothes for victims of the violence.[117]

Lower-middle-class Jewish women usually veiled themselves when they went out into the street. Reports on women's dress from 1929 noted that women covered their faces; by 1932 accounts indicated that this practice was being abandoned. Prior to World War I some Iraqi Jewish middle- and upper-class women had worn Western clothes; the 1930s and 1940s saw this trend widen. The change in styles of dress led to discussions about propriety, particularly with regard to young educated women. It should be noted, though, that Zionist emissaries complained that the covering of the women's faces in public, the segregation of men and women at dinners and social events, and the marriage of girls at a young age (which cut short their education), were still common practices in Baghdad during the 1940s (although their reports do not distinguish between various classes).[118]

The discourse about the behavior of Jewish women was conducted both within the religious sphere and beyond that community. Within the boundaries of the religious community, certain customs relating to Jewish women, such as marriageable age, arranged marriages, the expenses of wedding ceremonies, and the covering of heads (as Muslim women did), were all discussed in Jewish newspapers and magazines.[119] In their writing on the Jewish women's question, Jewish intellectuals were influenced by Muslim reformers, whose concerns seemed relevant to the Jewish context. The understanding that Jewish and Muslim women alike were Eastern women, and as such subscribed to certain cultural norms, was crucial to Jewish intellectuals. Marriage customs in particular were called into question in the mid-1920s: young Jewish intellectuals critiqued the practice of not allowing a groom to meet his bride before marriage and called for reform in dowry practices and Jewish family laws. Shim'on Mu'allim Nissim had founded a society in 1920 dedicated to the dissemination of modern ideas such as marriage without dowry. In 1925 he published a series of essays, *Letters Before Marriage*, in which he quoted Qasim Amin by way of calling on young Jewish men and women to act bravely and rebel against the old norms. Qasim Amin's name was also invoked by *Al-Misbah*'s writers who advocated that the education of Jewish women would benefit the entire Iraqi nation. In response to these concerns, during 1924 a committee of Baghdadi rabbis considered new pleas to modify divorce and inheritance laws so as to better serve the interests of Jewish women. Although its proposed reforms of Jewish family law never materialized, they did reflect new ideals of how educated young men should interact with women.[120]

Upon its inception, the journal *Al-Burhan* immediately plunged into the discussion of Jewish marriage customs. The editorial in the first issue, "Commercial Marriage in Iraq" ("Al-Zawaj al-tijari fi'l 'Iraq"), reminded readers that sociologists considered the institution of the family to be of the utmost importance. As human societies developed and battled for survival, the family had emerged as a key institution for the protection of the young. Consequently, the state should not neglect the marital affairs of its subjects, since a dysfunctional household would reduce the chance for a viable subsequent generation. The author of the editorial then referenced the science of eugenics in arguing that marriages should not be based on dowries but rather on biology and science. The Iraqi Jewish man looked for a suitable partner but needed capital in the form of a dowry, and thus marriage had become a commercial transaction between two parties, rather than a decision grounded in science. Capital allowed the weak, and those unfit to be married, such as individuals suffering from mental or physical defects, to form households, despite the fact that their marriages jeopardized human society. The article then bemoaned divorce practices among Iraqi Jews, detailing the physical abuse of women in some households.[121] Another article, dealing with children's mortality, put forth the opinion that this unfortunate phenomenon was "our fault." Despite access to modern medical treatment, which enabled human beings to live longer, Iraqi children still suffered from various hereditary health problems because the state did not enact laws stipulating who could marry whom. One wondered, the article concluded, why the state did not intervene more forcefully where eugenics were concerned.[122]

The points raised in *Al-Burhan* represented a new stage in the discussion of the condition of Iraqi Jewish women and their rights. On the one hand, the call for reform in dowry practices that had been voiced in *Al-Misbah* was echoed here as well. On the other hand, the reasoning offered for reform in *Al-Burhan* did not take into consideration the rights of women. Marriage was understood to be within the purview of the state, which ought to monitor the medical condition of its subjects so as to guarantee the viability of future generations. Muslim nationalists such as Sami Shawkat were especially eager to see the state intervene in the domain of marriage. Anxieties concerning demographic decline had inspired such suggestions as levying taxes on unmarried men and physical education for girls to ensure the health of the next generation.[123] The above-mentioned editorial rekindled these anxieties. Though addressing a Jewish audience, the editorial placed the responsibility on the state and its legislative bodies to enact the scientific solution to the Jewish marital problem.

It should also be added that *Al-Burhan*'s positions concerning women's liberation varied according to the issue at hand. Jewish women were advised to be modest, and to know that what mattered to a man were the health of a woman's body and the purity of her blood (*damm naqi*).[124] Yet the paper also called for an expansion of educational opportunities for girls. One of its editorials reviewed the proliferation of Jewish schools offering instruction in French, English, and Hebrew, and the cultural diversity within the nation (*ikhtilaf al-thaqafa bayn abna' al-balad*). This editorial reflected the journal's complicated stance toward women's rights. The writer held that girls' education was nothing but a means to cultivate a blissful family, but also critiqued the present state of that education, in which girls were taught only French, tennis, and piano.[125] In theory, the article expressed a very conservative view, namely, that Jewish girls should be educated solely for the purpose of being better mothers. The remedy for the inadequacy of girls' education, however, was quite radical, as it proposed complete equality between female and male education, which was unacceptable to many in the Iraqi community.

Al-Burhan's intertwining of local Jewish issues with national concerns was not unique to that journal. A number of Iraqi-Jewish writers moved beyond the "Jewish women question" and wrote *as Iraqis* to Iraqi audiences—Muslim, Christian, and Jewish. Anwar Sha'ul, Shalom Darwish, Esterina Ibrahim, and Miriam al-Mulla often did not identify the faith of female characters in their works of fiction. Their primary concerns were the reform of certain practices common in all of Iraq, such as arranged marriage, honor killings, limited educational opportunities offered to women, and women's poverty—all of which hindered the progress of Iraqi women. At the same time Jewish writers expressed their anxieties over the Westernized behavior of women and satirized their eager imitation of European women. As the discussion of women's issues became a marker of belonging to the national community, these Jewish intellectuals, who viewed themselves as modern Iraqi nationalists, addressed Iraqi, Arab, and Eastern women in their writings. They felt that the private domain of national authenticity in which gender relations were discussed was shared by all Iraqis. Consequently their reflections about women allowed them to comment on matters related to both the Islamic faith and the Jewish faith. Furthermore, the analysis of the progress of Iraqi women and the degree of their Westernization enabled Iraqi Jews to respond to a global context and to situate Iraqi society between East and West, and between the colonizers and the colonized. In these processes, however, they ceased writing about Jewish women and turned to discussing the affairs of Iraqi women, as gender became a more important category than sect.

At times, women writers seemed to subscribe to a national narrative that equated women's progress with the creation of a healthy household. The concern for women's education as a way of guiding them to be better mothers, and the critique of the Westernized norms of upper-class women, which supposedly annihilated women's morality, were oft-discussed themes in the Iraqi press and were discussed by Jewish writers like Esterina Ibrahim.[126] Miriam al-Mulla's "His Tragedy Is a Lesson" ("Ma'satuhu mathal") focuses on a pious peasant who stabs his landlord's Westernized son after the latter has raped the peasant's daughter. As the peasant refuses to admit the real reason for his crime, he is sent to jail. Upon his release, he discovers that his daughter died several months after his incarceration.[127]

Mulla, an urban-educated Jewish woman, wrote about protagonists who were presumably Muslims and rural. Her story touches upon many of the issues that preoccupied the Iraqi public sphere at the time, especially the abuse of the peasants by corrupt landowners.[128] Interestingly, however, it does not condemn the practice of honor killing—in fact, the story presents it as understandable and even honorable. Moreover, the heroism of the peasant and his daughter derives from their silence. By their refusal to speak about the rape (as epitomized in the actual silence of the father and the death of the girl) they maintain a sense of family honor and respectability. In contrast to Mulla's conservative position, male Jewish writers such as Ya'qub Balbul unequivocally condemned honor killings.[129] Balbul associated these horrific crimes with rigid patriarchal authority, abuse, and sadistic impulses. Despite their conservatism, however, Mulla and Ibrahim's stories exemplify the tendency of female Jewish writers to claim a place for themselves in the national discourse.

Women were also integrated into the larger efforts of the Iraqi state to change and modernize Iraqi society. As part of the state's efforts to discuss women's affairs in a Pan-Arab framework, the Iraqi state sent elite women (such as the wives of important politicians) and noted Iraqi female writers to represent their country in Middle Eastern conferences on Eastern and Arab women. Esterina Ibrahim participated in the Arab Women's Congress (al-Mu'tamar al-nisawi al-'arabi), which was convened in Baghdad in 1932.[130] Jewish women also took part in literary salons in which Christian and Muslim women participated; Maliha Sehayek led such a literary salon in Baghdad.[131] The late 1940s and early 1950s saw the most radical phases of secularization, which had a significant impact on the lives of Iraqi Jewish women, who became more educated and more politicized. The years 1945–58 were an important time for Iraqi feminists in general. After the end of World War II, Iraqi intellectuals from both the left (social democrats and communists) and from the ultranationalist camp demanded women's suffrage as part of their critique of Iraq's electoral and judicial systems. The Zionist movement also contributed to the secularization of Iraqi Jewish women by offering a vision of emancipation and equality.[132]

Some educated Jewish women turned to the outlawed ICP attracted by its advocacy of women's rights. Female communists distributed pamphlets, campaigned for suffrage and welfare rights, organized demonstrations and public meetings, and taught one another. Naziha Dulaimi, a Muslim activist affiliated with the ICP, who was the most dominant figure in the leftist women's movement, was in touch with Jewish women activists, when she was in charge of organizing women's activities in Baghdad.[133] The ICP's women's organizations counted seven Jewish women, thirty-two Muslims, and one Christian in their ranks.[134] Because of their education, Jewish women were exposed to communist activities in colleges and high schools, where the ICP was active.[135] British accounts make mention of Jewish female students who were ICP members, notably Rachel Zilkha at the law college, Albertine Menashe at the medical college, and Sa'ida Salman, who was an organizer.[136] Other female members attended the Teachers Training College.[137]

Jewish women joined the ICP for religious and gendered reasons. As educated women, their concerns were echoed by the communist agenda, which emphasized suffrage and women's integration in the labor market. As Jewish women, whose family members were often communist, the nonsectarian vision of the ICP was especially appealing. They faced more pressure from their families to refrain from political activity and were therefore closely monitored by both their families and their state. Nonetheless, because of their gender, Jewish women could conceal their identity more easily (by wearing an *'abaya* and pretending to be religious Muslim women, for example), and minimize the extent of their activities when questioned by the police. Like the men, they operated in both Jewish and nonsectarian settings, and they understood their actions within a communist and Iraqi-patriotic framework.

Jewish women in the ICP worked mostly as couriers and organizers of women's cells.[138] Some, such as Sa'ida Mash'al, 'Amuma Masri, and Madeline Mir Ezra-Ezer, converted to Islam, usually after marrying a Muslim party member.[139] Women who were married or engaged to Jewish ICP members joined the party through these connections. Sa'ida Sasson Mash'al, a student at the Teachers Training College, was engaged for a time to Sasun Dallal, a prominent Jewish communist, who encouraged her activities in women's circles. She was in charge of establishing women's cells.[140] A prime example of a Jewish woman who assumed a leading role in the ICP was Allen Yusuf Ya'qub Darwish (1925–65), the wife of a prominent party member, Ibrahim

Naji Shumail, who joined the ICP in 1946. Allen was a member of the women's committee and organized women's cells. She was also an important courier; during the years her husband was imprisoned in the Kut jail, she passed along letters from him, the party's leaders, and other Jewish communists, to other ICP members in Baghdad.[141] Another important female Jewish communist was 'Amuma Masri (b. 1923), who was a member of the women's central committee, acted as a courier, and worked in the ICP's printing house.[142]

The radical politics of Iraqi Jewish women and their growing participation in the workforce (as modest as it might seem from our perspective) did not escape the critical eye of writers. Shalom Darwish's short story "In the Year 2541" ("Fi sanat 2541") seemingly offers an exaggerated vision of what women's rights might lead to. The story is constructed as a letter addressed to a female doctor. The reader quickly realizes that in the year 2541 women control the world. The letter's addressee had just asked the male protagonist's parents for his hand in marriage. The potential groom writes to his future bride: "Marriage, my lady, is an important social event that should not occur, in my opinion, between two individuals who are unequal in their rights and duties. We, the gentle gender [*al-jins al-da'if*], as you know, are the slaves of our homes. We work to maintain our homes, and to educate the children, as if we are mere tools, with no opinion or will, destined to obey those who control us."[143] The letter writer, however, has thoughts of freedom, and wishes to avoid his father's fate. He argues that a man's morals are not endangered by the earning of an honorable living, and moreover, that men should not rely on their mothers, sisters, or wives: "Why is this contrary to honor? Why should one gender alone posses 'power, capital, and beauty'?" He points out that when men stand up for their rights, they are considered rebellious. The letter writer is also concerned that with his wife working long hours, she will have no time to be his partner in life (*sharikat hayati*). He wants his wife to possess spiritual qualities and not perpetuate the tradition of unhappy marriages of "hundreds of years ago," in which men took wives solely for the aim of "sexual pleasure and the production of children." Nonetheless, determined to continue the struggle to destroy all the old chains and traditions (*taqalid*), he decides to reject the marriage proposal.[144]

The story could be understood as reflecting the anxieties of male intellectuals, intimating that if women were granted more rights, male hegemony would be lost forever. I think, however, that another reading of the story is possible: it is a call for the granting of equal rights to women. By putting men in the position of women, as human beings whose freedom was curtailed under the presumption that equal citizenship rights might erode religiosity, Darwish exposed the preposterousness and absurdity of these ideas. Just as men would not have liked to be barred from working, out of concern for public morality, or be considered simple machines of reproduction, so did women reject the notion that one gender was superior to the other. Darwish here was echoing the radical voices of women that colored the public debate in this period, rather than ridiculing them. What made this satire so effective was Darwish's ironic representation of religious discourse—Jewish, Islamic, and Christian—relating to women's morality. The role reversal in the story was thus intended to unsettle a wide audience of Jews, Muslims, and Christians, and to argue that the oppression of women was embellished with references to tradition and morality in order to conceal the fact that their subordination related to sex, capital, and power. Considering himself an Iraqi intellectual, Shalom Darwish had no qualms about mocking the dated customs of his country.

In Hashemite Iraq, the debate about the rights and duties of Jewish women was connected to Iraqi and Arab debates on education, labor, and nationalism. The debate, therefore, was conducted both within the boundaries of the Jewish community (especially when matters relating to Jewish religion were concerned) and outside these boundaries. Jewish writers such as Darwish or Balbul assumed a readership of bourgeois Iraqis (Jews, Christians, Shi'is, and Sunnis), whose interests and anxieties were located within the framework of the Arab and Iraqi nation. The push for women's rights often met with resistance from conservatives, whether rabbis concerned about women's morality or certain nationalists who saw women as nothing more than mothers responsible for raising the next generation of Iraqi patriots. By appropriating national discourses and challenging them in equal degrees, however, Iraqi Jewish women had gained more rights. The nonsectarian and pluralistic outlook of some prominent Jewish intellectuals and especially the bravery of young women in challenging social norms grounded in religion and cultural norms deserved a fair amount of the credit for this. In the 1940s and the 1950s, radical voices took center stage among Iraqi Jewish women, who found new political avenues for the expression of their hopes, anger, and anxieties.

Conclusions

Iraqi Jews did not become atheists in the Hashemite period. On the contrary, most accounts from Baghdad indicate that Jews (even more so in the 1920s) observed Kashrut laws and generally thought of themselves as loyal to their religion. They identified themselves as Jews, and stricter adherence to religious law was practiced in the poorer classes. Likewise, educated Iraqi Jews took great interest in Jewish affairs around the world. Nonetheless, their conceptualizations of identity and their position in the modern world, as well as their relationship with the state, their education, their reflections on gender, and the socioeconomic milieu in they were active became increasingly more secular in nature.

Two comments made by Adolph Brotman are particularly illuminating in this regard. Writing on how he and his wife were regarded by Iraqi Jews, Brotman noted: "They could not understand that we were really Jews. . . . The idea that Jews coming from England could pay any attention to getting kosher meat or not riding on the Sabbath or anything like that was nothing less than a phenomenon which in their view was quite exceptional."[145] While maintaining that Iraqi Jews in general were "intensely religious" and that "everything was done in accordance with Jewish tradition," however, Brotman admitted there were divergences from what he understood to be the correct practice of Judaism:

> I had a friend in Baghdad to whom a son was born while we were out there, and the Brit Mila was due to take place on the second day of Pesach. . . . The Chacham came by car to perform the Brit Mila . . . , which, of course, is inconceivable here [i.e., in England], but it was apparently quite the thing there. . . . Generally traveling on the Sabbath and Yom-tov was not looked upon as anything outside orthodoxy. Then again rice, which is not permitted on Pesach here, was the usual sort of thing there.[146]

Both Baghdadi Jews and the Brotmans believed that they were Jewish, modern, and religious, yet they had differing conceptions of what that meant.

Baghdadi Jews were actually following the ruling of Rabbi Somekh that permitted limited travel on the Sabbath.[147] To the Ashkenazi British couple, this did not square with Jewish practice as they knew it. Similarly, some Iraqi Jews found it difficult to see how their customs were compatible with those of a couple who seemed to be more familiar with the culture of the colonial power ruling Iraq than with the local Judeo-Arab culture. Both the Brotmans and the Iraqi Jewish elites considered themselves modern, yet each had a view of Judaism that had developed in a particular context: Britain, for the Brotmans; Baghdad, Iraq, and the Arab world, for their Iraqi friends and colleagues.

Brotman's comments, however, may be misleading. During the twentieth century, the cultures of British and Iraqi Jews grew increasingly intertwined, and a certain belief system was shared by both. Love of European languages, Western education, the adoption of European social practices and dress, and the presence of Britain in Iraq rendered impossible the division between East and West. The context in which Iraqi Jews came to understand their religious beliefs shifted constantly between the local and the global. The national Arab Iraqi idiom and the Iraqi education system created a climate which limited religious expression to the privacy of the home. Jews did not object, believing that this secularization would ensure their integration in the state. Concurrently, the call to modernize Judaism so that it would fit the demands of the modern world was raised within Jewish communities around the world, and thus Iraqi Jews were engaged in debates similar to ones conducted in Eastern Europe and elsewhere in the Middle East. In part, the desired reform of Jewish practices was intended to reevaluate the newly acquired leisure habits and secularized education of the Jewish effendia. Furthermore, although the Jewish print media was dedicated primarily to Jewish readers, it seemed to have conveyed the message that all communities in Iraq needed to abandon older modes and accept the secular, the modern, and the contemporary.

In this chapter, I have used *Arabization* and *secularization* interchangeably. Of course, to be (or become) an Arab does not mean to be (or become) secular. In Iraq, a person could be an Arab Muslim, an Arab Christian, and an Arab Jew and still remain loyal to his or her religious beliefs. Arabization, however, did chip away at the boundaries of the Jewish community by demonstrating that there was another community, namely the nation, which was highly important to Iraqi Jews. This awareness motivated Jews to address issues that affected other communities as well. Arabization meant interacting with other Muslim and Christian children in a state education system, accepting the authority of non-Jewish figures in questions pertaining to social conduct (ranging from a Muslim Arabic teacher to the theories of Qasim Amin), and recognizing that their debates regarding faith paralleled similar discourses among Christian and Muslim Arabs.

4

FRIENDS, NEIGHBORS, AND ENEMIES
Fascism, Anti-Semitism, and the Farhud

Sha'ul Menashe recalled the events of May 1941, in Basra, years after they occurred:

> We lived . . . in a Muslim Shi'i neighborhood. . . . We had a good life in this district, where neighborly relationships prevailed. . . . On that day, before dawn . . . , we heard [the] strong knocks of hammers and axes on the door of our home. . . . My father . . . went downstairs and climbed up to the roof with an object that looked like a pistol. . . . He went to the mob, making sure they saw the "pistol," and threatened them. . . . They took this threat seriously, and began running in all directions. My father was concerned nonetheless. He told me: "They will be back, and they will have weapons."
>
> The houses [in the neighborhood] were close to each other, with tin barriers separating them. We had a Shi'i neighbor by the name of Sheikh 'Abd al-Razzaq al-Hammam, who owned a lot of property. . . . When the rioters knocked on our door again, shooting their guns, my father knocked on the small tin barrier. The sheikh came by himself and told my father: "I know you are in trouble. What do you want?" . . . My father moved to the side of the sheikh, kneeled, and grabbed the sheikh's knee, saying: "Honorable sheikh, we are twelve people. Leave the men and the boys alone, but please take the women and the girls. Leave us, but please, protect their honor." The sheikh was moved and answered my father: "I am a sheikh and you ask me for my protection. You ask me to leave the men and the children and take

the women and the girls. I will not do so. You have two options: either all of you or none of you." ... My father responded: "As you command." ... The men tore an opening in the tin barrier that separated the two houses. Some of the children were hurt when they moved inside.... The sheikh hid us in a Turkish bath that was near the house.... He, his four children, and three of his Baluchistani guards stood in front of our home, holding weapons.... The mob's leaders then asked the sheikh: "Where are the Jews?" ... The sheikh told them he is bestowing his protection on the Jews; he will not betray them and will defend them....

My father was a known man in the market, and the Muslim shop owner who leased a store to my father found him two days after the pogrom had ended, and wanted to help him to reconstruct his business. Therefore, he gave my father a stand in the market so that he could sell fruits and vegetables. Many Muslims purposely came to buy from my father, because they knew we had suffered the most during the pogrom.[1]

Sha'ul's accounts relate to the Farhud, a series of urban riots directed against Iraqi Jews during which nearly 180 were killed. In colloquial Iraqi, the word *Farhud* means looting or robbing; it came to designate specifically the killing, wounding, and robbing of Jews in Baghdad on the first two days of June 1941 and the looting of Jewish property in Basra the previous month. Sha'ul's descriptions echo feelings of fear, terror, and helplessness, brought on by the penetration of the mob into the private domain of the household. On the other hand, these accounts commemorate those who helped their Jewish neighbors, especially the sheikh, whose humanity and adherence to Islamic and tribal values moved him to protect his neighbors. In these sad times the barrier which symbolically and physically separated the Jewish and the Shi'i households was broken.

I chose to open the chapter with this account because it reflects, in a nutshell, the experience of the Farhud. The Farhud brought to the fore both the worst and the noblest aspects of Jewish-Iraqi relations. Essentially the first pogrom in a modern Arab state, it was a direct result of rampant nationalism, the violence of which reached epidemic proportions. At this time Iraqi Jews were attacked by their fellow citizens, and more importantly, came to realize that elements in the Iraqi nation-state, to which they had pledged their loyalty, had betrayed them. The Farhud, however, was also a moment of intercommunal solidarity. It was a time when Muslim neighbors risked their lives in order to protect their Jewish friends, neighbors, and business partners, and when friendship, loyalty, and religious and tribal notions concerning protection of the peoples of the book overcame nationalist xenophobia.

As is to be expected, both Arab and Zionist national memories have silenced important aspects of the Farhud. Within Iraqi national historiography, the event was highly embarrassing, predominantly because it led to the questioning of the conduct of the Iraqi army, in addition to tainting the memory of Rashid 'Ali al-Kaylani's coup as national symbol. Consequently, most of the Iraqi nationalists who figured in the events of this period have failed to mention the Farhud in their memoirs. Moreover, the state itself was unwilling to recognize the social tensions exposed by the Farhud. While it acknowledged that the army and the police should have been held accountable for their actions, it made little mention of the participation of the urban poor in the riots, since doing so would have meant acknowledging its failed social policies.[2] Zionist historiography, in contrast, has highlighted the Farhud as a watershed in the history of the Iraqi Jewish community. From the Zionist standpoint, the Farhud was the outcome of the anti-Semitism and Iraqi nationalist rhetoric in the 1930s. It was also viewed as having galvanized the Zionist movement in Iraq and ultimately as causing Iraq's Jews to recognize that their country had rejected their attempts at integration and assimilation. In some Zionist circles, the event came to be understood as an extension of the European Holocaust into the Middle East.[3] This connection is made manifest today by the archiving of certain documents relating to the Farhud in Yad Va-Shem, the Israeli Holocaust Museum, in Jerusalem.

Anti-Semitism and Nationalism

The Jewish community faced a few significant problems in the 1930s. The first had to do with a new trend in the Iraqi labor market, as the increase in the number of educated Iraqi Muslims resulted in the dismissal of Jews from jobs they had held since the 1920s. The Jews who lost their jobs blamed anti-Semitism as the main reason for their dismissals.[4] The second, more serious, problem was the conflation of Judaism with Zionism. Reflecting on the "evil days" which befell the Jewish community in 1941, the British ambassador, Kinahan Cornwallis, noted that "inevitably, though falsely,"

Iraqi Jews paid the price for Zionism, with their money and with their blood. Sheepishly, however, he added that it was "vitally necessary for us to be most careful how we assist them [the Jews], if both helper and helped are not to be involved in a common charge of being Zionist agents."[5]

The battle against Zionism did not start in 1941; it was, in fact, a major part of the Iraqi national discourse. Large anti-Zionist demonstrations had taken place in Baghdad as early as 1928 (upon the arrival of a prominent Zionist, Alfred Mond), and articles warning against the perils of Zionism and protesting the dislocation of and discrimination against Palestinians appeared frequently in the press during the 1920s. From 1929 on, a dangerous trend took hold in Iraq: whenever there were troubles in Palestine, they would be echoed in Iraq as events that affected the relationship between Jews and Muslims. In 1929, Palestinian nationalists were engaged in a full-fledged revolt against British rule. The Jewish community became anxious as to subsequent tensions in Baghdad.[6] In August that same year, two Jews were slightly injured in Baghdad following a pro-Palestinian rally. On August 31 rumors flew concerning an attack on the community's synagogues the following day—special measures taken by the authorities thwarted the potential assault.[7] Interestingly, Faysal's pan-Arab solution to the conflict relied on national narratives that depicted Jews and Arabs as brothers. He proposed that Syria, Palestine, and Iraq be united as a homeland for the Semitic race.[8] After the revolt in Palestine was crushed, the connections between Judaism and Zionism continued to be played up in the Iraqi public sphere.[9]

The atmosphere grew more hostile during the years of the Arab revolt in Palestine (1936–39), when the Iraqi public was galvanized in support of Palestine's struggle against the British and the Zionists. Demonstrations against British policies in Palestine were covered in the press and were the subject of discussion at a leading Pan-Arab club called al-Muthanna.[10] The British embassy received protest letters from the various organizations, most notably the Committee for the Defense of Palestine (Lajnat al-difa' 'an Falastin), an Iraqi organization founded to express solidarity with the Palestinian national struggle.[11] The arrival in Iraq of Palestinian leader Hajj Amin al-Husayni in October 1939, along with a large group of Palestinian exiles (teachers, lawyers, and intellectuals), further complicated the situation. The exiles tried to drum up support for the Palestinian cause and worked with Pan-Arab Iraqis. Some, including al-Husayni, projected their animosity toward Zionism onto Iraqi Jews, and supported Nazi Germany. However, they were hostile not only toward Jews but also toward Iraqis who opposed the Pan-Arab ideology, in particular, the social democrats and the communists.[12]

As the rhetoric of animosity grew sharper during the years of the revolt, the level of violence directed at the Jewish community increased. In 1936, six Jews were killed in crimes related to their Jewish identity.[13] A British account noted that "it is true that in most cases the murders [of Jews] were attributed to personal motives; they were nonetheless symptomatic of a diminution of respect for the sanctity of Jewish life at the time of popular agitation."[14] Zionist accounts mention the circulation of pro-Palestinian leaflets in Baghdad, which condemned the British and their Jewish partners. The Committee for the Defense of Palestine operated a publishing house which put out pamphlets warning Iraqis about the Zionist threat, arguing that Zionism and communism were one and the same; that Zionist goods were about to flood the Iraqi market; and that Jabotinsky was talking of a Zionist state whose boundaries would extend to Iraq.[15] Two bombings of Jewish clubs in August 1938 further aggravated the situation. C. J. Edmonds, a British adviser, admitted that there was no doubt that the "recent campaign of Jewish reprisals in Palestine" had stirred up public anger in Iraq and given rise to the notion that "terrorism is a game that two [sides] can play." Edmonds did not think that the expulsion of Iraqi Jews as a result of these tensions was likely, but did recall that Sa'ib Shawkat, president of al-Muthanna club, had mentioned the idea to him.[16] In 1939, British officials stated that there was an average of three to five attacks per day on Jews and that the hatred of Great Britain arose from the perception that the British were pro-Jewish, as evidenced by their policies in Palestine.[17]

The Iraqi Jewish intellectual elite responded by adopting a pro-Palestinian line, contributing money to, and publishing petitions on behalf of, the Palestinian cause. The chief rabbi, as well as Jewish intellectuals, journalists, and poets, professed their solidarity with their Arab brethren in Palestinians.[18] In addition to Jewish efforts on their own behalf, measures taken by the Iraqi state, in tandem with British pressure to increase censorship of anti-Jewish publications and to punish those who committed anti-Jewish crimes, were effective in preventing further violence. Nuri Saʻid promised the British ambassador that the state would redouble its efforts toward protecting Jews, and a local newspaper that was attacking the Jewish community had its permission to publish suspended.[19] British officials had a direct interest in silencing reports from Palestine, which typically represented the British as anti-Arab and pro-Zionist. Their push for a reduction in and censorship of articles on their Palestinian policy indirectly improved matters for Iraqi Jews, as less incendiary material made for less tension.

Most important, it was during the Arab Revolt in Palestine (1936–39) that a military coup, led by Bakr Sidqi (October 1936–August 1937), took place. The elites leading the coup were inspired by Kemalist models, and initially were open to cooperation with the social democrats and other reformist elements. They were proponents of Iraqi territorial nationalism, viewing the Pan-Arab tendencies of the previous governments with great suspicion. During the years of the military regime, Jewish rights were protected and respected. Zionist diplomat Eliyahu Epstein visited Iraq in 1937, pretending to be a journalist. Epstein was concerned about the Pan-Arab and pro-German spirit among the youth. Nevertheless, he heard time and again, from high-ranking officials such as the minister of finance Jaʻfar Abu Timman, the minister of transportation Kamil Chadirchi, and even Prime Minister Hikmat Sulayman (the only man who knew Epstein was a Zionist) that the regime was primarily occupied with social reform and modernization efforts within *Iraq*. The regime's antisectarian commitments were made clear to Epstein.[20]

Finally, the Palestinian exiles came in for criticism from various quarters, not just the Jewish community. The social democrats charged that the exiles denigrated Iraqi Kurds and in general were merely tools of corrupt Iraqi politicians.[21] Ezra Haddad also noted that the mufti al-Husayni did not manage to turn the masses against the Jewish population. In Haddad's view the anti-Zionist campaign in Iraq was not directed specifically against Iraq's Jews, but that the masses tended to confuse Judaism with Zionism.[22]

The third problem facing the Jewish community in the 1930s was German propaganda. The German goal was to sway Iraqi public opinion in favor of Germany by casting the latter as a power opposed to Great Britain and hence a possible strategic ally of Iraq. The Germans were able to get pro-

Nazi articles printed in the newspapers: the daily *Al-'Alam al-'Arabi* published pieces on German and Italian affairs, while the German ambassador, Fritz Grobba (1866–1973), visited newspapers' editors and financed the publications of stories that described Nazi Germany in positive terms. Officials in Germany pressured German firms with offices in Iraq to dismiss Iraqi Jewish employees and replace them with Iraqis who supported the German cause. In addition, the Germans provided an Arab cinema owner in Baghdad with a film projector so that he could screen pro-German propaganda, and sold printing equipment at ridiculously low prices to pro-German newspapers.[23] On October 24, 1940, the Iraqi press reported on Germany's declaration of sympathy with the Arabs, which was met with approval by journalists and was considered a great honor in certain nationalist circles.[24]

Some Iraqi intellectuals, officials, and policymakers were swayed by this campaign. They admired Germany's program of modernization, which had paved the way for its military and economic triumphs. Italy was more problematic as a role model because of that nation's occupation of Ethiopia—the Italian colonial danger was far closer to home. Fascist aesthetics and vocabulary began to take root in Iraq. Youth movements, in particular the paramilitary organization al-Futuwwa, were seen in nationalist circles as key to the cultivation of healthy notions of masculinity and manhood. Speakers at al-Muthanna club hailed the efforts of Germany to modernize and reform. A Mousuli writer, Yunis al-Sab'awi, translated parts of *Mein Kampf* into Arabic and worked for the German embassy as a translator of pro-German material.[25] The British noted that Nazi propaganda was effective among the Muslim Young Men's Associations and complained about the pro-German sympathies of Iraqi politicians Sami Shawkat and Sa'ib Shawkat.[26]

There is no doubt that the activity of the mufti al-Husayni, Sab'awi, and Sami Shawkat, among others, had done much to damage Jewish-Muslim relations. The Jewish community, however, knew how to meet these challenges, and tried its best to assume agency and respond to threats and accusations. Equally significant was the response of Muslim and Christian Iraqi intellectuals who articulated a democratic and pluralistic response to pro-Nazi and profascist activities and disassociated Zionism from Judaism.

Jews countered public expressions of anti-Jewish sentiment in a number of ways. First, they joined nationalist organizations such as al-Futuwwa.

Second, the community was quick to refute allegations that seemed to be anti-Semitic in the Iraqi press. This tradition started as early as the 1920s. When an Arabic translation of Shakespeare's *Merchant of Venice* appeared, *Al-Misbah* featured a long essay explaining the historical background which produced the character of Shylock.[27] In 1924, an Iraqi officer by the name of Rasul al-Qadiri published his memoirs in *Al-'Alam al-'Arabi*, contending that there existed an international Jewish conspiracy that aimed to take control of the world's economic resources through a series of revolutions, the most recent of which was the Bolshevik Revolution. Anwar Sha'ul attempted to respond to al-Qadiri within the pages of *Al-'Alam al-'Arabi*, but the editor refused to print his article. Undaunted, Sha'ul used *Al-Misbah* as the venue for his refutation of al-Qadiri's accusations. As a result al-Qadiri apologized, explaining that his intention was to expose Russian Jews only; Iraqi Jews were unquestionably loyal citizens who posed no danger to anyone.[28]

In the 1930s and early 1940s, Iraqi Jews heard of the Nazi persecution of Jews: from refugees, especially doctors, who had fled to Baghdad; from stories in the Arab and international media about the war; from British propaganda efforts; and from Jewish Polish soldiers stationed in Iraq. These soldiers belonged to units under the command of Władysław Anders, which were created by the USSR but passed to British control after 1942.[29] Communal prayers for the Jews suffering in Europe and for their survival were conducted in Baghdad and Mosul.[30] More importantly, Anwar Sha'ul, Ezra Haddad, and Shalom Darwish addressed their anti-German critiques to the Arab Iraqi community via the Arabic-language press, especially the journal *Al-Hasid*, and appearances on BBC anti-German broadcasts. Sha'ul included Italy in his condemnation of fascist regimes, particularly after that country's invasion of Ethiopia. He was also moved to compose a poem dedicated to an Ethiopian female warrior leading four hundred Ethiopian maidens into battle against the fascist invaders. The antifascist and anti-Nazi arguments of these Iraqi Jewish thinkers echoed what was said about fascism in Iraqi and Egyptian journals, namely, that totalitarian regimes endangered universal principles of democracy and freedom. Moreover, Haddad and Sha'ul underscored the fact that Italy and Germany were colonizing powers that imperiled the entire Middle East. Their overarching point was that Iraqis and by extension all Arabs should reject fascism since a racist, colonialist, and antidemocratic regime like that of Nazi Germany was antithetical to the values that all democratic Iraqis hoped their motherland would embrace.[31] *Al-Hasid*'s anti-Nazi line was of immense importance, because the journal published the writing of leading Muslim and Christian national intellectuals. The activity of the journal, moreover, bolstered the Jewish sense of belonging in Iraq. As Ishaq Bar-Moshe recalls: "One journal was always present in our home: *Al-Hasid*. I felt proud seeing the name of the leading editor, who was a Jew, and I read enthusiastically and with great interest his articles attacking the Nazi movement and its supporters. *Al-Hasid* was a literary journal but it did not hesitate to weigh in on political matters. All of its political articles supported the national government, and Jews were seen as part of the nation and the state."[32]

Iraqi Jews used their economic power to influence reporting on Jewish affairs and the war: Ishaq Bar-Moshe reports that his parents and relatives did not buy newspapers associated with the pro-Nazi camp.[33] The British war effort received contributions of various kinds from Jews. Gurji Levy established a society to help the British army and collected large sums of money on its behalf. The lawyer Hesqel Murad tried to buy a number of newspapers in order to challenge pro-German propaganda, but was unsuccessful. Mir Basri reports of similar attempts to publish anti-German propaganda in the Iraqi press that failed because of Grobba's interference.[34] On the other hand, it was difficult for the Germans to screen pro-Nazi films in Baghdad because the Jewish movie theater owners (who dominated the trade in the city) refused to show such films.[35]

Schools were another battleground between the anti- and pro-German factions in Iraq. Jews were quick to complain to the government and to the British about inappropriate behavior of teachers. 'Izzat Sasun Mu'allim, who lived in Diwaniyya, recalled that in 1937 all of the Jewish female students in the school in Diwayniay went on strike in protest of discrimination against Jewish students. The regional director of education asked the Jewish students to return to school and the schoolmistress had to apologize to her students.[36] In June of the same year, Grobba complained that Jewish students had been filing grievances concerning the spreading of propaganda by German teachers in Iraq. He contended that the Jews in Iraq were playing a dangerous game, forgetting that Iraq was not Germany, a land that wished to banish its Jews while still treating them in a humane fashion. Iraq, however, was an oriental country. When desires erupt within an oriental people, Grobba wrote, all boundaries collapse and the masses want to see blood. If the Jews continued with these tricks, a day would come when the masses' rage would erupt and would lead to a massacre.[37] Grobba's observations, written two years after the enactment of the Nuremberg laws, seem ironic, if not plainly horrific, considering the subsequent history. His grumbling, however, indicate that the attempts of Iraqi Jews to sabotage his propaganda efforts were sometimes successful.

It seems, moreover, that Grobba himself was not the major proponent of Nazi ideology in Iraq. He had come to Iraq before Hitler's rise to power in 1931. A Freemason, he frequented Masonic lodges in Baghdad and interacted with its elites. After the rise of the Nazis, Grobba had to defend the local German community against accusations that they associated too frequently with German Jews who had immigrated to Iraq, and was forced to go back to Germany and explain his conduct. In a letter to his superiors, he admitted that the local German community socialized with German Jewish migrants to Iraq and preferred them as doctors to Arab or British ones.[38] The British noted that reports on Germans in Iraq who worked with Jews were sent to Berlin, and that Grobba was recalled to Germany and "hauled over the coals for mixing too freely with the Jews and for attending Masonic lodges in Baghdad."[39] According to another account, Grobba's attitude toward Jews caused the British adviser to the Ministry of Justice to think that, although Jews were considered undesirable elements in Germany, German representatives abroad were being given instructions to help them.[40] Grobba helped Jewish merchant Salih Sasun Mukmal remain the agent for a German boot polish company in Iraq; he befriended Dr. Sausman, a German Jewish surgeon who had immigrated to Iraq, and dissuaded Sa'ib Shawkat, the director general of health, from deporting him; and he threw a party for the German Jewish Dr. Rosenthal, walking arm-in-arm with him and introducing him to various Iraqi nationalists, all of which led to Rosenthal's finding work as a doctor in Diwaniya.[41] This is not to suggest that the Germans did not play a major role in the dissemination of pro-Nazi propaganda. Grobba was central in these efforts. However, at least during the 1930s, he seems to have been a more complex character than he has been portrayed. The British, for their part, identified Jewish doctors who wished to come to Iraq as a possible danger. Ambassador Basil Newton wrote that it was difficult to bring the Iraqi authorities to take action against Jewish doctors of German or Austrian origin who had established practices in Baghdad.[42]

Iraqi Jews were aware they had allies in the struggle against Nazi sympathizers. Great Britain, through its presence in Iraq, supported the anti-Nazi campaign in a number of ways. The BBC invited Sha'ul to take part in its broadcasts because the British government and Iraqi Jews faced a common threat. Moreover, British pressure on the Iraqi state was able at times to thwart German propaganda efforts. Grobba's proposals to subsidize a German hospital and a German technical school, and to open a German club, of which Iraqis could become members, were all turned down. Grobba himself complained about anti-Nazi and anti-German publications in Baghdad.[43]

A number of prominent Iraqi voices came out in support of pro-Jewish and anti-German positions, beginning in the 1920s. The neoclassical poet Ma'ruf al-Rusafi wrote to the journal *Al-Misbah* to express his appreciation of the journal in general and the innovative work of the Jewish poet Murad Mikha'il in particular.[44] In an article published in *Al-Hilal*, Rusafi argued that the history of the Jewish people should serve as a model for Arabs under the yoke of colonialism. The Jews, he contended, had managed to make progress and to bring about reform both in the East and in the West without having political sovereignty. Thus it was possible that Arabs could revitalize their culture, despite being politically subordinate to British and French colonial interests.[45] Rusafi is perhaps the best example for the tensions embodied in the Iraqi intellectual elite. He supported the Kaylani movement and saw it as an anticolonial revolt, yet at the same time he was one of the most zealous proponents of a secular Iraq in which Jews would be full-fledged citizens. Rusafi, however, was not alone. The Christian intellectual Yusuf Ghanima, himself a graduate of the Baghdadi Alliance school, wrote a book on the history of Iraqi Jews, which was published in 1922.[46] The Shi'i poet Muhammad Mahdi al-Jawahiri supported radical Jewish intellectuals in their challenge of the high taxes on kosher meat in Iraq (the state imprisoned him for his poem on the subject, arguing that he had interfered in the local affairs of the Jewish community!).[47] The historian 'Abbas 'Azzawi contributed to *Al-Hasid* regularly, beginning with the very first issue, and also taught in a Jewish school, while the Shi'i intellectual Ja'far al-Khalili, the editor of *Al-Hatif*, recognized the literary talents of Ya'qub Balbul and maintained close contacts with Anwar Sha'ul and other Jewish intellectuals.[48]

The support for Iraqi Jews was not only based on the admiration of their literary and cultural contributions to Iraq. It was also bound up with the anti-Nazi stance taken by a small, albeit important, group of Iraqi intellectuals. Some belonged to the social-democratic party al-Ahali, which attacked Nazism and fascism in its publications. Religious intellectuals such as the Shi'i Hibat al-Din al-Shahrastani saw Nazism as a form of polytheism and thus as anathema to Islam.[49] The nascent communist party likewise took an anti-Nazi stance. When World War II broke out, the communists initially viewed it as a battle among imperial powers over spheres of influence, and counseled neutrality on the part of the Arab world. The communists, however, reminded Iraqi nationalists that Germany was an imperialist nation, whose military assistance should not be sought after.[50] Beyond Iraq's borders, Syrian and Egyptian newspapers expressed antifascist and anti-Nazi opinions. Egyptian intellectuals in particular, some of whom resided in Iraq, led a campaign against Nazism. Their views that Germany was a colonizing power, waging war against humanist culture, strengthened the perception that Germany was seeking to destroy liberty, both inside and outside of Germany.[51] Certainly, an anti-Nazi article published in the Egyptian journal *Al-Risala* could not have allayed the fears of Iraqi Jews regarding World War II or match the nationalist propaganda appearing in newspapers and articulated in al-Muthanna club. Nevertheless, the activity of the anti-Nazi Iraqi groups in this time testifies to a public sphere in which Iraqi Jews could make their views known and expect to reach some sympathetic listeners. Thus, when Iraqi Jewish intellectuals enunciated their anger against the Germans and Italians, they did so as Jews *and* as democratically minded Iraqis, who were fearful of what the implementation of a totalitarian model would do to their citizenship rights and to their pluralistic vision of the nation.

Rashid 'Ali and the Farhud in Baghdad

The Farhud erupted after a period of intense debate among intellectuals concerning Nazism and fascism, after German propaganda disseminated into the Iraqi print market, and after a heated anti-Zionist campaign. To fully understand the Farhud, however, it is necessary to consider the situation in Iraq in April and May 1941.

Iraq had experienced a period of continual political instability following the failure of the military coup orchestrated by Bakir Sidqi in 1936. A group of nationalist colonels, Salah al-Din al-Sabbagh, Kamal Shabib, Mahmud Fahmi, and Fahmi Sa'id, wielded tremendous political power so that they could ensure the installation of prime ministers sympathetic to their concerns. In September 1939, the pro-British Nuri al-Sa'id was appointed prime minister and declared that Iraq would not enter World War II unless attacked. He confirmed, much to the chagrin of many nationalists, including the four colonels, that Iraq would help Britain in the war, though only to the degree specified in the Anglo-Iraqi Treaty. Disagreements regarding the nature of Iraq's relationships with Germany led to the appointment of Rashid 'Ali al-Kaylani as prime minister in March 1940. He resigned, rather than cut off relations with Italy, at the end of January 1941, but returned to his post as the result of pressure from the colonels and the military. Upon regaining power, Kaylani announced the establishment of a military regime, a point at which Nuri Sa'id and the regent quickly made their way out of Iraq. This turn of events did not please the British, who were aware of the nationalist and pro-German sympathies of the new government and of the four colonels in particular. Kaylani proved to be unable to navigate between British pressure, on the one hand, and the nationalist demands of some of his supporters, on the other. He promised the British officials that he would honor the treaty with Britain, but they did not consider him trustworthy, and British forces entered Iraq on April.[52] After a short military campaign, lasting through April and May, the British reoccupied Iraq. Kaylani and his supporters fled Baghdad in late May 1941, leaving the capital's mayor, Arshad al-'Umari, to negotiate an armistice with the British.[53]

The Jews of Iraq were in a great state of anxiety as a result of the coup. On the surface, life was normal: Jewish schoolchildren collected money for the Red Crescent and Iraqi Jews drafted into the army fought with Kaylani's forces.[54] Kaylani himself was adamant about maintaining order and did not allow any harm to come to the Jews in Baghdad.[55] Nonetheless, the situation across the country was tense. Iraqis knew that British forces had invaded the country and were headed toward the capital, and they were speculating about the future of the military regime and that of their country. Accurate information was hard to come by, and people were unsure whether to believe accounts originating from their government or from foreign news services. The government seemed to have enjoyed a great deal of popular support in Baghdad, and was hailed by many intellectuals, who saw in the Kaylani movement a national and patriotic act of defiance against Britain and its influence in Iraq. Groups and individuals ranging from the communists to Hajj Amin al-Husayni, who disagreed on almost every political issue, all backed the regime. Their reasons for doing so naturally varied greatly: some saw the Kaylani government as leading the fight against colonialism, while others hoped for a more sympathetic attitude toward Germany. All, apparently, yearned for the departure of the British after two long decades of interference in Iraqi affairs.

During these two months of the disbelief and suspect, the coup's supporters trumpeted the heroic national battle against Britain through public speeches and essays in newspapers and journals. Paramilitary youth organizations, notably al-Futuwwa and Kata'ib al-shabab (Youth Brigades) as well as squads loyal to Yunis al-Sab'awi, patrolled Baghdad, presumably with the aim of keeping public order. The presence of these groups in the city, however, did more to create an atmosphere of fear. The press printed poems and articles glorifying the revolt and reported about events in the Arab world.[56] The radio was of particular importance as a barometer of the political leanings of the Iraqi populace. Radio Baghdad described the glorious achievements of the coup, and broadcasted poems and speeches lionizing the revolt. The ultranationalism which found a far-reaching voice in the radio had a darker side, however. Commentators warned about traitors from within, and it seemed to Jews that they were suspect in this regard. There was also an anti-British tone to much of what was broadcast at this time, which moved the British authorities to lodge complaints.[57] The station in Baghdad, for example, called upon Palestinians to rebel against the British who sided with the Jews.⁵⁸ At the same time, the British were careful to avoid referencing Jewish concerns in their own broadcasts. For this reason, the anti-Jewish stance of the Nazis was never emphasized and instead the BBC stressed that the minor anti-British, pro-Nazi faction in Iraq had no following among the Arabs themselves.⁵⁹ In their accounts of the time, Iraqi Jews have narrated "a battle of radios," as they would listen to the broadcasts of the BBC, while their neighbors listened to the Iraqi, German, and Italian stations.

During the months of the revolt, British citizens reported encountering a great deal of anti-British sentiment among the civilian population and soldiers.⁶⁰ The British bombing of Mosul, which killed a number of civilians (including women and children), and of a mosque in Faluja further inflamed anti-British feeling.⁶¹ Some Norwegians who happened to be staying in Baghdad from May 3 to May 19 observed that other than the Jews and the Christians, the Iraqi populace seemed to support the coup, and the Norwegian themselves were cheered because people thought they were Germans.⁶² Aware of the delicate situation, the British officials evacuated women and children from the British base in Habaniyya in late April, and warned of the "considerable jeopardy" faced by their subjects due to extremist propaganda.⁶³ British citizens in Baghdad sought and received protection at the American Embassy (in fact, 160 individuals of different nationalities took refuge there between April 30 and May 4).⁶⁴ Several British subjects were murdered during May and a cemetery for British soldiers was desecrated.⁶⁵ The Iraqi government informed the British that same month that if any government building in Baghdad were bombed, buildings in which British subjects were gathered would be bombed as well.⁶⁶ Late in May the British dropped forty thousand pamphlets critical of Kaylani in Iraq in order to challenge the anti-British sentiment.⁶⁷

The anti-German stance of the Jewish community was well known, and the assumption that Jews yearned for a quick British victory (which some Iraqi Jews later confirmed in their memoirs) made their lives very difficult. Elie Kedourie argues that German propaganda succeeded in characterizing the British as friends of the Jews.⁶⁸ Worse yet, it was thought that Jews were actively aiding the British war effort, despite the fact that they were serving in the Iraqi military. Jews, rumor had it, used their radios to broadcast information and to signal to British airplanes, and distributed British propaganda, especially the leaflets that the British dropped from their airplanes on Baghdad. There was no truth to these rumors, but they nonetheless circulated in the city. Gurji Barshan recalls how he met a Muslim friend, Ahmad, who had come to his neighborhood and told him he had heard that Jews were signaling messages to British planes: "I shook his hand and told him: 'My brother Ahmad, do you believe in this? . . . Could you think that I, your friend and comrade, will signal [to the British]? And how would I do this?'"[69] The two hugged and Ahmad left the scene. Not all were as understanding as Ahmad, however, and sporadically Jews were attacked by policemen and members of youth organizations who patrolled the streets. A woman with too shiny a pin on her cloak, housewives hanging laundry to dry on their roofs, and a man holding a violin case were all suspected of aiding the British.[70]

A British intelligence report indicated that small-scale looting in some neighborhoods in Baghdad had begun in May.[71] Another report, from May 1, noted signs of increasing anti-Jewish feeling in the city.[72] The accuracy of this assessment was underscored by the letter from the ICP, which had supported the coup, sent on May 7 to Rashid 'Ali. In it the communists admonished him to put a stop to the unjust attacks on Jews.[73] Jewish stores and homes had been looted in Basra in May and it was clear that Jews were being singled out, in the absence of order, as a target of mob violence. Moreover, donations to the Red Crescent and the war effort were extorted from Iraqi Jews, especially merchants, according to British reports.[74] On the other hand, Sylvia Haim notes that since the names of the donors were read on the radio, these contributions improved the image of Jews in the eyes of the public. In fact, the British seized upon this in claiming, after their reoccupation of Baghdad, that Jews had supported Rashid 'Ali(!).[75]

The quick defeat of Rashid 'Ali, after a short period of national euphoria, and the allegations that the Jews had aided the British, made for a volatile situation, which exploded violently on the first and second days of June. The accounts of Iraqi Jews contend that, going back to the beginning of the coup, Yunis al-Sab'awi had wanted to kill Jews, but Arshad al-'Umari, the mayor, and Rashid 'Ali himself had prevented him from acting on this desire. Nuri al-Sa'id had later argued that the riots were organized by pro-Nazi Iraqis. Among the grounds for this belief were Sab'awi's reporting on Hitler's career and his post in the coup government as the leader of the paramilitary youth groups. The most convincing evidence, though, was Sab'awi's warning to Chief Rabbi Sasun Khaduri shortly before the Farhud that Jews should not leave their homes for three days and should have enough food to do so. This was understood as reflecting his intent to murder the Jews in their homes.[76] Shalom Darwish met with Rabbi Khaduri shortly thereafter, and the rabbi said he had been treated with much respect, and that he was certain that Sab'awi would guarantee the safety of the Jews. Darwish recalled that this report did not allay his suspicions, and that the rabbi himself came to regret his trust in Sab'awi's promises.[77] Sab'awi may well have intended to harm Jews, but it is also possible that he was indirectly expressing his fear that something bad might happen to the Jewish community because of the anti-Jewish atmosphere that was prevalent in Baghdad. In any case, by the first of June, Sab'awi himself had left the city.[78]

Seemingly, the troubles of the Jewish community in Baghdad had dissipated by May 31. On May 25, reports still noted great confusion in Baghdad, as Rashid 'Ali was not sure whether to abandon the city or establish an alternative government in Mosul.[79] Five days later, however, it was clear to Baghdadi Jews that the coup had failed, that the regent and pro-British powers were about to enter the capital, and that an armistice would be signed with Great Britain. Rashid 'Ali and his supporters fled Baghdad, leaving the mayor, Arshad al-'Umari, to negotiate an armistice with the British. On May 30, after Kaylani's forces had left the city, a committee for public order was formed. The youth organizations were dissolved and were ordered to turn in their weapons. Soldiers began coming back to the city. Al-'Umari and the other officials leading the negotiations with the British did not declare a curfew, despite the recent tensions in Baghdad.

On June 1, Baghdadi Jews went to welcome the regent, who was rumored to return to Baghdad, or according to some accounts, to celebrate the holiday of Shavuot, and were attacked by groups comprised of policemen, soldiers, civilians, and young people. On a bridge called Jisr al-Khirr (between Karkh and Rusafa), they were met with a group of armed men. One Jew was killed, and sixteen others were wounded. A government hospital was then attacked by another group seeking to assault the Jewish nurses. In the neighborhood of Bab al-Sheikh Jews were dragged out of buses and beaten, some to death. Jewish stores on Ghazi Street and al-Rashid Street were looted. The rioters then proceeded to Abu Sifin, Tatran, the very poor section of the Jewish quarters, where eight more people were killed. The looting and the attacks in Jewish neighborhoods close to Ghazi Street and al-Rashid Street and in the old Jewish quarter of the city continued during the night and spilled over into neighborhoods that had mixed populations. The rioting ended around 3 P.M. the following day, when forces loyal to the regent reached the city. At the end of the two days the damage to the Jewish community was enormous: somewhere between 135 and 189 persons were killed; between 700 and 1,000 were wounded; there were at least 10 rapes; and around 550 stores and 900 apartments were looted. Two thousand families were reported to have suffered either physical harm or economic losses. Violent deaths, stabbing and knifing, and in some cases testimonies of beheading and dismembering, also appear in accounts.[80] According to the list of victims, most of the dead were from the Jewish neighborhood of Abu Sifin. However, killings and looting also occurred in the neighborhoods of Bab al-Sheikh, Tatran, Mahdiyya, 'Aquliyya, and Qabmar 'Ali.[81]

Military intervention could have put an end to the rioting as soon as it broke out. The regent did not send his forces into the city on June 1. Nor did the British act, though they knew that Jewish lives and property in Basra had been in peril less than a month earlier and they had received reports about anti-Jewish feeling in Baghdad.[82] Elie Kedourie has shown that the British did not want to risk their own soldiers and did not want to create the impression that the regent needed British help to return to power.[83] The regent for his part did not want to leave Basra at the end of May and was hesitant to assume leadership in Baghdad.[84] A British report on May 20 noted that despite the demonstrable progress of the British army, "Iraqi [pro-British] leaders [had] lost heart."[85] The desire to create the impression that the regent's return was predicated on "a broader basis" of support certainly played a role in deterring the British from entering the city.[86]

Evidence provided by most accounts identifies policemen, soldiers, and young people (members of paramilitary organizations and students) as the main elements in the mob that attacked Jewish neighborhoods.[87] However, a considerable change occurred on the second day, when the city's poor, which included the recent urban migrants who lived on the outskirts, joined the mob. These groups were mainly interested in looting and profiting from the sale of stolen goods. A racist British source reported that "the rabble of Baghdad, actively assisted by the army and police, were able to indulge in the favourite Arab pastimes of rapine and pillage; many Jews were murdered, and much commercial property looted before order was restored."[88]

Jewish sources do not provide much information about the soldiers who returned from the battlefield, disappointed at the failure of the coup, probably because Jews did not know them personally. One source also indicated that rioters on the first day were masses incited by a sermon they heard in the Kaylani mosque.[89] In contrast, much information is told about the policemen and their conduct during the Farhud. Policemen shot at Jews and participated in the looting. They likewise armed the rioters and shot off locks of houses and stores, after removing their badges so they could not be identified. One Jew was killed while negotiating with policemen concerning a bribe.[90] Demands for money, cigarettes, and food in return for the protection of Jewish homes were common; in the neighborhood of Tatran, Jewish residents sent handkerchiefs with money down from their rooftops to policemen below. Bribes did not guarantee the assistance of the police, however. The investigation committee's report and the British noted that the police refused to open fire on the rioters. Even at the top ranks, very few were willing to give orders that might force the police to fire on their fellow officers or on soldiers.[91] Eliyahu Epstein claimed that the American military attaché in Istanbul told him that there was a plan to loot Jewish property with the assistance of the police.[92]

British accounts seem to corroborate the testimony by Jewish witnesses as to the complete apathy of the Iraqi police:

> The army and police were largely sullen and resentful and the people in the streets looked angrily at those who passed on their turn from greeting His Highness at the place.... The police force was for a time useless ... and officers and men joined recklessly with the mob in breaking into and looting shops and houses all over the town. The Lord Mayor [Arshad al-'Umari] who, pending the formation of a new Government, was still nominally in control, begged the Director-General of police to use his reserve and to order them to clear the streets and shoot to kill, but the Director-General pleaded that he could not accept responsibility for such drastic action unless specific orders were given by the Regent.[93]

On the other hand, Jewish accounts do mention that other policemen tried to protect Jewish neighborhoods, even going so far as to open fire on rioters. The police defended the government hospital and did not allow harm to come to the Jewish nurses. Obadiah Gurji, fourteen years old at the time, recalled that he escaped from one of the buses which were attacked near Bab al-Sheikh and was saved by a policeman who told him, "Don't be afraid, my son," and took him to a police station. Twenty more Jews arrived at there, some by police cars. Outside a crowd gathered, demanding that the Jews be handed over to them, but they were driven them off by the police.[94]

In some instances, the policemen saw an opportunity to line their pockets. A case in point is the story of the Fattal family of Tatran, who paid a policeman to protect their home. The officer said he would stay until midnight, but the family convinced him to stand guard the entire night: "In exchange for an appropriate payment, food, drink, and the boosting of his ego, the policeman watched the home and its inhabitants for the night. Every once in a while one of us would go outside and watch the alley from the window to find the loyal watchman dozing off. It was not clear at all who was guarding whom—we him, or him us. At any rate, the night passed by calmly."[95] Affluent Jewish neighborhoods were not attacked, since their residents could rely on (or bribe, if necessary) the police to defend their neighborhood. In Batawin, the man in charge of the police force was a Jew called Naji Haqqaq. He made sure that Batawin was defended, while elsewhere in town, his own home was looted.[96]

Occasionally, the presence of a single policeman or soldier was enough to scare off rioters. A uniform of any kind (whether associated with the military, police, or youth organizations) could deter the mob. A Jewish man who was an officer in the Ottoman army and lived in Bab al-Sharqi went out in his uniform, armed with his sword and pistol, which, he indicated, he was more than willing to use. He managed to scare off the rioters.[97] In Karada, a man who had formerly worked for the Iraqi police sat with two guns in front of his home and no one dared to approach.[98]

On the second day of rioting, residents of the poor neighborhoods of Baghdad began to participate in the looting and killing. These were mostly recent migrants to the city whose living conditions were appalling, and they altered the direction of the Farhud. Looting was a major part of the Farhud.

The Bata Shoe Store, for example, was looted because the owner was Jewish. The rioters broke into a radio store and car dealership, but once it was discovered that the owner was not Jewish, the business was left in peace.[99] Accounts render the looting through the powerful images of people carrying objects, of any sort or kind. Abraham Kahila, who lived in al-Kishel, described his neighborhood the day after the riots: "Along the roads we saw a pacifier, dolls, pieces of furniture, torn books, a torn shoe—endless tools and objects that fell from the hands of the looters." The widespread feeling that everything was up for grabs emboldened women, children, and the elderly to take part in the looting: "I will never forget the sight of a blind man carrying on his back a dresser, and a young boy showing him the way."[100] Avner Ya'qov Yaron, who watched the looters from the roof of his home, provides a similar account:

> I asked myself: How come all the people in the streets are running as if they were porters? ...Why are all sorts of broken objects that have fallen from the hands of these running people scattered on the black asphalt road across from our house? Pieces of broken crystal mirrors, pots and pans.... No one had the answer to my questions and no one knew how to name the madness that took over the street on the night of the holiday of Shavuot, 1941.[101]

Many who looted on the second day of rioting were merely hoping to turn a quick profit. This is reflected in a popular song (in colloquial Iraqi Arabic) written at the time, in which poor looters boast at the goods they have taken from Jewish homes.[102] As Elie Kedourie confirms, the British did not guard the bridges, which meant looters could move freely from various parts of the city into Jewish neighborhoods.[103] Many of these criminals, however, did not intend to cause physical harm to the Jews, and even fought with policemen and soldiers over stolen goods. This escalation of the looting may have helped bring the Farhud to an end. The historian Avraham Twena (who also lived in Baghdad during this time) argues that fears that the more distant tribes would come to the city and that the looting would spread to non-Jewish neighborhoods motivated the state to stop the rioting. He recalls that his Muslim neighbor was concerned about what would happen if the Farhud continued, saying: "Until this moment you [the Jews] were the only ones in danger. But now all of us are in jeopardy because the Bedouins around the city have come in and they cannot distinguish between a Jew and a Muslim."[104]

The accounts of the Farhud indicate the rioters numbered in the hundreds. All the rioters and looters felt that there was no actual leadership that would punish them for their deeds. With respect to the looters, it should be mentioned that fears relating to the city's urban poor dominated political discussions in Baghdad throughout the 1930s. The urban poor were comprised of various groups, most notably the tribesmen and peasants who had migrated to the city and populated its new slums. There were public debates concerning the ability of these migrants as workers, their lack of hygiene, and their potential for violent behavior and criminality. They were one of the most underprivileged groups in Baghdad in terms of education, health services, employment opportunities, and housing.[105] Anxieties concerning the poor materialized in the Farhud, but the additional chaos created by the presence of large groups of the urban poor made the killings at times more difficult.

When the forces loyal to the regent entered the city on the second day of June to restore order, many looters and murderers were themselves killed: "After some delay the Regent sent the order in writing and also arranged for the dispatch of troops to take control. The soldiers did their work well. There was no more aimless firing into the air; their machine guns swept the streets clear of people and quickly put a stop to looting and rioting."[106] The British ambassador wrote that the second day of rioting was more violent than the first. Large number of rioters roamed the streets and "*Iraqi troops killed as many rioters as the rioters killed Jews*" (emphasis added).[107] Kedourie notes that the official investigation committee placed the number of Jews and Muslims killed at 130. One of the members of the committee believed that the number was closer to 600, but this was not made public for fear it would embarrass the government.[108] Zionist accounts estimated the number of non-Jews killed (rioters and looters as well as Muslims who helped the Jews) as quite high. Eliyahu Epstein, based on interviews with eyewitnesses, came with one thousand as the number of Jews and Muslims who died. This is certainly inflated, but the mention of non-Jews is important.[109] Other Zionist accounts venture that the number of rioters killed by the regent's army was three hundred to four hundred.[110] Again, while probably overestimated, these figures would seem to indicate that the last hours of the Farhud were complete and utter chaos, during which the violence directed initially at Jews came to affect a wide range of Baghdadis. This may be yet another reason for the later silence of the state regarding the Farhud.

While Jews reported that their non-Jewish neighbors joined in the riots and looting, a constant element that appears in most accounts of the Farhud is a narrative relating to a good neighbor. A Zionist account written shortly afterward also acknowledged the many instances of Muslims assisting Jews.[111] Judging by the lists of the Jewish dead, it seems that Jews in mixed neighborhoods stood a better chance of surviving the riots than those in uniformly Jewish areas. The reason for this is that their neighbors and their friends protected them. Avraham Twena lived in a mixed neighborhood in a commercial area on al-Nahr Street:

> Relatives who deserted their homes asked for my protection. At 8 P.M., three Jewish clerks from nearby offices escaped and came asking for shelter in my home. The sound of bullets was heard outside, and we sat, about thirty people, scared to death.... In our alley there were four Jewish families, and four Muslim families. One of them hated the Jews and its boys [had been threatening] us for a month. At 10:30 about fifty men entered the alley. My neighbor, the *mukhtar*, who was sixty-five years old, stood in front of them and said: "Over my dead body will you pass here." The other [three Muslim] families helped him. They talked to the rioters, at times kindly, at others intimidatingly, until the rioters left the place. We were later informed that the bad neighbors were the ones pushing the perpetrators to attack us.[112]

The proximity of the families and the friendship with the *mukhtar* (leader of the neighborhood) stood in the way of the mob. This narrative includes key elements that are repeated in a few different testimonies. Some Jews speak of a bad neighbor alongside a good one, or a few good ones, who came to their rescue.

Sometimes all that was needed was a single steadfast ally. Mordechi Ben Porat recalls his neighbor, a colonel by the name of Tahir Muhammad 'Arif, who came to his father a few days before and warned the family about a coming danger. On Sunday, June 1, a mass of people "enflamed and incited, armed with working tools, sticks, swords, and axes," attacked their home in al-A'zamiyya:

> We locked ourselves inside[,] ... climbed to the roof and watched what was going on outside. From the roof I could see our neighbors ... who ignored

our good relationships and led the criminals to our doorstep. I also saw the wife of Colonel Tahir Muhammad 'Arif. In the absence of her husband, and perhaps under his direct instructions given ahead of time, she decided to do something. She went from her home, armed with a gun and a hand grenade, and stood between the incited mob and the door of our home, threatening in a decisive voice, that if the house was attacked, she would not hesitate to blow up the grenade and use the gun. As she was talking, she displayed the weapons, and the attackers drew back from the house.[113]

Avner Yaron's family had previously helped their Muslim neighbors, Haydar and Hamdiyya. During the Farhud, Haydar stood in front of the Jewish family's house, pretending as if it was his own, in order to chase off looters: "Haydar shouted at them, released a few juicy curses . . . and frightened them away, saying [to the perpetrators]:' . . . You sons of bitches! Can't you see I'm a Muslim and my wife is a veiled Muslim? This is my home. Do you want to rob a Muslim?'" Haydar was shocked at the sight of Jewish shops being looted: "Haydar swore to my father by Allah that he would guard us, even if his head was torn from his neck. Hamdiyya kissed my mother and told her . . . [,] 'You once saved me from death and now it is my turn to save you and your children.'"[114] The Muslim neighbors' claiming ownership of the Jewish house physically but also symbolically made them a part of the Jewish household; the neighbors, in other words, thought of the Jewish family as part of their extended family and therefore under their protection. In fact, many Iraqis gave refuge to dozens of Jews in their homes. Some accounts mention people who sheltered up to seventy people or more, as Jews moved from one roof to another until they found a safe haven. Similarly, drivers who saw the lynching at Bab al-Sheikh warned Jews to stay away from the neighborhood.[115] Arab guards protected shops against looting because they knew the Jewish owners.[116] Not only familiarity, but also a sense that what was happening was morally wrong motivated these Muslims. Converts also helped their Jewish relatives. A Jewish woman, who had married a man from the Zahawi family (a Muslim family), and had been long shunned by her Jewish relatives, renewed her relationship with them following the coup. She and her grown children, who had become lawyers and judges, went to their Jewish uncles' homes and guarded them during the Farhud. They invited their mother's family to their own homes and protected them from the looters.[117] At times, ideology had very little to do with the assistance provided to the Jews. A man who worked for the rail company, whom a Zionist document identified as "a Nazi," refused to fire his Jewish workers and kept a close eye on them during the riots.[118] Sa'ib Shawkat himself opened his doors to Jews and gave them refuge.[119]

Occasionally, looters and criminals came to the help of the Jews. One man was executed after the Farhud for murdering a young Muslim woman who was looting with her sister. She saw the man attacking a young Jew and told him to leave the Jewish man alone. He responded by stabbing her.[120] A Jew, wounded by a rioter with an ax on Abbas Effendi Street, was taken by his son to the house of a neighbor. The house was full of goods looted by the owner, who nonetheless protected the Jewish man and the rest of his family.[121] A man known to be a thief protected around a hundred Jews in his neighborhood, and forced the local baker and the grocery store owner to provide them with food.[122]

When Jews were not aided by others, they defended themselves by a variety of means. Jews locked their doors and fortified them with heavy objects and furniture to prevent the looters and killers from entering. Because the houses in the poor Jewish neighborhoods were very close to one another, people jumped from rooftop to rooftop and escaped in this fashion. They used every weapon at their disposal, including knives, sharp objects, stones, bottles, pistols, and clubs. Of course such weapons were useless when armed policemen and soldiers entered their homes or threatened them with machine guns, but the throwing of stones or hot oil from the roof and the threatening of looters with pistols were additional tactics of Jewish resistance in the Farhud.[123]

This analysis of accounts of the Farhud reveals that it was marked by total disorder and the collapse of the state. Rumors replaced official media reports; rioters took advantage of the lack of public order; and the police were unable to act in any organized fashion. The government's investigation committee report on the Farhud conveys this sense of peril, as it repeatedly emphasizes the need to restore order in the city.[124] The Farhud was also a moment in which Jews saw representatives of the state—policemen and soldiers—turn against them; it was a moment in which the state's failed social policies surfaced in Baghdad, as the city's lower-ranking policemen and urban poor turned against their fellow Baghdadis, notably Jews, using force for economic gain, and at times, killing for such aims. The deaths of many Muslims in the Farhud (while protecting Jews, in fights related to looting, and as a result of police shooting) indicates that the uprising had very important social repercussions that extended beyond the Jewish community, repercussions that the state was unwilling to acknowledge.

However, the Farhud also testified to the resilience of certain norms of coexistence that typified interwar Baghdad. The victims of the violence often suffered at the hands of anonymous attackers, whereas those who survived the riots mention the names of familiar individuals who came to protect them. Friends, business partners, and neighbors were aware of religious differences between themselves and their Jewish neighbors, yet they felt the need to offer help and support. This sprang from a sense of intimacy in the mixed Baghdadi neighborhoods, where Jews and Muslims attended the same schools or worked in close proximity. No matter what nationalist ideas were broadcast on the radio, or what exclusionist images of the nation were projected by particular elements within the state, these neighbors and friends remained loyal to each other. Mordechi Ben Porat became one of the leading activists of the Zionist movement in Iraq, in part because he believed the Farhud signaled the destruction of the Jewish-Iraqi paradise. Yet he confesses in his memoirs that "the courageous action of our brave Muslim neighbors ... left an enormous impression on me ... burned in my memory, fresh, like it all happened yesterday."[125]

Religion and Tribalism: Basra, South Iraq, and North Iraq

The Farhud did not spread to other parts of Iraq, although a prelude to the Farhud occurred in Basra during the month of May and a few cases of looting were reported in Faluja as well. On May 1, 1941, the British decided to occupy the port area of Basra. After a brief engagement, the Iraqi forces retreated and the port was in British hands. On May 7 the British entered Basra from the commercial areas close to Shat al-'Arab, and moved through a suburb called al-'Ashshar. As groups of people gathered to watch, the soldiers locked up the shops and stirred the group's attention toward looting. While Muslims watched their shops, Jewish stores were looted freely. In central Basra residents stayed in their homes. When the police station was abandoned by Kaylani's forces, groups began looting Jewish residences as well as business. This continued through the night but the British did not enter the city. On May 8 a group of notables went to the British and asked them to take control of the city, fearing more houses would be looted and women and children would be harmed. The British refused. Most of the looting of Jewish property took place during these two days, though there were some isolated incidents a week or so later.[126]

Basra was not the scene of violence comparable to what was seen in Baghdad, notwithstanding the apparent parallels, especially the looting by a mob of both policemen and the urban poor. One reason was that the nationalist faction was not as prominent in Basra.[127] Moreover, assistance by Muslim neighbors based on religious and tribal values assumed immense importance in the city. A British account explained that the notables in Basra, with the spread of looting, recruited night watchmen to protect local property, and "many gave asylum in their own homes to Jews and other members of minorities who were in fear for their lives."[128] The British also reported that the situation in the south was different than in Baghdad. They noted in late April that support for Rashid 'Ali was eroding in the provinces where Shi'i sheikhs held sway, as they tended to be pro-British. Other reports, however, note that students in the secondary schools in Basra supported the revolt and that there were pro-Kaylani demonstrations.[129]

One of the most important persons in Basra was the notable Sheikh Ahmad Bash-A'yan, who had served in the Iraqi government and as the mayor of Basra. During the riots, he formed a militia of his Baluchistani guards to keep order. They and other armed groups loyal to the sheikh managed to stop the looting and restore peace in the old sections of Basra.[130] After the riots were over, the sheikh was to travel to Palestine to receive treatment for an eye ailment. The president of the Jewish community in Basra sent a letter to the Jewish Agency declaring that his highness, Sheikh Ahmad Bash-A'yan, belonged to one of the most respected Arab families in Iraq. During the riots, the president explained, the Bash-A'yan family had upheld its noble tradition of helping the weak and had protected Basran Jews whose lives and property were in danger. He therefore asked that the Hebrew press make mention of the arrival of this dignified and righteous guest and recount the kindness and bravery shown by this ancient royal family.[131]

Sheikh Bash-A'yan was not the only Basran to aid and protect Jews. When two individuals tried to break into the home of the Jewish Sofer family in order to assault a woman who lived there, a Basran notable, Sayyid Muhammad Salih al-Radini, came to the Sofer household with weapons and armed men. He threatened the two men and they left (according to some accounts, they were also beaten, as a "cautionary" measure).[132] After the riots the Hakham Bashi visited both the Bash-A'ayan and the al-Radini families, thanked them for their noble actions, and blessed them and their children. Shelomo 'Azariya, who was a young teacher at the Alliance in Basra, adds:

> There were many Arabs with whom Jews had friendly and neighborly relationships and they looked with disdain on the looting and the pillaging directed against the Jews. They came to defend their Jewish neighbors, carrying weapons. They did so in the houses of Jews, and in their own houses, into which they accepted the Jewish families. I, together with my family, was moved to a house of a Basran Arab who was a friend of my uncle, after he sent his two sons to escort us. They sheltered us until the afternoon of the following day when they realized order had been restored.[133]

Similarly, the Jewish Qattan family, who lived in Suq al-Hunud in Basra and made a living from selling alcoholic drinks in their shop, was saved by their neighbor, also a shop owner in the market, a Muslim and a Hajj. When the neighbor realized that the mob was very close to the Qattans' house, he stood in front of the rioters and told them that he would consider the looting of the house of his Jewish neighbors as the looting of his own, and suggested they kill him first. In another instance, the Jewish Sarraf family, who lived in a Christian neighborhood, was aided by a Muslim neighbor, Abu Tariq, whose own son was a staunch suppers of Kaylani. Abu Tariq, however, came with his other sons, all armed, to stand guard along the street.[134] Finally, after the looting ended, the Shi'i imam in Basra delivered a sermon in which he said that what had happened in the city was contradictory to Islamic law. It was forbidden, he said, to loot shops and to sell or buy stolen goods. Goods taken from Jewish homes were sold in the city's markets nonetheless.[135]

Though other parts of southern and central Iraq did not feel the impact of the Kaylani coup as much as Basra, Jews felt their repercussions. In

Diwaniyya, the provincial governor attempted to round up the city's Jews and arrest a member of the well-known Sasun-Mu'allim family in the city, but the provincial governor of Hilla prevented him from doing so. A Jew, Menashe Kalachi, was shot to death in Shamiyya on May 22, but this occurred in the context of local tribal conflict. Menashe's brother supported one tribe, and Menashe was killed by members of the other tribe.[136] In 'Amara, talk circulated about a possible attack against the Jews, and Jewish children were beaten. A map of Iraq was planted in a pocket of one Jew who was later attacked because of his "espionage."[137]

After Basra, the most important city in the south-central region of Iraq was Hilla, where a large Jewish community resided. According to most accounts, the governor (*qaimmaqam*), the local judge, and the local police assisted Jews, but the military governor was hostile to the community. Jews in Hilla thus had reason to be fearful. On a daily basis, the local police searched houses of Jews for radio transmitters that could be used to pass information to the British, and had to be bribed to leave.[138] As in Basra, religious and tribal leaders played an important role in keeping order, most notably Mirza al-Qazwini, the local *mujtahid*, and the sheikh who was the head of the tribe Bu Sultan. When the governor in Hashimiyya had weapons distributed to the Futuwwa paramilitary youth movement and told them to attack the Jews of Hilla, the sheikh threatened the governor that if this came to pass, his tribesmen would attack the city. The sheikh was able to prevent violence on a large scale, but three Jews were attacked while boarding the train in Hilla, with one dying in the hospital. Upon hearing this, Mirza al-Qazwini went to the governor to complain, arguing that the murder of a Jew was an act of sacrilege.[139]

Despite the support for the coup in the north and especially in Mosul, Arab nationalism never enjoyed a great deal of support in this region because of the large Turkish and Kurdish populations. Moreover, the religious justifications that Basrans had cited for protecting Jews were repeated in the north. In Kirkuk, the police saved a Jewish woman from a mob that believed she was signaling to the British while hanging her laundry to dry. The woman was taken to the police headquarters and the governor had her released within two hours.[140] British reports on the north mention extreme anti-British propaganda and rumors that the British intended to kidnap the young king.[141] The military governor Qasim Maqsud tried to blackmail the Jewish community by demanding a substantial amount of money to guarantee its safety. The leaders of the community managed to buy time by making excuses, so that Kaylani was defeated before the deadline for payment arrived. These examples notwithstanding, when Hajj Amin al-Husayni visited Mosul, he was told by Ra'uf al-Mufti, the chief judge, that the people of Mosul had no intention of attacking the Jews, because the latter were their neighbors and Islam commands Muslims to guard the neighbor and the friend. The mufti Sheikh Ibrahim al-Rumi promised the rabbi that the Jews would be safe, and the commander of police likewise guaranteed their safety. On June 1 the police were guarding the Jewish streets in the city; they remained at these posts through the following day.[142] In Sulaimaniya, the imam of the city, upon hearing that young men were planning to attack the Jewish population, attempted to dissuade them by saying those who had looted houses were criminals who did not believe in Allah and His Messenger and that the Jews were under the protection of Islam.[143]

In national discourses, the existence of tribal and religious values is juxtaposed with the seemingly superior national values. Nationalism, so it is argued, obliterates notions of tribal and religious difference between individuals and brings them together. Iraqi Jews, as we have seen, strongly believed in national values. Events outside of Baghdad during 1941, however, prove the opposite. The adherence to tribal values, especially the notion that a tribal leader should defend those under his protection, and religious values, which directed the Muslim faithful to protect the people of the book, proved far superior to the nationalist ideology, which paved the way for racism and discrimination. The Islamic faith, in whose name tribal and religious leaders spoke, managed to undermine nationalist propaganda and to serve as an ideological tool with which individuals could be addressed. Mujtahids, imams, and muftis acted powerfully against those who wished to mark Jews as traitors whose lives and property were at the mercy of the mob.

The linking of Jews with the British, conspiracy theories about Jewish espionage, and the desire of the urban poor and the youth to lay hands on Jewish property were not unique to Baghdad. The south and the center were characterized by political chaos; officials in Diwaniyya and Hashimiya pursued an anti-Jewish agenda, only to be challenged by an official in Hilla. The lack of centralized power, however, meant that tribal leaders and their tribes had retained their arms and as a result, tribal sheikhs wielded their own authority. The reasons for the differences between Baghdad and the other regions of Iraq relate also to the spread of nationalist ideology. Tribal leaders objected to the efforts of Baghdad to centralize the Iraqi state. Kurds, Turkmans (in the north), domiciled Persians, and Shi'i religious leaders (in the south) did not always look favorably on the idea that Arab ethnicity should be the sole basis of the national identity of the state. A variety of political, social, and cultural conditions thus made for a significant divergence between the Baghdadi center and its peripheries. More than anything, however, as in Baghdad, the strong relationships between people, neighbors and friends, and the bonds created by individuals living in the same locale were what spurred Iraqi Muslims to stand in defense of their Jewish neighbors and friends.

Immediate Responses, 1941–43

The immediate responses to the Farhud occurred on three levels: the Iraqi state, the Jewish Iraqi community, and the Zionist movement.

A few months after the Farhud, some steps were taken to punish criminals and perpetrators. The government of Jamil al-Madfa'i, which was set up after the coup, appointed an investigation committee to study what had happened. The committee recommended the firing of the chief of police, the chiefs of local neighborhood police stations, and army officials, as the committee's official report held the police and the army responsible for the violence. It listed more long-term factors, especially German propaganda (of which the primary source was Grobba), which had found a receptive audience in the army. Also singled out was Hajj Amin al-Husayni, who was blamed for distributing much of the anti-Jewish propaganda and for redirecting money given to him for the Palestinian cause to that propaganda campaign. The participation of young Iraqis in the Farhud was of special concern to the committee. As young people were understood to be very impressionable, the report zeroed in on those individuals and entities with the greatest influence: Syrian and Palestinian teachers; the German station which broadcast in Arabic and Iraq's state radio station; and the paramilitary youth organizations, especially al-Futuwwa and Kata'ib al-shabab, as well as youth squads loyal to Sab'awi.[144] The report's conclusions mirrored the British analysis of the events. Ambassador Kinahan Cornwallis argued that the riots were instigated by certain army officers and the police, and that Rashid 'Ali's propaganda, as well as pro-Nazi and pro-Italian propaganda, help sparked the riots as well.[145]

The recommendations of the investigation committee were carried out. Military courts were set up to try rioters: four rioters were convicted on charges of murder and were publicly hanged, and others were sentenced to prison. Some of the property that was looted was retrieved and returned. In some cases, Jews were asked to inspect the houses of suspected looters to look for their property, an act that probably increased sectarian tensions. Most property, however, was not returned; even those who knew which of their neighbors had looted their property were unable to reclaim it. In the days after the Farhud, soldiers and policemen threatened Jews that they would incite a second wave of rioting.[146] Sab'awi himself was hanged on May 5, 1942, for his role in the coup.

British accounts convey the sense that the punishments of the criminals did not match the crimes they committed. Cornwallis wrote that on July 13 three men were executed for the crimes they committed on June 1 and 2 and that a number of others were sentenced for imprisonment. He concluded that this could not be regarded as "just and adequate," given "the deplorable happening of these two days." In his view, too few of the police and military officers who took part in the looting and killing were punished, and even when disciplinary action was taken it seldom matched the enormity of the crime. He also noted that the the Madfa'i government waited a long time to release the report of the investigation committee and that it took no action against the high officials whose conduct the report condemned.[147] Furthermore, the British reoccupation did not dampen pro-German feeling in Iraq. Many "undesirable teachers" continued to work in schools in Mosul and many pro-Nazi civil servants retained their posts in the education ministry.[148]

The halfheartedness of the state's propaganda efforts and the unwillingness to take a position that could be construed as pro-Jewish are exemplified by the pro-British daily called *Sawt al-Haqq* (The Voice of Truth), which made its debut in Baghdad shortly after the Farhud. It condemned Rashid 'Ali and his supporters and strongly denounced fascism and Nazism as hostile to democracy, freedom, and religiosity. Articles in the paper strove to demonstrate that Islam as a Semitic religion was anti-Nazi in its very essence, given Nazism's hatred of Semitic peoples and cultures. Moreover, Islam allowed for freedom of thought and expression, which Nazism did not tolerate. Finally, Islam made no distinction between blacks and whites or Persian and Arabs, whereas Nazism privileged the Germanic races and considered Arabs, Jews, and blacks as inferior races.[149] Consequently, of all people, the Arabs had the most reasons to fight Nazism, being the leaders of the Islamic and the Semitic world.[150] As an example of Nazi oppression, the paper reported how Nazi Germany was a police state controlled by the Gestapo.[151] What was more, when Germany conquered other nations, they put everyone—men, women, and children, old and young—in camps and jails, as the case of Greece showed.[152] The paper listed the victims of Nazism, among whom were many Muslims.[153] Jews, however, were omitted from these accounts, and were only hinted at when the paper referenced the Semitic race.

Sawt al-Haqq had no qualms about denouncing the Palestinians, who had recently arrived in Iraq. One story about Hajj Amin al-Husayni linked him to a fifth column that was operating in Iraq. He was compared to Iblis (the devil in Islamic tradition), who was first an angel and then became a devil; the mufti, too, appeared at first to be a committed anti-Zionist leader, but turned out to be a manipulator who did nothing but spread hate and promote his own interests. Worse yet, those who had come with him from Palestine, notably Darwish Miqdadi and Akram Zu'aytar, had found jobs as bureaucrats and teachers that should have been given to Iraqis. Arabism for these men was simply a means to deceive the people of Iraq and rise to prominence.[154]

Sawt al-Haqq's editorials reflected the new state's ideology. On the one hand the paper was committed to an anti-Nazi and antifascist agenda, and attempted to rally Iraqi opposition, under the unifying banner of Islam, to these secularizing doctrines. A key point of emphasis was that Nazi anti-Semitism was directed at Arabs and Islam. Yet whereas the liberal press in Egypt courageously condemned Nazi Germany's persecution of its Jewish subjects, the editors of *Sawt al-Haqq* seemed to feel that certain topics, especially racism directed against Jews, were still too sensitive for the Iraqi public.

Nonetheless, by the end of 1942 the British Embassy reported that the flow of hostile propaganda was diminishing and that confidence in an eventual Allied victory had steadied, in part due to Stalingrad's resistance against the Germans.[155] Accounts from June to August 1941 also reveal that many Muslims felt guilty about the treatment of their Jewish neighbors. In July, Zionist diplomat Eliyahu Sasson (Sasun) had a conversation with the new Iraqi consul in Palestine, Jamil al-Rawi. Rawi told Sasson that he regretted the attacks on the Jews, who had lived in peace and friendship with Iraqi Muslims. These, he said, were contrary to the Arab tradition and the Islamic faith and did not add much honor to Iraq as a state that ought to have protected its minorities. Rawi noted that the rioters had assaulted Muslims as well; that Jews had won the compassion and understanding of their Muslim neighbors; that the riots had not spread beyond Baghdad; and that the looters had been sentenced to long prison terms.[156] Shortly after the Farhud, Sheikh Jalal al-Hanafi spoke on the radio about the need to respect one's neighbors and the *dhimmi*s. The *'ulama* in Najaf and Karbala issued fatwas urging the faithful not to fight for the Nazis. Madfa'i and the regent secretly donated money to assist the Jewish community. Acting quickly, the cabinet passed a decision on June 3 to expel all undesirable foreigners, especially Syrian, Palestinian, and Egyptian nationals, and many pro-German teachers were dismissed from their jobs as a result. The government of Nuri al-Sa'id, which succeeded the Madfa'i regime in October 1942, initiated a second crackdown on Rashid 'Ali's sympathizers. One hundred and twenty supporters of the coup were deported, seven hundred arrested, and many Palestinian teachers were exiled.[157] As part of the British-Iraqi retaliation against the coup's leaders, three were executed in 1942. Although the charges brought against these men did not mention the Farhud, it may have eased the minds of Iraqi Jews who blamed Kaylani's supporters for the riots.

As always, matters became increasingly complicated when money was involved. Under Jamil al-Madfa'i, the Jewish community was promised 30,000 dinars as compensation for the looted property (it should be noted that the community felt this amount was inadequate). A Zionist report noted that Madfa'i was attempting to dissuade the Jewish community from seeking assistance from Jews in other countries. Within the government, however, this decision was the subject of a lengthy debate. Finally, under Nuri al-Sa'id, a sum of 20,000 dinars was allotted, as a portion of the 120,000 dinars paid to British citizens whose property had also been looted during Kaylani's regime. People who had suffered because of riots in other cities such as Basra were compensated as well.[158]

The Jewish community likewise worked to help the victims of the Farhud. In the weeks afterward, the community saw to the immediate needs of the victims and their families: identifying bodies in a mass grave and hospitals, based on a list of photos that the chief rabbi had (and bribing the police in order to locate additional bodies); finding women who had been abducted or abused; and estimating the financial damage. Women's societies assisted the needy, especially orphans. Rabbi Khaduri distributed a leaflet calling for members of the community to help each other in these difficult times.[159] Other accounts, however, speak of animosity toward the chief rabbi, as he was faulted for not doing enough to prevent the riots. Merchants in particular were incensed that the bribes they had paid to ensure the community's security meant nothing during the Farhud.[160] The community's leaders worked with the state in order to identify both perpetrators and victims, and to handle the monetary compensation. Jews in other countries made contributions as well: the Jewish community in India donated two thousand dinars, while Zionist organizations sent four hundred Palestinian liras. The funds were distributed by the local Jewish community, with individuals who had lost property receiving one to two dinars. Yusuf al-Kabir dedicated the money given by Zionist organizations to collective charity.

The leadership of the Iraqi Jewish community was criticized for having downplayed the conclusions of the investigation committee, having prevented people from gathering at the mass graves, and for being unwilling to ask the Iraqi government for more compensation.[161] According to Ezra Haddad, the state put pressure on the Jewish leadership to avoid enflaming the passions of the community. A copy of the investigation committee's report was indeed made available to the leaders, but it was labeled "top secret" and community members were not allowed to respond to it publicly. Haddad also reported that on the Sabbath and on Jewish holidays hundreds of Jews used to visit the mass grave to mourn the victims of the Farhud. This did not sit well with the government, which feared the political implications of these mass gatherings, and thus the Jewish leaders put an end to the visits.[162] In response to the behavior of the leadership of the community, some young Jews organized a small organization, Youth to the Rescue

(Shabab al-inqadh), which was dedicated to the self-defense of the Jewish community. A number of the members eventually became either Zionists or communists, although the names of the latter have been omitted from most official accounts of the organization written in Israel. The communists left Shabab al-inqadh once Zionist emissaries began to make their influence felt. One pamphlet distributed by Shabab al-inqadh read:

> Jewish young men and women! . . . When will you awake, cease to be cowards, and arise, as one, to protect your honor that is about to be desecrated by dishonorable men? Oh youth! The enemy has harmed all that was sacred to you; they murdered your relatives and robbed all that you had. But do not cry for the past. We need to prepare for the next massacre. Those who live with you in this country, await the opportunity to eat you alive. But you care about making a profit and not about protecting your own lives—and this is the reason for our destruction and demise. The money has made you forget what has happened. . . . Do not claim all was done by the act of God. No! God did not want this! God did not want a three-day-old baby butchered! God did not want us butchered as sheep!¹⁶³

One can clearly see how the fears about future violence, and anger that the Farhud had been forgotten, colored the viewpoint of Jewish youth. It is thus no wonder that they were drawn to radical options. Most significant, however, is that the solution offered was to increase the Jewish capacity for self-defense within Iraq, not outside of it. Moreover, it was not entirely true that Iraqi Jews pretended as though the Farhud had never taken place. One consequence of the violence was that many Jews sought to acquire weapons, whether from relatives, drivers, or arms dealers.¹⁶⁴

The Farhud altered the Jewish community's relationship with the British. Ironically, Iraqi Jews, who were blamed for supporting Great Britain during the coup, now resented the British for not intervening to stop the riots. Some speculated that the British profited from the riots, and most were angered at the British for not sending forces into Baghdad to stop the looting and killing. A Zionist emissary reported: "Feelings of animosity exist between the Jews and the British. The Jews are bitter that the British had done nothing to save them. They are therefore extremely reserved towards the British and do not invite them to any official event."¹⁶⁵ A British report from 1944 confirms that Iraqi Jews tended to belittle Britain's war efforts while lionizing the Americans and the Russians because they felt that British forces did not protect them during the Farhud and that the British government did not press the Iraqi authorities to execute more of the murderers and looters.[166]

After the Farhud the Zionists stepped up their activities in Iraq, but this did not result in a Jewish exodus to Palestine. Those who wanted to leave Iraq during the coup and shortly thereafter set their sights on Iran, India, and especially America, as well as Britain.[167] In most cases, these nations refused to take in Jewish immigrants.[168] Some Iraqi Jews did go to Iran, but returned within a few months. Yet the redoubled efforts of Zionists to bring more Jews from Iraq to Palestine ended in failure.[169] Zionist emissaries complained that Jewish young people were integrated into Iraqi society to such a degree that convincing them to join the Zionist project was almost impossible. Eliyahu Epstein, who went to Basra and Iran to meet with Iraqi Jews, reported on the unenthusiastic reaction to his suggestion concerning the founding of a village in Palestine named after the victims of the Farhud and on the general lack of interest in immigration to Palestine.[170] The emissary Enzo Sereni came to the conclusion that middle-class Iraqi Jews had no desire to come to the land of Israel and bemoaned the fact that Iraqi Jews aged eighteen to twenty-five were very difficult to influence.[171] As it turned out, despite a few difficult months after the Farhud, when the community still lived in fear, the years following the British reoccupation and especially after the defeat of the Axis forces at El Alamein were marked by economic prosperity. Jews, along with the Iraqi population as a whole, benefited as a result. Iraqi Jews therefore had no desire to leave the Iraqi homeland, especially during such good times, for an uncertain future in Palestine. As one emissary observed, "Many [Jews] are getting rich. Business is booming, and many work for the British army. The Iraqi [Arabs] are getting rich as well."[172]

Esther Me'ir's insightful analysis showed the complexity of responses within the Yishuv (the Jewish community in mandatory Palestine) itself. Moshe Sharet (head of the Jewish Agency at the time) rejected the idea of allocating migration licenses (the number of which was limited because of British regulations) to Iraqi Jews in May 1941, fearing that it might actually jeopardize the Iraqi Jewish community. News of the Farhud did not reach Jews in Palestine until early June, when *Ha-Aretz* reported that many civilians of all religions had been killed in Baghdad. In July, truck drivers on the

Haifa-Baghdad route brought more information concerning what had happened. Based on these sources, Zionist leaders estimated the number of people killed at one thousand.[173] On July 19, Moshe Yatah, who lived in Iraq and was active in education within the community, met with Sharet and told him that the number of those killed was less than 110 and provided some details on the extent of the property damage. On July 9, MAPAI (Mifleget po'aley eretz Israel: Party of the Workers of the Land of Israel, the main leadership of labor Zionism at the time) began to discuss the riots. Party members believed that similar riots could occur in Syria, and that Britain was not to be trusted as willing to protect Jews anywhere in the Middle East, including Palestine. Sharet felt that the tragedy supported the Zionist argument that Arabs should not be granted independence. This type of political arrangement was clearly perilous to minority rights; the Zionists pointed to the massacre of the Assyrians as further evidence to support their claim. Me'ir lists some of the more shocking comments of the participants, such as, "This is more terrible than what has happened in Germany, even in the most horrible days of Hitler."[174] An internal document of the Zionist agency discussing "this *sho'ah*" argued that the public should know about "these sights of horrors, which were worse than the horrors of Tsarist Russia and Nazi Germany."[175]

The Irgun (the underground political organization of right-wing Zionists) weighed in on the Farhud, from which it drew the lesson that collaboration with Britain and the Arabs was to be avoided at all costs. A leaflet printed by the Irgun stated that twelve hundred people had been killed in the Farhud, and that the Jewish women had committed suicide to save themselves from fates worse than death. Jews should not enter into pacts with murderers: the Farhud, the leaflet cautioned readers, was a warning to all those who had forgotten the Arab gangs in 1921 and 1929 in Palestine. The leaflet ended with the promise that the "Hebrew sword shall take revenge from the bloodthirsty daughter of Arabia."[176] Government authorities associated with labor Zionism feared that the Irgun would provide Iraqi Jews, those remaining in Iraq and those who had immigrated to Palestine, with weapons. In response, they sent emissaries to Iraq in the fall of 1941 to recruit candidates for immigration, while also increasing the number of immigration permits available to Jews from Iraq. These emissaries, as we have seen, encountered immense difficulties in persuading Iraqi Jews to immigrate.[177]

Memorials for the victims were held in Palestine.[178] A month after the Farhud, Baghdadi rabbis in Jerusalem and the committee of Babylonian Jews in Palestine (*va'd 'adat ha-bavlim*) called on their fellow Iraqi Jews to mourn "the killings of hundreds of our brethren . . . by an organized attack from their neighbors who pretend to be noble and just."[179] The rabbinic leadership of the Land of Israel called on the Jews of Palestine to dedicate the afternoon hours of the seventh day of Av 1941 in honor of "the victims [*hallal*] of the riots [*pera'ot*] in Baghdad." In these hours, the public was asked to convene in synagogues and offer prayers for "the pure martyrs, killed by the people of Rashid 'Ali, the people of the ex-mufti of Jerusalem, and other Nazi agents."[180]

The responses to the Farhud were varied, yet overall they seem to negate the idea that the Farhud caused Iraqi Jews to cease thinking of Iraq as their homeland. Most of the effort toward reconciliation was made within Iraq, with the Iraqi state playing a significant role. It made no sense for Iraqi Jews to migrate to Palestine, where the prospects for earning a livelihood and for Jewish political sovereignty were unknown. Jews thus wished to remain in Iraq, where economic opportunity abounded during the latter years of World War II. The youth responded differently; they were shocked by the violence, angry with the British and the nationalists, and displeased with what they saw as an extremely sheepish Jewish leadership. Anti-British sentiment and intense resentment of the nationalists would drive some to Zionism. Others would seek a different direction, both patriotic and anti-Zionist, namely, communism.

Conclusions

The Farhud was a moment in which all boundaries were dissolved and the state's failed social policies and its ultranationalist discourses ended in a fiasco. Consequently, there are many silences that need to be unpacked by our reading of the events, in particular the state's silence regarding the great number of Muslims killed in the riots. In the context of Jewish Iraqi history, moreover, a distinction should be made between an analysis of the Farhud and the Farhudization of Jewish Iraqi history—viewing the Farhud as typifying the overall history of the relationship between Jews and greater Iraqi society. The Jewish community strived for integration in Iraq before and after the Farhud. In fact, the attachment of the community to Iraq was so tenacious that even after such a horrible event, most Jews continued to believe that Iraq was their homeland. This vision was shattered only by the realities created following the 1948 war in Palestine.

Sectarian relationships during the Farhud were constructed by and against the state. Particular individuals within the Iraqi national elite, such as Sami Shawkat or Yunis al-Sab'awi, promoted an undemocratic and racialized vision of Iraqi society that was often exclusivist (and not just with respect to Jews). The collapse of this vision resulted in sectarian strife. However, these Arab nationalists found difficulties arguing for racial difference between Jews and Arabs, as many secular Arab writers praised the entire Semitic race as a superior race. Not only the Arabs, but the Nazis themselves were aware of this problem. Although Hitler referred to the Arab peoples in extremely racist terms, he permitted the omission in Arab translations of *Mein Kampf* of sections that might seem insulting to Semites. Grobba also ordered that certain phrases from the original be dropped, and the word *anti-Semitic* replaced by *anti-Jewish*.[181] More crucially, alongside these exclusionist narratives, there was another vision of Iraqi society, of people who lived in the same neighborhoods, worked together, and were friends, business partners, or neighbors. Iraqi Muslims and Jews were aware that their neighbors did not necessarily share their religious faiths. And yet, being friends, neighbors, and partners created a sense of belonging that could withstand the racism and chauvinism promoted by certain elements within the national elite. It is this shared notion of community from below that led Muslims to protect their Jewish neighbors during the Farhud and prevented the violence from spreading throughout Iraq.

The conduct of these brave Iraqis was inspired not only by the national principle according to which religious differences were ignored for the sake of the nation, but also by religious principles that maintained that Jews and Christians deserved the protection of Muslims, and by the commonly held belief that a neighbor is a sort of a relative who deserves protection and care. The medieval category of Jews as *ahl al-dhimma*—a minority whose rights should be protected by the majority Muslim community—ought to have disappeared in Iraq by this time, as the state's constitution guaranteed equality before the law to all citizens, regardless of their religion. And yet, in this ultranationalist context, it was the concept of the *dhimmi* that was often evoked in order to counter nationalist violence. Throughout this period, Muslim religious leaders (both Sunni and Shi'i) objected to the implementation of racial hierarchies within the Iraqi state. One testimony suggests that individuals in the Kayalni mosque incited against Jews and Hajj Amin certainly propagated anti-Jewish ideas, yet the rest of the testimonies and even state-sponsored propaganda efforts confirm that the Islamic faith was used as a means to counter chauvinistic, exclusionist, and authoritarian discourses coming from the state and to challenge notions of ethnic nationalism. Similarly, tribal leaders expanded the notion of protection to include local Jewish communities. At times, ideology had little to do with the conduct of individuals during the Farhud. Muslim neighbors (even those who supported the Kaylani movement) helped their neighbors because they knew them. This intimacy could not be overpowered by the actions of the state and its national elites, and was resilient in the face of the chaos that ensued when the state collapsed.

As depicted in Chapter 2, the national vision which was promoted by Jewish intellectuals, as well as by Iraqi social democrats, communists, and certain nationalists, assumed that nationalism was not constructed out of ethnicity alone, but rather out of language, literature, geography, and history. Arab culture, moreover, could be acquired through schooling, coexistence, and shared linguistic practices. This view called for a democratic nation-state, equal rights based on equality before the law, and a social contract between the community's different religious and ethnic groups. This vision was severely challenged in the 1930s and early 1940s. The failure of the Kaylani movement marked its initial revival and the rise of the left as an alternative. The next outbreak of street violence in Baghdad would pit Iraqis of all religions against the state itself. In January 1948, Iraqi Muslims, Christians, and Jews would demonstrate together against the state's pro-British agenda, its unjust social policies, and the lack of democratic freedoms in Iraq.

5

RED BAGHDAD

Iraqi Jews and the ICP, 1941–51

Salim Fattal (b. 1930), a poor Jewish student from the neighborhood of Tatran, joined the Iraqi Communist Party in 1948. He explained his motivation for joining the party as follows:

> I kept a warm spot in my heart for the Soviet Union, the homeland of communism, for giving the world the gift of victory over Nazi Germany, for overcoming the greatest enemy of the Jewish people, and for saving the Jews from total annihilation.[1]

Salim was not alone. It is no great secret that the ICP had assumed a major role in Iraqi politics since the early 1940s. Not unlike their counterparts in Europe, Iraqi Jews entered the ranks of their country's communist party because they believed in its vision of equality and social justice. Nonetheless, apart from Yosef Me'ir's ground-breaking study in Hebrew,[2] very few studies have addressed this phenomenon. The noted historian Hanna Batatu downplayed the role of Jews in the ICP, pointing to the small number of Jews in the ICP leadership and questioning the patriotism of two prominent Jewish Iraqi communists, Yehuda Sadiq (1914–49) and Shelomo Sasun [Sasson] Dallal (1927–49).[3] Nonetheless, while very few Iraqi Jews held high positions of authority in the ICP, police records list many who were rank-and-file members during the 1940s. The Iraqi researcher Fadhil al-Barrak, by no means a great historian but a man who did gain access to additional police files, likewise identified many Iraqi Jews as communists.[4] Letters written by Zionist agents in the mid-1940s expressed concerns about the difficulty of attracting young Jews to the illegal Zionist underground because of their ties to communism. Moreover, the League for Combating Zionism ('Usbat mukafahat al-Sahayuniyya), another communist organization, successfully recruited many Jewish supporters, raising fears in Iraqi, Zionist, and British circles.

The Jewish Iraqi communist experience is indeed of immense significance, despite its short timespan (1941–51). First, it adds new dimensions to the concept of the Arab Jew. In the communist context, Jews employed the term *Arab Jew* not only as a means of elucidating their ethnicity, but also to indicate that such questions as the problems of the Jewish proletariat, the class struggle, and the anti-imperial struggle could, and should, be solved in the communities in which Jews lived. Thus, Iraqi Jews, as Arabic-speaking Iraqis, should remain in Iraq and fight alongside their Iraqi brethren. The goal of this struggle would be to end sectarianism and anti-Semitism. Communist ideology therefore enabled Iraqi Jews to cope with the shock of 1941 and critique the Iraqi state and its nationalist elites, while remaining loyal to the Iraqi people. Second, postwar Iraq was characterized by sociopolitical turmoil, as strikes, demonstrations, and constant critiques of the state's pro-British affiliations and unjust social policies loomed large in the public sphere. Iraqi Jews, like their Muslim and Christian compatriots, looked for political options that would provide an appropriate answer to these socioeconomic and political challenges. They found one in communism. The postwar years seemed initially promising: in 1945, the regent called for the establishment of political parties in Iraq, and by 1946 five political parties had come into being. In 1947, this short democratic interlude came to a halt, yet the expansion of the public sphere spurred growing criticism of the state and the formation of a stronger opposition, which could not be intimidated by violence and surveillance. The major strikes and demonstrations of 1945–47, reflecting this increasing socioeconomic unrest, culminated in a major uprising against the state, the Wathba, on January 1948.

Iraqi Jewish involvement in the ICP was most marked in the 1940s. The ICP, however, had been active since the 1930s. Its roots were in local groups that had coalesced around communist and socialist causes in Baghdad and the south beginning in 1929. These groups united on March 1935, a unity that led to the formation of the ICP. From 1941 to 1945, the British turned a blind eye to communist activities, because of the communists' fierce anti-Nazi stance. Many communists were released from prison, and labor laws were amended to permit the establishment of a number of unions. Moreover, the mass waves of jailing and deportation of radical Pan-Arabists in 1941 created a vacuum in the intellectual scene. The small ICP was well positioned to fill that void, and it successfully did so, especially under the charismatic direction of its Christian leader Yusuf Salman Yusuf, known as "Fahd." After the war, the ICP was quick to seize the moment during the short time democratic freedoms were granted to Iraqis. Although never a legal entity, it managed to expand geographically and attract workers and students. The socioeconomic turmoil that overtook Iraq in 1945–47 served as an opportunity for the ICP to organize strikes, and its power reached its zenith in the Wathba. That event, however, provoked a national backlash against communism, and the state arrested many activists; the leaders of the party, Fahd, Zaki Basim, and Muhammad Husayn al-Shabibi, were executed in 1949.[5]

As with communists in third world countries, still divided by sect, tribe, and religion, the question of how to disseminate communism in a mostly illiterate society was paramount to the ICP. The party adjusted to the Iraqi milieu by advocating an antisectarian and antitribal vision and a struggle shared by all religions and ethnicities. In Iraq, communist ideology also offered a specific critique of the elites—the landowners, the Sherrifians, and the monarchy—and a constant emphasis on socioeconomic injustice, of which the Iraqi peasantry and workers were the primary victims. The ICP adopted a strong anticolonialist line, arguing that Iraq was independent in name only, given that its financial system was subordinated to international capitalism and that it constantly faced the danger of occupation by foreign powers. As the ICP saw it, Britain and the Iraqi ruling elites worked together to further their joint economic and geopolitical interests. Britain had forced the capitalist order on Iraq, through the presence of many British companies in Iraq and that of the British economic advisers who plotted the future of the Iraqi oil industry and the development of its economy.

Since the socioeconomic privileges of the ruling elites depended on British support, Iraq's battle for equality entailed a struggle against both its local elites and its colonizers.[6]

Becoming Communists: Reasons and Motivations

Iraqi Jews had shown interest in socialist organizations formed in Baghdad that predated the ICP. In 1932 some Jews participated in campaigns against illiteracy orchestrated by the social-democratic party al-Ahali. When the party was reincarnated as the recognized NDP, Jewish intellectuals such as Murad al-'Umari, Menashe Somekh, Salim al-Basun, and Shalom Darwish supported it (Darwish was a party's representative in parliament). When the ICP was founded, the number of Jewish members in the party in general and on its central committee in particular was limited. The journalist Na'im Tweig (1909–89), however, did become a member in 1941.[7]

Membership in the ICP and Jewish support for communist causes increased during World War II. Zionist emissary Enzo Sereni reported in 1942 that Jewish merchants read the communist newspaper *Al-Sharara*. A Jewish merchant told him that *Al-Sharara* reported what was really happening in other regions of the country and other parts of the world. Sereni met with second-rank communist activists, and inferred that communism had spread among the Jewish intelligentsia and the upper classes. He observed that the poor also admired the Soviet Union, and that one saw the Soviet Star and the Star of David in Jewish stores, because of the admiration of the Soviet Union as the power that had defeated Germany.[8] In 1943 he offered the opinion that communist propaganda and the economic situation in Iraq would thwart the attempt to convince Jews to migrate to Palestine.[9] Sereni sensed that communism was "fashionable" among the Arab population as well, because of the Soviet victories. After the failure of "bourgeois assimilation" (*hitbolelut burganit*), underscored so dramatically by the Farhud, Iraqi Jews had turned to "red assimilation" (*hitbolelut aduma*). He reported that in the summer of 1942, "there was a period when the communists were very active" and sought to discredit Zionist propaganda. He advocated that Zionist anticommunist efforts be maintained, cautioning that "the danger of red assimilation is serious."[10] In 1944, another emissary complained bitterly that many young Jews were attracted to communism, and that the movement had spread like a disease in Jewish life. In the schools, he argued, 80 to 90 percent of Jewish youth were communists.[11] During the war years, Jews did assume positions of leadership in communist splinter groups from the ICP, but returned to the united ICP in 1945.[12]

In 1945–48, when the party widened its ranks, Jewish involvement became even more vigorous. A British intelligence report from 1948 noted, "Although there is no significant percentage of Jews amongst communists in Iraq, the Jews are probably rather more interested in communism than the other minorities."[13] Another report, from 1949, concluded that "it will be evident that the Jews have played no small part in the ICP, although no exclusively Jewish organization within the party's framework is apparent."[14] Zionists were likewise aware of the increasing number of communists among Iraqi Jews, saying that even communist British soldiers found ways of reaching out to Iraqi Jews.[15] A report to David Ben Gurion mentioned the Railway Company, the electric company, the tobacco industry, and institutions of higher education as hotbeds of communist activity. Moreover, the report argued that the ICP was very popular among the Shi'is and the Christians, and was likely to spread among the Jews and the Kurds.[16] Another account singled out the educated Jewish community, especially students in high schools, as the target audience of the ICP. It noted that the attraction of Jews to communism was consistent with the general socialist and leftist tendencies of the Iraqi population, and that many Jewish journalists and reporters leaned leftward. Cheap versions of communist literature in book form were available in the markets, while Jewish communist teachers introduced propaganda in classes. The report also observed that although the ICP was not led by Jews, the Jews were a "lively element in the party."[17]

It is difficult to determine how many Jews were actual members of the ICP. Historian Yosef Me'ir estimates that there were a few hundreds in Baghdad, less than a hundred in Basra, and fewer in the north.[18] Using the three-volume collection that includes confessions and police files on members of the ICP, known as *A Secret Encyclopedia Concerning the Iraqi Communist Party* (*Mawsu'a siriyya khassa bi'l hizb al-shuyu'i al-'iraqi*; 1949), and data collected by Fadhil al-Barrak, we arrive at a number of around 250–300 Jewish communists in 1947 (according to Batatu the ICP had about 3,000–4,000 members in 1948).[19] The ICP's stronghold was Baghdad, where most

Iraqi Jews lived, and where hundreds of young Jews were susceptible to radical ideals. It should be pointed out that according to Batatu, Jews also joined the ICP in the south, especially in Basra, albeit in smaller numbers; Jews were an active component in the ICP in that region from 1943 to 1949.[20] The data Batatu collected about the number of Jews in the party's institutions further shows that the percentage of Jews in the party's leadership was slightly higher than in the population of Iraq as a whole (about 14.9 percent in 1947).[21] Interestingly, one of the communist organizations affiliated with the ICP, the League for Combating Zionism, had, according to British estimates, thousand members. If accounts about the league's membership being at least 50 percent Jewish are correct, then the estimated number of Jews in communist organizations should be higher.[22] Zionist accounts, as we have seen, gave different numbers and tended to stress the growing number of Jewish communists, especially in the war years. It is difficult to ascertain, however, how many of these Jews were actual ICP members and how many were favorably disposed toward the Soviet Union but did not join the party. The Zionist emissaries do confirm that large segments of the Jewish youth, as well as parts of the middle classes, adopted very positive opinions regarding communism and the Soviet Union.

A list of 245 Jewish communists compiled by Fadhil al-Barrak, based on data gathered around 1947,[23] indicates that over 90 percent of Iraqi-Jewish communists were Baghdadis, mostly in their twenties. Workers made up the largest number of Jewish communists, followed by students, clerks, and teachers.[24] The party thus drew supporters not only from the Jewish effendia, but also from poorer strata of Jewish society. At least 30 percent of its members lived in Jewish neighborhoods, such as Tatran, Tawrat, Suq Hanun, and Abu Sifin, which were anything but well-off districts. Clearly, then, the ICP attracted a broad spectrum of Iraqi Jews.[25]

Iraqi Jews joined the ICP for a variety of reasons, some "purely Jewish"—such as the Farhud and the conflict in Palestine—and some that were common to all Iraqi communists. A few key reasons are identifiable from the writings of these communists. Ya'qub Mir Masri (b. 1920), who played a leading role in the activities of women and workers in the ICP, lists the party's antifascist struggle as one of the main reasons that led to his involvement in the party.[26] After the battle of Stalingrad, the heroic Soviet

War against Nazi Germany was a much discussed topic in the Iraqi public sphere in general, as Iraqi intellectuals, like the celebrated Shi'i bard Muhammad Mahdi al-Jawahiri, applauded Soviet resistance. Iraqi Jews shared the prevailing sentiment. A Zionist emissary complained, "When you enter a house of a Jewish merchant, you might find a son named Stalin. . . . They [the Jewish merchants] say that England will not give us the land of Israel, the Germans will kill us, and hence Russia remains the only redeemer. When you ask a Jewish merchant like this: 'But they will take your money if there is a communist regime,' he says, 'I'll get by.'"[27] Further evidence for the popularity of the Soviet Union within the poor segments of Jewish Iraqi society is found in accounts from Tatran. In this neighborhood, poor Jews admired Stalin whom they named Abu Shawarib, "Mr. Mustache." Not only Stalin, but also Molotov and other Russian communists, whose names were often mispronounced, became the objects of a great deal of "love and admiration."[28]

Like many communist parties elsewhere in the war and postwar years, the ICP set out to represent itself as the only true opposition to Nazi imperialism. In its publications from the early 1940s, it attacked the Iraqi nationalist elites as profascist, and as willing to betray Iraq's national interests to whatever colonial power most suited to fit their interests. The communist journal *Al-Majalla* (published by Dhu Nun Ayyub), to which Jewish communists Yusuf Harun Zilkha (b. 1921), Na'im Tweig, and Ya'qub Mir Masri contributed, printed stories on the need to unite against fascism, an imperialist monster whose aims were stifling individual freedom and conquering the Middle East.[29] Tweig called on Iraqi students to emulate the efforts of their peers in China, Yugoslavia, Spain, America, and the Soviet Union, to fight fascism.[30] Furthermore, the radical Jewish youth active during the 1940s often identified radical Pan-Arabism with a pro-German stance, which, they contended, was partly responsible for the Farhud; the anti-Nazi and anti-right-wing position of the ICP was thus very appealing.[31]

The ICP was a crucial ally for Iraqi Jews in the face of anti-Semitic attacks by radical nationalists, which increased as the situation in Palestine worsened.[32] In 1946 the communists assured Jews that they would take action to prevent anti-Jewish riots.[33] In early 1948, during a nationalist demonstration, the slogan "Death to the Jews" was heard; the ICP responded by organizing a counterdemonstration in solidarity with Iraqi Jews. In April of that year, the Zionist emissary Yerahmiel Assa wrote to his wife that the situation of Iraqi Jews was grave, especially due to the escalation of the conflict in Palestine. He also noted that Iraqi leftists were pushing back against the anti-Jewish propaganda campaign being waged by the nationalists: "The communists and the social democrats demonstrated carrying signs saying, 'Long live Judaism! Long live Jewish-Arab brotherhood!'" The outcome, according to Assa, was that "Jews see in the communists [their] new protector."[34] Party members anticipated a wave of violence against Jews on the day that the state of Israel declared its independence (May 1948), and thus organized the guarding of Jewish neighborhoods in Baghdad by both Jews and non-Jews.[35] Similarly, in Basra, the left positioned itself as the protector of Jews. The British consul reported that Jews who supported the NDP were persecuted by the right-wing party al-Istiqlal and local notables.[36] When al-Istiqlal organized anti-Jewish demonstrations, the NDP organized counterdemonstrations during which the slogans "Long live Stalin" and, more importantly, "Long live the Iraqi Jews" were repeated.[37] In 1950, the ICP denounced the law that allowed Jews to emigrate from Iraq provided that they renounce their citizenship, arguing that this would support the Anglo-American plot to expand their influence in Israel and Jordan. The party, however, did not object to the departure of its Jewish members to Israel, understanding their difficult circumstances in Iraq.[38]

More generally, the ICP's antisectarian stance was very appealing to Jews. As Moshe Huri (b. 1922) recalls: "I found there what I was looking for: human solidarity and internationalism." Eliyahu Ezer (b. 1928) believed the ICP "could save us all: the Jews, the Arabs and the Kurds." Its power, he added, reflected the mentality of the Iraqi people, who were not prejudiced against minorities such as the Jews or the Kurds.[39] Zionist emissary Enzo Sereni felt that the "red youngsters" and "Bolshevik merchants" did not desire the installment of a Soviet-style regime in Iraq, but thought of communism as a means to attain equal citizenship rights in Iraq.[40]

The shortcomings of the Iraqi state also drove Jews to the ICP. The strikes, demonstrations, and what Jewish communist Menashe Khalifa called "the national wave for liberation" from 1945 to 1952 struck a chord with them.[41] Protests concerning abuses of human rights and citizenship rights in Iraq encouraged many Jews to join the ICP, which claimed to be fighting for "democracy and peace."[42] The Soviet Union at this time was admired for being a progressive nation that had institutionalized labor rights, the emancipation of women, and a secular regime. It thus offered a model that Iraqis and their fellow Arabs ought to emulate. Iraqi Jews, like their fellow Iraqis, resented British interference in their country's domestic and foreign policies, and desired complete independence. Sasun Dallal mentions that his joining the party was inspired by his desire to fight Anglo-American imperialism in Iraq and in the Middle East, and to attain complete sovereignty for his country.[43] The hours of delay before the British came to the assistance of the Jews during the Farhud had also done much to stir anger against them. Their willingness to cooperate with certain Iraqi right-wing nationalists after the war, in the hope of maintaining anti-Soviet alliances, was yet another strike against the British—and the list was already long in Jewish eyes.[44] Here, the generational component is important. While their parents had sometimes welcomed British involvement in Iraq as a mark of Westernization, the communist Jewish youth considered British intervention in Iraq's domestic and foreign affairs intolerable.

Iraqi Jewish interest in joining the ICP spiked in 1948. The communists played a major role in the Wathba, in which young Jews felt their hopes for equality and a shared nonsectarian and patriotic battle against the regime were materializing. Slogans of Arab-Jewish solidarity and Arab-Jewish-Kurdish brotherhood were chanted during the Wathba and the participation of rabbis, qadis, and other religious authorities in the demonstrations contributed to their nonsectarian nature.[45] In subsequent years the ICP used the memory of the Wathba to drum up support for its organization: Sasun Dallal, for example, urged that it be mentioned whenever possible in public speeches and in unofficial ceremonies.[46] The outcome of the Wathba was not all positive for the ICP, however, as massive waves of arrests and subsequent imprisonments of communists occurred in Baghdad. Many Jews were victims of this campaign.[47] The year 1948 thus marked the pinnacle of communist success in Iraq as well as the beginning of the end of the communist Jewish Iraqi experience due to the persecution of leftists throughout the country.

Being Communists: Jewish Activities in the ICP

Upon joining the ICP Jews worked together with Muslims and Christians. It does not seem that there was a particular Jewish segment within the party, with the exception of the League for Combating Zionism. Like the Christians, Jews were mostly from urban areas and spoke Arabic, and thus communication with them did not involve an additional language, such as Turkish, Kurdish, or Armenian, or organization in separate cells (as was sometimes done in the northern regions). Yet joining the ICP did not sever Iraqi Jews from their social networks: on the contrary, Jewish activists recruited in their neighborhoods, stores, and schools. One significant nexus was the Jewish family, as Jewish communists urged their relatives to join and recommended their membership to the ICP. Notable pairs of brothers who joined the party were Yehuda and Hesqel Sadiq (b. 1921), Sasun and Da'ud Dallal, Ya'qub and Hesqel Qujman, and Moshe and Eliyahu Huri. At other times cousins convinced one another to join the party. Sisters and wives of members entered the party's ranks with their male relatives.[48]

In 1948, one of the party's key non-Jewish leaders, Malik Sayyif, was arrested. To save his life, he implicated many members in his confessions. Sayyif made much of a network of Jews within the party, but his account should be taken with a grain (or rather a heap) of salt. He competed with a fellow Jew, Yehuda Sadiq, for the leadership of the ICP, and fought with him frequently. The British believed that one could not rely on his anti-Jewish statements because he may have felt he was expected to denounce the Jewish element in the ICP.[49] At the same time, some of the information he provided has been corroborated by other sources. Jews collected money from fellow Jews, including merchants and store owners, on behalf of the ICP. The hub of this particular network was the Jori Drug Store on al-Rashid Street, at which Jewish activists gathered. The store's owners, Ibrahim Naji Shumail (b. 1912) and Ya'qub Ephraim Sehayek (b. 1912–92) (who were related) were communists.[50] Their initial cell included four members, all of whom were Jewish.[51] Shumail and Sehayek were major funders of the ICP; the support they provided to the party was considerable, which caused their names to appear in British reports concerning the communist danger beginning in the late 1940s. The British also noted that the socialist newspapers *Al-Watan* and *Al-Sha'b* were backed by the Jewish credit bank and the Jewish Zilkha bank, respectively.[52] Batatu notes that in 1945 the largest amounts collected for the ICP were from party members among Jewish shopkeepers.[53] Outside of Baghdad, activists did recall cells that were exclusively Jewish. In Irbil, for example, some Jewish party members worked in the shoe-making business (especially in the Bata store), according to one source.[54] Jewish connections also proved helpful as they formed a network of support within the Jewish community. Relatives who were not communists were willing to bribe the authorities to release jailed communists. Families (knowingly or unknowingly) hid communist materials or even actual activists when they were being persecuted. For example, Sami Michael (b. 1926) recalls that Zionists helped him when the police were harassing him.[55]

Despite the existence of these Jewish networks, the party was not divided according to sectarian or religious lines. In fact, the ICP was a nonsectarian organization par excellence. In many cells, unions, and ICP branches, Jews worked with fellow Iraqi Muslims and Christians. Communist Jews worked in primarily Muslim regions, such as the south, or in Muslim neighborhoods in Baghdad (like the Shi'i neighborhood of al-Karkh) and in Basra.[56] Jews were also active in organizing shoemakers, tailors, and workers unions that were typically nonsectarian in nature.[57] Many Jews worked closely with one of the party's leaders, Muhammad Husayn al-Shabibi, on the publication of *Al-Qa'ida*.[58] When Jews contributed to communist journals, they tended to address non-Jewish themes. The League for Combating Zionism was unique in that it published essays on issues specific to the Jewish community. Most Jewish writers, however, did not write as Jews and for Jews. For example, Ya'qub Masri's stories in *Al-Majalla* centered on the trials of the simple folk and their humiliation by upper-class Iraqis.[59] Party members (including leaders like Fahd and Zaki Basim) were put up by Jewish members and certain key meetings were held in Jewish homes.[60] Muslims hid Jewish communists in their homes; thus, with the Sayyab family in the south or with prostitutes in Baghdad following a big communist anti-Zionist rally, Jews found shelter in non-Jewish homes.[61]

The colleges in Baghdad (pharmacy, law, teachers training), as well as some high schools in Basra, Baghdad, and Mosul, were attended by Jews,

Sunnis, Shi'is, and Christians alike. The ICP made a strong effort to recruit in these settings, with the mixed religio-ethnic student bodies making for mixed cells, rather than cells comprised of members of one ethnicity or religion. Jews were recruited to the ICP by non-Jews with whom they studied, and helped to recruit others. These encounters with other minorities made Jews aware of the difficulties faced by other communities, such as the Kurds.[62] The Teachers Training College in Baghdad was one of the most fertile grounds for communist activities. 'Aziz al-Hajj, a Kurd and a key ICP leader, recalls that this particular college during the 1940s had a very diverse student body—Jews, Arabs, Sunni, Shi'is, Kurds, and Turkmans—from which the party recruited members.[63]

The activities of Jews in the ICP varied. The most important organizational unit within the party was the cell. Each cell included three to four members who studied the party's decisions, read its newspapers and publications, and distributed newspapers and posters which were taken from hiding places.[64] Autobiographies provide interesting accounts of what transpired in these cells. Jewish communist Shim'on Ballas (b. 1930) describes the café in which he met his comrades: "In this café ... [, I] began a new chapter in my life, a chapter that took me out from the isolated world in which I was living, the world of a student in a Jewish school, who did not have the opportunity to form bonds of friendship with non-Jews, and positioned me, for the first time, with people I had no contact with in the past."[65] The secretary of his cell was a primary school teacher, and another cell member was a shoemaker. When Ballas was asked by the secretary to explain the differences between historical materialism and idealism, he gave what he thought was a comprehensive answer. To his surprise, however, the shoemaker was much more knowledgeable; he quoted Lenin and Marx and showed Ballas who the true intellectual in the cell was.[66]

Salim Fattal's detailed accounts depict the communist activities in a cell led by a member referred to as 'Adil (the party ordered members to use pseudonyms because of security concerns). Its meetings concentrated on 'Adil's explorations of current events, although 'Adil's passionate speeches often made little impression on Salim and his comrade, Ra'uf. Upon learning about Husni Za'im's coup in Syria (March, 1949), 'Adil was filled with enthusiasm, and exulted that the coup was indeed a sign of the uprising of the poor and the coming revolution. "He examined the coup according to the intricacies of Marxism-Leninism. In a celebratory meeting of the cell he investigated the bursting political volcano in the Arab world and referenced the *Communist Manifesto*, which sounded to us like an accurate prophecy of what had happened in Syria and what was about to happen in our region."[67] Sadly, the expectations of the cell's members for a revolutionary movement that would topple the pitiful Arab comprador regimes soon vanished. Nonetheless, the activities of the cell were important in that they allowed the young students to place current events within a larger communist narrative, and to make sense of the changing realities surrounding them.

The cell members participated in demonstrations, with one such action taking place near the Ghazi cinema, where they met with other cells, having brought with them posters protesting against imperialism and the Iraqi "blood government." The small convoy of some forty people began picketing and marching. It converged with yet another gathering to form a group of about a hundred young men, who rallied in the street against "Anglo-American imperialism."[68] A young communist activist known as Zahi held a piece of bread in one hand and a shoe in the other. He addressed the crowd: "Iraq is a country rich with oil and water. Its treasury is full with money. But the Iraqis are poor. Thousands of families are unable to buy bread for their hungry children or shoes for their barefoot kids. Why? Because the government and its ministers, the tools of British imperialism, rob the treasury."[69]

The performative elements of the speech are important when compared with the writings of Fahd. Iraq, wrote Fahd, is rich, but the Iraqi people were famished as the main possessions of the country and its natural resources were subordinated to the capitalist colonizers: "Our people strive and work to pay taxes which are not spent in the interests of the people, but are raised to support an army of bureaucrats and governmental mechanism."[70] Fahd's words were written a few years before; at the time of the above-mentioned demonstration he was in jail, and was executed shortly afterward. Nevertheless, his statements were paraphrased to address the needs of the public who gathered at the demonstration. In Zahi's shorter speech the word *capitalism* was omitted, yet Fahd's message came across clearly in his improvised sermon. In addition, Zahi carried two artifacts that symbolized what the urban poor so badly needed, bread and shoes. Importantly, the shortage of grain and bread was a key factor that ignited the Wathba.[71]

Within the general ranks of the party, roles of writers and translators were often assigned to Jews. The ICP's leadership made it a priority to produce publications on Marxist theory, current politics, and local strikes and demonstrations to be sent to the colleges and party members nationwide. According to Sasun Dallal, and before him Fahd, publications were crucial to the intellectual battle (*nidal fikri*) with reactionary forces in order to influence the political actions of the masses (*suluk al-jamahir al-siyasi*). Printed materials helped inform members in the north and in south-central Iraq about party activities elsewhere in the country. Both Yehuda Sadiq and Sasun Dallal, themselves avid readers of leftist literature, spoke of the need to expand the party's printing network to make available publications in Kurdish. Cell members often taught and informed fellow students about the ICP, using booklets distributed by the party.[72] Vital to the dissemination of the ICP's message was its press, especially its illegal newspapers *Al-Sharara* (from 1940) and *Al-Qa'ida* (from 1943).

Many Jewish members were students in or graduates of high schools, and some had attended university or had academic degrees, making them well prepared to contribute articles to the party's journals, and help with the printing and distribution of materials. Na'im Salman (1916–92) was one of the founders of Dar al-Hikma, the ICP's publishing house. Yehuda Sadiq likewise played a dominant role in the publishing of communist books. Ya'qub Masri, who was actually trained as a printer, not only translated works by Lenin and Harold Lasky but assisted with production as well.[73] Jews were able to serve in the crucial capacity of translators for the ICP because of their bilingual education and resultant command of foreign languages. Most times, an entire work was not translated, but rather extracts from the classics of communist literature. Because of their education, communist Jews were also drafted to take part in the ICP's literacy campaigns. The Ministry of Education approved of these initiatives, which enabled hundreds to learn how to read and write, and ICP members used them as an opportunity to present its ideology.[74] Some members, such as Yehuda Sadiq, Yusuf Zaluf, and Ya'qub Bechor, were teachers who introduced communist ideas in their educational institutions.

In addition to being cell members and translators, Jews were active in women's, shoemakers', tailors', and workers' unions, as well as among railroad workers and among port authorities in Basra.[75] The ICP workers' committee in 1946–47 included four Jewish members out of the total of seven. Jews held the rank of *ma'sul* (a party member in charge of regional committees, unions, and student and women's organizations) in the north, south, and in certain neighborhoods in Baghdad, and they appeared in every organization of the party, from lower-rank leadership to the top command, the party's central committee.[76]

The state did not remain blind to the fact that Jewish members were found in all ranks of the ICP during the years 1941–48. Communist Jews did not typically come in for worse treatment than other members of the ICP. However, it seems that Jews, because of the imagined association between communism and Zionism, were often blamed for supporting communism, although they had nothing to do with that movement. The Iraqi law number 51 was called to punish those engaged in anarchy, communism, and Zionism. As a result, sometimes Jewish communists were accused of being Zionists.[77] Moreover, the authorities occasionally underscored the Jewish nature of the ICP. For example, in the 1949 encyclopedia of Iraqi communists produced by the police, all the photos of arrested communists are of Jewish activists, although many members of varying religious affiliations were arrested in this period.[78]

Undoubtedly, the years most difficult for Iraqi Jewish communists were 1948 and 1949. Jewish involvement in the ICP helped deflect to some extent the ill will generated by the war in Palestine, because the ICP offered Jews a patriotic Iraqi framework in which they could act. The Wathba symbolized this involvement. On the other hand, during this period the state was engaged in an anti-Jewish campaign, and the fact that young Jews were engaged in an illegal operation against the state drew even more attention. The state's fear of communism manifested itself in a system of surveillance, especially at schools attended by Jews (both Jewish-only and mixed schools). This system was quite effective; the Iraqi police had information on Jewish students who possessed copies of the party's newspapers, attended meetings, or were suspected of paying party dues. Outside the schools, the police searched the houses of suspected communists for documents and papers and arrested many members.[79] Those convicted received long prison terms: Ya'qub Ephraim Sehayek was sentenced to fifteen years in jail, Ibrahim Naji Shumail was sentenced to life imprisonment, and others were jailed for three to ten years. Women received long imprisonment sentences as well.[80]

The prisons became important hubs for communist activities. Jews were not separated from their communist comrades in jails, nor were they accorded special treatment. Unlike jailed Zionists, who were often isolated, Jewish communist prisoners were able to communicate with other prisoners and participated in their activities.[81] Jailed ICP members had access to communist publications such as *Zionism: The Enemy of Arabs and Jews* (*Al-Sahayuniyya 'aduwat al-'Arab wa'l Yahud*) published by the League for Combating Zionism. Activities in jail often convinced noncommunist Jews who were imprisoned at the time to join the party. The Kut jail in particular was key in this respect, because the leaders the ICP (Fahd, Shabibi, and Basim) led the party from there before their executions. Another jail which was an important communist center was the notorious Nuqrat al-Salman, a southern fortress to which many communists were sent.[82]

Most communist prisoners were organized and managed to have their own medical clinic, participate in sports activities, and initiate a host of cultural events. The secrecy that typified the small cells outside of jail could not be maintained inside, and thus cell members came in contact with higher-ranking members of the party. A Zionist prisoner in Nuqrat al-Salman (imprisoned in 1951) ironically commented on communist activities in the jail:

> They [the communists] wished to keep morals high, and had a party every fourth or fifth day. There were always plenty of reasons: Labor Day in Mongolia, Revolution Day in Czechoslovakia. . . . They had a calendar where all these events were listed. Their parties were successful. They spread their mats and bedcovers on a stage and had a celebratory dinner. Their leader would deliver a congratulatory speech, while his subordinate explained the reason for the celebration. They would then start singing communist songs, chanting communist lyrics to the tunes of popular Iraqi songs.[83]

In jails, communist Jews often met Zionist prisoners. Reasons for resentment between the two groups were ample. Jewish communists report that Zionists did not share food that they received on Jewish holidays or that they ate while the communists went on hunger strikes. Zionists speak of great suspicion on part of their communist brethren based on ideological reasons (to such a degree it was easier to befriend a Muslim communist than a Jewish one). On the other hand, the need to withstand state's persecution often encouraged collaboration between Zionists and communists. More often, a common sense of humanity, and bonds of friendship, tied Jewish political prisoners of various inclinations, and we find many instances in which communists helped Zionists to survive torture and abuse.[84]

Jails were also spaces of resistance and Jews, imprisoned as communists, took part in strikes, hunger strikes, and protests within jails.[85] One such protest took place in Nuqrat al-Salman. In 1951, the prison had 162 political prisoners; 50 were Jewish, of whom 8 had been stripped of their citizenship. On July 12, 1951, all the Jewish prisoners and a number of others began a hunger strike. They alleged that the courts that had tried them were illegal, and they demanded that their sentences be rescinded and the jail closed down. All political parties, including the NDP and even the nationalist al-Istiqlal, reported on the strike and the torture in the prison. There were demonstrations in Baghdad and Basra in the last week of July in support of these prisoners. On July 31 the directorate of the press and propaganda published stories that dismissed the prisoners' complaints as baseless.[86] In Baghdad's central women prison, a group of fifteen communist women, fourteen of them Jewish, who were serving long sentences (from seven to twenty years), along with one Zionist girl from Irbil, Regina, declared a hunger strike. The female prisoners demanded special cells, visitation rights, and books. After three days of striking, three male policemen beat the girls for about an hour and a half, but were unable to break their spirits. On the fifteenth day of the strike the girls were taken to the hospital to be force-fed. On the road to the hospital, the girls shouted that they were political prisoners. The newspapers in Baghdad reported on the event.[87] In 1953, when communist hunger strikes were brutally crushed in the Baghdad and Kut jails, the communists were no longer able to maintain their hegemony in jails. Worse yet, Jewish prisoners were now separated from other prisoners, and sent to Nuqrat al-Salman. At this point, the relationship between Muslim communist prisoners and Jewish ones (who remained practically the only Jewish communists in Iraq, as many of their Jewish comrades had escaped the country) deteriorated, especially after the persecution of Jewish doctors in the USSR.[88]

In the period following Fahd's arrest, two Iraqi Jews, Yehuda Sadiq and Sasun Dallal, served as party secretary and the head (*mas'ul awwal*) of the ICP's central committee, the highest leadership position in the ICP. It was, as Batatu calls it, a period of "children communists" as a new, relatively inexperienced generation led the party, because of the vacuum created in the leadership by the waves of arrests and imprisonments. Both paid with their lives for their beliefs and their mistakes.

Yehuda Sadiq was born 1914 in Samawa into a lower-middle-class family. In February 1948 he became the leader of the ICP. He believed that it was critical to extend the party's influence in the north, to which end he sought to have ICP publications printed in Kurdish and Armenian (Fahd was moved to remind Sadiq that the south was of great importance as well, and that the Wathba had actually taken place in Baghdad). The state accused him (based on a confession from Malik Sayyif and his own letters) of organizing communist activities involving the army. His relationships with workers in the north, as well as with Sayyif, however, were unstable. Although Yehuda put Sayyif in charge of the editing of *Al-Qa'ida*, he was surprised when Fahd ordered him from jail to resign the leadership of the party in favor of Sayyif. He delayed in obeying Fahd's order, and when Sayyif found out, he was quite angry. In August, Sayyif became *mas'ul awwal* of the ICP.[89]

Opinions vary as to Sadiq's role in the ICP: while Batatu presents him as young and inexperienced and evidently favors Sayyif (whom he interviewed), Me'ir notes, based on interviews he conducted with Jewish communists, that Yehuda and his brother Hesqel possessed excellent organizational skills. Other sources, including Sayyif himself, have corroborated this.[90] Nonetheless, many believed that the battles between Sayyif and Yehuda led to the destruction of the party.[91] When Yehuda was arrested he gave some details to the police; his confession was much shorter and much less detailed than that of Sayyif. An MI5 report noted, "It is clear from the statement of Yehuda Sadiq that he evaded on a number of important points and by no means told all he knew," and therefore the police did not question him further.[92] Certain party members, such as Ya'qub Masri and 'Aziz al-Hajj, accused him of giving information to the police, yet even al-Hajj describes Yehuda as a friend, and depicts, with much sympathy, the fear that overcame Yehuda upon his arrest. He refers to him as a national hero.[93]

Shelomo Sasun Dallal joined the ICP in 1946. From December 1948 to February 1949 he led the party. Dallal, according to many who knew him, was blessed with a sharp mind and was interested in Marxist-Leninist theory. Like Sadiq, he was very much involved in the production of printed ICP propaganda: he translated articles for *Al-Qa'ida* and was responsible for about thirty publications on Marxist theory and the party's positions on socioeconomic and political affairs (strikes, student affairs, political prisoners, and demonstrations). Dallal was arrested on February 20, 1948, and was charged with disseminating communist propaganda in the army. Like Sadiq, he was executed for this crime.[94]

Ishaq Bar-Moshe, who attended the same high school as Dallal, depicts him as a stubborn and uncompromising idealist. When asked about the state's persecution of Iraqi Jews by Ishaq, Dallal answered that it was just one element of the Iraqi state's campaign of terror undertaken to further the interests of British imperialism. The blame for this persecution, he explained, should not be placed on the Iraqi people, because the Iraqi government did not represent them. Bar-Moshe responded that the Soviets themselves recognized the state of Israel, to which Dallal replied: "I do not argue with the Soviet government but *as a man born in Iraq I find myself owing much more to Iraq*" (emphasis added).[95]

It seems that Dallal was inexperienced and strayed from the path laid out by Fahd. His theoretical skills seem to have been far superior to his organizational skills. Nonetheless, Dallal's opinions resembled Fahd's on many matters. The goals of the party, as he saw it, were forming a national front based on an anti-imperialist agenda that included the abolition of military courts and treaties with England and other imperial forces, pressing for the release of political prisoners and countering racial and sectarian tendencies.[96] He, like Fahd, was convinced of the significance of the intellectual battle, in tandem with the need to organize, and called for the creation of a revolutionary cadre that would radicalize the peasantry and the workers and adapt Marxist-Leninist theory to the conditions of Iraq.[97] References to the struggle against imperialism were common in his letters, and indicate the prominence of this theme in the ICP's rhetoric. For example, the strikes by the oil company workers were seen as a step in the anticolonial struggle against Anglo-American interests.[98] All of these goals and statements closely resemble those articulated by Dallal's predecessors (especially Fahd) who had also attempted to modify the theories of Marxism-Leninism to the Iraqi context.

Dallal, however, seemed to have been more radical on certain issues. Rafiq Jalak contends that Dallal believed that Stalin and his supporters had betrayed the communist ideal, and was more loyal to Marx, Mao, and Lenin than to Stalin.[99] Some have made the claim that Dallal threatened to execute traitors.[100] According to a few accounts, including letters, Dallal was interested in Lenin's writing on terrorism and believed that the party should respond to the state's violence with violence.[101] The communists, he wrote, should assume a more militant posture and fight to the death.[102] When planning the commemoration of the Wathba, he ordered all members in a particular district to join a general strike, and that those who refused were to be forcibly convinced. Dallal was certainly not the only ICP leader to be accused of advocating terrorism. The goal of a revolution in Iraq, even by violent means, united many communists. In the investigations, communists were asked about Dallal's terrorist intentions, naturally of concern to the police.[103] Yet Dallal's apparent extremism might indicate that he was responding to changing conditions. The state was already engaged in a bitter anticommunist campaign, and Dallal had witnessed the harsh persecution of his colleagues. This may account for the references to terrorism in his writings, which grew out of his despair in the face of a battle whose outcome seemed hopeless.

Both Sadiq and Dallal were executed for their "crimes." The willingness of Sadiq and Dallal to die for the causes they believed in inspired some Jewish communists, but also deterred many from joining the ICP or remaining members.[104] Sadiq's trial was kept secret; it was alleged by the prosecution that Sadiq had written to Fahd naming two army officers as members of the ICP. The British ambassador, however, admitted that information received from secret sources indicated that "the trial was not conducted in accordance with British ideals of judicial impartiality."[105] Even more troubling than the trial was the gruesome public execution of Sadiq on February 13, 1949. The sight of Sadiq's body, left hanging for hours and surrounded by crowds observing the spectacle, shocked many Jews.[106] The execution became a topic of conversation in the community, even for Jews who had never heard of him before. Some Jews believed that Sadiq was executed because the government felt that it needed to add a Jew to the list of the party leaders it had executed, a list that included a Christian (Fahd), a Shi'i (Shabibi), and a Sunni (Basim).[107]

In the spring of 1949 Sasun Dallal was sentenced to death by a military court for having worked for a secret subversive organization and having had contact with the armed forces to incite them to act in support of that organization. The trial was held in a secret military court. Having been attacked by the USSR for its public executions, the Iraqi government faced pressure from the British not to execute Dallal in a similar fashion. He was therefore executed in jail on May 3 and the press reported on the execution.[108] Bar-Moshe characterizes the execution as "a despicable crime demonstrating the disgraceful nature of Nuri Sa'id's regime and its moral level,"[109] and adds that Jews believed that Dallal and Sadiq were executed because they were Jewish.[110]

The accused men were not executed for being Jews. They died as communists; their deaths were intended by the state to serve its campaign against the communist peril, whereas the men saw themselves as martyrs in the struggle for freedom and justice. Nonetheless, their deaths came at a time when other Jews were being persecuted for a variety of reasons, especially on charges having to do with Zionism. A sense of betrayal had taken hold in the community, and the execution of two Jews, albeit communists, by the state, contributed to a growing feeling of despair. The fact that the families of both Sadiq and Dallal had been unsuccessful in getting the sentences of the two men overturned by means of bribes and appeals to politicians they knew was further cause for alarm. By 1949, the executions, together with the jailing, imprisonment, and other forms of persecution of ICP members made it clear to many Jewish communists that there was no hope for an Iraqi Jewish patriotism. If they remained in Iraq, their lot might end up being that of their imprisoned friends. Leaving Iraq seemed to be the only option.

The Question of Palestine: The League for Combating Zionism

In September 1945, eight Jewish communists requested a license from the Iraqi Ministry of Interior to form a political organization, the expressed aim of which was to oppose Zionism. They were: Salim Menashe, who worked with the shoemakers union; Ibrahim Naji Shumail; Ya'qub Ephraim Sehayek; Nisim Hesqel Yehuda, a proprietor; Moshe Ya'qub, the president of the tailor workers' union; Ya'qub Cohen, a clerk in al-Fattah's cloth factory; Masur Qattan, an editor of the newspaper *Al-Sha'b*; and Ya'qub Masri. The license was eventually granted, paving the way for the League for Combating Zionism, as the organization was called. This organization came to be very influential in both communist and the Jewish circles, and in 1946 managed to draw the attention of a wide range of actors in Iraq—Iraqis, Jews, and the British alike.

The league's conceptualizations focused on three domains: Jewish, Iraqi, and Arab. In the Jewish domain the league attempted to present its criticism of Zionism from a Jewish vantage point, maintaining that the Jewish religion could not form the basis for a national community and that the solution to the Jewish problem should be sought within the communities in which Jews lived. In the Iraqi domain, the league argued that Iraqis who equated Judaism with Zionism were fomenting sectarianism and suggested that the struggle against colonialism within Iraq, as well as the domestic campaign for democratic freedoms and social justice, should be viewed as part of a comprehensive battle for liberation, of which the struggle against Zionism was one aspect. On an Arab Palestinian level, the league called for the creation of a free and democratic Palestinian state. The league's pamphlets and publications deployed the term "Arab Jew" to mark the identity of its members, thus giving us an idea as to the meanings ascribed to this term in the communist context. As many members of the league were Jews themselves (although its ideas were favorably received by Muslims and Christians), its activities illuminate the ways in which Jewish communists imagined their Arab community.

The secretary of the league and the editor of its journal was Yusuf Harun Zilkha, a former member of a communist splinter group called Wahdat al-nidal, who returned to the ICP in 1941. His day job was a clerk in the rail authority. The league's ideas were most lucidly outlined in his book *Zionism: The Enemy of the Arabs and the Jews*, which endeavored to provide a historical narrative for the Jewish problem that attended to Arab, Iraqi, and Jewish concerns. Zilkha argued that the Jewish problem was not abstract, but rather ought to be contextualized within specific periods and socioeconomic conditions. In his opinion, the existence of Jews as a minority within non-Jewish societies had a very long history, going back to Assyrians' exile of the people of Israel from their land. This trend had solidified under the Babylonians, when the people of Judah became one of the ancient communities of the Near East. Notably, even when given permission to return to Palestine in antiquity, not all Jews had chosen to leave Babylon and resettle in their place of origin. Jews had continued living in exile from that moment on, being affected by, and affecting, each community in which they lived.

Zilkha believed that the Jewish problem was related to the class struggle. Whenever the ruling classes felt threatened by a new class, they used the Jews as a convenient scapegoat in order to distract the masses from their real problems. This global practice was particularly noticeable when either a state or a ruling class was on the verge of collapse. In the modern age, the Jewish problem had become more acute. The French Revolution had sown the seeds of liberty in modern Europe, causing the reactionary movements which emerged after the Napoleonic wars to unleash a racist campaign against European Jews as part of a more general attempt to curtail the democratic rights of the subjects of European empires. As the class struggle intensified, Jews suffered increasingly from racist and anti-Semitic campaigns. Continuing into the twentieth century, the most obvious manifestation of this phenomenon was the Nazi regime. Capitalist Germans, facing threats from the workers, turned against Jews who were blamed for all the ills of capitalism, in particular unemployment and the global economic crisis. Germany and Italy, however, were not the only places where the toxic mixture of anti-Semitism and capitalism took root. In Britain, fascist groups, such as that of Oswald Mosley, adopted similar ideologies. Dangerously, pro-Nazi movements had spread in the colonies and in semicolonized countries, such as Egypt, Iraq, Syria, and Lebanon. Even with the defeat of Nazi Germany and the Axis, anti-Semitism did not disappear. Presently, wrote Zilkha, anti-Semitic propaganda focused on breaking down the unity of national liberation movements in the colonized world and separating the ranks of the working classes.[111]

Zilkha's analysis, however, provoked the following question: if anti-Semitism and racism were so dominant in European culture and history, why not turn to Zionism and seek a solution in Palestine, where the Jews could have a sovereign state of their own? In response, Zilkha argued that when Jews joined a shared struggle with the working classes in the countries in which they lived, their conditions improved and anti-Semitism declined. Jews and non-Jews should therefore fight together against anti-Semitism and strive for the attainment of democratic freedoms.[112] More importantly, Zionism in itself could only lead to an increase in anti-Semitism.

Zilkha's critique of Zionism included a few components. To begin with, he contended that religion alone could not serve as a basis for a national community. He defined a nation as a group of people who share a common history, language, territory, economic life, and collective mentality. From this perspective, Jews could not be considered a nation:

> Jews do not have a shared history. The history of Arab-Jews [al-yahud al-'arab] . . . is different than the history of Russian or British Jews. The history of German Jews is different from the history of Turkish or American Jews and so on. For example, British Jews are part of the British nation [umma], just as the Arab Jews are part of the Arab nation. The Jews do not have a common territory. They do not have a shared language, because German Jews speak German, British Jews speak English and Arab Jews speak Arabic. . . . They do not have a shared mentality [takwin nafsi] that manifests itself in a shared culture, because they lived for thousands of years in various communities, and became part of the societies in which they lived.[113]

Zionism, moreover, was an antidemocratic movement, since it did not seek to give equal freedoms to all the inhabitants of Palestine, privileging only one group, the Jews, over the Palestinian Arabs. From its very inception, the movement's leader, Theodor Herzl, had sought the help of authoritarian rulers, such the Ottoman sultan 'Abdulhamid II and the German kaiser, to support its exclusionist agenda. Although labor Zionism claimed to be socialist, whoever considered himself a socialist could not but object to a regime that preferred one ethnicity over the other in the labor market. The Histadrut, supposedly a labor union, was in fact an organization which employed workers in the same companies it controlled and only respected the rights of Jewish workers. Consequently, Palestinians suffered from high unemployment because of the unfair competition between Arabs and Jews in the market.[114]

Zionism served the interests of British and American imperialism. The connection between Zionism and Great Britain dated back to the nineteenth century but the Balfour Declaration (*al-Wa'd al-mash'um*) marked a new stage in these developments, in specifying the means by which Palestine was be colonized, namely, under the hegemony of the Zionist movement.[115] Zionist leaders fully recognized the colonialist potential of their movement. For example, the movement was offered Uganda as a Jewish homeland (1903), while territorial Zionism, led by Israel Zangwill (1864–1926), actively supported the colonialist project in many places across the globe. Furthermore, the Zionist desire to build a Jewish state in Palestine was grounded not only in the Jewish cultural and historical connections to the land, but also in the eagerness to exploit Palestine's natural resources and its position as a geostrategic center that was important to the colonial project. Jews, moreover, should not be misled by the American and British resistance to Nazism and their sympathy for the horrific state of Jews who survived the Holocaust. In America, prominent capitalists such as Ford were anti-Semitic, while in Britain a fascist party was allowed to speak out against the Jews. Thus, Great Britain and America had taken up the Zionist project not out of humanitarian concerns but rather because of economic and political interests.[116]

Most importantly, Zionism posed a problem to world Jewry in its presumption to speak in the name of all Jews and to blur the differences between Judaism and Zionism. Zilkha argued that it is important for whoever wanted to battle Zionism to distinguish between Zionism and Judaism. While Zionism was a political movement which aimed at "hegemonizing [*saytara*] Arab Palestine, exiling its original inhabitants, and forming a Zionist government in it," Judaism signified "a famous Semitic religion" that had no connection with Zionism.[117] As a matter of fact, many Jewish social and political movements objected to Zionism. Weizmann himself was concerned about the extent of anti-Zionist sentiment among Soviet Jewry, who believed that the solution to the Jewish question could be found in the Soviet Union. American Jewish groups objected to Zionism as well, and even Jews who had migrated to Palestine wished to return to their countries of origin. For this very reason, the Zionist movement continually equated itself with Judaism, so that it could "falsely claim that it represents world Jewry." Hence, whoever equated Judaism and Zionism was "in effect serving, whether willingly or unwillingly, none other than Zionism itself."[118]

Equating Judaism and Zionism imperiled Jewish communities in Arab countries. Rather than thinking about the ways in which Arab regimes served colonialism, Arabs began worrying about whether the Jews living among them were serving the interests of Zionism. In this sense, British colonialism created a Jewish problem in countries where there had not been one before. There were no conflicts between Arabs and Jews in Ottoman Palestine prior to the arrival of British colonialism and Zionism. Moreover, in Palestine itself, German and Polish Jews looked down upon Eastern (*sharqi*) Jews.[119] Arabs should consequently remember that Jews in Arab countries had professed their objection to Zionism and expressed their contempt toward it: "The racist slogans which certain segments in Palestine and in Arab countries call for, slogans which are always created by the agents of colonialism and inspired by them, like 'the need to banish the Jews from Palestine', 'Jews and Arab will never live together' and other such bigoted slogans, serve no one but Zionism and colonialism."[120] To Zilkha, such slogans provided the British with a reason for their stay in Palestine and the Middle East, supported by the claim that they were defending the Jews from the Arabs. There was, however, no need to banish Jews from Arab states, since Arabs and Jews could have democratic rights in each Arab nation-state where they lived, including Palestine.

Zilkha contended that the solution to the question of Palestine was the creation of an independent Palestinian state, which meant "the abolishment of the mandate, the banishing of foreign armies from Palestine, and the formation of an independent democratic state that will respect the rights of all its present inhabitants."[121] Naturally, all Arabs should support this struggle, yet it seemed doubtful whether the Arab regimes of the day were up to the task. Zilkha's historical analysis suggested that the leaders of the Arab regimes that came into being after World War I collaborated with colonialism, and therefore all Arab states suffered from a social crisis at the core of which was the question of liberation (*al-qadiyya al-taharruriyya*). The subjects of states such as Iraq, Egypt, Syria, and Lebanon sought to expel foreign armies from their lands, attain national sovereignty, and solve the Palestinian problem. However, Britain, aided by its new partner, America, as well as the reactionary Arab governments, sabotaged their efforts. Although Arab regimes expressed their concerns regarding Palestine, they suppressed popular democratic movements that truly battled for the Palestine cause.[122] Targeting his home audience, Zilkha stressed that the Iraqi regime permitted the presence of foreign powers in the country for the purposes of controlling Iraq's oil production. Iraqi Jews, moreover, could not express their abhorrence of Zionism since the state persecuted the league's members, as well as members of other democratic parties. Iraq was a nation in which the security forces opened fire on workers and demonstrators, where there was no freedom of expression, and where censorship on the press was heavy and unrelenting. The league, then, believed that fighting the ruling elites of Iraq and protecting the democratic rights of Iraqi citizens was part of its battle against Zionism.[123]

The ideas expressed in Zilkha's book represent an interesting mélange of national and leftist ideologies. On the one hand, many of Zilkha's arguments had been articulated by Jewish Arab nationalists in the past. The notion that the Iraqi environment had created an Iraqi Jew whose culture was both Eastern and Arab was crucial to the league's arguments that Iraqi Jews should join other Iraqis in a shared battle for the liberation of their country. As a corollary to these ideas, Jewish Arab nationalists of the 1930s had contended the Jewish question was particular to the European context alone. On the other hand, the linkage between anti-Semitism and the class struggle and the argument that the Iraqi regime had created conditions favorable to the rise of Zionism (primarily by collaborating with British and, later, American interests) were entirely new.

The league strove to achieve these ideas, although, as could be imagined, the propagation of these ideas was not a simple matter. As noted, the league was founded by eight Iraqi Jews who were all communists. In September 1945 they requested a license from the Ministry of Interior to form a party, but were denied because of their communist connections. A British intelligence report noted that the signatures of the petition included "many notorious communists with anti-British leanings."[124] Despite this initial setback, the league was still able to make the public aware of its existence, thanks to declarations of support from Iraqi politicians and some positive press coverage (especially through Masrur Qattan's activities in *Al-Sha'b*). The members opened an office and published a pamphlet on the day of the Balfour Declaration, which ended with the following words: "Long live the struggle of the Arabs for freedom and independence! Long live independent, democratic, Arab Palestine! Long live the Iraqi people!"[125]

The political climate at this time was very much influenced by the question of Palestine. Prior to a visit of an Anglo-American investigation committee on the question of Palestine in March 1946, the league used the debates about the arrival of this committee to Iraq to ask its supporters to boycott the committee's discussions. In response, the Iraqi police used the fact that the league was not a licensed organization as a pretext for arresting its members, who were tried in March 1946. The league's members were acquitted, however, since the court accepted the arguments of the defense that the league's members had acted as an establishing board and not as a legal association. That same month, the league was granted a license from the state and was permitted to print a journal called *Al-'Usba* (The League). The publisher was a Muslim communist lawyer, Muhammad Husayn Abu al-'Is, and the editor was Yusuf Harun Zilkha. The first issue appeared on April 6, 1946. That same month the league held its first public congress. The league's executive committee included, among others, Yusuf Harun Zilkha, Ya'qub Masri, Salim Menashe, Muhammad Abu al-'Is, and Zaki Khayri (all of whom were members of the ICP).[126]

The connections of the league to the ICP were clear. The British classified the league as an organization with communist influence,[127] whose members were "known by the police for their communist activities."[128] Another British account saw the league as an "important subsidiary organization of the communists" which was "funded and controlled by Jews" and served as a useful cloak for extreme left-wing activities.[129] Ambassador Stonehewer-Bird characterized the league as a "small stick" beating the British and as an organization that could easily be part of "a fifth column" by various anti-British troublemakers.[130] Consequently, the league "could prove troublesome to the British, since under the cloak of anti-Zionism, the left can take common ground with the extreme nationalists."[131] This organization, the British believed, "offers [an] excellent clearing house for all those who dislike us, namely all members of the left-wingers tied up with other communist organizations in Baghdad." The Soviet Union or any other unfriendly power, the British feared, might encourage the league to "foster an anti-British spirit here."[132]

The league's members likewise connected the league to the ICP. Menashe Zaluf, in his confession to the Iraqi police, confirmed that the ICP was involved in the league's activities. According to Zaluf, the league's purpose, the fight against Zionism and colonialism, meant they had common cause with the ICP, as both organizations considered themselves antiracist and progressive.[133] In fact, many Jewish members of the ICP arrested in 1947–1948 were known to be or have been members of the league as well.[134] The league worked with the Liberation Party (Hizb al-Taharrur), an organ affiliated with the ICP and with the communist newspaper *Al-Qaʿida*. One of the league's members, Ibrahim Naji Shumail, was an important financial backer of the ICP, and Dar al-Hikma, the ICP's publishing house, printed its publications.[135] Yehuda Sadiq admitted that the ICP intended to use the league in order to expand its influence in the Jewish community.[136]

The league seems to have been a successful organization. According to the historian Yosef Me'ir its membership numbered three hundred, although others have put forth the figure of two thousand. A British account from the time speaks of a thousand members.[137] Initially the British authorities predicted that no leading members of Baghdad's Jewry would back the league.[138] This assessment, however, proved to be quite wrong, as Jewish support of the league increased during 1946. Zionist agent Me'ir Shilon-Shlank complained in a letter to Eliyahu Sasson that the league had branches in every city, and that it had managed to attract a considerable number not only of educated Jewish youth but also Muslims and Christians.[139] Indeed, in May 1946, the league established a branch in Basra. Eighteen Jews from Nasiriya pledged their support of the league in the pages of the press.[140] The league received donations and support from Iraqi Jews as well as from Muslims and Christians, and was in contact with the mechanics', shopkeepers', workers', and clerks' unions.[141] Yaʿqub Masri similarly argues that the league had members from various communities.[142]

The league's pamphlets and various publications testify to its audience. At times, they described themselves as Arab Jews. Pamphlets stated in no uncertain terms that league members, "as Jews and Arabs at the same time, are the enemies of Zionism."[143] Speaking as Jews (and at times as "progressive Jews"), and on behalf of Iraqi Jews, the league objected publicly to the attempts to make the Jews "pawns in the colonialist game."[144] The

British, too, identified the league as a Jewish organization. Shortly after the establishment of the league, it was viewed as an organization with the goal of demonstrating to Arabs that Iraqi Jews sided with the Palestinians. This position, the British maintained, was a "form of insurance against possible anti-Jewish rioting in case things change in Palestine."[145] Other reports noted that the league was controlled by Jews and served their interests.[146] On the other hand, the league claimed to speak in the name of all progressive Iraqis. In a memorandum to Joseph Stalin, for instance, it argued it represented "thousands Iraqi citizens, of all religions and ethnicities [*qawmiyyat*]."[147] Some pamphlets were addressed to the noble people of Iraq as a whole and some were addressed to specific groups within the Iraqi nation: workers, peasants, students, merchants, and the educated elite.[148] A letter to the Minister of Interior identified the league as embodying the progressive consciousness (*wa'i mutanami*) of Iraqi Jews and the Iraqi masses (*al-jamahir al-sha'biyya*).

The league also characterized itself as a transregional communist organization and boasted of receiving letters of support from Palestinian labor organizations. One of its pamphlets included the following telegrams:

> [From] the association of Arab workers of Gaza: "Your battle as progressive Jews [*ahrar*] against colonizing Zionism is a blow to any reactionary movement."
>
> [From] the executive committee of the workers' conference in Jaffa: "You have demonstrated that you are noble citizens. We support you in your battle against Zionism, your enemy and ours."
>
> [From] the National Liberation League in Haifa: "We support you; your actions will have a good impact in Palestine."[149]

Similar telegrams were sent from workers in Bersheeva and Beit Jalla. Members contributed essays and articles to *Al-Fajr al-Jadid*, the journal of the Egyptian communist party, as well as to the Egyptian newspapers *Al-Damir* and *Um Durman*.[150] The league addressed Jewish communists throughout the Middle East, and particularly those in Palestine, and sent a letter to the Hebrew communist newspaper *Kol ha-'Am* in April 1946, written in the name of the progressive Jewish youth, and delineating the league's goals.[151] In appealing to both Arabs and Jews via its publications, the league evidently considered its audience to have been anyone who supported the workers' struggle in the Middle East.

The league also reached out to Arab audiences who were not necessarily communist. When Zilkha was arrested, the league printed letters of support from individuals affiliated with the Palestinian cause, including Shukri al-Quwatli and Jamal al-Husayni, representing the Supreme Arab Committee in Palestine, as well as letters from Syrian politicians and representatives from the Arab League. These were meant to show that the league's message that Zionism was the enemy of both Arabs and Jews had been heard loudly and clearly across the Arab world and to demonstrate that the Palestinians themselves made the distinction between Judaism and Zionism. The league similarly held up letters of support from leading Iraqi politicians to legitimize its positions. Hamdi al-Pachachi, Ahmad Baban, and Tawfiq al-Suwaydi were cited as having argued that the Jews of Iraq were loyal citizens.[152] The nationalist Mawlud Mukhlis observed that European Zionists felt nothing but contempt for the Jews of the East. Even the much-abhorred Nuri al-Sa'id was mentioned, for having said that Zionism was not to be found in democratic countries where citizens enjoyed equality.[153] The fact that a communist publication would quote Sa'id, Baban, Suwaydi, and Mukhlis might seem peculiar since all were criticized in communist publications. And yet, doing so was intended to illustrate that the league's ideology was commonsensical and familiar to any Iraqi nationalist. The publication of these statements also put Iraq's leadership in a precarious position, as it was difficult for nationalist officials to object to an organization that called for a unified Iraqi campaign against Zionism.

The league's activities focused on a few projects. The first was addressing the public via printed materials, initially via pamphlets, and later via their newspaper, *Al-'Usba*. Estimates of the numbers of copies of *Al-'Usba* sold ranged between two thousand and six thousand. The editorials of the newspaper were written primarily by Yusuf Harun Zilkha, who had prior experience in the field of journalism, as he had written for both *Al-Sha'b* and *Al-Majalla*. League members, such as Zilkha, Yehuda Sadiq, Menashe Zaluf, and Ya'qub Cohen, translated anti-Zionist publications from English and other European newspapers such as the *Jewish Clarion*. Some editorials were written by Fahd.[154] Open letters to prominent individuals were yet another means through which the league broadcast its ideology. Zilkha wrote to leaders of Arab countries, the heads of the Iraqi senate, the secretary of the Arab League, and the head of the Arab High Committee in Palestine. All were published in *Al-'Usba* or in pamphlets. Zilkha likewise wrote a memo to the British prime minister and the president of the United States, asking them to halt Jewish immigration to Palestine and assist with the formation of a national democratic government in the country. Another letter was addressed to Joseph Stalin, advocating that the Soviets take up the struggle against Zionism and imperialism.[155] A memorandum sent to the United Nations called on that organization to cut off relations with both the United States and Britain to protest their conduct in Palestine.[156]

The league held public meetings in order to disseminate their ideas, once it had obtained an official license from the state (on March 16, 1946). On April 13, it held its first conference and reported that the event was attended by as many as three thousand individuals. The league claimed that one of its major achievements was drawing many Jewish citizens, who had previously stayed clear of politics, into the national struggle. Between March and August 1946, members managed to hold twenty public meetings, as well as more modest gatherings. The number of participants in these meetings, based on the league's accounts, was as high as five thousand. The league's meetings in Basra, according to its own assessment, attracted thousands of participants as well.[157] The meetings were usually held on the Sabbath in the neighborhood of Karada in a building that belonged to the league. Other meetings were held at Dar al-Hikma.[158] The league had a dramatic group which performed plays and arranged sport gatherings and cultural activities, all open to the public.[159] Iraq's most celebrated poet, Badr Shakir al-Sayyab, then a communist, identified with *Al-'Usba*'s aims in Basra. He admits that the league was well supported in the city, and that he was invited to read a poem in a crowded meeting held at a primary school whose principal was a communist.[160] Sayyab's uncle helped distribute the *Al-'Usba* while Sayyab himself protested when *Al-'Usba* was canceled by the state.[161]

The league was in contact with other organizations in Iraq, yet such connections were difficult to maintain because of the communist leanings of its members. As noted, it was very close to Hizb al-Taharrur and organized a few activities in conjunction with it.[162] The league, however, was attacked by nationalist papers such as *Al-Yaqdha* and *Al-Ba'th*.[163] The nationalist daily *Al-'Alam al-'Arabi*, for example, opined that the league's members should be talking to the Anglo-American Investigation Committee rather than boycotting its discussions. The daily therefore wondered whether the league was, in fact, serving Zionist interests. The five legal parties in Iraq also refused to allow the league to join their shared committee for the defense of Palestine, presumably because of its communist connections.[164]

The league organized demonstrations in solidarity with the Palestinians and in order to present its domestic socioeconomic agenda. Fahd was fully aware of these demonstrations and assisted in their organization. The first major public demonstration was held on June 6, 1946. On June 11 the league organized a demonstration in which men wearing blue shirts called for a just solution to the Palestinian problem and the evacuation of foreign armies from Iraq. Eighteen of its members were arrested in response.[165] On June 28, the league and Hizb al-Taharrur held their largest joint demonstration in the main streets of Baghdad. Three thousand workers, students, and other supporters marched toward the British Embassy and began throwing stones at the statue honoring General Maude.[166] Eighty to one hundred soldiers were deployed to suppress the demonstration. The police opened fire on the demonstrators, killing one, Sha'ul Tweig.[167] Following Sha'ul's death, the league printed an obituary in honor of "the patriotic martyr [*shahid*], Sha'ul Tweig, who fell in the battle against Zionism and colonialism, in front of the statue of General Maude, the symbol of British colonialism in Iraq, in the time of the government of Mr. al-'Umari, during the bloody demonstration of June 28th."[168] Major newspapers wrote about the death of Sha'ul, with one journal arguing that Tweig's death laid the foundations for brotherly solidarity in Iraq. Mourners from various religious communities came to his parents' house in large numbers.[169] At other times, the league's demonstrations were not sanctioned by the state. After the Anglo-American Investigation Committee arrived, members wanted to demonstrate, but were prevented by the authorities (they managed to hold the rally nonetheless).[170] Despite the suspension of the league's license in August 1946, it held its last demonstration in December that same year.[171]

Since the league's argument was that anti-Semitism turned the attention of the working classes away from their true concerns toward hatred of Jews, and that the struggle for democracy and workers' rights related to its anti-Zionist platform, it addressed the abuse of human rights in Iraq in particular, and across the world in general, in its publications. *Al-'Usba* therefore ran stories about the suffering of Iraqi peasants under the present feudal system and the persecution of leftists in Spain and in Greece.[172] British intelligence reports noted that the league was linked to attacks on the government, criticized the Iraqi upper classes, and was generally engaged in "propaganda ... similar to [that of] Moscow."[173] In the north, it was involved in strikes organized by workers of the Iraqi Petroleum Company in Kirkuk.[174] In 1946, one of the workers in the Iraqi Petroleum Company's oil field in Basra was burned alive in a work-related accident. The communists were present at his funeral in Najaf, where Sayyab read a poem in his memory. *Al-'Usba* printed the poem and reported on the event.[175]

As part of its struggle for democracy and sovereignty, the league claimed the harsh treatment it endured attested to the lack of freedom within the Iraqi state itself. The league protested when the director of propaganda, Naji Qishtayni, shut down *Al-'Usba*, on June 6, 1946, and complained about the restrictions on the political activities of Hizb al-Taharrur.[176] It reminded its supporters that citizens had a right to hold demonstrations for the causes in which they believed and to publish their opinions, even if these opinions were not regarded favorably by the state. These limitations on freedom of speech and freedom of assembly were thus illegal.[177] Similarly, when the police confiscated a pamphlet calling for the termination of the mandate in Palestine, and arrested twelve people (including Zilkha and an eight-year-old boy) for its distribution, the league printed a protest arguing that these arrests were unlawful.[178] As the league was blamed for carrying out actions that threatened public safety, it printed a proclamation arguing that it had simply criticized Arab governments for having too kind an opinion toward colonialism, and that such criticism did not justify the detention of citizens.[179] In June and July 1946, activists from Hizb al-Taharrur and the league were arrested for demonstrating in support of the Palestinians; the league protested, saying that the action had been peaceful and that no arrests were warranted.[180]

The league's activities were crushed by the state. After the pro-Palestinian demonstrations during the month of June, many members were arrested, the right to publish *Al-'Usba* was suspended for a year, and the league was blamed for serving the aims of Zionism.[181] The arrested members were acquitted after spending thirty-one days in jail. On June 11 Ya'qub Masri presented a petition of 539 signatures addressed to the council of ministers to end the suspension of *Al-'Usba*, questioning the legality of the act. As many as fifteen lawyers defended the league in court.[182] A more serious case was the subsequent arrest of Masri (the league's secretary), Masrur Qattan (its accountant), and three other members. A pamphlet critical of the government's stance with regard to Palestine suggested that the Iraqi regime, which was at the beck and call of British colonial interests, could not possibly challenge British colonialism in Palestine. The authorities responded by charging the leagues' members with endangering the public safety by inciting sectarian hatred. In his defense, Masri argued that all his criticisms against the reactionary powers in Iraq were intended to discredit those who equated Judaism and Zionism, and that his views merely reflected the sentiments of the Iraqi people.[183] Masri's Muslim lawyer, the left-leaning politician 'Aziz Sharif, contended that Zionism endangered Jews in Arab countries, because of the Zionist assumption that Jews could not live under anything but Zionist rule. To support this contention, the Zionist movement propagated lies about the deep hatred between Jews and their brothers, the Christian and Muslim Arabs. The league, however, did not act against the Iraqi government or any of its officials, or incite sectarian hate in Iraq. On the contrary, it did not attack any particular Iraqi sect or ethnicity, such the Sunna or the Shi'a, the Kurds or the Arabs, but rather took issue with the pro-British policies of the government—but not the government itself.[184] The Muslim lawyer Mahdi al-Arazi, also part of the defense team, contended that his Jewish brothers were simply struggling to dispel the myths of colonialism. The Iraqis as a nation had fought this same battle in 1920. Moreover, the right to wage this battle was protected by the Iraqi constitution, and the natural rights of citizens to fight dictatorships. Similarly, the people in Palestine possessed the right to fight against their own ruling elites and to advocate democracy. The league's actions, when viewed in this light, were not illegal. Those who endeavored to convince people that every Jew was a Zionist—they were the parties guilty of fomenting sectarian hatred.[185]

Predictably, the Iraqi court was unimpressed by such arguments. The court of Baghdad ruled in September 1946 that the league was actually acting in the service of Zionism. The aim of the pamphlet was to "evoke feelings of hatred and abhorrence between the denizens of Iraq" by dividing them into "patriots, colonizers, and reactionaries" and thus harming public safety. The court, however, used a rather original line of reasoning:

> Had the league really wanted to fight Zionism it would have been called the League for Combating **Against** Zionism [*'Usbat al-mukafaha* **did** *al-sahayuniyya*]. The [grammatical construction of the] name chosen [*'Usbat mukafahat al-sahuyuniyya*], however, indicates clearly that the league is the league for the sake of the Zionist struggle, [which acts] by spreading feeling of hatred between the people of Iraq . . . so that the government will be busy with such matters rather than carry out its actions on behalf of Arabs of Palestine.[186]

A pamphlet arguing that the government served Great Britain, the court maintained, had led the people to believe that the government and the people were not united: "Zionism comes in different shapes and forms in every country. . . . In Palestine, they are engaged in assassinations against the British and in acts of nihilism. . . . In Arab countries they . . . spread division and hatred between the people and endanger the public peace, so that every Arab country is busy with its internal affairs and could not be freed to defend Palestine."[187] The judge Khalil Amin al-Mufti also wrote in his ruling that the league, as an organization directed by foreign interests, had duped the simple-minded Iraqis in order to achieve its goals. He sentenced both Ya'qub Masri and Masrur Salih Qattan to a year in jail with hard labor.[188]

Mocking the idea that it had been founded to spread Zionism, the league suggested that the judge was in urgent need of a lesson in Arabic grammar. Referring to another Iraqi organization, the League for Combating Illiteracy ('Usbat mukafahat al-ummiyya)—a name with the same grammatical structure—the League for Combating Zionism's pamphlet wondered whether the former was attempting to increase illiteracy. Finally, the point was made that if the league was pro-Zionist, then all the Iraqi leaders who supported the league must be clandestine Zionists.[189] Ya'qub Masri and his comrades expressed similar grievances concerning the judge, arguing that from Amin's comments during the court's hearings, it was clear that he believed Jews were constantly betraying their fellow Iraqis, and thus could not under any circumstances be considered loyal citizens.[190] Referencing the judge's understanding of Arab grammar again, Ishaq Bar-Moshe drew attention to the "almost comic" moment in which the anti-Zionist communists were labeled as Zionists. Sibawahi [a medieval Arabic grammarian], he wrote, must be turning in his grave.[191]

During the last months of 1946, the league's activity gradually came to an end. With its license canceled, its daily newspaper suspended, and several of its leaders arrested, the organization found it very difficult to operate. Some league members left to join the ICP, and still more were arrested over the course of the next two years. Zilkha himself was arrested in 1947 and sentenced to four years in jail. Upon his release, he and other members were exiled from Iraq. They refused to board the airplanes, and were beaten and abused until they gave in. Zilkha was flown to Cyprus and from there—to Israel.

The league represents a unique moment in the history of Jews in Iraq. Its critique of Zionism was not original—various groups of Jewish communists across the globe were making the same point, as were Arab nationalists. Nonetheless, as the leaders of the ICP recognized, the league's positions resonated with Muslim and Christian Iraqis. Moreover, the advancement of an anti-Zionist agenda enabled the ICP to appropriate the question of Palestine from nationalist organizations such as al-Istiqlal, and represent itself as Iraq's leading anticolonial party. It should be remembered that there was much resentment within the Jewish community toward some Palestinian exiles in Iraq, most notably Hajj Amin al-Husayni, his family, and his supporters, whose actions had helped to spark the Farhud in Jewish eyes. The fact that the league recruited its supporters from the Jewish community shows that Iraqi Jews themselves were able not only to separate Judaism and Zionism, but also to distinguish between the conduct of particular Palestinian leaders and the Palestinian cause itself. There was substantial opposition to Zionism in Iraq already in the 1930s, yet in the 1940s it also entailed criticism of Iraqi state policy. The league viewed the Iraqi regime, and all the regimes in the Middle East, as beholden to British interests. These regimes, they felt, permitted Zionist activities within their borders, violated human rights, and were in constant conflict with one another, and as such, would not be able to save Palestine.

The ICP position on Zionism would change in the coming years. The ICP's publications joined those of the league in voicing their objections to

Zionism. However, following the USSR decision to support the partition decision, the ICP was forced to change its opinion and support partition in Palestine. The ICP's stance was now that while a binational state in Palestine was preferable, British and Zionist activities created a situation in which there was no hope for a peaceful binational solution, and thus partition was the only choice. The time it took the Arab communists to affirm their agreement with the Soviet position shows the difficulties they had with respect to the decision. The Soviet foreign minister had stated in May 1947 that the USSR supported partition and indeed the USSR voted for it in the United Nations on November. The communist Arab Democratic Committee, convened in Paris on June 11, 1948, supported this view.[192] The committee's decision circulated in Iraq in the month of August and ignited much criticism. Fahd himself could not understand why the Soviets had recognized the Jewish state, as he constantly argued that Jews should not be considered a separate national group. Other ICP members were demoralized and questioned the logic behind the USSR's action. Worse yet, this decision enabled the ICP's opponents, especially the radical nationalists, to present the ICP as supporting colonialism and Zionism, and as nothing more than a puppet of the Soviets.[193] Indeed, the Iraqi state continued to use this support of partition against the communists in the coming years.[194]

The response to the ICP's support for partition among Jewish members was mixed. Salim Fattal reports that his Jewish comrades in the poor neighborhood of Ttaran were overcome with happiness, as they viewed Stalin's support of partition as a sign of Soviet support for the Jewish people. Batatu, however, argues that the Jewish members of the ICP were perplexed, given the ICP's anti-Zionist position.[195] Shim'on Ballas speaks of the great embarrassment and confusion he and his friends felt, following this decision, which was inexplicable and suggested collaboration with the Zionists.[196] Given the support to the league among Iraqi Jews in general, it seems that Ballas's views were those of a larger segment of the Jewish communists. The loyalty of Iraqi Jews to the ICP, therefore, was not a result of the party's position on partition, but rather the communists' protection of Jews in the wake of partition and their willingness to take on nationalists who equated Judaism with Zionism. The ICP's treatment of Jews as equal members during the turbulent years of 1947–49 was the major source of Jewish attraction to the party and not their position on partition that was imposed on the party from above.

Conclusions

To conclude this chapter, I would like to return to a few comments made by the great (if not the greatest) historian of the ICP, Hanna Batatu, on the role of Iraqi Jews in the ICP:

> Iraqis of the Jewish faith took no part whatever in the founding of the communist party..., and came into the picture only after 1940. Even then..., they were of no considerable account in the top layers of the party command.... They do not appear to have minded much their exclusion from certain political or social roles and in an economic sense were better off than all the other communists. Indeed their relative prosperity amidst general distress became a source of danger to them. This factor, and to a much greater extent the aftereffects of the advance of Zionism in Palestine, combined to place their entire position in Iraq in jeopardy. It is, therefore, in the first place to a growing sense of insecurity that has to be attributed the drift of Jews toward communism in the forties.[197]

Batatu writes of Sadiq's leadership of the ICP, "People close to the party later wondered whether he had been a bona fide Communist: Zionist feelings were taking hold of many Baghdadi Jews at the time. But this is a line which, in the absence of concrete indices, cannot profitably be perused."[198] Batatu's claims become bolder when he describes Dallal's leadership of the ICP:

> Perhaps the "frenzied" and "suicidal" demonstrations [Dallal initiated] ... were really in the nature of diversion and ought to be read in connection with what was going on at the time in Palestine. Perhaps..., the authorities were right in suspecting the he was a Zionist. Dallal's first "important appeal"... was issued on 25th December 1948. On the twenty first Fahd had been transferred from the Kut Prison to Baghdad for retrial. On the twenty second the Israelis had launched their offence in the Negev against the Egyptian army. Did Dallal's initiative relate to one or to the other of these events? Was it all a coincidence? Here again, as in the earlier case of Yehuda Siddiq [Sadiq] we found ourselves on the unprofitable and dead-end alley of conjecture.[199]

Batatu's book is usually considered the "Bible" for all historians of the left in Iraq—but was he wrong about what he wrote on the Jewish role in the party? He was certainly correct in pointing out that Iraqi Jews were not founding members of the party, and that they joined it as a result of their minoritization by the Iraqi state. He was wrong, however, to assume that Jewish membership in the ICP was unimportant and to insinuate a possible connection between Iraqi Jewish communists and Zionism. Zionist emissaries to Iraq do refer to the communism of the Jewish youth during the 1940s, yet they speak about Jewish Iraqi communism as a danger, not as a potential partner. Zionists in Iraq felt that their greatest challenge in the competition for the souls of Jewish youth was the communist organizations. Dallal and Sadiq paid with their lives for their communist and patriotic beliefs. Moreover, Iraqi Jewish communists did contribute to the ICP. Jewish men and women were cell members, union leaders, and party secretaries. An urban-educated community, they played a major role in the party's translation and educational efforts. Membership in the ICP gave them a sense of belonging and was consonant with their nonsectarian outlook.

The Jewish Iraqi experience shares much in common with the experiences of communist European Jews. Both looked to the Soviet Union as a power offering a vision of equality and the ability to battle anti-Semitism, right-wing nationalism, and discrimination in the domain of citizenship rights. Accounts written by Iraqi Jewish communists are similar to tales narrated by communists across the globe at the time, and the clichés they invoke about the power of communism to appeal to the hungry and the oppressed were common tropes in leftist discourses of postwar Europe, Africa, and Latin America. At the same time, the Jewish experience reflects the ways in which the international ideas of communism were localized in Iraq, and how such ideas were further reinterpreted in Jewish schools, cells, and in poor Jewish neighborhoods in Baghdad. In these processes of localizing communist ideology, the ideals of brotherly love and social justice blended with notions of Iraqi patriotism; and anti-Nazi, Soviet-inspired propaganda served to counter pro-German Iraqi nationalists and to attract more Jews to the party. Stalin himself became a local, mustached hero in Tatran. Thus, when certain Iraqi nationalists interpreted notions of religious difference as markers of disloyalty to the state and the nation, communism enabled Jews to demonstrate their devotion to the community in which they lived. While it is perhaps true that "the working men have no country," Iraqi Jewish communism came into being in an Iraqi context: in Baghdad's neighborhoods, streets, and cafés; its schools, high schools, and colleges; and in its prison cells and on its gallows.

Iraqi Jewish communists, in fact, acted within three circles. The first was the ICP itself, a body organized into a clear hierarchy (groups divided into districts, cells, and cell leaders). Outside the party, there existed a second circle, a lively public sphere composed of left-leaning intellectuals and networks of radical students who labored to spread the ideals of the party or at least identified secretly with it. The third circle was the city and its neighborhoods. Many individuals in these neighborhoods—be they Jewish pro-communist merchants or the Jewish urban poor—felt great sympathy toward the ICP; although they did not fully comprehend its ideology or commit themselves to its causes, they recognized its importance as a mechanism that critiqued the state's policies. Jewish ICP members were often situated between these circles: as young men who came from a Baghdadi and Basran neighborhoods, they identified with the third circle. As students, translators and journalists, they were in contact with fellow students and read books composed by leftist intelligentsia. Finally, as cell members they received orders from their cell leaders and other commanders in the ICP's hierarchy. Their familiarity with each circle, however, enabled them to survive: ordinary Iraqis aided them at times of trouble, and the party provided them with a framework to understand current events.

The communists were Iraqi patriots who, during the period under study (1941–51), condemned the Pan-Arabism promoted by comprador Arab regimes in the Middle East and critiqued the right-wing Pan-Arabism of Iraqi parties such as al-Istiqlal, which they felt opened sectarian and religious divisions within the Iraqi people. They also believed in a shared battle with non-Arab minorities in Iraq, like the Kurds. Nevertheless, despite these critiques of Pan-Arab policies, Iraqi Jews contributed to Arab culture within the ranks of the ICP. It was under the auspices of the ICP that Jews translated communist and Marxist publications into Arabic. Jewish Iraqi communism, moreover, produced one of the most rigorous criticisms of Zionism, as understood by Jewish intellectuals who defined themselves as Arab Jews. The collaborative activities of Iraqis of various faiths and ethnicities within the ICP, especially the activity of Jews in mixed cells, reproduced the experience of religious coexistence in Iraqi neighborhoods and schools, and confirmed the notion that Iraqis, regardless of their religious beliefs, could share the same sociopolitical agenda. Jewish communists worked with Muslim and Christian communists in cells, unions, schools, and prisons; they hosted fellow Muslim and Christian communists in their homes, and they took refuge in homes of Jewish and non-Jewish Iraqis. I do not wish to romanticize the ICP: there were disagreements, internal battles, and splits, and the division between Sadiq and Sayyif proved particularly lethal for the party. This was not a democratic organization, but rather a Stalinist one. Nonetheless, many Jews came to the ICP looking for a nonsectarian, anticolonial, and secular vision for Iraqi society, and they found it in its ranks.

The fact that many Iraqi Jewish communists immigrated to Israel was not necessarily a Zionist triumph but rather the failure of the antidemocratic monarchy to tolerate criticism of its regime. As part of a brutal anticommunist campaign conducted by the state, many Jewish communists were jailed and arrested, and some were even stripped of their citizenship. These Jews did not foresee an end to this persecution, and thus emigration was the only option. The fact that the Iraqi state, which declared itself to be vehemently anti-Zionist, persecuted and exiled Jewish members of the League for Combating Zionism is the best illustration of Iraq's shortsightedness with respect to its Jewish minority.

6

AN END?

Iraqi Jews and the Iraqi State, 1946–51

Before his arrival in Israel, Sasson Somekh went to visit his friend the poet Akram al-Witri. Witri was surprised that Sasson chose to leave Iraq:

> He could not imagine that a person like me, so bound to the Arabic language and close to its culture and literature, would decide to abandon his homeland and the homeland of his ancestors to jump into an unknown territory of strangeness and mystery, war and insecurity.
>
> I tried to explain to him that the situation in Iraq had become unbearable, and that I had no chance of being accepted into an institution of higher learning in Baghdad, merely because I was Jewish. Above all, I explained that there was no democracy in Iraq. . . . Akram stopped me gently, then continued to admonish me: How will you manage in a country whose citizens are a mixture of all the communities and languages, he asked, the future of which is not at all certain?[1]

The concerns raised by Akram were not unfounded. The departure of Jews from Iraq is puzzling in retrospect, considering the degree to which the Iraqi Jews were immersed in Iraqi life and culture. This emigration, however, was spurred by the increasingly volatile situation in the years 1948–51. The desire of the state of Israel to bring Iraqi Jews to Israel, in conjunction with a brutal right-wing nationalist activity and the ineptitude of the

Iraqi leadership, provided the impetus for emigration. A vicious circle was set in motion during these years. The escalation of the conflict in Palestine prompted Iraqi right-wing politicians to mark Iraqi Jews as Zionists. The state did not make much of an effort to discredit these right-wing propaganda efforts, and at times even incited anti-Jewish acts, with the result that younger Jews turned to Zionism. The state of Israel for its part seized upon the Iraqi government's actions as the ultimate proof that Arabs and Jews could not live together.

When describing this vicious circle, the reasons behind the Iraqi state's actions are not readily apparent. The Israeli motivations are easier to explicate. As laid out by the important works of Esther Meir, Abbas Shiblak, Haim Cohen, Moshe Gat, and Yehouda Shenhav, as well as by Zionist agents in Iraq, it is clear why the state of Israel wanted Iraqi Jews to come to Israel and why Zionist Iraqis wished to leave Iraq. The central tenet of Zionist ideology was that Israel was the homeland of every Jew. Events such as the Farhud indicated to Zionist officials that Jewish communities in the Middle East were in peril and needed to be saved by a Jewish state.[2] Furthermore, after 1942 the realization of the dimensions of the Holocaust caused the Zionist movement to turn its attention eastward, namely, toward the 750,000 Jews who lived in the Muslim world, 135,000 of whom lived in Iraq (0.7 percent of the world's Jewry).[3] Therefore, I do not focus in this chapter on the activities of Israel as much as I do on things that have happened in Iraq itself.

It is less clear, however, why the Iraqi state pursued policies and a course of action that alienated a productive segment of its citizenry. In this context, it is important to address the often-blurred boundaries between anti-Jewish and anti-Zionist policies. The Iraqi public was troubled by the tragedy of the Palestinian people, and many an Iraqi intellectual, Arab nationalist and communist alike, wrote pro-Palestinian articles and demonstrated in support of the Palestinians. In the spring of 1948, Iraq fought a war against the newly established state of Israel. Not surprisingly, the Iraqi authorities were greatly concerned about the existence of an illegal Zionist underground in Iraq, and attempted to crush it. Nonetheless, to underscore its commitment to the fight against Zionism, the state engaged in a process of collective punishment. It arrested Jews who had nothing to do with Zionism, and, in effect, unjustly designated an entire community as second-rate citizens.

These undemocratic measures did not achieve their goal of rooting out Zionism, however, and in fact pushed Jews to emigrate from Iraq and tore asunder the bonds of education, nationalization, and cultural hybridity that I depicted in the previous chapters.

The Difficulty of Being a Jew

With the end of the Second World War, the insolubility of the conflict in Palestine became a Middle Eastern reality that affected the lives of Iraqi Jewry. Testifying to the connections between the Palestinian and Iraqi Jewish arenas is a conversation that took place in January 1943 between Prime Minister Nuri Sai'd and some leaders of the Jewish community, among them Senator Ezra Menahem Daniel, Rabbi Sasun Khaduri, Gurji Shalom Levy (deputy director of the Ottoman Bank), and Khaduri Shukr (a merchant and member of parliament). Sa'id told his Jewish guests that he was familiar with the Zionist movement. He had met with a Romanian Zionist representative in Istanbul in 1909, and later had contacts with Chaim Weizmann on a number of occasions, the last of which was in London in 1935. When he was in Palestine, he met with Dr. Magnes and discussed with him the possibilities for ending the conflict. Sa'id then asked these Jewish leaders to publicly declare their position on the situation in Palestine. Gurji Levy replied that he had come to hate the word *Palestine* since it now stood for the disagreement between Jews and Arabs outside Palestine, and added that he did not understand why the prime minister wanted to identify Iraqi Jews with Zionism, a movement with which they had no involvement. Khaduri Shukr echoed Levy, arguing that the problems in Palestine were created by Great Britain: "He pointed to the building of the British Embassy, saying: Why don't they—the British—find an agreeable solution for both sides? Why do you ask for the solution from Iraqi Jews who never concerned themselves with this problem?" Sa'id said that he knew that Iraqi Jews were loyal Iraqis, and that Ezra Menahem Daniel would never leave Iraq, even if a Jewish state was established. However, he insisted that Iraqi Jews, being influential merchants, could and should solve the problem of Zionist propaganda, especially in America.[4]

The meeting spoke to the precarious position of Iraqi Jews. On the one hand, the prime minister wanted his country's Jews to declare their opposition to Zionism, and set forth what they believed was the best way to resolve the conflict in Palestine. The position of the Jewish leadership of the community, which was not Zionist, was different. They wanted to distance themselves from the conflict as much as possible, feeling that any plan they offered, even one counter to Zionist interests, would link them to the Palestinian arena. Nonetheless, as the situation in Palestine escalated, this attitude changed, and in 1946, the Jewish leadership adopted a more resolute pro-Palestinian stance. Ibrahim al-Kabir's memo to the Anglo-American Investigation Committee argued that Iraqi Jews, as lawyers, traders, doctors, and writers, had helped build the economy and society of Iraq. The hatred of Jews in Iraq, he claimed, was the result of Nazi propaganda and the prominence of the question of Palestine in the Iraqi public sphere. Yet al-Kabir maintained that Jews were not discriminated against, and thus did not wish to leave Iraq.[5]

With the end of the Second World War, a few steps were taken to discourage Iraqi Jews from considering Zionism as a political option. In 1945, limits were imposed on Jews wishing to enter Iraq (out of fear of the possible entrance of Zionist agents), and a number of non-Iraqi Hebrew teachers were expelled from Iraq.[6] In the time between the United Nations vote on the partition of Palestine in November 1947 and the declaration of the foundation of the state of Israel in May of 1948, the situation of Iraqi Jews worsened noticeably. Pro-Palestinian articles appeared in the press and demonstrations occurred in Iraq, especially in April 1948, following the death of Palestinian leader 'Abd al-Qadir al-Husayni in battle. The situation continued to deteriorate after Iraq sent armies to fight Israel in May 1948, after the establishment of the state of Israel. Iraqi Jews responded by contributing funds to Palestinian causes (although some have reported that they were forced to do so), while Rabbi Khaduri, the official leader of the community at the time, declared that Palestine belonged to the Arabs, and that the Iraqi Jewish community was loyal to the Iraqi nation.[7] Jews, however, worried that the pro-Palestinian climate did not bode well for them. After the massacre in Dir Yasin, Jewish schools and shops were closed out of fear of retribution.[8]

With Iraq's entrance to war against Israel, the Iraqi government, headed by Prime Minister Muhammad al-Sadr, announced a state of emergency within Iraq, which meant that military rule was in effect nationwide. Military courts were set up in Baghdad, Basra, and Kirkuk, supposedly to safeguard the Iraqi home front. In June 1948 Sadr's government fell and Muzahim al-Pachachi became prime minister, with Sadiq al-Bassam as the minister of defense. Pachachi's government held power until January 1949, when it was replaced by a government led by Nuri Sa'id. The events that happened under these three governments paved the way for the mass emigration of Jews from Iraq in the early 1950s.[9]

The pressure on Jews in Iraq increased and lessened continually in the years 1948–51, with two especially difficult periods being May–September 1948 and October–November 1949, following the exposure of a Zionist underground in Iraq. Indeed, a British official in Iraq described the summer of 1948 as a period of an "anti-Jewish campaign," during which Jews were blamed for disrespecting both Iraqis and Palestinians.[10] In mid-July 1948 the parliament defined support of Zionism as a crime, equal to support of communism and anarchism, to be punished by imprisonment (with a minimum sentence of seven years) and in extreme cases, by death. Trips abroad by Iraqi Jews were severely curtailed, as families had to provide a financial bond when one of their members traveled outside of Iraq. This measure, intended to prevent immigration to Palestine, was a great burden on merchants who did business outside the country and greatly limited the ability of Jewish students to enroll at foreign universities, even if they had been awarded fellowships.[11] Letters between Iraqi Jews and their relatives in Palestine were seen as proof of the Zionist leanings of the former, even if the letters dated from the 1920s, when Zionism had not yet been outlawed in Iraq. The government confiscated mail addressed to Jews, and arrested, fined, and jailed the intended recipients. Visits to Palestine, even if made in the 1920s, were likewise viewed with suspicion. In fact, it took very little to prove that someone was a Zionist: a sixty-year-old man was sentenced to five years in jail for getting a letter from his son in Palestine; a seventeen-year-old youth was imprisoned for two years when a teacher reported that he had insulted the Iraqi army; and a fifty-five-year-old man was jailed for three years after two witnesses said he had contacted his son in Israel.[12]

A more serious concern for Iraqi Jews was job security. Large numbers of Jews employed at governmental ministries were let go from their positions, beginning in the spring of 1948. By the end of 1949, 159 Jews had been fired from the Ministry of Foreign Affairs, 57 from the Ministry of Finance, 261 from the Iraqi State Railway, 109 from the Directorate General of Ports, 138 from the Directorate General of Posts, 24 from the Public Works Department, 11 from the Ministry of Economics, 21 from the Ministry of Interior, 4 from the Ministry of Defense, 117 from the Ministry of Education, and 1 from the Department of Civil Aviation. In this same period, the government made it more difficult for Jews to get import licenses (although influential Jews had less trouble getting such licenses).[13] Jewish doctors found it harder to be placed in hospitals, while Jewish bankers could not conduct business as freely as before because of the limits on foreign trade. A Zionist account from October 1949 estimated that fifteen hundred Jews in the private and public sectors combined lost their jobs.[14]

Jews encountered increased limitations in other arenas as well. Their enrollment in high schools and universities in Iraq and abroad was curtailed, beginning in the period 1949–51.[15] Rabbi Khaduri reported that during 1948–49, Jewish homes could be and were searched at night if it was suspected that Zionist activities were taking place; an unofficial ban on the selling of real estate by Jews was in effect; and Jewish conscripts for the army were assigned noncombatant roles.[16] The matter of diminished military service is important because it shows that in Rabbi Khaduri's view, Iraqi Jews still wanted to express their patriotism by serving in the army, but were denied the chance to do so by the state. The house searches, arrests, and jailing were clearly related to the state's hunt for Zionist activists, and the Iraqi authorities did succeed in capturing a number of Zionists in October 1949. Yet even non-Jewish observers viewed the state's anti-Zionist campaign as problematic. The British ambassador was concerned about the lack of fair trials as well as the possibility that detainees were tortured, and feared that the decline of the Jewish community in Iraq would soon follow.[17]

The situation became much graver in September 1948, with the execution of the Jewish businessman Shafiq 'Adas for selling military supplies to Israel. 'Adas was an extremely wealthy Syrian Jew who had settled in Basra and become the principal agent for the Ford Motor Company in Iraq. He maintained good relationships with the Iraqi upper classes, as well as with several ministers and the regent. He and his business partners bought British scrap metal, which was later exported to Italy; according to the military court that tried 'Adas, it was then shipped to Israel to be used in weapons' manufacture. As Sylvia Haim perceptively notes, "The official story cannot be altogether discounted, but it is doubtful whether there was prior knowledge about the eventual destination of this material. The significant part of the episode, however, is that 'Adas, the only Jew in the partnership, was also the only man to be punished."[18] The nationalist press was the first to accuse 'Adas of supporting Zionism, and even went so far as to call for his execution. In August 1948, 'Adas was arrested and tried in a military court, which sentenced him to death for supporting Zionism and communism and fined him one million dinars. The trial itself was somewhat of a mockery; 'Adas's three lawyers resigned halfway through because the judges allowed only witnesses from the prosecution to appear. Government ministers and district governors protested how the trial was conducted as well. 'Adas's family hoped until the last minute that his sentence would be commuted, because they believed the charges against him were unfounded and that his business connections and his prominent position in the community could somehow save him. Yet it was all to no avail.[19] On September 23 'Adas was executed publicly at the entrance to his home. The British Consul in Basra provided the following account:

> The graph of anti-Semitism continued to rise sharply until everything seemed to crystallise in the farcical trial of Chafiq Ades, against whose person the whole hatred of Arabs for the Palestine Zionists seem to burst. His execution on the 23rd September 1948 was really an anti-climax. He met his death bravely. . . . When offered the usual privilege of a final speech he merely turned to the President of the Court Martial, who stood at the steps of the gallows, and said: "I have no speech to make, but I hold you . . . personally responsible for my unjust execution, and within one hour I shall accuse you before God.[20]

Ezra Haddad points to this as the event that changed the mentality of Iraqi Jews. "Many believed that from now on the rift opened between Jews and their Arab neighbors would get deeper and deeper."[21] Even more troubling was that the execution was turned into a spectacle meant to celebrate the killing of a Zionist traitor by the state; individuals were invited to watch it and see the body, and in the day after the execution photos of the hanged man were scattered near the shops at the commercial center of al-'Ashshar.[22] 'Ozer Benjamin, a Basran Jew, described the atmosphere in his city during the day of the hanging: "A big demonstration of an incited riffraff passed by our home in the neighborhood of al-'Ashshar. . . . They carried a dead dog hanged on a stick saying, 'This is the lot of the Zionist 'Adas. During the demonstration, the participants started throwing stones at our house.'"[23] The wife of their neighbor, a Shi'i cleric, a highly respected man in the city, went out, shouted at the demonstrators, and managed to scare them away. 'Ozer's wife, Marcel, was a tailor, and one of her costumers called her husband, a policeman, to come to the aid of the Jewish neighbors, which he did. 'Ozer's account sets forth the forces in Iraqi society that impacted Jewish life: the state, responsible for the sense of terror the Jews felt because of the hanging of 'Adas, and the neighborly friendships and business connections in Basra, which helped Jews cope. Nonetheless, the general sentiment was that if a man as well connected and powerful as 'Adas could be eliminated by the state, other Jews would not be protected any longer.

The targeting of high-profile Jews by the state did not let up following the execution. In January 1949 lawyer Reuben Battat, a former member of parliament and an author of a book on Iraqi constitutionalism, was sentenced to three years in jail for conducting business on behalf of one of his clients with the Jewish National Fund. The fact that these dealings had occurred in the 1920s, when Zionism was still legal in Iraq, was ignored by the court. Ironically, an influential man, who was identified with one of the pillars of Iraqi democracy, the constitution, was now charged with treason.[24]

Things improved when Nuri Sa'id resigned in December 1949, and Tawfiq al-Suwaydi was appointed prime minister on February 1950 and Salih Jabr his minister of the interior. Suwaydi had had business dealings with the leader of the Jewish community, Hesqel Shemtov, while Jabr lived in a neighborhood with Jews and befriended Jewish politicians such as Abraham Haim and Moshe Shohet.[25] Following Sa'id's resignation, martial law was lifted. With travel restrictions relaxed, Jews began immigrating (illegally, for the most part) to Israel. In the second half of 1949, 1,243 Iraqi Jews passed through Iran on their way to Israel, and between December 1949 and March 1950, 4,500 more left Iraq. The emigrants managed to take their property with them, at a cost to the country of some four hundred thousand pounds. America, at the request of Israel, pressured Iraq and Iran not to jail those caught smuggling at the border or send them back to Iraq. Iraq, for its part, was not interested in using force to stem the tide of illegal emigration.[26]

In an attempt to control the exit of Iraqi Jews, Suwaydi and Jabr passed a law in March 1950, to be effective for a year, giving the Jews the option to register for emigration provided that they would renounce their Iraqi citizenship.[27] This denationalization law was passed after negotiations between the Zionist emissaries and Suwaydi.[28] The law was framed as a liberal act, since the government hoped to allow Jews to leave Iraq legally. The government also hoped to be rid of radical Jews, especially communists and Zionists, as well as the poorer classes of Jewish society. The state estimated that only about ten thousand would actually choose to leave via Iran.[29] The law was attacked by nationalist parliament members and ministers, by the nationalist press, and by prominent Palestinians.[30] The Zionist movement, for its part, welcomed the law. In April 1950, on the last day of Passover, it printed an Arabic leaflet entitled "O Zion in Babylon Escape!" It called on Jews to follow the visions of their prophets and leave Babylon, and for the second time in 2,488 years to expedite the redemption of the Jewish people.[31] After a period of relaxation that following the winter of 1949, Iraqi Jews encountered again difficulties in conducting business, finding employment with the state, and in being accepted in schools in the period between March 1950 and March 1951.

The government, which expected that a small number of Jews would emigrate, was surprised when 47,000 Iraqi Jews had registered to leave by May; by September 70,000 had registered; and the final tally was 104,000 Jews.[32] As the government had hoped, some of these were poor Iraqi Jews. Jonah Cohen, who observed the masses who came to register in the synagogues, depicted them as people who "dwarfed themselves as they walked alone the narrow alleys," people whose daughters could not marry due to the poverty of their families and who hoped that in Israel their fate would be different.[33] The potential emigrants, however, also included Jews from the upper and middle classes. The large number of potential emigrants suggests that these Jews had lost all hope of attaining equal rights in Iraq, a country they once considered a homeland. Zionist emissary Shelomo Hillel provides a list of motivations for this departure: messianism, fear of the state because of the persecution, and an element of public psychosis. While the messianic tendencies among Iraqi Jews are questionable at best (as most accounts from the period accentuate the secular nature of the Iraqi middle classes), the idea of public psychosis seems plausible. When Jews saw their relatives (even their own children), as well as their friends, neighbors, rabbis, and butchers, leaving Iraq, the fear of isolation drove them to emigrate too.[34]

In September 1950, Nuri Sa'id replaced Tawfiq al-Suwaydi as prime minister, and immediately took steps so that Jews would leave Iraq as rapidly as possible. Ben Gurion wrote that Nuri demanded that Israel take in ten thousand Iraqi Jews a month. In January 1951 Sa'id agreed to let Jews fly out of Baghdad.[35] On March 10, the government passed a law freezing the assets of all Jews who emigrated. The law was rushed through parliament on the grounds that Jews were smuggling their wealth outside the country. This law impoverished the Iraqi Jewish community. Some estimate the value of the property frozen to have been 150–200 million U.S. dollars.[36] By the end of the mass migration to Israel, Iraq had lost 130,000 of its Jews. One of the largest Jewish communities in the Arab world had been destroyed.

Accounts from Basra for the years 1949–51 testify to the processes which instigated this mass migration, as the Jewish community of that city in particular experienced many hardships. In 1949, the British Consul in Basra reported that Jews were being blamed for being either Zionists or communists. He did note that several had been caught trying to leave the country via Fau, but added that they were probably looking for a safer place to live.[37] In February 1950, the consul argued that whoever claimed that there was no discrimination against Jews in Basra was speaking "pure nonsense." Jews, he wrote, were being driven out of every department of the municipal government and swept out of the Port Administration; Jewish merchants were refused import licenses and their goods were subject to delays in Iraqi ports. Later that year he reported that the number of Jews in schools was declining, that Jewish doctors could not renew their licenses, and that merchants were forbidden to sell to non-Jews.[38] In October 1950 the Basran teachers' union and the right-wing press attacked a Jewish woman teacher who was appointed to a senior post; as a result she was transferred to 'Amara a week later. In late 1950 four Jewish schools in the south were shut down.³⁹ As of late 1952, the consul reported that the Jewish employees of the State Railways who chose not to leave Iraq had found that their hopes of being left alone as useful citizens were baseless. All but one of the twenty-one employees were placed on temporarily dismissal, which meant that their cases would not go before any board and that they would lose all pension rights. Many of them were near retirement age, and consequently their prospects for work and an acceptable standard of living in Iraq were minimal.⁴⁰ This situation led to increasing illegal emigration by Jews in 1949–50.⁴¹ In April 1950, however, the consul reported that Jews did not want to register to leave, as they hoped for better times.⁴² At the end of that month, eighteen hundred out of the ninety-seven hundred Jews in Basra had registered to emigrate, as well as three hundred from 'Amara.⁴³ The numbers of Basran Jews wishing to migrate seems to have fluctuated throughout the year, partly because of government restrictions and partly because of Jewish hesitation.⁴⁴

As I have noted before, Iraqi anti-Jewish policy was not unrelenting; it happened mostly during the summer of 1948, October–November 1949, and, to a much lesser degree, the period after March 1950. It is understandable that Iraq, as an Arab country that was at war with Israel, wanted to minimize the influence of a pro-Israeli organization, the Zionist movement, among the Jewish population. However, the indiscriminate nature of these measures drove the majority of Iraqi Jews, who were neither Zionist nor communist, to leave the country. The potential repercussions of these anti-Jewish actions, in particular the harm to the Iraqi economy that would be caused by the departure of Iraqi Jews, were known at the time.⁴⁵ Furthermore, the arrival of immigrants in Israel made solving the Palestinian refugee problem much more difficult. What, then, motivated the Iraqi state to undertake such a policy, knowing it might lead to mass emigration that would eventually strengthen Israel?

Right-wing activity in the public sphere was certainly a factor. In May–September 1948, the state was greatly concerned that nationalist propaganda in addition to the pro-Palestinian sentiments of the Iraqi people would lead to anti-Jewish riots. Anxious to avoid another Farhud, the state actually implemented increased security measures in Jewish neighborhoods in Baghdad.⁴⁶ In Mosul, the army and the police set up a cordon around the Jewish neighborhood.[47] Ezra Haddad has argued that the police knew things would not be as they had been in June 1941; Jews had armed themselves and the Zionists were ready to defend the Jewish neighborhoods.[48] The communist were also willing to defend the Jews.[49] Therefore, the possibility of clashes in the Jewish neighborhoods between Zionists and communists, on the one hand, and right-wing protesters, on the other, seemed immediate and alarming. The Iraqi authorities might have wanted to make clear that the state alone would "take care" of its Jewish problem and crush Zionism within Iraq, fears that led to the punishment of the community as a whole. The fact that the nationalist al-Istiqlal party was a part of some Iraqi government coalitions in the years 1948–51 further intensified the anti-Jewish stance.

The nationalist press was particularly vociferous. Two prominent nationalist newspapers, *Al-Nahda*, and al-Istiqlal's mouthpiece, *Al-Yaqdha*, played a dominant role in the spreading of anti-Jewish propaganda. To get a sense of the ways in which nationalist rhetoric destroyed the possibility of an Arab Jewish identity let us turn to articles published in *Al-Yaqdha* after the denationalization law went into effect.[50] By this time many Jews had lost their positions in state ministries, as the right-wing nationalists had demanded. Moreover, Jews were now leaving Iraq in large numbers, for which the nationalist press had been clamoring since 1949 (since it perceived all Jews as pro-Zionist). *Al-Yaqdha*—especially its editor, Salman al-Safwani—was not satisfied, however, and remained relentless in its attacks against Iraqi Jews. The attacks took the form of editorials, letters to the editor, and a gossip and news column located on page 2 of the newspaper, which included short, anonymously published items about crimes, misdemeanors, and rumors. In these sections, *Al-Yaqdha* frequently printed the names of Iraqi Jews whom it deemed as involved in some sort of Zionist activity. Ordinary men and women—teachers, clerks, and administrators—who probably never imagined that they would be mentioned in a newspaper were all of a sudden shamed in public for their alleged Zionist crimes. Since most of the news items had no author attached to them, it was very difficult to press charges against the paper for libel or slender, especially in a context in which the Jewish community was accused of being unpatriotic. The mention of crimes by Jews (who often had Jewish-sounding names such as Moshe, Hesqel, Ezra) in the newspapers nearly every day created a sense that the Jewish population in Iraq presented a grave and immediate danger.

The basic working assumption in *Al-Yaqdha* was that all Iraqi Jews were Zionists and thus should not be treated as equal citizens. At one point the paper even insinuated that Jews who renounced their citizenship should be treated as prisoners of war; their having done so meant that they were Zionists, with whom Iraq was at war.[51] This suggestion was also put forward by an al-Istiqlal member, Fa'iq al-Samara'i. The proclivity of Jews toward Zionism was interwoven into a general narrative underlining the Jewish propensity for criminality and wrongdoing. According to the paper, when granted permission to leave Iraq, Jews sold their lands at prices that were much higher than their market value.[52] Referring to the book of Exodus, *Al-Yaqdha* informed readers that the Jewish women who had left ancient Egypt wished to steal the property of other Egyptian women. Beware of the Jews as they are all thieves, *Al-Yaqdha* concluded.[53] A letter to the editor from a reader in Faluja complained about the wrongdoing by the company of one Menashe Mash'al. He then criticized the audacity of Jewish senate members, in particular Ezra Menahem Daniel, who called the Jews "persecuted", saying, "We are the ones who are persecuted, oh Ezra Menahem!" The resources of the state, he concluded, should be guarded, when dealing with people whom Iraqis considered to be citizens but who were actually following instructions from Tel Aviv.[54]

Al-Yaqdha's articles drove home the point that the Iraqi state had made a great mistake in allowing Jews to keep their citizenship rights. When four Iraqi students at the American University in Beirut were arrested for being communists, *Al-Yaqdha* reported that one of them was a Jew. The news item ended with the following question: "At whose expense has this student studied there?"[55] The paper alerted readers that Jews controlled the Iraqi economy, as exemplified by the fact that many markets and businesses were closed on Jewish holidays and on Saturdays.[56] A story that three banks in Baghdad had announced they would be closed on Yom Kippur was proof that Jews ran the Iraqi economy at the expense of Iraqi capitalists and entrepreneurs.[57] Moreover, Jews had no opportunity to refute *Al-Yaqdha*'s allegations. When a Jewish doctor published a letter in which he declared he was not going to renounce his citizenship, the paper's editors insisted he had already registered to immigrate to Israel.[58] Criticizing the Iraqi government, the paper positioned itself as the guardian of the interests of the Iraqi people. It assured its readers that Jews were secretly assisted by Arab governments in Lebanon, Sudan, and Jordan, where British and American influence was predominant.[59] *Al-Yaqdha*, however, would make sure that things were different in Iraq.

Al-Yaqdha's most vociferous campaign was against the employment of Jews in state ministries and public institutions. Salman al-Safwani's editorial, "Get the Jews out of government ministries," reported that Jews employed by the Iraqi State Railways had registered to leave for Tel Aviv (all Jews in *Al-Yaqdha*'s articles were bound for "Tel Aviv"), and the State Railways had turned to Pakistan looking for trained personnel to replace them. This was proof, Safwani argued, that the Jews held too many positions at the State Railways, as they did in the Port Authority. Safwani called to hire Iraqis in their stead. All nations realized, he continued, that Jews could not be trusted to be loyal citizens. The Europeans, for example, supported Zionism because they wanted to rid themselves of their Jews.[60] The paper also pointed to specific sectors in which the Jewish presence was problematic: there were too many Jewish doctors and pharmacists in state hospitals and in the Baghdad medical college,[61] while Jews were influential in the chamber of commerce and the Jewish intellectual and economist Mir Basri was irresponsibly placed in a position of financial importance.[62] The Ministry of Education came under the most scrutiny, because it permitted Jews to teach the ideals of Arabism and patriotism to Arab and Muslim students.[63] One story drew attention to the astonishing fact that two hundred Jewish teachers worked for the ministry, while two hundred Iraqis with academic degrees, including some who had studied abroad or graduated from the Teachers Training College, were unemployed. *Al-Yaqdha* proposed that the Ministry of Education fire the Jews and replace them with Iraqis, Palestinians, and Egyptians.[64]

The pro-Palestinian Iraqi position was translated into the argument that as Israel had had wronged the Palestinians, so should the Iraqi state treat its Jewish citizens.[65] *Al-Yaqdha* advocated the confiscation of Jewish property as the Israelis had confiscated Arab property in Palestine, and pointed out that the Jewish departure from Iraq via trains and airplanes was much more pleasant than what the Palestinians had experienced in being driven out of their villages.[66] Discussing the so-called high number of Jews in the Ministry of Education, *Al-Yaqdha* wrote: "Ask Tel Aviv if they have in their schools one Arab teacher? No! But in Iraqi schools there is a big number of *Hasaqila* (the plural name of Hesqel, a Jewish name)!"[67] The logic behind these stories was crystal clear: since the Palestinians had been exiled from their homeland, the Jews should be expelled from Iraq.[68] Shafiq Hasan al-Dik's piece, "To Every Palestinian Refugee," assured the Palestinians that "each and every one of you knows that Iraq expels the sons of Zion [*banu sahyun*] from its country." Al-Dik then called on the Jews to get out of Iraq and find a king or a people who would welcome them.[69]

Most newspapers in Iraq did not print such racist accusations against Iraqi Jews; they separated between Judaism and Zionism, and their editorials never called for the ethnic cleansing of Jews. Moreover, *Al-Yaqdha*'s articles did not make much sense from a Palestinian perspective. On the one hand, the paper assured readers that all that Iraqi Jews ever wanted was to immigrate to Israel. On the other hand, the very same paper called for the forced immigration of Jews to Israel, knowing that they might be settled where Palestinians used to live. This anti-Jewish campaign allowed *Al-Yaqdha* to appropriate a national cause (namely the battle for Palestine), and claim that a racist agenda served the interests of the Iraqi, Palestinian, and Arab peoples. For *Al-Yaqdha*, there was no point in promoting hybrid categories such as Arab Jews or Iraqi Jews, since Jews were separated—ethnically, religiously, and culturally—from the Arab Iraqi population. The opinions voiced in its articles alarmed many Jews. Furthermore, the Iraqi government censored communist and leftist newspapers, especially when the latter mocked government officials or were too critical of the state's pro-British or social policies. The fact that the state did not censor such articles in *Al-Yaqdha* indicated to Iraqi Jews that it supported the nationalists. Rabbi Khaduri, for example, complained bitterly that the government had failed to restrain attacks on Jews in the press.[70] The British noted with concern "some degree of fanaticism" in the public sphere when the paper printed a sermon by Shi'i cleric Muhammad Mahdi al-Khalisi calling on the people of Baghdad to close their businesses on Fridays, as ordered by the Muslim faith, and not on Saturdays, as the Jews did.[71]

Another explanation of the state's position toward its Jewish subjects had to do with the Wathba and the fear of communism in Iraq. The significant level of Iraqi Jewish participation in the Wathba did not go unnoticed by the government. In August 1949, Nuri Sa'id met with a Jewish delegation and showed them photos of Jews demonstrating in the Wathba and attending public funerals of its victims. In his view, Iraqi Jews, given their opposition to the government, did not deserve the protection of the state.[72] In his memoirs, Tawfiq al-Suwaydi elaborates on the narrative that connected Zionism, communism, and the Wathba: "The communists . . . pushed the masses, using various means, to protest against the [Portsmouth] treaty, being aided by the Zionists, who feared the treaty because they knew that it encompassed a significant victory to the Arab problem in Palestine over the interests and hopes of Zionism."[73] Suwaydi never explained how the Portsmouth Treaty, meant to solidify British hegemony in Iraq, was to help the Palestinian people, but he did point to a link between the Zionists and communists. This association was often evoked by the state, as Jews were arrested for being *both* Zionists and communists. This also helped the state discredit communism. Minister Sadiq al-Bassam explained that Zionism and communism were twins, and therefore the governments of Iraq and other Arab nations should combat both: "Communism is Zionism and Zionism is Communism. . . . If the Palestinian problem develops, and Jews are successful in forming an internationally recognized entity, we, and other Arab governments, must produce a firm policy of cleansing [*tathir*] our countries from elements which form a fifth column."[74] The linkage between the conflict in Palestine and Iraqi Jews was not new, yet the evocation of communism in this context, even for propaganda purposes, meant that the Jews were now affiliated with not one, but two, subversive movements. This linkage also served the aims of the state which, in the attempt to crush the leftist movement following the Wathba, used all the means at its disposal. In this context, it is worthwhile to mention that pro-government newspapers depicted Israel as a communist heaven, populated by communist Jews and posing a threat to the entire region.[75] As late as 1953, Iraqi Prime Minister Arshad al-'Umari equated Zionism with communism, arguing that Israel was a foothold through which the USSR would gain dominance in the Arab world.[76]

The third factor that led to the emigration of Iraqi Jews in the years 1950–51 was the idea of population exchange and transfer, which came to the fore in the Iraqi public sphere and in diplomatic circles at this time. Israelis, Iraqis, and members of the international community treated Iraqi Jews and the Palestinians as pawns in a possible solution for the Arab-Israeli conflict, without any regard as to what the Iraqi Jews and the Palestinians might have wanted. In January 1949, in a conversation with British Ambassador Mack, Nuri Sa'id raised the possibility of expelling Iraqi Jews, saying that if the Palestinians were not allowed to return to their homes and were not compensated, he would send 150,000 Iraqi Jews to Palestine. The British, however, tried to convince him that such a move would give Israel an excuse not to compensate Arab refugees for the loss of their property.[77] In February 1949, the British ambassador to Israel warned Iraqi officials that the Israelis would welcome this move because it would allow them to obtain people prepared to work hard for low wages, and, significantly, to insist that Iraq take displaced Arabs in return.[78] The British ambassador in Iraq further argued that Iraq would suffer economically and politically if Jews were expelled, and that Israel would not benefit from Iraqi Jews who were mostly townsmen who had done clerical work. He also did not believe that Israel had the means to impose the absorption of Palestinian refugees on Iraq.[79] The ambassador seemed convinced that Sa'id had no intention of proceeding with this measure immediately, and that he regarded this as a step of retaliation, if the Israelis were unreasonable concerning Arab refugees. "I shall do my best to dissuade him from any action alone these lines," he pledged, yet he also predicted "some measure against the Jews here, if Israelis do not agree to a satisfactory solution of the refugee problem."[80]

The possibility of the transfer of Iraqi Jews in the context of solving the Palestinian problem was raised later that year.[81] In July Sa'id made a similar proposition and was again convinced by the British not to follow through. The British ambassadors in Israel, Jordan, and Iraq objected to this policy but noted it had one advantage, namely, that it would create official relations between Israel and the Arab countries and therefore lead to regional stability.[82] The Americans also reported that extreme nationalists had from time to time put forward the idea that Iraq should force all of its Jews to leave. However, they felt that any Iraqi government in the future would be reluctant to do so. They also noted that the departure of Jews would cause severe economic problems since 75 percent of Iraqi trade was in Jewish hands.[83]

These proposals of Nuri Sa'id, despite the fact that Sa'id had never acted upon such threats, indicated a clear break with his previous policies. In the past, Sa'id had been committed to the welfare of Iraqi Jews whom he respected. Kaylani and his supporters were also Sa'id's political opponents, and consequently he was quick to punish them for their hand in the Farhud. In 1949, Sa'id was discredited by many Pan-Arab politicians as one of the region's most pro-British leaders. An achievement connected with the resolution of the Palestinian refugee problem could have strengthened his position as an important regional figure, and consequently he was willing to consider the fate of Iraqi Jewry within the arena of Middle Eastern diplomacy and the struggle for regional hegemony.[84]

The idea of population exchange, however, was not advanced by Sa'id alone. Zionists, Israelis, and foreign diplomats were discussing it concurrently. The revisionist Zionist writer Joseph Schechtman advocated exchanging a hundred thousand Iraqi Jews for two hundred thousand Palestinian refugees.[85] Edwin Samuel, the son of the first British high commissioner to Palestine, Herbert Samuel, published an article in the *Middle East Journal* in 1949, suggesting a population exchange between Jews and Arabs.[86] His views were known in Iraq: when Muzahim al-Pachcaci objected to the denationalization law, he argued that even the Zionist Edwin Samuel had said that Arab refugees should be taken into consideration when the Jews left Iraq, and thus he did not understand why the law did not include the Palestinians.[87] The Iraqi press showed great interest in population exchange as well. *Al-Sha'b*, *Al-Zaman*, and *Al-Hawadith* reported on Sa'id's opinions, although their editorials expressed the opinion that Iraqi Jews should stay in Iraq and that Palestinian refugees should be allowed to return to Arab Palestine.[88] Regardless of the feasibility of exchange, however, the debate in the press indicated to Iraqi Jews that emigration was a possibility, and that their lives and their property were now connected to the future of the Palestinian refugees.

There is an old Yiddish expression, "schwer zu zein ein yid" (It is difficult to be a Jew). In the years 1948–51 it was indeed very difficult to be a Jew in Iraq (although it was also very difficult to be a communist, Kurdish nationalist, Shi'i tribesman, or feminist). Some of the anti-Jewish measures taken by the state were driven by an anti-Zionist logic: the Iraqi authorities denied passports to Jews because they feared Jews would emigrate. They attempted to prevent Jews from sending letters to Israel, fearing Zionist espionage. But while these measures may have ostensibly targeted a specific group of Zionists, the hysteria that accompanied them and their generalizing nature caused them to become collective acts of sectarian and religious discrimination. The Jews who were dismissed from their positions and were attacked in the right-wing press were middle-class merchants and clerks who had very little to do with the Zionist movement. Yet the state's actions conveyed the general sentiment that a Jew in Iraq was a Zionist and hence a second-class citizen.

From the perspective of the Iraqi state, these measures backfired and were ultimately harmful to Iraq's national interests. They pushed some of the Jewish youth toward Zionism and convinced Iraqi Jews that emigration was a possible solution for their problems. Israel also benefited. As Esther Meir has shown convincingly, the Israeli media campaign on behalf of Iraqi Jews was intended, in part, to increase financial contributions to Israel from around the world and demonize the Iraqi state in the Israeli mentality.[89] Initially, Israeli representatives did not work directly on behalf of Iraqi Jews, but preferred to use international Jewish organizations, especially those based in England and America, as channels. In October 1949, when word of the arrests of Zionist activists reached Israel, the Israeli Foreign Office was ordered by Prime Minister David Ben Gurion to turn global opinion against the persecution of the Jews in Iraq. Shortly thereafter, articles protesting this mistreatment were published in France, America, and England, and Zionists held demonstrations in those countries and in Iran, at the American Embassy in Teheran.[90] Israel also threatened to raise the issue at the United Nations; British diplomats, however, saw this as a way for Israel to protect itself during discussion of the Palestinian refugee question in the UN and to raise money in the United States.[91] Moreover, as brilliantly shown by Yehuda Shenhav, Israel itself had openly linked the question of Iraqi Jewry, their status and their property, to the question of the Palestinian refugees.[92] Back in July 1948, Moshe Sharet had mentioned that the issues of the Palestinian refugees and the future of the Arabs in Israel were to be resolved in tandem with the issue of the Jewish communities in Arab countries. Knesset member Eliyahu ben Elisar suggested (in a Knesset meeting which discussed the lot of Iraqi Jews in March 1949) a "Jewish transfer," which would include the resettlement of Arab refugees outside of Palestine and the immigration of persecuted Middle Eastern Jews to Israel. His proposal was rejected, but it set in motion a dangerous trend.[93] Ironically, Israel and right-wing Iraqi nationalists seemed to have been speaking in the same voice.

Becoming an Exile

The Iraqi state's desire to root out Zionism, as we have seen, led to the antidemocratic campaign of 1948–49. But how much support did the Zionist movement really have in Iraq? Was it able to shape the mindset of an entire population, as the Iraqi right argued? Did the movement endanger the nation, as state authorities suspected?

Zionism was a minor movement in Iraq until the early 1940s. From the perspective of the Zionist organizations, the lack of interest in Zionism shown by Iraqi Jews and British limitations on Jewish immigration to Palestine made European Jewry preferable as immigrants.[94] Iraqi Jewish leaders were indeed unenthusiastic about the effects of Zionism on their lives. Senator Ezra Menahem Daniel had expressed the opinion as early as September 1922 that Zionism might occasion friction between Jews and Muslims. Iraqi Jews who migrated to Mandatory Palestine in the years 1919–20, moreover, experienced many difficulties. Nonetheless, during the 1920s Zionist activities were permitted in Iraq. Jews contributed to the Jewish National Fund, and newspapers such as *Al-Misbah* reported on events related to the Yishuv, such as the opening of the Hebrew University in Jerusalem. In July 1921, an Iraqi Zionist group, the Hebrew Literary Society, was established; a year later the Zionist Foundation of Aram Naharyarim (Ha-Aguda ha-zionit le-Aram Naharyim) was organized. In 1924 attempts to teach Hebrew in Jewish schools by Zionist teacher Moshe Sofer were successful, although in 1929 some Hebrew teachers were expelled from Iraq. In 1929, a small group of students at Shammash, with the encouragement of their Hebrew teachers, founded a society to promote the study of Hebrew and to collect money for the Jewish National Fund. Ten of its members came to Palestine in 1934 and settled in the Sharon district.[95]

Most Zionist activity in Iraq came to a halt in 1932, with the announcement of the official independence of the Iraqi state and the banning of Zionism.[96] This remained the case until the Farhud, in response to which young Jews began collecting weapons and forming self-defense societies. Most of these groups came into being spontaneously. In Hilla some young Jews formed the Movement for Jewish Resistance (Harakat al-muqawama al-yahudiyya), and similar groups were formed in Baghdad and Basra.[97] In 1942–43, Zionist emissaries Shemaryahu Gutman, Ezra Kedourie, and Enzo Sereni were sent to Baghdad from Palestine and were able to establish cells. The first two were established in Basra and Kirkuk. Zionist activities were divided between the "Movement" (Ha-Tenu'a; or Tenu'at ha-Halutz, the "Pioneer Movement"), which focused more on emigration and Hebrew education, and the creation of an armed organization (Ha-Shura or Ha-Hagana) for self-defense. In 1943 the first Zionist conference took place: a council was set up, and the Zionist movement was named "a socialist pioneering movement."[98]

Zionist emissaries initially encountered a great deal of resistance from local Jews. Enzo Sereni reported in 1942 that the latter did have a favorable impression of the Land of Israel, but that anti-Zionist pamphlets were also a source of information for them. He went on to comment that the merchants in Iraq were uninterested in agricultural work, and that the more rural Kurdish Jews were more suitable immigrants to Mandatory Palestine.[99] The complaints about the unwillingness of Iraqi Jews to emigrate were typical. Shemaryahu Gutman felt that the Farhud had forced Jews to consider leaving Iraq, yet they were unwilling to go to a place where they would be forced to change their lifestyle. Moreover, many of those who made the Aliya came back, because there was no prosperity to be had in Palestine.[100]

By 1944 the movement had become more organized and hierarchical. Iraq was divided into districts, and in each a number of cells were established. The cells were headed by guides who lectured the youth about socialism and the Land of Israel and provided them with publications in Hebrew. Meetings were often held in the houses of cell members. A subbranch called Young Pioneer (Ha-Halutz ha-tza'ir) was established for members under the age of eighteen. By Passover 1944 there were 550 members and

30 guides. Zionism also spread rapidly in the north, where many of the Hebrew teachers in Jewish schools were Zionists. The much smaller self-defense organization became more formidable in 1946, due to the arrival of arms from Palestine and the purchase of weapons from local dealers, especially in the south. Its members learned how to use hand grenades and guns and prepare Molotov cocktails. By 1945, according to one account, the Zionist movement consisted of about seven hundred members in Baghdad and central Iraq, and two hundred in the south. According to some estimates, in 1948–49, membership in the movement rose to two thousand, being primarily young people.[101]

While Zionism gained adherents in Iraq, Zionist and Israeli politicians were not always enthusiastic about the immigration of Iraqi Jews, as Dafna Simhoni has shown convincingly. Undoubtedly, there was a desire to help the community, especially after the Farhud, as well as the acute realization that Middle Eastern Jewry had become an important pool of immigrants after the Holocaust. Nonetheless, Israeli officials saw the Holocaust refugees and Jews living behind the Iron Curtain, particularly in Romania, Hungary, and Poland (where forty thousand Jews signed up for emigration in 1950) as more desirable candidates for immigration. They felt that negotiations about the future of Iraqi Jews were hopeless until the question of Arab refugees was solved; they faced severe financial pressures because of the increasing number of immigrants to Israel; they feared that the balance of power between the Ashkenazi majority and the Sephardi minority would crumble; and they were worried about the number of communist sympathizers among Iraqi Jewry. There were always tensions within the Zionist leadership as to how many Iraqi Jews should be brought to Israel, and similarly there were tensions between the local Zionist leadership in Iraq, which pushed for mass emigration, and the Israeli state, which wanted to control the flow of Iraqi Jews to Israel.[102]

With the outbreak of the war in Palestine, Iraq authorities became concerned about the weapons in Iraqi Jewish hands, and initiated an anti-Zionist campaign that reached its peak in October 1949, when the Jewish underground was discovered by the police. The campaign involved drastic measures, such as the issuing of death sentences and long prison sentences. By late October, a hundred Jews had been sent to Abu Ghraib and seven hundred brought in for questioning. Nonetheless, the authorities were not always successful in catching actual Zionists. They were able to dismantle the structure of the movement, but many of the Zionist guides, for example, managed to escape arrest.[103] The state, in other words, was able to curtail the movement's activities, but many of the Jews taken into custody were not affiliated with Zionism.

The attitude of the more established members of the Jewish community, like Ezra Menahem Daniel and Yusuf al-Kabir, toward Zionism remained negative. Since Zionism had been outlawed, they believed that the institutions of the community must keep a safe distance from Zionist activity.[104] When the Zionists were arrested in October, they were told by one of the leaders of the community that the Zionists in Iraq had not consulted the Jewish leadership when setting up cells and buying weapons, and therefore there was no need to ask for Jewish protection after they had been arrested. They better surrender themselves to the police.[105] In their accounts of the period, young Zionist activists mention that their parents did not approve of their political engagement. When Emile Murad's parents discovered that he and his brother were Zionists, their mother burst into tears. Their father (who later became a Zionist himself) told his sons to forsake the Zionist cause: "You come to me to tell me that you decided to leave home, despite all the dangers that await you. Leave to where, children, to what place? To a road with no end?"[106] Young female Zionist activists encountered even more challenges because their parents were upset that they spent many hours outside of the home.[107]

One consequence of the wave of arrests in October was a change in the community's leadership. That same month 150 to 300 Jews demonstrated in front of the house of Rabbi Khaduri, asking him to secure the release of Jewish political prisoners. The demonstration was organized by the Zionist movement, and according to one account included only female protesters, who entered the rabbi's chambers, broke furniture, and dragged him into the street. An employee in the rabbi's chambers called the police, and forty Jews (including some bystanders) were arrested. Fifteen of them, including two women, were tried for their involvement in the affair. The events were reported by *Al-Sha'b, Al-Umma, Al-Hawadith, Al-'Alam al-'Arabi, Sawt al-Ahali, Al-Zaman, Al-Hatif, Al-'Ahd,* and *Al-Yaqdha*—which claimed the incident proved the Jews of Iraq did indeed support Zionism.[108] On October 25 the community declared a day of solidarity with those arrested. This was followed by a boycott on kosher meat. Both moves were organized by the Zionists. Taxes on meat were used to cover some of the expenses of the Jewish community, and the boycott's organizers threatened that they would continue the strike until a new leader to the community was appointed. These events led to the resignation of Rabbi Khaduri and the appointment of the Zionist Hesqel Shemtov in November as the new leader. Shemtov had had business dealings with Naji al-Suwaydi, and was personally acquainted with Salih Jabr.[109] The Zionist underground used these connections to speak directly to the Iraqi government. In 1950, for example, it sent messages via Shemtov to the Iraqi leadership threatening to flood the trains to the north and the south with Jews headed to the border if the Iraqi government did not issue permits allowing Jews to emigrate.[110] Clearly, the emissaries from Israel and the local Zionist Iraqi leadership had grown bolder, to the point that they seriously weakened the anti-Zionist Jewish leadership that had been in place for some time.

It might seem surprising that the Zionist movement was as successful as it was, given the harsh security measures taken by the state. One of the contributing factors was the pervasive corruption in Iraq. The availability of weapons, the ease with which police officers and government officials could be bribed, and the relatively easy access across the borders, created a fertile ground for Zionist activities. The most acute problem, from the authorities' perspective, was the smuggling of people out of Iraq, as smugglers of cigarettes and other goods began to transport Jews to Iran and Jordan. Iraqi officials were especially worried from the flow of emigrants to Basra, and had trains to Basra from Baghdad watched. In February 1950, the Basra train station was closed to Jews; any Jews who arrived by train from Baghdad were sent back. In 1949, the number of illegal emigrants increased considerably. Although Zionist activists were coordinating the migration of Jews with the smugglers, some managed to leave Iraq without being under the supervision of the Zionists, who threatened Jews remaining in Iraq that anyone else who did so could expect no help from the Zionists in Iran.[111]

On April 8, 1950, and January 14, March 14, May 10, and June 5–6, 1951, bombings (typically involving hand grenades) occurred at Jewish centers in

Baghdad. In an attack on the Mas'uda Shemtove Synagogue on January 14 five people were killed.[112] The nationalist press suggested that individuals in the Jewish community were responsible, as they hoped to draw attention to the plight of Iraqi Jews, but a rumor also circulated in the bazaars that an Iraqi army officer has been arrested.[113] The British complained that it was difficult to discover the facts behind the affair because the Iraqi police were unwilling to divulge what information they had.[114] In the summer of 1951, the Iraqi police claimed to have discovered a Zionist spy ring and arrested eighty of its members.[115] The police suggested that Zionists were behind the attacks, which were intended to remind the Israeli authorities of the situation in Iraq and spur rich Jews to leave. These arguments made sense since the denationalization law was about to expire (in March 1951), and Jews who did not declare their intention to leave had no choice but to remain in Iraq. The arrests of the Zionist underground members caused the nationalist press to call for the expulsion of the remaining Iraqi Jews as the underground threatened the security of the entire city of Baghdad.[116] Two Zionists, Salih Shalom and Yusuf Basri, were executed as a result; others were charged with collecting arms and forming secret terrorist groups, and sentenced to varying prison sentences.[117]

The debate as to who bombed the Jewish centers has persisted into the present. An Israeli investigation committee concluded that the Zionists could not have carried out the bombings, although many of the witnesses brought before the committee argued that they, or other members of the Jewish community, knew at the time that Jews were behind the bombings.[118] There was additional evidence: Zionist activists threatened Ezra Menahem Daniel that they would use violent means, if necessary, to bring about the mass emigration of Iraqi Jews.[119] It seems plausible that the Zionist underground in Iraq could have been responsible, as these acts of provocation could have had two purposes. First, the local Iraqi Zionists may have hoped that the Israeli government would increase the quotas of Iraqi Jewish immigrants, with the bombings serving to make clear to the Israeli authorities what lay in store for Iraqi Jews. Second, the Zionists may have sought to frighten Iraqi Jews into leaving for Israel, especially as the denationalization law was about to expire and the numbers of Jews signing up for migration was declining. On the other hand, Iraqi Zionists have steadfastly maintained they were not behind the attacks, and offered to go before Israeli courts and governmental investigation committees to prove their innocence. Elements within the Iraqi state also wanted to scare the Jews into emigrating, and there was no shortage of right-wing propaganda against them. Nuri Sa'id himself decided that once Jews had registered to emigrate, they should leave as soon as possible. The Iraqi economy was suffering due to the state of limbo created when Jewish merchants and traders, having registered for emigration, sold all their property and were uncertain as to when and how they would leave Iraq.[120] Again, there seems to be more circumstantial evidence that suggests Zionist involvement, but I do not think historians can provide a decisive answer at this point. These explosions in any case were just the final chapter in a longer process that had been initiated in 1948. If it were not for the antidemocratic campaigns of 1948–49, Israeli intervention in Iraqi politics, and the growing boldness of the Zionist leadership in Iraq, these explosions would not have been enough to trigger Jewish emigration. As we have seen, the Farhud, a much more violent episode, did not do so. However, at this point, after the loss of so many jobs and the abrupt change in the Jewish leadership in Baghdad, many Jews did not see any reason to stay.

Most of the young individuals who joined Zionist groups were products of an Arab educational system and were deeply immersed in Arab culture. What, then, made these young men and women answer the call of Zionist emissaries in the years 1943–46, while most of their peers, as well as their parents, sought to distance themselves from Zionism and other young Jews turned to communism? The answer to this question has to do with the disappointment young Iraqi Jews, like their Muslim and Christian peers, felt with their nation at the end of the Second World War. These young Iraqis (Muslim and Jewish alike) associated the previous generations with the unsolved ills of the Iraqi state: the miserable situation of the peasants and workers, the lack of democracy in the country, British interference in Iraqi affairs, and the lack of women's rights. They thus looked for radical alternatives that would respond to their critique of society. Some Iraqi youth found the answer in communism, others in radical Arabism, and a minority group of Iraqi Jews found it in Zionism. A few essays published by young Iraqi Zionists in the years 1943–46 shed some light on how Iraqi Zionists represented themselves. These accounts, moreover, give us a sense of how such young individuals modified European Zionist ideology to fit Iraqi realities.

Within the context of growing socioeconomic tensions in Iraq, Zionism promised socialism and with it socioeconomic justice and the liberation of women. Significantly, these could be realized only *outside* of Iraq, in the Land of Israel. Members wrote that Zionism would lead to a rebellion against the existing order and the prevailing societal norms. In the new Jewish socialist community Jews would become productive workers, and enjoy liberty, justice, and equality.[121] Female Zionist activists underlined the differences between the unfair realities of life in Iraq and the feminist message of Zionism: Esther Darwish and Evelyn Salton-Zilkha, for example, characterized the lives of Jewish women in Iraq as typified by middle-class shallowness and empty values. The Jewish Iraqi girl was forced to live an idle life, since she was ashamed to work for a living; her only occupation was to make herself beautiful so that her family could marry her off to a rich man. Only Zionism could save the Jewish girl and her people, give her full rights, and allow her to shape her own future.[122] Many of the young women who were attracted to Zionism were educated, and shared the same socioeconomic profile of the Muslim and Jewish women who called for suffrage and women's emancipation in Iraq. These women became guides and secretaries in Zionist cells and took pride in their achievements and independence.[123]

The social ills young Jews saw in Iraq in general, and in the Jewish community in particular, such as poverty, social conservatism, and the gap between rich and poor, became in their writings the markers of Jewish life in exile.[124] The European Zionist portrayal of the Jew in exile as weak, dependent on the graces of gentiles, and fearing for his life was thus transported to the Iraqi context. Gideon Golani explained:

> For generations the exilic Jew lived in the city, far from nature.... This is the source of the weakness of the Jew and his incapacity for hard work. The narrow long alleys [in the poor Jewish quarters], dark and crooked, had led the Jew to physical weakness, and internal fear. Our houses are built so that they are closed and sealed.... Sunrays do not arrive anywhere. Under such conditions Jewish children are raised ... the children of the Ghetto, the children of alleys. Thus the Jew grows with no connection to nature ... and without knowledge of country-life that provides health for the body and tranquility for the soul.[125]

Such activists believed that Jewish life in Iraq was doomed to fail, as the poor led miserable lives while the rich and the bourgeoisie were selfish and idle. In the words of Violet Ben Porat:

> I wandered in the streets of the city; I walked about in the alleys of the ghetto. The willingness to know my people drove me to do this. I went to the markets and to the dark and narrow alleys of poverty, and my heart was filled with sadness and excitement. There [one sees] dirty children, children of poverty, and pale women carrying their thin children. The houses are crowded, and sunrays do enter inside. . . . The people's hearts are empty, aimless. On one side of the streets there are synagogues. Religious people are occupied with learning, and sometimes you hear a sigh from a heart full of misery and suffering: when will the Messiah come, when will salvation come? . . .
>
> I left the ghetto and moved to the streets of the rich. . . . The houses are clean and neat, but the people become assimilated and distance themselves from their Judaism. . . . They deny [what is in] their own hearts and their ears are deaf to the call for help and assistance. All they worry about is the [money in their] pockets, their fine dresses and delicious food. . . . The rich have already forgotten the events of the past. They know well that the gentiles hate them, but they never think about their fate in the future. . . . These Jews do not aspire light and freedom, they do not want to end our exile, and they even fail those who wish to be saved.[126]

Berta Sofer likewise wrote that before her Zionist brethren came to rescue Iraqi Jewry, she thought there was no hope for world Jewry because she imagined that all Jews were like Baghdadi Jews, "egotistical and weak." Moreover, before the arrival of the Zionists, Iraqi Jews had accepted the history of a foreign people as their own. Now, however, they learned about Jewish history and about the Land of Israel, the land God ordered them to conquer.[127]

These descriptions introduce a new vocabulary that had originated in the writings of European Zionists. First, the poor Jewish neighborhoods are signified by the word *ghetto*, a concept that was used to depict European Jewish life, and a word that in 1944–45 conveyed important ideological meanings. Second, the depictions of Jewish life in Iraq were associated with darkness, especially the dark alleys where children are raised in ignorance and poverty. Darkness, however, is also symptomatic of the lives of rich Baghdadi Jews, who were submerged in a superficial and sterile existence. Interestingly, the solutions offered—physical exercise and closeness to nature—had been advocated by Iraqi Arab nationalists during the 1930s as part of the Iraqi national project. In the minds of these young Zionists, however, a return to nature and liberation were possible only in the Land of Israel.

Life in Iraq was portrayed as a temporary experience. For this reason, names of particular branches of the Zionist movement were borrowed from important Zionist sites. Baghdad was renamed Tel Aviv; Basra, Haifa; Mosul, Tiberia; Kut was called Kineret after a famous Jewish settlement by the Sea of Galilee; Khanakin bore the name of a famous kibbutz, Hanita; and Halabja (for some reason) was renamed Tel-Hai, one of Zionism's most hallowed sites. Moreover, every person in the movement was given a Hebrew name, and Jewish holidays, such as Passover, which were normally observed in the households of Jewish families, were now celebrated with other Zionists. The transfer of the celebration of holidays from the private domain of the home to the space of the collective indicated to young Zionists that the Jewish nation was now their extended family and that the Judaism they knew would be modified by Zionist ideology.[128]

Another important theme in the writings of these young activists was the linking of Iraqi Jewish history to European Jewish history and, moreover, the universalization of Jewish history. Viewed according to this framework, the Farhud in particular had shown that Jews and Iraqi Muslims, just like Jews and gentiles in Europe, could not live side by side. The Yizkor (collective prayers in memory of members of the community who had perished) for the victims of Farhud conveys this idea most lucidly:

> May the people of Israel in this exile remember those bitter days, days of pillage and murder, rape and disgrace. . . . We shall remember that in these days we were surrendered to the hands of a blood-thirsty mob and greedy policemen, and even the mighty army stood by and watched. . . . We shall remember, the only ray of light, the few Jews who defended themselves, with all that they had, saving their honor and their lives. Let us remember and know: our exile is like the exile in Yemen, and the one in Yemen is like the one in Germany: our lot is the same in the world.[129]

The passivity emblematic of the exilic Iraqi Jew was thus fully articulated in the Farhud. The Yizkor ignored the Muslims who helped Jews in the Farhud, and emphasized self-defense instead. Most significantly, the Farhud was understood as the ultimate proof that the destiny of Jews all over the world was the same. The implication, therefore, was that what had befallen European Jews could befall Iraqi Jews, and therefore that Iraqi Jews should emigrate from Iraq. This was not just the lesson of the Holocaust; this was the lesson of the entire history of Jews in exile. Shelomo Shina observed that before the destruction of the Jewish people in Europe, Jews had been butchered in Spain and in Russia, yet they tended to forget this shared heritage. The conclusion with regard to Iraq was clear: Jewish economic success and tranquility were a mere illusion. The Farhud, writes Shelomo, "is just the beginning."[130] 'Aliza Qattan invoked the same logic: "Let us learn from . . . the disaster of our brethren in Europe. . . . May our brothers who defended themselves in the Ghettos [in Europe] be our guides."[131]

The 1948 war and the anti-Zionist campaigns in 1948–49 turned the Iraqi-Zionist discourse more militant. In 1949 a book was published in Iraq explaining the meaning of a new holiday, Israel's Independence Day, and describing how Iraqi Jews had celebrated it in May 1949. The movement published a call (in Arabic) for Iraqi Jewry to observe the holiday by wearing special clothes and having family dinners during which candles were to be lit and the wine was to be blessed. The book featured descriptions of tearful women in the "ghetto" who prayed "for the next year in Israel." The fact that secular Zionists felt bold enough to amend Jewish religion and offer special prayers that they had composed for fellow Jews underscores their self-confidence and the new hybridization between Jewish religion and Jewish nationalism within the Iraqi milieu.[132]

Stories in the book explicated the significance of the holiday. One essay suggested that once the Jewish state overcame the seven wolves (i.e., the seven Arab countries that fought against Israel), Jews in Iraq could take pride in the defeat of Goliath by David.[133] A poem (possibly written by Ezra Haddad), "To the Freedom Fighters ("El lokhamey ha-hofesh"), aired its author's hopes for the redemption of "our people" and "our nation." It applauded the armies of Israel, led by "the cubs of the Maccabbites," that defeated "all the tribes of the invader." These freedom fighters had managed to dry the waters of the Nile, the Jordan, the Tigris, and the Euphrates, and made the Galilee, Mount Carmel, and the Negev rejoice.[134] These depictions rendered Jews and Arabs as enemies. The Tigris and Euphrates, once symbols of Iraqi patriotism, now epitomized the defeat of Iraq in the 1948 war. This was seen as an event to be celebrated, since it indicated the victory of the Jews. The new opposition between Jews and Arabs was also played up in a pamphlet celebrating the first meeting of the Knesset in Jerusalem, at which the Jewish Iraqi community was depicted as "the oldest of exiles, which swore the eternal pledge of allegiance to the motherland, and which contributed the Babylonian Talmud [to our] exilic spiritual creation."[135] The Babylonian Talmud, an emblem evoked by Iraqi Jews to mark their contribution to Iraqi culture, thus came to signify Jewish *exilic* existence.

The 1948 war was recast so that it involved all Jews, including those in Iraq. A speech delivered at an independence party in Baghdad expressed the happiness of the youth in exile, who were chosen to be the defenders of the nation and the Jewish people: "We know that this holiday cost us rivers of blood of those holy and scared, yet there was no other choice. It is worthy to die for the motherland."[136] Ilan Lev called on his brethren in Israel, who were protecting the country from those who robe it (i.e., the Arabs), to accept the greeting of their Iraqi (Jewish) peers who were fighting for the Jewish people and were willing to endure hardship—even torture—for the sake of their nation. He vowed to break the chains of prisons and battle the enemy until the hour of victory was at hand, in order to help in the building of the holy land: "O brethren, bless us in our difficult war!"[137] The arrests of Zionists in Iraq and the imprisonment of some of the movement's members were consequently associated with Israel's War of Independence, as both were battles for Jewish liberation. Arabs—Palestinians in particular—were thought of as the enemy. Their suffering did not matter.

The writing of Iraqi Jews about the exilic Jews and their debased existence echo the themes in the writing of European Zionists. Moreover, when Iraqi Jews wrote about establishing a new and just socialist community in the Land of Israel, there was no mention of the Palestinian inhabitants of the country. However, most essays by young Zionists before 1948 did not focus on Iraqi Arabs, Muslims, or Palestinians, but rather on their own parents and their Jewish "exilic" existence. The relative success of the movement in attracting the youth can be attributed to the fact that it offered a very simple solution to all societal ills. Leftist Jews, who were similarly concerned with ending poverty, discrimination, and class disparities in Iraq, were bogged down in heated debates about the merits of a range of approaches: socialism, social democracy, communism, Marxist-Leninism, and Stalinism. The Zionists, on the other hand, said that all that was necessary was emigration to Israel. Of paramount importance was the opposition the Zionist activists created between Arabs and Jews after 1948. Where Iraqi Jewish writers in the 1930s had underscored the differences between Eastern and Western Jews, arguing that the former had enjoyed a comfortable life (unlike their European brethren), under the protection of Islam, now all Jews shared the same history and destiny. The Arab Jew, once a desired concept, had become an oxymoron.

Lure of Baghdad: Let My People Stay!

The troubles Jews faced did not mean that Arab-Jewish coexistence had come to an end. A few mechanisms of support still existed, since some elements in Iraqi society reassured Iraqi Jews that not all Iraqis equated Judaism with Zionism or saw Jews as a fifth column. Thus, although some Jews were beaten in the streets and it seemed that their fellow Iraqis were generally indifferent to their plight, many Jews felt that the state's anonymous power, not the Iraqis themselves, was responsible for the ill treatment they suffered (dismissal from employment, trials, denial of admission to universities). Consequently, Jews felt betrayed not by their neighbors, friends, and colleagues, but rather by the state and the right-wing nationalist factions.

A few mechanisms helped Iraqi Jews to cope with the realities of 1948–51. The first was that the educated Iraqi elites, especially those affiliated with the left, often expressed sympathy for their Jewish compatriots.[138] Nor did the press did speak in a unanimous voice. On the one hand, Jews who wanted to work as journalists, such as Menashe Somekh, did have to use pen names to conceal their Jewish identity. On the other, newspapers not associated with the nationalist camp offered other interpretations of Jewish Iraqi life. Menashe Somekh's articles in *Al-Sha'b* and *Sawt al-Ahali*, for example, were critical of the trial of 'Adas and reflected a more balanced perspective on events. *Al-Yaqdha*, in fact, often grumbled about journalists who refused to label every Jew a Zionist. Not all newspapers attacked the right-wing press and very few reported on the persecution of Jews; and yet the racist vilifications that characterized *Al-Yaqdha*'s rhetoric did not appear in such publications.

Al-Sha'b, a paper edited by Yahya Qasim, critiqued Zionism, yet made the distinction between Zionism and Judaism. Qasim was close to Hesqel Shemtov, acted as the lawyer of the community, and negotiated many of the deals regarding the denationalization law. Menashe Somekh came to work for Qasim after being employed at *Sawt al-Ahali*, and quickly became one of *Al-Sha'b*'s leading workers. The paper's coverage challenged the racist overtones that typified the reporting in *Al-Yaqdha* and *Al-Nahda*. In a story about a discussion in the British House of Lords concerning the sufferings of the Palestinian refugees, *Al-Sha'b* published an article about a prominent Jewish author who sought ways to alleviate their misery. The story ended with the following words: "Based on the call of this eminent Jewish personality, we hope that the Arab countries and their league will find an incentive to invest every effort for this goal [i.e., helping the Palestinian refugees], if they cannot find any other incentive!"[139] The article suggested that a Jew, despite his religion, could sympathize with the plight of the Palestinians, since ethics and compassion, and not religion, were what determined how one responded the refugee problem. Similarly, *Al-Sha'b* considered Iraqi Jews as part of the Iraqi nation. It ran, for example, a photo of the members of the Iraqi chamber of commerce, which included several Jews. Where *Al-Yaqdha* protested the substantial number of Jews in Iraqi officialdom, *Al-Sha'b* posted their group photo on its front page.[140] *Al-Sha'b*, moreover, insinuated to Jewish readers that immigration to Israel would be a grave mistake. The new Jewish state, according to some news reports, was in the throes of an ongoing economic crisis and on the verge of bankruptcy. Although aided by America, Israel lacked natural resources, and had been experiencing growing unemployment, leading to a series of workers' demonstrations in Safad, Teaberries, Lod, and Ramla.[141] Unlike the right, which urged Jews to leave Iraq as soon as possible, *Al-Sha'b* implied that leaving for Israel would not solve their problems.

Other newspapers in Iraq, such as *Al-Zaman*, *Sawt al-Ahali*, *Iraq Times*, and *Al-Hawadith*, were generally fair in their coverage of Israeli politics. These dailies did complain about the fact that Jews were taking their money out of the country when they emigrated; they printed stories on Jewish domination in America; and in news articles rather than opinion pieces they quoted right-wing politicians who advocated cleansing Iraq of its Jews.[142] *Al-Zaman* and *Al-Hawadith* were not very helpful from a Jewish perspective for yet another reason—they supported the government's contention that Jews were not discriminated against in Iraq.[143] *Al-Hawadith* suggested that Jews in Iraq faced neither pressure nor terror. They were not arrested or harassed; they controlled the economy; they lived in beautiful houses; and they enjoyed a comfortable life.[144] On a normative basis, these papers seemed to have recognized the fact that it was wrong to discriminate against citizens because of their religion. However, their response was not to face the allegations, but rather to deny them, and to highlight the fact that Israel manipulated such stories for its propaganda wars and to avoid discussing the Palestinian refugee problem and its own Arab citizens.

Generally speaking, there was a great deal of reliable information about Israel in the Iraqi press. News about Israel in the Iraqi press did not serve propaganda aims in all cases, and Iraqi dailies quoted responsibly from Israeli newspapers such as *Herut, Ha-Aretz, Ha-Zofeh, 'Al Ha-Mishmar*, and *Davar*. However, the depiction of Israel as a country on the verge of collapse was commonplace in the Iraqi media, representing Israel as the last place to which Jews, especially those living in the Middle East, would like to immigrate. *Al-Hawadith* and *Al-Zaman* reported on the flow of newcomers to a state that could not provide for their most basic needs, since its resources were allocated almost exclusively to security concerns and the military.[145] *Al-Hawadith* covered the demonstrations against the government's treatment of the recent arrivals, especially the protests concerning unemployment which targeted the minister of labor, Golda Meir; the lack of appropriate schools and sufficient nutrition; the reactionary party led by an exterrorist, Menachem Begin (meaning the revisionist Herut Party); and the tensions between religious and secular Jews, as well as the fact that Israel was comprised of different ethnic and ideological elements which had very little in common with one another.[146]

Special attention was devoted to Middle Eastern Jewish immigrants. Editorials promoted the idea that while Israelis spoke of the ill treatment of Jews in Iraq, Egypt, and the rest of the East, it was the Jewish state that treated Middle Eastern Jewry as slaves of the Russian Ben Gurion. These Jews, as a matter of fact, were on the verge of rebellion against Israel.[147] Eastern Jews lived in twenty-three transit camps (*mu'skar*), in which living conditions were so hellish that many Jews wanted to leave Israel for Europe.[148] *Al-Hawadith* depicted Israel's main transit camp, Sha'ar ha-'aliya (correctly translated by the paper as *bab al-hijra*, the Gate of Aliya), as a hub for Jews from various countries. The camp was guarded at night, and was racked by tensions between Jews of various persuasions. Jews from Iraq lived in tents, while Kurdish Jews endured even more difficulties, partly because no one could communicate with them due to their unique dialect.[149] Israel dedicated no resources to these immigrants, and in fact planned to settle them in the arid Negev region.[150] *Al-Zaman* reported that Iraqi Jews who left for Israel sent news about their difficult conditions: they could not work in their professions, they faced military service, and they did not enjoy political freedom.[151] Life in Israel was so harsh that Jews were returning home from Palestine and a Jew from Marrakesh even committed suicide after coming to Israel.[152] The sheer number of items on the lot of Iraqi Jews in Israel indicated that people were still curious about the experience of Iraqi Jews after they left Iraq.

Immigration to Israel was often represented in the mainstream Iraqi press as counterproductive to the Palestinian cause, as serving the interests of Israel. *Al-Zaman* dismissed one report that the Iraqi government had decided to send Jews to Israel as a form of population exchange as coming probably from Jewish sources, because Israel needed more Jewish immigrants, especially due to limitations on Jewish emigration from Russia.[153] An editorial by *Al-Hawadith* in the winter of 1949 likewise suggested that rumors about population exchange should be considered Zionist propaganda.[154] Moreover, these transfer plans negated the logic that formed the core of the demand to the right of return. In a report about the proposal of a British delegation in Israel that Iraqi Jews and their property be exchanged for Palestinian refugees and their property, *Al-Zaman* contended that it ignored the desire of the refugees to return to their homes.[155]

Al-Zaman voiced opinions similar to those of *Al-Sha'b* regarding the place of Jews in Iraqi society. In the modern world, according to an editorial written by the paper's editor, Tawfiq al-Sam'ani, religion is a matter for Allah, while the homeland is for all.[156] Like *Al-Sha'b*, the paper took pride in Jews who considered themselves loyal Iraqi citizens. From 1949 to 1950 it serialized articles by Mir Basri (the same Mir Basri who was sharply criticized in

Al-Yaqdha), on the economy as a whole, and on specific issues such as taxes, workers' conditions, and unemployment.[157] Moreover, when the exminister, Christian intellectual, and Alliance graduate Yusuf Ghanima died, it was Basri who wrote the obituary, which appeared on the paper's front page.[158] *Al-Hawadith*, although following Nuri Sa'id's line, also ran stories that testified to the desire of Middle Eastern Jewry to remain in their original homelands. One story quoted a Syrian Jew who complained that Eastern Jewry had become pawns in the game of solving the Palestinian problem.[159]

The mainstream Iraqi press did not attack *Al-Yaqdha* directly. In the eyes of the Jewish community, the stories in the mainstream press were certainly not enough, because these newspapers would not make the claim that Jews were being treated badly. And yet these newspapers did put forth a much different perspective, according to which population transfer was ethically wrong; Jews in Iraq ought not to emigrate because they were loyal Iraqi citizens and because Israel was unsuited for their needs; and above all, not all Jews were subversive Zionist agents; their presence in Iraq was welcome.

In addition the mainstream press, an important institutional mechanism for challenging discrimination and racism was the Iraqi parliament and the Iraqi senate. There Arab and Muslim politicians continued to maintain that Iraqi Jews were loyal Iraqi citizens and objected to the freezing of their property. For example, on September 28, 1948, Muzahim al-Pachachi (who espoused both pro- and anti-Jewish positions) attacked the minister of defense, Sadiq al-Bassam (who was forced to resign over the loss of the war against Israel), arguing that Zionism was not Judaism, and that Iraqi Jews were part of the motherland.[160] Even in the debates leading up to the denationalization law, the interior minister, Salih Jabr, contended that most Jews were still loyal citizens and should not be seen as enemies of the country. When Pachachi contended that if the relatives of those Jews who emigrated to Israel remained in Iraq, they would become a fifth column, Jabr replied that families should not be forced to emigrate and that there was no need to exile Jews who wished to remain in Iraq.[161]

Iraqi Jews also made use of the parliament and the senate to make their concerns known. Sasson Semah, the parliamentary representative for Mosul who served for the last time in 1948–51, witnessed the arrests of Jews from his district (such as a group of Kurdish Jews who mentioned the name "Israel" when dancing and consequently were charged with espionage). In response, Semah used his connections in parliament to make sure that the police and the army protected the Jewish quarter, as well as to secure the release of Jews who had been arrested, and help his community cope with dismissals and discrimination.[162] The most important figure in this regard was the courageous senator Ezra Menahem Daniel. In a discussion about the 1948 law criminalizing Zionism, Daniel reminded the Iraqi leadership that it was the Iraqi state, under British guidance, that had allowed the Zionists to set foot in Iraq in 1922, despite the protests of prominent Iraqi Jews. Moreover, the state should remember that poor Jews were emigrating to Israel because they hoped for a better life. When Nuri Sa'id suggested, in 1949, the death penalty as punishment for anyone who aided the Zionist cause, the senator objected, asking him whether he planned to arrest Jews who mentioned Zion in their prayers. In 1950, in a discussion of the denationalization law, the senator said that the state ought to address the root causes of Iraqi Jewish emigration: discrimination with regard to entry in educational institutions, limitations on traveling abroad, and the inability to obtain a decent position as a government clerk. Jews in Iraq, said Daniel, were loyal citizens but the government did nothing to reassure them safety and well-being. He repeated the well-known narrative: Jews were the original inhabitants of Iraq; their forefather, Abraham, had come from Iraq; and they had lived there for thirty-five hundred years. The true solution to the problems faced by Iraqi Jews, he maintained, was to allow the courts to operate freely and fight state corruption.[163] Daniel's points fell on deaf ears, yet they indicate that the senate still served as a democratic arena for debating Jewish concerns. His remarks were very important for the Jewish community since Iraqi politicians such as Fadhil al-Jamali continued to argue that Jews enjoyed comfortable lives in Iraq and faced no discrimination.[164]

The leaders of the Iraqi Jewish community also made known their dismay at the status quo. On October 28, 1948, they submitted an official protest to the minister of interior affairs, which stated that they were loyal Iraqi citizens who enjoyed full constitutional rights, and should therefore not be punished because of the war in Palestine.[165] In the winter of 1949, a Jewish delegation (which included Rabbi Khaduri and Ibrahim Haim) to the Iraqi government complained that Jews were being dismissed from employment for racist reasons and were unable to buy or sell property. The acting prime minister, 'Umar Nadhami, replied that the numbers they presented were exaggerated and that there was an ongoing war which had left eight hundred thousand Arabs homeless.[166] Khaduri and other leaders also addressed international organizations asking for improvement in their living conditions. The demands made by Khaduri were not meant to pressure Iraq to let its Jews emigrate, but rather to ensure that Jews could live in Iraq as equal citizens.

The mechanisms which created a space for Jews to remain in Iraq were not effective in preventing mass emigration, but did achieve some degree of success. Some six thousand Jews chose to stay in Iraq. As Sylvia Haim notes, by 1951 the economy had picked up again and the state had initiated new projects of building and development. Emigration had lost some of its attractiveness: "Western countries were not so welcoming (to Iraqi Jews), nor so easy to settle in; reports from Israel were not always reassuring, especially when examined with a mind devoid of Zionist zeal."[167] Moreover, Jews who chose to stay in Iraq continued their daily activities; Ezra Menahem Daniel, Mir Basri, Anwar Sha'ul, and Yusuf al-Kabir, among others, continued working and publishing. After the mass emigration, and the freezing of Jewish assets, the press asked to help the Jews who had not left Iraq to be reincorporated into the nation's life.[168] Leading members of the Jewish intellectual elite who saw Iraq as their homeland thus remained loyal to their beliefs, staying on only to be driven out in 1968 by the violence of the Ba'th.

The evidence provided by autobiographies and memoirs corroborates the contention that Arab-Jewish coexistence survived in this period. These texts certainly lay bare the marginalization of Iraqi Jews, yet they also recall Iraqi friends, neighbors, politicians, and business partners who wanted Jews to stay in Iraq. In these narratives the dominant sentiment is not that Jews left because they wished to, but because they were forced to—and that this forced emigration was lamented not only by Jews, but also by their fellow Iraqis. Two texts in particular illuminate this line of thinking: *The Exodus from Iraq (Al-Khuruj min al-'Iraq, Yetzia't Iraq)*, a novelistic memoir by Ishaq Bar-Moshe, and "Iya," a short story by Shim'on Ballas.[169]

Ishaq Bar-Moshe is an Iraqi journalist and novelist who immigrated to Israel in 1950 and worked in Israel's broadcasting station in Arabic. *The

Exodus from Iraq, essentially a collection of short depictions, and dialogues, focuses on the life of its narrator, a young Jewish law student in Baghdad during the years 1945–51. Bar-Moshe's daily reality was shaped by politics, as is evident on almost every page of the book. He provides ample examples of the discrimination he encountered: petty and inconsiderate comments made by fellow students, being bullied by a nationalist professor, and being constantly asked to speak to his Iraqi friends on behalf of the Israeli side in the 1948 war. The text records instances of the betrayal of Jews by people whom they loved and trusted. The memoir, however, offers no black-and-white divisions. One episode, for example, focuses on the story of Salih, a young man who landed a position as a clerk through the intervention of the exminister Yusuf Ghanima. In his new position, Salih found himself in confrontation with a fellow Christian worker, Mikha'il. Salih's coworkers demanded that Mikha'il stop insulting their Jewish friend. Nonetheless, Mikha'il managed to publish a story in *Al-Yaqdha* that insinuated that Salih had disparaged the Iraqi army in Palestine, and Salih was subsequently arrested and imprisoned for a time. The story encapsulates the powers that Jews faced, as the state and the nationalist coworker stand in the way of Salih's integration into society. This, however, does not mean that bonds of friendship and mutual help ceased to exist. Salih's coworkers and family friends are represented as supportive and understanding, though their attempts to make their Jewish colleague feel like an equal citizen failed.

Although Bar-Moshe recognizes the love of Iraqi Jews for the Land of Israel, and the feeling of communal solidarity between Jews, he accentuates how much Jews loved Iraq. Iraqi Jews were bitterly disappointed when their country denied them their citizenship rights: "They [the Jews] used to say: she [Iraq] is the country where we grew, and in whose institutions we studied, and under whose skies we lived. We read her books, and sang her praises, and felt that we are a part of her, and that she is a part of us. And there she is, betraying us."[170] Iraq, like an unfaithful woman, spurned the affection and attention of those who loved her, the Jews. Bar-Moshe, however, also cites the Iraqis who assisted their Jewish compatriots. Politically, he underscores the fact that the Iraqi intellectuals affiliated with the left provided a sense of comfort within a climate of increasing isolation and fear. He recalls that the leftist journalist 'Abd al-Rahim Sharif, the editor of *Al-Watan*, published an article criticizing the discrimination against Iraqi Jews in the Law College.[171] Bar-Moshe singles out one of Iraq's most interesting thinkers, 'Abd al-Fattah Ibrahim, whom Bar-Moshe befriended. A social democrat, 'Abd al-Fattah feared the effects of the anti-Jewish campaign on Iraqi society, as it appeared to be the first step in the silencing of all voices of opposition.[172] Through 'Abd al-Fattah's voice we learn about the harsh undemocratic realities in the post-Wathba era and observe how secular and democratic Iraqis sympathized with Jewish Iraqi citizens and identified the persecution of the left with the persecution of the Jews.

Beyond the realm of politics, Bar-Moshe describes friends, business partners, and neighbors who sensed shared the community's pains:

> What we did not dare to utter in these days, our non-Jewish neighbors did. We were surprised at their audacity to speak so fearlessly, while we were shaking and trembling when turning what was concealed in our hearts into words.... They knew well that the Jews were wronged. They understood well the mentality of the Jewish individual.... The government initiated these prosecutions and planned them, [but] these events affected non-Jews as they affected the Jews. The fear and humiliation were the backbones of the persecution. To be truthful, the same fear and humiliation were the lot of every [Iraqi] citizen.[173]

The same Muslim neighbors tried to convince Jews to stay in Iraq, telling them that the bad days would come to an end, and that Israel was an unknown entity. They emphasized that other religious and ethnic minorities had suffered in Iraq, but that eventually their situations had improved.

Through such conversations readers also become acquainted with the Muslim-Iraqi perspective on the question of Palestine. When Bar-Moshe said to his friend 'Adnan that the Land of Israel was mentioned in the Bible many times, 'Adnan replied that the Qur'an did not come with a homeland attached to it.[174] 'Adnan also told his friend frankly that he was offended by the fact that Iraqi Jews identify with Israel. The dialogues with 'Adnan record the fears of both friends in 1950, as they realize that Bar-Moshe's departure from Iraq is near. One such conversation begins with 'Adnan's question:

> ['Adnan:] Imagine that you are already there, and that you are drafted to the army, and I am drafted to the army here. If a war breaks out, we will face one another.
> [Narrator:] I find it difficult to imagine such a situation.

['Adnan:] But the possibility exists.
[Narrator:] Only in theory, because in practice neither you nor I can recognize each other's faces in the battlefield.
['Adnan:] Meaning ...
[Narrator:] Meaning: the war is blind, deaf and mute.
['Adnan:] But the possibility is horrifying.
[Narrator:] Then we need to make sure there will be no war.
['Adnan:] True, at least for both of us.[175]

War requires faceless, anonymous soldiers. Recognizing the face of the enemy renders war impossible because both sides are acknowledging the humanity of their foes. This brief interchange articulated the end of the Arab-Jewish experience as it points to a time when Jews and Arabs were marked as enemies based on new national affiliations. In Bar-Moshe's text, the dissolution of this hyphenated identity, Arab and Jewish at the same time, is depicted as horrifying and almost unimaginable for both Arabs and Jews. The only outcome that could prevent it, as indicated by the two friends, is peace.

Another text that has much in common with Bar-Moshe's reflections on Iraqi Jewry is Shim'om Ballas's short story, "Iya." This story, which includes some autobiographical elements, is told from the point of view of an Iraqi Shi'i nanny, Zakiyya. Born into a poor family, Zakiyya was married at the age of twelve to a violent and abusive man. She was "rescued" by the Ottoman army, which drafted her husband, and managed to support herself by going to work for a Jewish family; Iya is what the children call her. This experience changed her life as she slowly became integrated into Iraqi Jewish society: she visited the Jewish synagogue, and lit candles in memory of the Jewish saints, as she had done in the Shi'i shrine of Imam Musa al-Kazim. She became familiar with Jewish dietary laws, so that she could cook for the family, and even picked up a few Hebrew words. Having no children of her own, Zakiyya, as mentioned several times in the text, came to see the Jewish family as her own.

The story takes place on the day the family is about to leave for Israel. Zakiyya seems incapable of finding ways to process the horrible reality and come to terms with the fact that she will never see the family again: "The three children she raised in her arms: she will not rejoice when they marry.... She will not see their offspring."[176] The child closest to Zakiyya is Ephraim, a Jewish communist. She wonders why he feels the need to leave for Israel: "What pushed you to abandon everything and leave? . . . To work in agriculture? Did you go to school for this?"[177] Zakiyya's doubts about the future of the family in Israel mirror the doubts of the Jewish family itself; they know that where they are going they might live in tents, without electricity and running water.

Zakiyya refers to religion, as she endeavors to convince herself that this inexplicable mass migration is a sign of the wonders of God, incomprehensible to human beings. Yet elsewhere in the text she appears fully conscious of the sociopolitical realities that pushed the family to emigrate: "the demonstrations and the fears . . . and the hanging of the leaders of the communists. And the damned war in Palestine."[178] Zakiyya, moreover, hears from her fellow Iraqis that all the recent troubles facing Iraq have to do with the Jews, who brought the evils of communism and Zionism on the country. These accusations leave her speechless. The story, however, also portrays those Jews who chose not to leave. They have a variety of motives for remaining in Iraq: fear of leaving their elderly parents; reluctance to lose their property or jobs (especially in journalism); or anxieties about the unknown realities in Israel.

The final paragraph of the story leaves no doubts as to the nature of the connection between Iya and her "son," Ephraim:

> She sat in the darkness of the kitchen, drained of thoughts, numb as if she fainted. After a few moments she heard Ephraim's steps coming up the stairs and then saw his shadow at the door. "Why are you sitting in the dark?" He turned on the electricity switch and entered the room "Sitting like this, all alone in the dark?" She blinked her eyes from the light and did not reply. "I brought you something," he said, and handed her a book with a green cover, decorated in golden letters. "I give you the Qur'an."[179]

The story is unique in that it tells of the Jewish departure from Iraq in the voice of an Iraqi Muslim. The story evokes two images that were commonly used in national narratives: the nation as a woman and the nation as a family. Both were employed in essays, short stories, and poems from the interwar period and in the 1950s.[180] Zakiyya seems to encapsulate many of the features of ordinary Iraqis: She is Shi'i (like the majority of the Iraqi population), she comes from a rural environment (again, like most Iraqis at the time), and she is deeply religious. On the other hand, her religiosity is never translated into zealotry. On the contrary, she is willing to learn new things about Judaism, and observes Jewish customs as part of her social milieu. Moreover, Jews and Muslims are presented as being part of the same family, and hence the departure of Jews from Iraq leaves a void that cannot be filled. Thus the story evokes the image of a grieving mother to represent the emigration from Iraq as a loss imposed on a family's matriarch, as her sons and daughters are forced to abandon her. As we have seen, Jews adopted the Qur'an as a maker of their Iraqi and Arab identity. Iraqi Jews such as Ezra Haddad proposed that Jewish children be taught the Qur'an as a way of teaching them Arabic grammar. The last scene begins when Zakiyya is sitting in the dark, a darkness symbolic of the gloom that will fill her life when the family departs. Light is associated with the Jewish communist Ephraim, whom she raised and loved as a son. And it is the Jewish communist who gives her an artifact which binds them together culturally: the Qur'an.

Let us now return to Somekh's meeting with his friend Akram al-Witri, which opened this chapter. Writing on why Witri was disappointed when Somekh chose to leave Baghdad, Somekh explains:

> Akram's basic assumption was that a man . . . who had been torn from his culture could not immerse himself in a new culture. . . . Akram repeatedly reminded me of my "cultural roots," and from time to time even hinted that young people like me were needed by Iraq and its culture. I came to realize that his somewhat angry tone was not directed against me personally, but rather sprang from his anger at an entire, successful community that resolved one day to abandon its past and its future and to exile itself (as he put it at one point) to an unknown place.[181]

Akram, we note, does not blame Somekh for being a Zionist. Culture and language, not religion, are the ingredients which determined, in Akram's mind, the belonging to the Iraqi, and indeed to the Arab, national community. Thus he accuses Somekh of betraying the Arab culture to which he feels Somekh belonged. Somekh, for his part, immigrated to Israel not out of a perpetual yearning for the Land of Israel, but because of the denial of his citizenship rights in Iraq. Akram's position, however, is that despite this discrimination, Jews should have stayed, because their past and their present were shaped by Iraqi Arab culture. To people such as Akram, Iraq was still home for the Jews, and Israel, a place of exile.

Conclusions

This was a chapter that dealt with an end, but not *the* end, of Arab Jewish and Jewish Iraqi identity in Iraq. This end was caused by a chain of events in the years 1948–50. The Iraqi state was fearful of Zionism: Iraq had been defeated in a war with Israel, during which most Palestinians became refugees, and Iraq's leaders wished to uproot Zionism from their midst and were concerned about the weapons in the Zionist underground. The steps taken by the state in its anti-Zionist campaign, especially their collective nature, were often unjustified, unconstitutional, and incompatible with democratic principles. These actions moreover, alienated the people who were the most unlikely to emigrate, the Jewish upper classes and the Jewish Iraqi effendia. Hashemite Iraq was never a full-fledged democracy. It was clear that the hegemony of the Arab Sunni elites would never be endangered, despite the existence of an electoral process. But some minority communities in Iraq did have certain expectations regarding freedom of religion and employment. These rights, which the Jewish community enjoyed during the years 1921–48 and expected to enjoy in the future, were now denied.

The Zionist movement was a minority movement in Iraq. At its height (1948–49) it counted some 2,000 members, out of a total number of 150,000 Iraqi Jews. This upsurge in interest can be traced in part to the crackdown on the communists following the Wathba; prior to this, radical Jewish youth had been more attracted to communism. Not all Zionists belonged to the armed self-defense organization; many were Ha-Tenu'a members who did not know how to operate weapons. Moreover, those weapons, at least until 1950, were not used against Muslims or fellow Jews. The Iraqi Zionism of the years 1943–47, although initially inspired by agents from outside the country, can be understood as a reaction to the Farhud and as a mechanism for critiquing the Jewish bourgeoisie and upper classes. Turning away from their parents' social conservatism, and dismayed by the socioeconomic inequality that pervaded Iraq, Iraqi Zionists believed that they would find socialism, equality, and feminism in the Land of Israel. In 1948, however, the movement became militant, as its members identified with the victorious Israelis and became greatly concerned about the fate of their fellow Jews in Israel, whom they idolized and regarded as model pioneers. Training members in how to use weapons might have seemed, at the time, as a way to prevent another Farhud, yet when the weapons were found by the Iraqi police, they served as proof of the threat posed by Zionism. Israel used Iraq's policies for its propaganda aims, while some Israeli politicians toyed with the idea of population exchange and others devised plans to bring Iraqi Jews to Israel. In tandem, Iraqi Zionists attempted to position themselves as an alternative leadership of Iraqi Jewry, realizing that even courageous leaders such as Senator Ezra Menahem Daniel had lost their powers. The ties that Iraqi Zionists cultivated with the state of Israel were crucial, because these ties allowed them to discuss with the Iraqi government concrete plans to transfer Iraqi Jews to Israel.

The end of Arab-Jewish relations was only partial. Memoirs, autobiographies, and short stories reflect the split between the Iraqi state and Iraqi society: friendships, partnerships, and neighborly relations still existed in this context. Not all Iraqis were happy to see their Jewish friends and neighbors leave, although some interpreted this emigration as a betrayal of the Arab culture they felt Jews shared with other Iraqis. Unlike the Farhud, however, friendship and neighborly relations could not withstand the efforts of not one, but two states, to dictate the fate of Iraqi Jews.

Some scholars point to the connections between the Farhud and the realities that emerged in 1948–49.[182] There is certainly a connection between the vociferous campaigns of al-Istiqlal and the writings of pro-German ultra-nationalists in the 1930s. Whereas the ultranationalist camp saw Jews as British spies in 1941, *Al-Yaqdha* and al-Istiqlal alleged that Jews were Zionist agents in 1948–50. However, the Kaylani movement was an anti-British reaction against Iraq's pro-British elites, and the Farhud happened in the chaos instigated after its fall. The very same pro-British elite endeavored to crush the supporters of the Kaylani movement, and therefore many Jews chose to stay in Iraq after 1941. Conversely, in the years 1948–49 anti-Jewish sentiments were voiced by elements within the pro-British Iraqi elite itself. It was the pro-British Nuri Sa'id who suggested that Iraqi Jews be expelled in order to solve the Arab-Israeli conflict and bolster Iraq's reputation in the Arab world. This elite did not move to muzzle racist right-wing newspapers, even taking the lead from these nationalists. The fact that the state brutally crushed the ICP meant that a patriotic Jewish Iraqi option no longer remained.

The emigration of Iraqi Jews was a result of many misunderstandings, vicious circles, bad calculations on the part of the Iraqi political elites, and Israeli and Iraqi moves that turned Iraqi Jews into mere pawns. Yet I feel that the term "ethnic cleansing," used by some scholars and especially by so-called pundits in the popular media today, is inappropriate for this context. The Iraqi state was interested in avoiding riots in Jewish neighborhoods. When the denationalization law was passed, leaders such as Tawfiq Suwaydi and Salih Jabr hoped that the majority of Jews would stay in Iraq. After 1951, the remaining Jewish community was able to recover to some degree. Thus, despite the tragic nature of the events, a term taken from civil wars in Yugoslavia, Rwanda, and Palestine should not be applied to this case. I used the word "tragic" in the last sentence to characterize the departure of Iraqi Jews, as this was indeed a devastating tragedy. A community that had existed in Iraq for over twenty-five hundred years was all of a sudden displaced. Wealthy and middle-class Iraqi Jews, who became penniless because of the freezing of their assets, endured horrendous living conditions in Israeli transit camps. And it is tragic for yet another reason. Much of what happened in Iraq during these years, such as the national elite's labeling of political opponents as Zionists, in order to discredit them; the ways in which Iraqi politicians manipulated the pro-Palestinian sentiments of the Iraqi people simply to increase their own power (without doing much for the Palestinian people themselves); and the total collapse of the distinctions between the terms *Jew*, *Zionist*, and *enemy*, such that they became one, prevailed in the coming years. In the Israeli version, every Jew was also a Zionist and the impossibility of Arab-Jewish coexistence became a narrative that shaped the past and affected the present. Arabs and Jews, it seemed, could no longer see each other's familiar faces, and remained blind, deaf, and mute. The Qur'an left in Zakiyya's hand had long been forgotten.

CONCLUSIONS

The Iraqi Jewish singer Salima Murad was one of the most celebrated performers of modern Iraq. Her songs, mostly composed by the Jewish brothers Da'ud and Salih al-Kuwaiti, became part of the Iraqi musical canon. In recent years, her songs have appeared online, especially as videos posted on YouTube. In comments (mostly in Arabic) posted in response to these videos, Iraqis recognize Salima's Jewish heritage, nostalgic for a time when Jews and Arabs shared the same Iraqi space and shaped its cultural vision. Another Iraqi Jewish woman, Reene Dangur, appears on Google Images, and stories about her 1947 selection as a Baghdadi beauty queen are scanned and posted online. Dangur's elegance and beauty seem to be commemorated in order to celebrate a moment when a dazzling Jewish woman, holding a statuette of Aphrodite, could symbolize the exquisiteness and splendor of modern Iraq. The recent interest in Reene and Salima might suggest that despite the realities of the Arab-Israeli conflict, some Jews, Muslims, Iraqis, and Arabs reject the conspiracy theories and racist vocabulary that have colored the discourses of the conflict, and privilege in their stead other sentiments: nostalgia for a shared Arab-Jewish past, longing for a different kind of Iraq, and a vernacular remembrance of Jewish-Arab coexistence not mediated by nation-states. The Jewish Iraqi experience for these people is very meaningful, and there is a sense that it could inspire a new imagining for the future of Iraq, Palestine, and Israel.

Things have not always looked this promising. With the revolution of 'Abd al-Karim Qasim in 1958, the state adopted a very positive approach toward the Jewish community—the reintegration of Jews into Iraqi society was one element of Qasim's national vision. But with Qasim's fall in 1963 state policy once again become oppressive toward the Jews, and the situation became even worse after the Israeli victory in the 1967 War and the rise of the Ba'th to power in 1968. Between 1967 and 1969, three hundred Jews were arrested (10 percent of the Jewish Iraqi population), Jewish property was confiscated by the state, and Jews were fired from government positions. In 1969, dozens of Jews were thrown in jail. Forty of them died either in gruesome public executions or as a result of torture. By 1971 only fifteen hundred Jews remained in Iraq; a year later this number had declined by two-thirds. The most passionate supporters of Arab-Jewish nationalism, including Mir Basri and Anwar Sha'ul, left Iraq during these years.[1]

Even so, Iraqi Jewish and Arab-Jewish experiences did not come to an abrupt end. Iraqi Jews kept in touch with Iraqi Muslims and Christians in the diaspora, especially the communities in England and North America. True, politics caused a rift between many exiles, but an ongoing dialogue between Iraqis of various religions was maintained. Mir Basri, for example, continued to publish books on Iraqi history and culture, which were cited by many Iraqi historians and intellectuals. Interest in Arab-Jewish history has also had an impact the cultural activities of the Iraqi diaspora in recent times. The rise of postcolonial and postnational approaches to Iraqi history in academia and the immense literary and cultural productivity of the Iraqi diaspora have generated a great deal of interest in Iraqi Jewish history on the part of non-Jewish Iraqis. The novels in which Jews figure as prominent characters, the memoirs reflecting on Jewish neighbors and friends, the studies on Iraqi Jewish history (produced inside and outside of Iraq), the journalistic articles on Iraqi Jews, and the websites on Iraqi music and culture testify to the fact that contemporary Iraqis do not subscribe to nationalist mythologies, but are rather fascinated by the Jewish-Iraqi coexistence of the past.

In Israel, despite the horrendous living conditions Iraqi Jews experienced in transit camps during the early 1950s and the discrimination that was directed generally against Jews of Middle Eastern origins, Iraqi Jews were able to integrate into Israeli society, largely because of their high degree of education and professional training. More importantly, a minority group of Iraqi Jews continued speaking and writing in Arabic in various contexts. Arabic had a very negative connotation in the eyes of the Israeli public, yet it was still an important language. True, the children of Iraqi, Egyptian, and Syrian Jews were too ashamed to speak Arabic, and were often embarrassed when their parents did so. Nonetheless, unlike the much-abhorred Yiddish—the other major language of "the exile"—Arabic was an official state language and a means of communicating with the Palestinian Arabs who became Israeli citizens. Moreover, as the language of "the enemy," its study was crucial to the state's security interests. Thus, while Yiddish was marginalized as an academic language, classical Arabic, as well as Middle Eastern and Islamic studies, were taught in most Israeli universities and Arabic was offered as an elective in Israeli high schools and middle schools. The significance of Arabic enabled certain Iraqi Jews, especially the intellectuals, to find niches where they could be of service to the state of Israel: some worked for Israel's Arabic broadcasting station and others found positions with the state-sponsored Arabic press or taught in schools attended by Palestinians. The orchestra of Israel's Arabic broadcasting station, composed mostly of Iraqi and Egyptian Jews, became very popular with Jewish and Muslim audiences and was a source of pride for many Jews from the Arab world who settled in Israel. Under state patronage, former members of the Zionist underground in Iraq founded a museum dedicated to Iraqi Jewish history, which possesses rich archives documenting the history of the community. Most Iraqi Jewish immigrants adopted Hebrew as the means of communication, yet these Iraqi cultural elites kept their Arabic voice alive within the new state.

Not only within, but also outside the state apparatus, radical Iraqi Jews strove to keep Arab Jewish culture alive. Under the umbrella of the Israeli Communist Party, Iraqi Jews and Palestinian Arabs fostered important cultural and political initiatives. The party was a prominent cultural hub, and counted many Palestinian writers and poets, such as Emile Habibi and Mahmud Darwish, among its members. Iraqi Jews, like Shim'on Ballas, Sami Michael, and Sasson Somekh, consequently came in contact with the leading voices of the Palestinian intellectual elite who had remained in the state of Israel. The cultural conversations between Arabs and Jews which began in the party lasted many years, and continued even after 1968, a time when many Jewish members left the party. A collection of poems by David Semah, *Until Spring Comes* (*Hatta yaji al-rabi'*), testifies to these historical trends. Semah joined the party after arriving in Israel from Iraq, and published poems dedicated to Palestinian and Arab causes. His poem "He Shall Return" ("Sawfa ya'udu"; 1956) took as its subject the victims of the massacre in Kafar Qasim, focusing on a daughter who lost her father. Another poem addressed to Tawfiq Ziyad ("Akhi Tawfiq"; 1959) spoke of the hope of finding light and liberty in the skies of the east in general and in the Galilee in particular. Semah's other poems treated Algeria's battle for independence ("The Battle of Algeria" ["Nidal al-jaza'ir"; 1958]), commemorated the Wathba and Baghdad's fearless rebels, and celebrated the July revolution of 1958 in Iraq. These fine verses echoed the sentiments of Semah's Arab contemporaries all over the Middle East. In Israel, however, an Israeli Jew could publish them only within the framework of the communist party.

The communist party was not the only venue in which Iraqi Jews turned Israeli citizens were able to remember their Arab past(s). Ishaq Bar-Moshe, Samir Nakkash, Anwar Sha'ul, and Ibrahim Obadiah wrote literary works in Arabic, often about their lives in Iraq, while Sami Michael and Shim'on Ballas explored Jewish Iraqi life in their Hebrew novels. The field of modern Arabic literature in Israeli academia was promoted by Iraqi Jews: Sasson Somekh in Tel Aviv University, David Semah and Shim'on Ballas at the University of Haifa, and Shemu'el Moreh at the Hebrew University. Iraqi Jews retained their position as important cultural mediators, working as translators of Arabic texts into Hebrew. Sasson Somekh's Hebrew translations of Arabic poetry and narrative prose, Sami Michael's translation of Nagib Mahfuz's Cairian trilogy, and more recently Moshe Hakham's masterful rendition of *Bab al-Shams*, by Iliyas Khouri, are a few examples of the great productivity of the Jewish Iraqi community in the literary domain. The Society of Exiled Academic Jews from Iraq (Rabitat al-jami'iyin al-yahud al-nazihin min al-'Iraq) printed dozens of books in Arabic on Iraqi Jews (in the form of memoirs, historical studies, and works of literature). From the 1970s on, as interest in the history of Mizrahi communities has grown, much more attention has been devoted within Israeli academia to the histories and cultures of Iraqi Jews, especially after their arrival in Israel.

Iraqi Jewish life, then, fascinates Iraqis, Israelis, as well as other scholars and intellectuals across the world, as a way of encountering another Iraq, one which is more pluralistic and tolerant. This story, despite its many tragic features, seems to offer some hope. For historians, Iraqi Jewish history offers much insight regarding monarchic Iraq, Iraqi-Arab nationalism, Arab-Jewish identity, and sectarian conflict in Iraq.

The study of Middle Eastern Jewish history and culture in recent decades has been influenced by the much-welcomed desire to write a post-Orientalist history of Arab-Jewish communities. Many scholars have rejected the universalizing approach to Jewish history, as though there was no variation in the Jewish experience across the globe. This novel approach has enabled scholars to see that the relationships between Jews and non-Jews in the Middle East differed from those in Europe, and that the nature of these relationships dictated different political options regarding the place of Jews within non-Jewish societies. Hashemite Iraq, however, was affected by modern and Western ideologies such as democracy, social democracy, communism, and fascism. Some of Iraq's elites were educated in Western schools, and Iraqi politics were shaped by the state's interaction with the colonial powers. In this context, the Western and the global were very much a part of the Iraqi local context. I therefore do not think it is productive to write about Jewish Iraqi history without taking into account these modern phenomena, for if not, we will reduce such a history into a new essentialism that isolates Iraq and its Jewry from the rest of the globe. The Saidian and postcolonial project, in many ways, has pointed to the impossibility of imagining a stable East and West in a globalizing and capitalist world. When thinking about the Iraqi Jewish experience, it is therefore better to consider the constant dialogue between various cultural centers in Iraq, the Middle East, Europe, and America. What I have tried to show in this book is how cultural elements such as the Islamic faith, Arab nationalism, and the ethno-religious composition of Iraqi society created a unique Jewish Iraqi experience, which was nonetheless intertwined with global and Western discourses. Comparing Iraqi Jewish communists to their Jewish "comrades" in Russia, Argentina, or Poland, as well as looking into the adoption of the national language by Jewish intellectuals in countries such as Germany and France, could therefore highlight the distinctiveness of the Iraqi context, yet also locate it within a modern and global one.

This book has delineated the ways in which Iraqi Jews took up Arab nationalism. In the Iraqi Jewish context, Arab nationalism and Iraqi patriotism coexisted, and Iraqi Jewish writers considered Arab-Islamic history and Arabic literature their own. Like their fellow Iraqis, they read books and journals from Egypt and Lebanon, and shared the literary and musical tastes of their Arab contemporaries. Theoreticians of Arab nationalism at the time, like Sati' al-Husri, emphasized that education and urbanization could make Arab nationalism an acquired (rather than a racially inherited) feature of modern Iraqis. While political parties such as al-Istiqlal appropriated Arab nationalism to promote a host of ultranationalist and racist agendas, the notion of Islam as a civilization and culture rather than just a religion, advanced by many Muslim modernists, appealed to Iraqi Jews. For intellectuals such as Ezra Haddad the writings of medieval Arab historians or the wording of the Qur'an were germane to the understanding of Jewish history in Iraq and the Middle East. Moreover, the state's institutions, especially its schools, introduced a certain dynamic of their own, where students and teachers debated the definitions of Arabism and nationalism, in ways different from the original schemes designed by Iraqi bureaucrats and politicians. These constant negotiations of Arab and Islamic cultures and their relationship to Judaism inspired a variety of expressions of Arab Jewishness. Thus, the Arab-Jewish experience of Iraqi communists was very different from the Arab-Jewish reflections of nationalists such as Anwar Sha'ul. Still others did not call themselves Arab Jews, although they were fully immersed in Arab culture and felt they were an integral part of the Arab Islamic society in which they lived. In addition to the concept of the Arab Jew, the transregional categories of the East (*sharq*) and the Eastern Jew were also employed by Iraqi Jews in order to construct a national narrative that underscored the contrast between the experience of the fortunate Eastern Jews who lived under the tolerant rule of Islam and their less-than-fortunate European brethren who lived under oppressive Christian rule.

On the other hand, Jews in Iraq felt loyal to that country in particular, and often regarded themselves as Iraqi Jews, rather than Arab Jews. Some Pan-Arab policies adopted in Iraq, such as the teaching of Arabic and Islamic history in schools, solidified the communal bonds between Jews and Shi'is, Sunnis, Christians, and Kurds *within* Iraq itself. More generally, the Iraqi context was marked by specific conditions that distinguished Iraqi Jewry from other Middle Eastern communities. The Iraqi Jewish community, for instance, did not have a large Ashkenazi or Karaite component as did the community in Egypt, and was much more secular than the community in Yemen. Iraqi Jews responded to debates about nationalism, gender, sectarianism, and religiosity that were engendered by the tribal, ethnic, and religious composition of Iraqi society. The fact that in Iraq, Jews were one minority among many religious communities—Armenians, Chaldeans, Orthodox and Catholic Christians, Shi'is, and Sunnis—meant that their religious difference was not marked as peculiar. Considering the local (Iraqi, Egyptian, Yemeni, and so on) and the Pan-Arab component in Middle Eastern Jewish identity suggests a rejection of Israeli policies which treated Jews from such various locations as Morocco, Yemen, Egypt, and Iraq as one oriental lot, and, more importantly, reveals various kinds of Arab-Jewish experiences—note the plural here—in diverse Middle Eastern contexts.

Zionism posed a challenge for the Iraqi-Arab nationalism embraced by Iraqi Jews, especially since the Iraqi state's policies with respect to the Jewish community were largely determined by how its elites viewed the impacts of Zionism on the Middle East, Palestine, and Iraq. Iraqi Jews, however, responded differently to Zionism: intellectuals (whether nationalists or communists) vehemently opposed the movement; the upper and middle classes were indifferent to it in the 1920s and fearful of its destructive potential in the following decades; some radical young Jews enthusiastically adopted it in the years 1948–51; and their parents accepted it as a possible solution to their predicament after 1948. The response of the Iraqi state to Zionism was far from monolithic, shifting from indifference in the 1920s to opposition in the 1930s and 1940s, culminating in a war against Israel in 1948. Furthermore, Iraqis imagined the connections between Judaism and Zionism in various fashions, and only after 1948 did the association of Jews and Zionism became entrenched in the mindset of the Iraqi authorities. Eventually,

Zionism "won" the battle with Iraqi Judaism, as most of the community left for Israel after 1948. The children of these Jews no longer spoke Arabic and saw themselves as Israeli citizens. This victory, however, should not be projected onto the past, that is, onto the Iraq of the 1920s through the 1940s, when most Iraqis, Jews and non-Jews alike, still believed in the vitality of a shared Jewish-Iraqi project.

The history of Iraqi Jews bears on an ongoing debate in the discussion of Iraqi sectarianism. Sectarianism in Hashemite and post-Hashemite Iraq is a modern phenomenon, constructed by the state and the colonial powers. Iraqis of the same faith, as recent studies have shown, did not subscribe to a sociopolitical vision based solely on their religious orientation. An important response to sectarianism within Iraqi society was secularism. By pointing to the secularization of Iraqi Jews, I am not arguing that Jews forsook their religious heritage, but rather am suggesting that discourses relating to modernity and secularity in the Arab East shaped the thinking of Iraqi Jews about the connections between religion and society. These modern discourses led many Jewish intellectuals to believe in the virtues of a secular democracy, that is, the separation between state and religion in the public sphere, or as they put it, "Religion is a matter for God and the homeland is for the community." Jewish Iraqi secularism was further encouraged by the state's new institutions, especially its education system. There were many debates about the degree to which the community ought to be secularized and as to the definition of secularism itself. Yet, the conversations about secularism and the espousal of new Western practices by Iraqi Jews altered the ways in which they were educated, how they dressed, what they ate, how they passed their leisure time, and how they perceived the role of women in society. Although secularism dovetailed the national aspirations of the Iraqi Jewish community and its desire to participate in the development of the Iraqi state, its most radical manifestation was actually directed against the state, as young Jews took up the cause of the radical left. In Iraq, as in Egypt, Syria, and North Africa, communism was a crucial patriotic avenue for Jews; it permitted them to critique the state while underscoring their loyalty to the people among whom they lived.

Secularism, however, was not the only vision for Jewish integration within Iraqi society. Tolerance and pluralism were also meaningful modes for advancing a shared coexistence. In the mixed neighborhoods, in which Jews lived together with Muslims and Christians, religious differences were not obliterated in favor of national unity. On the other hand, residents in these mixed neighborhoods all spoke Arabic, read the same journals, books, and dailies, worked together, gossiped with one another, and often sent their children to the same schools. These integrated spaces cultivated friendships, business partnerships, and neighborly relations. What was fostered in these milieus was not secularism as much as tolerance and the understanding that the community was composed of people of different religions. These very same surroundings protected the Jews during the Farhud.

As I write these conclusions, I encounter dozens of conferences, books, academic papers, websites, media debates, and videos on YouTube dedicated to dhimmitude, Arab and Muslim anti-Semitism, jihad and Jewish hatred, and Holocaust denial in the Arab world. This new discourse, however, ignores contemporary Arabs and Muslims who believe in a democratic future for the Middle East and reject anti-Semitism, or the Arabs and Jews who shared similar democratic visions prior to, and even after, 1948. Most dangerously, this discourse attempts to highjack the Jewish-Arab past. It ignores the history of Jewish communities in the Middle East and dehistoricizes Arab-Jewish experiences. The alternative is not the construction of a false paradise of Arab-Jewish harmony, but simply to document and study periods in which Jews and Arabs did not look at each other as enemies, but rather as neighbors, compatriots, and friends.

REFERENCE MATTER

Notes

Chapter 1: Brothers and Others

1. Sha'ul, *Wa-baza'*, 69.
2. Brubaker, "Ethnicity," 169.
3. Spivak, "Nationalism and the Imagination," 84.
4. On nineteenth-century Iraqi Jewish life see: Simhoni, "Kavim le-re'shit"; Kazzaz, "Political Activities of Iraqi Jews"; Kedourie and Shohet, "Jews of Baghdad"; Haqqaq, *Igrot ha-rav Shelomo Bekhor Hotzin*; Haqqaq, *Nitzaney ha-yetzira ha-'ivrit ha-hadasha be-Bevel*; Obermeyer, *Modernes Judentum*; Bashkin, "Why Did Baghdadi Jews Stop Writing."
5. On the public sphere of the interwar period, see Davis, *Memories of the State*; al-Musawi, *Reading Iraq*; Bashkin, *Other Iraq*.
6. On the internal domain, see Chatterjee, *Nation and Its Fragments*.
7. Asad, *Formations of the Secular*, 2–13.
8. Chatterjee, "Secularism and Toleration"; see also Gil Anidjar, "Secularism."
9. Chakrabarty, *Provincializing Europe*.
10. For the Arab national narrative, see 'Abd al-'Aziz, "Al-Nashat al-sahayuni fi'l 'Iraq fi dhill al-intidab al-baritani"; al-Ma'adidi, *Al-Sahafa al-yahudiyya fi'l 'Iraq*; Barrak, *Al-Madaris al-yahudiyya*. For Zionist representations: Moreh and Yehudah, eds., *Sin'at yehudim*; H. Cohen, *Ha-Pe'ilut*; Atlas, *'Ad 'amud ha-teliya*; Hillel, *Ruh qadim*; Ben Porat, *Le-Baghdad ve-hazara*; Barshan, *Yehudi be-tzel ha-Islam*; Ya'qov-Yaron, *Shalom lakh Baghdad*.
11. Kazzaz, *Yehudim*.
12. Ella Shohat has discussed the ways in which Zionist historiography undermined the richness of the Arab Jewish experience by subjecting it to a universalizing model of Jewish oppression under non-Jewish sovereignty, showing that Iraqi Jews did not cease to be Iraqi and Arab once they became Israeli citizens, but framed their Arab Jewish identity in a new fashion. She illustrated how these diasporic, transregional, and liminal forms of identity can challenge national mythologies. Nancy Berg has drawn attention to the rich commemoration, by Iraqi Jewish novelists, of the Jewish Iraqi world in Israel. Yehouda Shenhav's discussion of the concept of "the Arab Jew" has lain bare the relationships between the Zionist movement, the state of Israel, and Iraqi Jewry, by studying such phenomena as the activities of Zionist emissaries and Jewish Ashkenazi workers in Iraq, the organizations of Iraqi Jews in Israel and the manners which in Israel handled

the question of Jewish property seized by the Iraqi state. See Shohat, *Taboo Memories*; Shohat, "Sephardim in Israel"; Berg, *Exile from Exile*; Berg, *More and More Equal*; Shenhav, *Arab Jews*; Hever, *Ha-Sipur ve-ha-le'om*.

13. Snir, *'Arviyut, yahadut*.

14. Simon, *Iraq Between Two World Wars*; Haim, *Arab Nationalism*; Eppel, *Palestine Conflict*; Marr, "Development of Nationalist Ideology in Iraq"; Tibi, *Arab Nationalism*.

15. Zubaida, "Fragments Imagine the Nation"; Davis, *Memories of the State*; al-Musawi, *Reading Iraq*; Bashkin, *Other Iraq*.

16. Watenpaugh, *Being Modern*.

17. Gelvin, *Divided Loyalties*; Thompson, *Colonial Citizens*.

18. Wien, *Iraqi Arab Nationalism*; Davis, *Memories of the State*; Eppel, "Elite, the Effendiyya."

19. Matthews and Akrawi, *Education in Arab Countries*.

20. Wild, "National Socialism in the Arab Near East"; Gershoni, *Or ba-tsel*; Gershoni, "Beyond Anti-Semitism"; Gershoni, "Egyptian Liberalism"; Gershoni and Jankowski, *Confronting Fascism in Egypt*; Nordbruch, *Nazism in Syria and Lebanon*; Achcar, *Arabs and the Holocaust*.

21. Simon, *Iraq Between Two World Wars*; Marr, "Development of Nationalist Ideology"; Tarbush, *Role of the Military*.

22. Wien, *Iraqi Arab Nationalism*; Bashkin, *Other Iraq*, chap. 2.

23. Bashkin, *Other Iraq*, chap. 2; Ibrahim, *Muqaddima fi'l ijtima'*; al-Amin, *Jama'at al-Ahali*; H. Jamil, *Al-Hayat al-niyabiyya fi'l 'Iraq*; al-Wakil, *Jama'at al-Ahali*. See the short story collections by Ayyub, *Rusul al-thaqafa* (Messengers of Culture; 1937), *Burj Babil* (Tower of Babylon; 1939), and *Duktur Ibrahim* (Doctor Ibrahim; 1939), all in Ayyub, *Al-Athar al-kamila*.

24. For an excellent analysis of narratives concerning Jewish identity in the Middle East, see Beinin, *Dispersion of Egyptian Jewry*; For an analysis of these historiographical trends, see also Cohen, *Under Crescent and Cross*; A popular representation of the myth of persecution is Bat Ye'or, *Juifs et chrétiens sous l'Islam*. On the inability of modern Muslim Arab societies to accept the ideas of coexistence, see in particular the last chapter in Lewis, *Jews of Islam*; Wistrich, *Anti-Zionism and Anti-Semitism*. Much has been written on Jewish-Islamic relations in the medieval period. The best-known work is S. D. Goitein, *Mediterranean Society*; on cultural interactions see in particular Lazarus-Yafeh, *Intertwined Worlds*; Adang, *Muslim Writers on Judaism*. In recent years scholars suggested innovative ways in which Arab Jewish relations could be imagined beyond the binaries of Zionism and Arab nationalism: Alcalay, *After Jews and Arabs*; Anidjar, *Our Place in al-Andalus*; Anidjar, *Semites*; Hochberg, *In Spite of Partition*; Levy, "Jewish Writers in the Arab East."

25. Bashkin, "Looking Forward to the Past."

26. On the Nahda see: Hourani, *Arabic Thought in the Liberal Age*; Saree Makdisi, "Postcolonial Literature in a Neocolonial World"; Samah Selim, "People's Entertainments;" Starkey, "Nahda."

27. Lital Levy, "Jewish Writers."

28. The dichotomy between "other" and "brother" is taken from Neta Shtahl's in-

sightful book that discusses the transformation of the image of Jesus from an "other" to a "brother" in modern Jewish literature. Shtahl, *Tselem yehudi*.

29. Sehayek, "Demut ha-yehudi"; on the *salafi* journal *Al-Manar* and its support of Dreyfus and Christian missionary journals which adopted an anti-Dreyfus approach: Haim, "Arabic Antisemitic Literature."

30. Sehayek, "Demut he-yehudi"; Levy, "Jewish Writers," Bashkin, "Arab Revival."

31. Dawn, "Formation of Pan-Arab Ideology"; Bashkin, "Arab Revival"; Tamari, "Lepers, Lunatics, and Saints," in *Mountain Against the Sea*, 93–113.

32. Me'ir-Glitzenstein, *Zionism in an Arab Country*; H. Cohen, *Ha-Pe'ilut*, Hillel, *Ruh qadim*; Ben Porat, *Le-Baghdad ve-hazara*; Sha'shu', *Yemey Baghdad*; Bibi, ed., *Me-Araba' kenafot ha-naharayim*; Gat, *Jewish Exodus*.

33. Al-Rawi, *'Usbat mukafahat al-sahyuniyya*; Zilkha, *Al-Sahayuniyya*.

34. Zubaida, "Fragments Imagine the Nation"; Nakash, *Shi'is of Iraq*; Bashkin, *Other Iraq*, chap. 5.

35. Batatu, *Old Social Classes*; Ismael, *Rise and Fall of the Communist Party*; Gabbay, *Communism and Agrarian Reform*. For list of Jews killed from the ranks of ICP, see Al-Hizb al-shuyu'i al-'iraqi, *Shuhada' al-hizb*.

Chapter 2: Nationalism and Patriotism

1. Mubarak, *Layla al-marida fi'l 'Iraq*, 52–53, 103; Mubarak, *Wahi Baghdad*, 287.

2. Davis, *Memories of the State*; Zubaida, "Fragments Imagine the Nation"; Amatzia Baram, "Case of an Imported Identity."

3. On Iraq ethnic relationships see: Nakash, *Shi'is of Iraq*; Abdul-Jabar, ed., *Ayatollahs, Sufis, and Ideologues*; Abdul-Jabar, *Shi'ite Movement in Iraq*; Abdul-Jabar and Dawod, eds., *Tribes and Power*; Farouk-Sluglett and Sluglett, "Some Reflections"; Luizard, *La formation de l'Irak contemporain*.

4. Rizk Khoury, *State and Provincial Society*; Abdullah, *Short History of Iraq* (see in particular chap. 4); Çetinsaya, *Ottoman Administration*; Luizard, *La formation de l'Irak contemporain*; Fattah, *Politics of Regional Trade*.

5. Bashkin, *Other Iraq*; Dodge, *Inventing Iraq*; Sluglett, *Britain in Iraq*; Wilson, *Loyalties*; Wilson, *Mesopotamia, 1917–1920*; Ireland, *Iraq: A Study in Political Development*; Longringg, *Iraq, 1900 to 1950*.

6. On Iraq in the 1930s, see: Bashkin, *Other Iraq*, chap. 2; Wien, *Iraqi Arab Nationalism*; Tarbush, *Role of the Military*; Majid Khadduri, *Independent Iraq*; Eppel, "The Elite, the Effendiyya"; al-Wakil, *Jama'at al-Ahali*; al-Amin, *Jama'at al-Ahali*; Simon, *Iraq Between Two World Wars*.

7. On Iraq in the 1940s, see: Davis, *Memories of the State*, chap. 4; Bashkin, *Other Iraq*, chap. 3.

8. The division between central/southern and northern Jews was noted by the British: AIR 23/806: secret report, app. A, "The Jews of Iraq," 9 July 1934.

9. Simhoni, "Kavim le-re'shit"; Kedourie and Shohet, "Jews of Baghdad"; Kazzaz, "Political Activities"; Haqqaq, *Igrot ha-rav*; Obermeyer, *Modernes Judentum*; Haqqaq, *Nitzaney ha-yetzira*; Bashkin, "Why Did Baghdadi Jews Stop Writing"; Levy, "Jewish Writers," 321–77; Sassoon, *Masa' Bavel*.

10. *Ha-Levanon*, 11 February 1870, 54–55; Bashkin, "'Religious Hatred Shall Disappear from the Land.'"

11. Al-Suwaydi, *Mudhakarati*, 64–65, 71; Bashkin, "Why Did Baghdadi Jews Stop Writing"; "A Talk with Sassoon Effendi: The Jewish Representative from Baghdad," *Ha-'Olam* 3:8, 10 March 1909; Bashkin, "'Religious Hatred Shall Disappear from the Land.'"

12. Basri, *A'lam al-yahud*; AIR 23/806: app. A, "The Jews of Iraq," 9 July 1934; Kedourie and Shohet, "Jews of Baghdad."

13. AIR 23/806: "Jews of Iraq"; Simhoni, "Kavim le-re'shit"; Kedourie and Shohet, "Jews of Baghdad." For demographical details on Iraqi Jews, see: Kazzaz, *Yehudim*, 27–33; FO 371/75183, 12 December 1949, Henry Mack (British Embassy, Baghdad) to Clement Attlee (Foreign Office).

14. Agasi, *Mi-Baghdad*, 94–95; Somekh, *Baghdad*, 57–58; Naggar, *Bab al-Sheikh*, 74; J. Cohen, *Hilla*, 92; Kazzaz, *Yehudim*, 67. The Syrian teacher 'Ali al-Tantawi, who was teaching in Iraq during the 1930s, reported that (much to his chagrin) his Jewish students in the 1930s excelled in their knowledge of Arabic and Islam. See 'Ali al-Tantawi, *Al-Sharq al-Awsat*, 24 May 1984, 10; for analysis, see Snir, *'Arviyut, yahadut*, 57–60.

15. Basri, *Rihlat al-'umr*, 22.

16. Ibid.

17. Salman Darwish, *Kull shay*, 200–201.

18. The reference here is to the Arabic renditions of the detective novels *Arsène Lupin* by Maurice Leblanc (1864–1941), which were extremely popular in the Middle East from the 1930s till the 1950s, and to Taha Husayn's *Al-Ayyam* (The Days). See also: Agasi, *Mi-Baghdad*, 94–95; Bar-Moshe, *Bayt be-Baghdad*, 109; Zubaida, "Being and Iraqi and a Jew"; Somekh, *Baghdad, Etmol*, 17, 57–61; Ballas, *Be-Guf rishon*, 20–22; Kahila, *Hayinu ke-holmim*, 61.

19. Somekh, *Baghdad, Etmol*, 132–35; on the new modernist movement in Iraq, see: DeYoung, *Placing the Poet*; Jabra, "Modern Arabic Literature and the West"; Jabra, *Princesses' Street*.

20. *Al-Hatif*, 4:161, 31 March 1939, 1 (the author then bemoaned the fact that a talented writer like Balbul needed the aid of his father in order to publish his works).

21. See the articles of Suhil Idris in *Al-Adab*, 1:2 February 1953, 22–25; *Al-Adab*, 1:3, March 1953.

22. Yusuf Mukmal was on the staff of the newspapers *Al-Mabda'*, *Al-Zaman*, and *Al-Ahali*; Na'im Salih Tweig worked for *Al-Zaman*; Menashe Somekh edited *Sawt al-Ahali* and *Al-Sha'b*; Menashe Za'rur was chief editor of *Al-'Iraq*; and Salim al-Basun (of *Al-Sha'b*), Murad al-'Umari (of *Sawt al-Ahali*), Suhil Ibrahim (of *Sawt al-Ahrar*), and Ya'qub Sha'ul also filled important posts at the nation's newspapers. Nissim Kazzaz, "'Itona'im yehudiyim be-'Iraq"; Me'ir, *Hitpathut tarbutit*, 298–310; *Al-Hatif*, 4:161, 31 March 1939, 1.

23. Sha'ul, *Qissa*; Bashkin, "*Al-Misbah*: A Jewish Iraqi Newspaper"; Bashkin, "Un arabe juif."

24. Sha'ul, *Qissa*; Bashkin, "Un arabe juif."

25. Sha'ul, *Qissa*, 185–87, 211–12; see also the poem Sha'ul wrote in honor of Mubarak, "Al-Adib" (The Intellectual; 1937), in Sha'ul, *Wa baza'*, 170–71.

26. Obadiah, *Sittin 'amman*; the poem first appeared in the collection *Fi sukun al-layl* (Cairo, 1947).

27. *Al-Misbah*, no. 1, 10 April 1924, 3; *Al-Misbah*, no. 104, 10 July 1926, 1; *Al-Misbah*, no. 4, 1 May 1924, 3; *Al-Misbah*, no. 50, 30 May 1925, 2.

28. *Al-Hasid*, 1:6, 21 March 1929, 1.

29. *Al-Hasid*, 1:5, 14 March 1929, 1.

30. Snir, *Arviyut, yahadut*, 75.

31. *Al-Burhan*, no. 3, 31 October 1929, 1.

32. *Al-Burhan*, no. 2, 24 October 1929, 1.

33. Levy, "Jewish Writers."

34. Dawn, "Formation of Pan-Arab Ideology."

35. *Al-Misbah*, no. 94, 22 April 1926, 5; *Al-Misbah*, no. 101, 6 October 1926, 1.

36. On approaches to the Ottoman past and the Ottoman background of Iraqi ruling elites, see: Simon, *Iraq Between Two World Wars*; Bashkin, *Other Iraq*, chap. 5.

37. Hourani, *Arabic Thought*, 222–45; Kerr, *Islamic Reform*; Commins, *Islamic Reform*.

38. *Al-Misbah*, no. 17, 31 July 1924, 6; *Al-Misbah*, no. 2, 17 April 1924, 4; *Al-Misbah*, no. 57, 28 June 1926, 1–2; *Al-Misbah*, no. 87, 4 February 1926, 2.

39. *Al-Hasid*, 1:11, 18 April 1929, 1.

40. *Al-Hasid*, 1:12, 9 May 1929, 1.

41. Bashkin, "Iraqi Afghanis and 'Abduhs."

42. Ibid.

43. Snir, *'Arviyut, yahadut*, 79–135.

44. Twena, *Golim u-ge'ulim*, 5:51.

45. Balbul, "Thawrat al-jahl" (originally published 15 August 1937), in: Balbul, *Mukhtarat min al-jamra*, 65–67.

46. Bashkin, *Other Iraq*, chap. 6.

47. MacDonald et al., "Djinn"; Grunebaum, "I'djāz."

48. Darwish, "Tahrir 'abd," in *Ahrar wa 'abid*, 18.

49. Ibid., 17–22.

50. Twena, *Golim u-ge'ulim*, 5:52.

51. Balbul, "Sura tabq al-asal" (An Accurate Portrait), originally published 18 June 1937, *Mukhtarat min al-jamra*, 40. See also Bashkin, "Iraqi Women, Jewish Men," 124–29.

52. Balbul, "Sura tabq al-asal," in *Mukhtarat min al-jamra*, 38; see also Bashkin, "Iraqi Women, Jewish Men," 124–29.

53. Sha'ul, *Wilhelm Tell*, 1. See also Sha'ul's Pan-Arab poem expressing his admiration to Sa'd Zaghlul in his 1927 poem: "Sarkha min wara al-qabr—Sa'd Zaghlul yatakallam" (A Cry from Beyond the Grave, Sa'd Zaghlul Speaks), in Sha'ul, *Wa baza'a*, 152–57.

54. Sha'ul, *Qissa*, 95–97; Bashkin, "Un arabe juif."

55. FO 371/14524: R. Brooke-Popham, Acting High Commissioner, Baghdad, to Colonial Secretary, London, 1930.

56. Ibid.

57. Susa, *Hayati*, 245–48; see Bashkin, "When Dwelling Becomes Impossible."

58. *Al-Istiqlal*, 8 October 1936, quoted in Khaduri, *Ra'i wa-ri'aya*, 389.

59. *Al-Mustaqbal*, 6 August 1938, no. 29. On the petition and the Jewish intellectuals who signed it, see Kazzaz, *Yehudim*, 258.
60. Kazzaz, *Yehudim*, 68, 228–29; Obadiah, *Sittin 'amman*, 23–26.
61. Salman Darwish, *Kull shay*, 202.
62. Kazzaz, *Yehudim*, 151; Darwish, *Kull shay*, 202.
63. Gertrude Bell, letter to her father, 20 July 1921, Gertrude Bell Archive, Newcastle University Libary, www.gerty.ncl.ac.uk/letter_details.php?letter_id=491 (accessed 4 January 2012).
64. Faysal ibn al-Husayn, *Faysal ibn al-Husayn*, 247–48.
65. Ibid., 249.
66. *Al-Misbah*, no. 56, 18 June 1925, 7; *Al-Misbah*, no. 28, 30 October 1924, 7; *Al-Misbah*, no. 73, 25 October 1925, 2; *Al-Misbah*, no. 55, 11 June 1925, 2.
67. *Al-Misbah*, no. 125, 6 December 1928, 4–5.
68. Asia, *Ha-Gesharim shel hayay*, 34.
69. Basri, *Rihlat al-'umr*, 20.
70. Me'ir, *Hitpathut tarbutit*, 41.
71. Sagiv, *Yahadut*, 166.
72. Bar-Moshe, *Bayt be-Baghdad*, 175.
73. Moreh, *Ha-Ilan*, 258–82, 296–345; Snir, *'Arviyut, yahadut*, 135–244.
74. Balbul, "Al-'Awda" (The Return; originally published in October 1937), *Mukhtarat min al-jamra*, 66. See also Orit Bashkin, "Iraqi Women, Jewish Men," 130–31.
75. See the poem by Murad Mikha'il, "Ya watani!" (Oh My Homeland!), originally published in *Dijla* no. 130, 11 April 1922, reprinted in Mikha'il, *Al-A'mal al-shi'riyya al-kamila*; Snir, *'Arviyut, Yahadut*, 86, 94, Kazzaz, *Yehudim*, 66; see also Sha'ul's poems: "Ila al-jundi al-majhul" (To the Unknown Soldier; 1928), *Wa-baza'a*, 125–26.
76. Obadiah, "Ya biladi" (Oh My Country), in *Sittin 'amman*, 236.
77. Ibid., 255–56.
78. Obadiah, "Baghdad," *Sittin 'amman*, 256.
79. *Al-Hasid*, 1:6, 21 March 1929, 1.
80. Wakil, *Jama'at al-Ahali*, 260–61; Zu'aytar, *Bawakir*, 595–96, 603, 615–19.
81. *Al-Hasid*, 1:7, 28 March 1929, 5.
82. *Al-Hasid*, 1:14, 26 May 1929, 1.
83. *Al-Burhan*, no. 1, 17 October 1929, 2.
84. *Al-Burhan*, no. 4, 12 November 1929, 1.
85. *Al-Burhan*, no. 2, 24 October 1929, 4.
86. Bashkin, *Other Iraq*, chap. 1.
87. Basri, *Rihlat al-'umr*, 81.
88. Ibid.
89. Kazzaz, *Yehudim*, 54–55.
90. J. Cohen, *Hilla*, 214.
91. Kazzaz, *Yehudim*, 151.
92. 'Aqabiya, *Al-Ta'ifa*, 6.
93. Ibid., 7.
94. Ibid., 9.

95. Ibid., 9–11.
96. Benjamin, ed., *World of Benjamin of Tudela*.
97. Haddad, *Rihlat Binyamin*, 10.
98. Ibid., 14.
99. The introduction was followed by a bibliography, which included Hebrew sources like *Toldot Israel*, by Benjamin Dobnov (the 1929 Tel Aviv edition). His modern sources on Jewish history consisted works like Israel Abrahams's *Jewish Life in the Middle Ages*, Elkan Alder's *Jewish Travelers*, Jacob De Hass's *Encyclopedia of Jewish Knowledge*, W. Bacher's work on Benjamin, Pomeranz's work on the Babylonian Ge'onim, and William Winston's 1912 translation of Josephus Flavius. This was followed by Arab sources, both medieval (Ya'qubi, Ibn Batuta [d. 1369], Ibn Sa'ad al-Andalusi [d. 1070], and Muhammad ibn Jarir al-Tabari [d. 923]), and modern (Muhammad Kurd 'Ali's *Al-Islam wa'l hadara al-'arabiyya*; 'Abbas 'Azzawi's *Ta'rikh al-'Iraq bayn ihtalalyn*; and Shakib Arslan's *Ta'rikh ghazawat al-'Arab fi Uruba*). The European works on Islamic history included *Encyclopédie de L'Islam*, the works of Le Strange on Palestine and the caliphate, the essays of William Muir, and Gibbon's *Decline and Fall of the Roman Empire*.
100. Haddad, *Rihlat Binyamin*, 50.
101. Ibid., 60.
102. Ibid.
103. Ibid., 142.
104. Ibid., 133.
105. Ibid., 140.
106. Ibid., 188.
107. Ibid., 191.
108. Ibid., 199.
109. Haddad also thanked Muslim Iraq historians 'Abbas al-'Azzawi and Mustafa Jawwad for their help in preparing the edition. 'Azzawi has also written an introduction to the text.

Chapter 3: The Effendia

1. Somekh, *Baghdad, Etmol*, 95–96.
2. On secular discourses in the Arab world, see: Elshakry, "Darwin's Legacy"; El Shakry, *Great Social Laboratory*; Hourani, *Arabic Thought*, 245–460; von Kugelgen, "Call for Rationalism."
3. Wien, *Iraqi Arab Nationalism*; Cleveland, *Making of an Arab*; Bashkin, *Other Iraq*, chaps. 5, 7.
4. Great Britain, *Special Report by His Majesty's Government in the United Kingdom of Great Britain and Northern Ireland to the Council of the League of Nations on the Progress of Iraq During the Period 1920–1931, Iraq Administration Reports*, 10: 279–82; Hooper, *Constitutional Law of Iraq*.
5. Butti, *Dhakira 'iraqiyya*; Bashkin, *Other Iraq*, chap. 5.
6. Somekh, *Baghdad, Etmol*, 93–94; Aziza Khazzoom, "Great Chain of Orientalism."
7. For lists of Jewish importers, insurance agents, car dealers, pharmacists, newspaper publishers, owners of shops and industrialists, and the addresses of their businesses,

see Kuriyya, *Yahud al-'Iraq*, 233–83. For their involvement in the economy see Me'ir, *Hitpathut tarbutit*: on commerce and imports, 345–53; on role in industry (especially in the shoes and food sectors), 353–63; on Jews as movie theaters owners and film producers, 363–65, 375–77; on Jewish banking, 368–73; on Jewish printers, 373–74; on Jews in the chambers of commerce, 575; on Jewish medical doctors, 537–41; on engineers, 541–49. See also Kazzaz, *Yehudim*: on Jewish clerks, 76–87; on role in foreign trade and the economy, 93–107; on Jewish finance and banking, 107–10.

8. AIR 23/806, secret report, app. A, "The Jews of Iraq," 9 July 1934.

9. *Al-Misbah*, no. 1, 10 April 1924, 8; *Al-Misbah*, no. 2, 17 April 1924, 8; Me'ir, *Hitpathut tarbutit*, 332–33, 427.

10. Somekh, *Baghdad, Etmol*, 55–61, 78; Me'ir, *Hitpathut tarbutit*, 316–19.

11. Me'ir, *Hitpathut tarbutit*, 440; Basri, *A'lam al-yahud*, 25–61; *Al-Misbah*, no. 56, 18 June 1925, 7; *Al-Misbah*, no. 28, 30 October 1924, 7; *Al-Misbah*, no. 73, 25 October 1925, 2; *Al-Misbah*, no. 55, 11 June 1925, 2.

12. Gershoni and Jankowski, *Egypt, Islam, and the Arabs*; Bozdogan and Resat Kasaba, eds., *Rethinking Modernity and National Identity in Turkey*; see also the articles by Camron Michael Amin, Mary Ann Fay, Kathryn Libal, and Charlotte Weber, in the edited volume on interwar feminism in: *Journal of Middle East Women's Studies* 4:1 (2007).

13. *Al-Misbah*, no. 6, 15 May 1924, 5.

14. *Al-Burhan*, no. 5, 19 November 1929, 2.

15. *Al-Misbah*, no. 4, 1 May 1924, 1; Me'ir, *Hitpathut tarbutit*, 429–30.

16. Susa, *Hayati*, 136–37.

17. *Al-Hasid*, 7 March 1929. Reprinted in Sha'ul, *Qissa*, 169–70.

18. *Al-Burhan*, no. 2, 24 October 1929, 2.

19. *Al-Burhan*, no. 3, 31 October 1929, 3.

20. On Bergson's influence on Egyptian intellectual Muhammad Husayn Haykal and his generation, see Smith, *Islam and the Search for Social Order*, 132–35.

21. Balbul, *Mukhtarat min al-jamra*, 80–82.

22. Zohar, "Yahaso shel ha-rav 'Abdallah Somekh."

23. On the position of the chief rabbi in the Ottoman context, see Har'el, *Ben tekhakhim le-mahpekhah*.

24. *Bayan hakhami Baghdad hawla qadiyat wakil al-hakhambashi* (The Opinions of the Rabbis of Baghdad Concerning the Problem of the Post of the Hakham-bashi) (Baghdad: Matba'at al-adab, 1929), reprinted in Khaduri, *Ra'i wa-ra'iya*; see also ibid., 48; Marmorstein, "Hahkam Sasson in 1949," 364–68.

25. Me'ir, *Hitpathut tarbutit*, 5–7.

26. Marmorstein, "Hahkam Sasson in 1949," 366; Me'ir, *Hitpathut tarbutit*, 426.

27. *Al-Hasid*, 1:11, 18 April 1929, 1; *Al-Hasid*, 1:12, 9 May 1929, 1.

28. Al-Majalis al-jismani al-isra'ili, *Na'im Zilkha*, 37–39.

29. Ibid., 22.

30. Theosophy is an ecumenical group established in New York in 1875 with the aim of searching for the meaning of the universe. Iraqi Jews were first exposed to the group in India. Sagiv, *Yahadut*, 73–89; H. Cohen, "Teosofim yehudim," 401–6.

31. Twena, *Golim-u ge'ulim*, 5:86.

32. Me'ir, *Hitpathut tarbutit*, 32–36; Al-Majlis al-jismani al-isra'ili, *Taqrir 'an al-madaris al-ahliyya al-isra'iliyya, sanat 1950*, 3–5; Ghanima, *Nuzhat al-mushtaq* (English trans.), 139–41.

33. Basri, *A'lam al-yahud*; al-Majlis al-jismani al-'isra'ili, *Na'im Zilkha*; Bashkin, "To Educate an Iraqi-Jew."

34. Monroe, *Report of the Education Inquiry Commission*; Matthews and Akrawi, *Education in Arab Countries*; Simon, *Iraq Between Two World Wars*, chap. 4; Cleveland, *Making of an Arab Nationalist*; al-Dujayli, *Taqaddum al-ta'lim al-'ali*.

35. For details on schools, number of students, and types of institutions see Me'ir, *Hitpathut tarbutit*, 551–61.

36. Ibid., 10.

37. Twena, *Golim u-ge'ulim*, 5:216; Murad, *Mi-Bavel ba-mahteret*, 13–17; Great Britain, *Report by His Britannic Majesty's Government to the Council of the League of Nations on the Administration of Iraq for the year 1927*; reprinted in: *Iraq Administration Reports, 1914–1932*, 1992, 8:499; Great Britain, *Report by His Majesty's Government in the United Kingdom of Great Britain and Northern Ireland to the Council of the League of Nations on the Administration of Iraq for the year 1929*, *Administration Reports*, 9:312–16; Great Britain, *Report by His Majesty's Government in the United Kingdom of Great Britain and Northern Ireland to the Council of the League of Nations on the Administration of Iraq for the year 1930*, *Administration Reports*, 9:486, Great Britain, *Special Report by His Majesty's Government in the United Kingdom of Great Britain and Northern Ireland to the Council of the League of Nations on the Progress of Iraq During the period 1920–1931*, *Administration Reports*, 10:279–82.

38. Great Britain, *Report to the Council of the League of Nations for 1927*, ibid., 8:499.

39. Me'ir, *Hitpathut tarbutit*, 447; Bashkin, "To Educate an Iraqi-Jew."

40. Al-Majlis al-jismani al-isra'ili, *Taqrir 'an al-madaris al-isra'iliyya fi Baghdad li sanat 1929–1930*, 1–2; on members of the committees and their relationship to the community, see Twena, *Golim u-ge'ulim*, 5:26, 35–55.

41. The schools not supported by endowments included the following: the Alliance network: a school for boys named after Albert Sasun and the elementary and middle school for girls named after Laura Kedurie; Rachel Shahmon primary school for boys (previously, *al-Ta'awwun*), *al-Wataniyya* school for boys (established 1923); Shammash high school (established 1928); Mas'uda Salmah primary school for boys (established 1930); Manashe Salih primary school for boys (established 1935); the high school for girls (al-Thanawiyya al-ahliyya, established 1941–42); the Frank 'Ayni middle school for boys (established 1941–42); the Mas'uda Shem Tov primary school for boys (established 1946); the primary school for girls named after Abraham Tweig (established 1946); the middle school for boys al-Mutawasita al-ahliyya (established 1948–49); the public high school for night classes (al-I'dadiyya al-ahliyya al-masa'iyya, established 1948–49); the public high school for boys (al-'Idadiyya al-ahaliyya, established 1939–40); and the Midrash schools. Schools that were supported by endowments included the elementary school for boys named after Rebecca Nur'el (established 1902); the primary school for girls named after No'am and Tova Nur'el (established 1924); the elementary school Menahem Salih Daniel (established 1909); and the professional girls school (established 1947). The Ministry of Education established additional three schools at the request of the community. The first was a primary school for girls named after Menashe Salih (established 1930),

whose teaching staff was mostly Muslim; the second was Ra's al-qarya (established 1929), whose director was Muslim, although the teaching staff was mostly Jewish; but since 1932 turned into a public school for all religions and al-Sama'wal primary school (established 1936). Al-Majlis al-jismani al-isra'ili, *Taqrir 'an al-madaris al-ahliyya al-isra'iliyya, sanat 1950*, 3–28; *Taqrir 'an al-madaris al-isra'iliyya fi Baghdad li sanat 1929–1930*, 1–10; Me'ir, *Hitpathut tarbutit*, 105–37;Ya'qov-Yaron, *Shalom lakh Baghdad*, 22; *Rapport du comité des écoles israélites sur les écoles israélites de Baghdad, 1930*;Twena, *Golim u-ge'ulim*, 5:59–151.

42. Sagiv, *Yahadut*; Me'ir, *Hitpathut tarbutit*, 141–79.

43. Me'ir, *Hitpathut tarbutit*, 179–80; on Jewish education in the villages, see ibid., 190–205.

44. Al-Majlis al-jismani al-isra'ili, *Taqrir 'an al-madaris al-isra'iliyya fi Baghdad li sanat 1929–1930*; Al-Majlis al-jismani al-isra'ili, *Al-Nizam al-dakhili*, 4–5; Al-Majlis al-jismani al-isra'ili, *Taqrir 'an al-madaris al-ahliyya al-isra'iliyya, sanat 1950*, 28–33.

45. Al-Majlis al-jismani al-isra'ili, *Taqrir 'an al-madaris al-ahliyya al-isra'iliyya, sanat 1950*, 36–41.

46. Ibid., 50–53, 177; *Al-Nizam al-dakhili li-madaris al-ta'ifa al-isra'iliyya bi-baghdad, 1930*, 1; Me'ir, *Hitpathut tarbutit*, 88–89, 92–98.

47. Bashkin, "To Educate an Iraqi-Jew."

48. Bar-Moshe, *Bayt be-Baghdad*, 229.

49. Great Britain, *Report by His Britannic Majesty's Government to the Council of the League of Nations on the Administration of Iraq for the Year 1925, Administration Reports*, 8:136.

50. Twena, *Golim u-ge'ulim*, 5:20; *Rapport du comité des écoles israélites*, 4–5; *Taqrir 'an al-madaris al-isra'iliyya fi'l Baghdad li sanat 1929–1930*, 5.

51. In 1949, the committee began holding special classes for teachers in order to expand their pedagogical training in the fields of psychology, educational theory, and the history of education; Al-Majlis al-jismani al-isra'ili, *Taqrir 'an al-madaris al-ahliyya al-isra'iliyya, sanat 1950*, 50–53, 177; *Al-Nizam al-dakhili li-madaris al-ta'ifa al-isra'iliyya bi-Baghdad, 1930*, 1; Me'ir, *Hipathut tarbutit*, 88–89, 92–98.

52. Salman Darwish reports that one group of Jewish students even considered converting to Islam, but the plan was short lived and never saw the light of day: Darwish, *Kull shay*, 201–2.

53. Simon, "Teaching of History in Iraq."

54. See, for example, the testimony of Naggar, *Bab al-sheikh*, 74.

55. Al-Majlis al-jismani al-isra'ili, *Taqrir 'an al-madaris al-isra'iliyya fi Baghdad li sanat 1929–1930*, 7; Me'ir, *Hipathut tarbutit*, 39–41.

56. Twena, *Golim u-ge'ulim*, 5:87.

57. Basri, *Rihlat al-'umr*, 22.

58. Shammash had 1,087 books in Arabic, 1,164 books in English, al-Mutawasita al-ahliyya li'l banat had 950 books in Arabic and 326 in English; Albert Sasson had 1,691 books in French, 950 in Arabic, 847 in English, and 364 children's books; Laura Kedourie had 168 books in English, 570 books in French, and 150 children's book; Frank 'Ayni had 410 books in Arabic and 1,070 books in English; al-Thanawiya al-ahliyya li'l banat had 273 books in Arabic and 214 books in English; Rachel Shamon had 536 books in Arabic, 120 books in English, and 344 children's books; al-Wataniyya had 1,032 books in Arabic,

350 books in English, and 523 children's books; Mas'uda Salman had 562 books in Arabic, 376 books in English, and 393 children's books; Menashe Salih had 1,770 books in Arabic, 260 books in English, and 640 children's books; Rivka Nurel had 107 books in Arabic, 105 books in English, and 116 children's books; No'am and Tova Nur'el had 424 books in Arabic, 144 books in English, and 199 children's books; Mas'uda Shem Tov had 145 books in Arabic, 82 books in English, and 232 children's books; Rina Tuwiq had 191 children's books. *Taqrir 'an al-madaris al-ahliyya al-isra'iliyya, sanat 1950*, 44.

59. Former students have recalled in particular their love of books by the Egyptian author Kamal Kilani. See: Somekh, *Baghdad, Etmol*, 17; Agasi, *Mi-Baghdad*, 94–95; Bar-Moshe, *Bayt be-Baghdad*, 109.

60. *Al-Misbah*, no. 91, 4 March 1926, 7; *Al-Misbah*, no. 93, 31 March 1926, 7; Sagiv, *Yahadut*, 166.

61. *Al-Hasid*, 1:13, 16 May 1929, 3; see also Morhen, *Ha-Ilan*, 358–80; Bashkin, "To Educate an Iraqi-Jew."

62. Lajnat Ta'awun al-Tullab fi Madrasat al-Alliance, *Ma'asi al-hayah bi qalam al-shab al-adib al-marhum*, 5, 7, 10–12.

63. Ya'qov-Yaron, *Shalom lakh Baghdad*; Bashkin, "To Educate an Iraqi-Jew." 22.

64. J. Cohen, *Hilla*, 202.

65. On the trip of student Emile Murad to the North, see Murad, *Mi-Bavel bamahteret*, 14–15. On trips in the Alliance high school in Basra, see Drori, *Mi-Bavel la-Carmel*, 60–61.

66. J. Cohen, *Hilla*, 157.

67. Ibid., 159.

68. Ibid., 193.

69. Ibid., 195.

70. Ibid., 196.

71. Ibid., 205. The reference here is to Psalm 137.

72. Ibid., 206.

73. The fact that Jonah reports that he was excited or moved in such trips is of great importance. During the 1930s and 1940s, the Ministry of Education advocated that emotion and feelings should be incorporated into the teaching of history, as teachers were urged to help their students relive their nation's past. See: Shawkat, *Hadhihi ahdafuna*, 12, 48; Reeva Simon, "The Teaching of History in Iraq," *Istiqlal*, 24 November 1939, no. 3512, 2.

74. Al-Majlis al-jismani al-isra'ili, *Taqrir 'an al-madaris al-isra'iliyya fi Baghdad li sanat 1929–1930*, 3; *Al-Nizam al-dakhili li-madaris al-ta'ifa al-isra'iliyya bi-Baghdad, 1930*, 1–2; *Rapport du comité des écoles israélites*, 1–8.

75. Twena, *Golim u-ge'ulim*, 5:220–21.

76. Ibid., 80–81.

77. Sagiv, *Yahadut*, 159–60.

78. Somekh, *Baghdad, Etmol*, 62–63; 133–34; Sami Zubaida, "Being Iraqi and a Jew," 271.

79. Moshe Sofer, "Jewish Education and the Zionist Movement in Baghdad in 1924–1929," an interview conducted by Haim Cohen, 3 May 1963 (in Hebrew), 6; in OYA.

80. Agasi, *Mi-Baghdad le-Israel*, 185.

81. Twena, *Golim u-ge'ulim*, 5:106; Me'ir, *Hitpathut tarbutit*, 124–27.
82. Barshan, *Yehudi be-tzel ha-Islam*, 112–13.
83. Dawn, "Formation of Pan-Arab Ideology"; Simon, *Iraq Between Two World Wars*, chap. 4; Bashkin, *The Other Iraq*, chap. 5, 7.
84. Wien, "Who Is 'Liberal' in 1930s Iraq?"
85. Twena, *Golim u-ge'ulim*, 5:102, 199–200; *Taqrir 'an al-madaris al-ahliyya al-isra'iliyya, sanat 1950*, 41–45; Me'ir, *Hitpathut tarbutit*, 77–80; Al-Majlis al-jismani al-isra'ili, *Taqrir 'an al-madaris al-isra'iliyya fi Baghdad li sanat 1929–1930*, 41–44; on reports about such competitions in the Shammash school, see: *Al-Akhbar*, 31 March 1947, located in the Shammash file in OYA; Madrasat Shammash, *Minhaj al-hafla al-riyadiyya al-sanawiyya li-madrasat Shammash al-thanawiyya* (1945), Madrasat Shammash, *Minhaj al-hafla al-riyadiyya al-sanawiyya li-madrasat Shammash al-thanawiyya* (1947).
86. Naggar, *Bab al-Sheikh*, 76–78; Sha'shua', *Yemey Baghdad*, 40–42; Barshan, *Yehudi be-tzel ha-Islam*, 94–96; on the Futuwwa, see Wild, "National Socialism," 136–37.
87. Me'ir, *Hitpathut tarbutit*, 77–79.
88. Sha'ul, *Qissa*, 76; Basri, *Rihlat al-'umr*, 22; Ballas, *Be-Guf rishon*, 9, 16–17.
89. Al-Majlis al-jismani al-isra'ili, *Taqrir 'an al-madaris al-isra'iliyya fi Baghdad li sanat 1929–1930*, 35–36.
90. Great Britain, *Report by His Britannic Majesty's Government to the Council of the League of Nations on the Administration of Iraq for the Year 1925*, Administration Reports, 8:136.
91. Great Britain, *Report by His Majesty's Government in the United Kingdom of Great Britain and Northern Ireland to the Council of the League of Nations on the Administration of Iraq for the Year 1928*, Administration Reports, 9:130–31.
92. Ibid., 312. On the opening of Shammash and the transformation to English, see also *Rapport du comité des écoles israélites*, 6–7.
93. OYA, "Jewish Education in Iraq," interview recorded in the home of Mr. and Mrs. Adolph G. Brotman, Wembley Park, London, August 5, 1962; interviewer: G. Wigoder.
94. Ibid.
95. Somekh, *Baghdad, Etmol*, 58–61.
96. J. Cohen, *Hilla*, 23.
97. The school was founded in 1909 with the aim of being an institution for Turkish instruction, which would teach the same subjects taught in the government military school in order to qualify Jewish students for military service. FO 195/2338, file 79, in Kedourie and Shohet, "Jews of Baghdad," 359; Me'ir, *Hitpathut tarbutit*, 38.
98. Snir, *'Arviyut, Yahadut*, 38. The authorities suspected, correctly, that some of the teachers, especially those who had come from Mandatory Palestine, were Zionists.
99. Sofer, interview, 9–10.
100. S 2/104 II (1927), a letter to the education department of the Zionist leadership in Tel Aviv, June 1929; letter from the schoolmaster of Alliance israélite universelle, College A. D. Sasson, 28 June 1927, letter from Ezra Haddad, the principle of al-Wataniyya, 20 June 1929.
101. S 2/102 I (1926), a letter to the education department of the Zionist leadership in Tel Aviv, Baghdad, 2 January 1926.

102. S 2/104 II (1927), a letter to the Dr. Lurya, Education Department, Zionist executive from A. G. Brotman, 24 June 1927.

103. J. Cohen, *Hilla*, 192–93; Bashkin, "To Educate an Iraqi-Jew."

104. On these regulations, see Al-Majlis al-jismani al-isra'ili, *Al-Nizam al-dakhili li-madaris al-ta'ifa al-isra'iliyya bi-Baghdad, 1930*, 8.

105. Zubaida, "Being Iraqi and a Jew," 271.

106. Bashkin, "Representations of Women"; Bashkin, "Iraqi Women, Jewish Men"; al-Sheikh Da'ud, *Awwal al-tariq*; Efrati, "Women in Elite's Discourses"; Efrati, "The Other 'Awakening' in Iraq"; Efrati, "Competing Narratives"; Woodsmall, *Study of the Role of Women*; 'Alwaji, *Al-Intaj al-nisawi fi'l 'Iraq*; Ende, "Ehe auf Zeit"; Ingrams, ed., *Awakened*; Wiebke, "From Women's Problems."

107. OYA, "Jewish Education in Iraq."

108. Al-Majlis al-jismani al-isra'ili, *Taqrir 'an al-madaris al-ahliyya al-isra'iliyya, sanat 1950*, 4–5; Twena, *Golim u-ge'ulim*, 5:76; Me'ir, *Hitpathut tarbutit*, 35–36.

109. Al-Majlis al-jismani al-isra'ili, *Taqrir 'an al-madaris al-isra'iliyya fi Baghdad li sanat 1929–1930*; Al-Majlis al-jismani al-isra'ili, *Taqrir 'an al-madaris al-ahliyya al-isra'iliyya, sanat 1950*; Twena, *Golim u-ge'ulim*, 5:35; Mei'r, *Hitpathut tarbutit*, 41; on the number of girls in the Frank 'Ayni Shammash system, see *Hiptahut tarbutit*, 557; on Rima Khaduri school, ibid., 559; on girls' education in the north, ibid., 167–71.

110. Gabbai, *Ha-isha*; Sehayek, "Changes in the Social Status of Urban Jewish Women."

111. Levi, *'Al Em ha-derekh*, 41.

112. Agasi, *Mi-Baghdad le-Israel*.

113. Ibid., app. 7.

114. An Arabic popular epic.

115. Gabbai, *Ha-isha*, 85–89.

116. Ibid., 92; Snir, *Arviyut, Yahadut*, 393–94.

117. Kuriyya mentions the following Jewish women as important philanthropists: Toya Nure'l, Mas'uda Salman, Laura Khaduri, Jane Menahem Salih Daniel, Hadiyya Menashe Saleh, who established schools, Rachel Simhon, Mas'uda Eliyahu Reuben, and Mas'uda Shemtov who established synagogues, and Jurjia Ezra Ishaq Salih, Farha Harun Khazzam, Rachel Sehayek, and Rachel Salman Daniel who raised funds for the Red Cross in 1918. See: Kuriyya, *Yahud al-'iraq*, 230–32; Gabbai, *Ha-isha*, 103–8.

118. S 25/5289, 3 February 1943, report by Enzo Sereni, *MZH*, 1: 168–73; report by Shemaryahu Gutman, 4 February 1943, *MZH*, 1:177; Sofer, interview, 9–10.

119. Bashkin, "Iraqi Women, Jewish Men"; Me'ir, *Hitpathut tarbutit*, 279.

120. A discussion of the issue of women's rights in the Jewish community started as early as July 1924 with a letter sent to *Al-Misbah* by a girl called R. S. Alias, who complained about the obstacles confronted by a young Jewish girl, which produce a wide range of encouraging responses from Jewish intellectuals, especially Anwar Sha'ul. See: *Al-Misbah*, no. 16, 24 July 1924, 2; *Al-Misbah*, no. 17, 31 July 1924, 1; *Al-Misbah*, no. 18, 7 August 1924, 2; *Al-Misbah*, no. 21, 28 August 1924, 3; Me'ir, *Hitpathut tarbutit*, 424–26; Gabbai, *Ha-isha*, 128–30.

121. *Al-Burhan*, no. 1, 17 October 1929, commercial marriage in Iraq, 1, 2.

122. *Al-Burhan*, no. 6, 30 December 1929, 1.
123. Shawkat, *Hadhihi ahdafuna*, 6–9; 79–80.
124. *Al-Burhan*, no. 6, 30 December 1929, 2.
125. *Al-Burhan*, no. 3, 31 October 1929, 2.

126. For example, Esterina's short story, "The mother," depicts the neglect of a child by his mother who left her baby in the care of others while she shared her nights and days with various lovers. For Jewish authors works on Iraqi women, see: Sha'ul, *Al-Hisad al-awwal*; Darwish, *Ahrar wa 'abid*; Snir, *Arviyut, yahadut*, 377–79; Sehayek, "Changes in the Social Status of Urban Jewish Women."

127. Mulla, "Ma'satuhu mathal"; originally published in *Al-Musawwar* (1951), reprinted in: Moreh, *Al-Qissa al-qasira*. Hebrew translation available in Snir, *Arviyut, Yahadut*, 540–41.

128. On the theme of honor killing in literature, see Bashkin, "Representation of Women," 71–75.

129. Balbul, "Sura tabq al-asal" (An Accurate Portrait), originally published on 18 June 1937, in *Mukhtarat min al-jamra*, 40.

130. Bashkin, "Representations of Women"; Kuriyya, *Yahud al-'Iraq*, 231.

131. Kuriyya, *Yahud*, 230; on the involvement of Jewish female writers in the Iraqi literary field, see Snir, *'Arviyut, Yahadut*, 377–97.

132. On rates of women's education, see Me'ir, *Hitpathut tarbutit*, 550–51, 557. Kuriyya mentions in this context prominent educated Jewish women such as Juliette Hesqel Naji, Simha Yamin, and Rahma Tweig, who graduated from the college of commerce and economy in 1951; Josephine Salih, who graduated from the Teachers Training College in 1941; and the nurse Rina Ishaq. See Kuriyya, *Yahud al-'Iraq*, 230–32. See also: Bashkin, "Representation of Women," 64–75; Efrati, "Competing Narratives," 546–62; on women in the Zionist party, see: Me'ir-Glitzenstein, *Zionism in an Arab Country*, 116–34; Carmela [Berta Sofer], "Our Movement in Iraq," December 1944, *MZH*, 2:397; Esther, "Girl in the Movement," December 1944, *MZH*, 2:406–8; Evelyn Salton-Zlikha, "Until When Shall We Wait?" *MZH*, 2:564–65.

133. "Confession of Malik Sayyif," 10 November 1948, *MS*, 1:37–38.
134. Me'ir, *Be'ikar*, 103.
135. Noticeably, Shammash was one of the few mixed high schools in the city.
136. FO 371/75131, March 1949, "The ICP," *MS* (5) to Foreign Office.
137. "Entry on Ezra Fu'ad Sasun Mash'al," *MS*, 3:694–96.

138. The activity of the women of the Qujman family is especially noteworthy, as two brothers, two sisters, and the wife of one of the brothers, were all party members, while the mother hid ICP documents in their home. Entry Hesqel Menahem Qujman, *MS*, 3:691–93; "Entry on Ezra Fu'ad Sasun Mash'al," *MS*, 3:694–96; Me'ir, *Be'ikar*, 101; "Entry on Rafiq Jalak," *MS*, 3:597; on the Masri family, see "Confession of Doris Sha'ul," *MS*, 3:696.

139. Me'ir, *Be'ikar*, 100.
140. Ibid.; "Confession of Fu'ad Bahjat," 27 February 1949, *MS*, 3:603–15.
141. "Confession of Malik Sayyif," 10 November 1948, *MS*, 1:37–38, 66; FO 371/75131, March 1949, "The ICP," MI5 to Foreign Office; Me'ir, *Be'ikar*, 100.

142. FO 371/75131, March 1949, "The ICP," MI5 to Foreign Office; "Confession of Malik Sayyif," 10 November 1948, *MS*, 1:37–38; Me'ir, *Be'ikar*, 100; see also Me'ir, *Hitpathut tarbutit*, 74.

143. Shalom Darwish, "Fi sanat 2541," *Ahrar*, 37–38.

144. Ibid.

145. OYA, "Jewish Education in Iraq."

146. Ibid.

147. Zohar, "Yahaso shel ha-rav 'Abdallah Somekh."

Chapter 4: Friends, Neighbors, and Enemies

1. Quoted in Sagiv, *Yahadut*, 109.

2. For the text of the report of the state's investigation committee, see al-Hasani, *Al-Asrar al-khaffiyya*, 246–56.

3. Representatives of this narrative include: Atlas, *'Ad 'amud ha-teliya*; Ben Ya'qov, *Yehudey Bavel*, 250–54, H. Cohen, *He-Pe'ilut*. The argument that the Farhud evoked pro-Zionist feelings among the Jewish youth appears in many memoirs of Zionist activists: Hillel, *Ruh qadim*; Ben Porat, *Le-Baghdad ve-hazara*, 132–35; Sha'shu', *Yemey Baghdad*; Bibi, *Me-Araba' kenafot ha-naharayim*, 11–12; Ya'qov-Yaron, *Shalom lakh Baghdad*.

4. FO 371/17874, British Embassy, Baghdad, to G. W. Rendel, Foreign Office (London), 13 December 1934; Sir Humphreys (Baghdad) to Sir John Simon (London), 13 December 1934; CO 733/274/4, 27 December 1934, Sir F. Humphreys (Baghdad) to John Simon (London); FO 371/20016, 18 April 1936, Clark Kerr (Baghdad) to Anthony Eden (London); Salman Darwish, *Kull shay*, 200–201.

5. FO 371/27116, 25 September 1941, Kinahan Cornwallis (Baghdad) to Sir Horace Seymour (London).

6. CO 730/149/5, Air Vice Marshall Robert Brook-Popham, H.Q. Royal British Air Force (Iraq), to Marshall of the RAF, 31 August 1929; FO 371/13758, 1 September 1929, High Commissioner to the Secretary of State for the colonies.

7. CO 730/149/5, Gilbert Clayton, High Commissioner to Iraq (Baghdad), to Lord Passfield, Secretary of State for the colonies (London), 11 September 1929.

8. CO 730/149/5, King Faysal to Major Young, Acting High Commissioner, Iraq, 8 December 1929.

9. CO 733/275/4, 27 December 1934, Sir F. Humphreys (Baghdad) to John Simon (London).

10. FO 371/20016, 19 May 1936, Clark Kerr (Baghdad) to Anthony Eden (London); 'Imad Ahmad al-Jawahiri, *Nadi al-Muthanna wa-wajihat al-tajammu' al-qawmi fi'l 'Iraq, 1934–1942*; FO 371/20016, 2 June 1936, Muhammad Mahdi Kubba, Muthanna Club (Baghdad), to Clark Kerr (Baghdad).

11. FO 371/20016, 14 June 1936, Young Men's Muslim Association (Mosul) to Clark Kerr (Baghdad); FO 371/20016, 24 June 1936, Sa'id Thabit, President, Palestine Defense Committee, to Clark Kerr (Baghdad). Other letters of protest were directed to the League of Nations.

12. Zu'aytar, *Bawakir*, 592, 595, 603, 616–19, 620–23, 629, 640, 695–97.

13. FO 371/20016, 17 October 1936, Clark Kerr (Baghdad) to Anthony Eden (London).

14. FO 371/21861, 22 August 1938, C. J. Edmonds (Iraqi Ministry of the Interior, Baghdad) to W. E. Houstoun-Bowswell (British Embassy, Baghdad).

15. S 25/3265, report from 29 November 1936. A month before, Haim Weizmann contended that Iraqi Jews would be in great danger if the British did not put pressure on the Iraqi government to come to their aid. S 25/9788, 20 October 1936, report by Haim Weizmann, Zionist Bureau (London), to Va'ad Leumi.

16. FO 371/21861, 22 August 1938, C. J. Edmonds, Iraqi Ministry of the Interior (Baghdad), to W. E. Houstoun-Bowswell, British Embassy (Baghdad); see also: CO 732/85/14, 11 July 1939, A. W. G. Randall (Foreign Office) to Basil Newton (Baghdad); CO 732/85/14, 22 July 1939, Basil Newton (Baghdad) to A. W. G. Randall (Foreign Office).

17. FO 371/23303, 11 April 1939, Mr. Mackereth (Damascus) to Halifax (Foreign Office, London); FO 371/23203, 11 July 1939, Sir Basil Newton (Baghdad) to Halifax (Foreign Office, London); FO 371/23203, 18 July 1939, Captain H. M. Merry, Air Ministry to Foreign Office.

18. *Baghdad Times*, 25 August 1938.

19. FO 371/20016, 17 October 1936, Clark Kerr (Baghdad) to Anthony Eden (London); FO 371/20016, 30 September 1936, Colonel Wedgwood to Secretary of State; FO 371/20016, 20 October 1936, Clark Kerr (Baghdad) to Mr. Bateman (Baghdad).

20. S 25/3522, 28 February 1937, report on a visit to Iraq by Eliyahu Epstein.

21. Al-Wakil, *Jama'at al-Ahali*, 260–61; Zu'aytar, *Bawakir*, 595, 603, 611.

22. YS:O3/1406, Ezra Haddad, letter to Itzhak Ben Tzvi, President of the State of Israel (Jerusalem), 13 October 1959; Ezra Haddad, testimony given on 18 July 1960, reprinted in Arazi et al., eds., *Yehudey 'Iraq*, 50; FO 371/23303, 15 April 1939, Mr. Houston-Boswell (Baghdad) to Baxter (Foreign Office, London); FO 371/23203, 11 July 1939, Sir Basil Newton (Baghdad) to Halifax (Foreign Office, London); FO 371/23203, 18 July 1939, Captain H. M. Merry, Air Ministry to Foreign Office.

23. YS:O3/1406; Ezra Haddad, testimony: 13 October 1959; FO 371/23303, 15 April 1939, Mr. Houston-Boswell (Baghdad) to Baxter (Foreign Office, London); FO 371/23203, 11 July 1939, Sir Basil Newton (Baghdad) to Halifax (Foreign Office, London); FO 371/23203, 18 July 1939, Captain H. M. Merry, Air Ministry to Foreign Office; Arazi et al., eds., *Yehudey 'Iraq*, 24.

24. FO 371/37063, 15 February 1941, C. J. Edmonds to Embassy.

25. Wild, "National Socialism in the Arab Near East"; al-Jawahiri, *Nadi al-Muthanna*.

26. FO 371/23303, 11 April 1939, Mr. Houston-Boswell (Baghdad) to Halifax (Foreign Office, London); FO 371/23203, 18 July 1939, Captain H. M. Merry, Air Ministry to Foreign Office.

27. *Al-Misbah*, 24 April 1924.

28. *Al-Misbah*, 16 October 1924; *Al-Misbah*, 25 September 1924; *Al-Misbah*, 2 October 1924; *Al-Misbah*, 25 September 1924; Kazzaz, *Yehudim*, 211–12; Sha'ul, *Qissa*, 108.

29. Sehayek, *Parasha 'aluma*, 68–151. For a list of the doctors, see Darwish, *Kull shay*, 189–91.

30. Sehayek, *Parasha 'aluma*, 105, 111.

31. Sha'ul, *Qissa*, 216–19, 251–56; Ezra Haddad, "Mihnat al-dimuqratiyya fi'l qarn al-'ishrin" (The Trails of Democracy in the Twentieth Century), *Al-Hasid*, 4:1, 28 July 1932, 12–14, 51.

32. Bar-Moshe, *Bayt be-Baghdad*, 255.

33. Ibid., 283.

34. Basri, *Rihlat al-'umar*, 74.

35. FO 371/20010, 4 June 1936, Sir A. Clark Kerr (Baghdad) to Anthony Eden, Foreign Office (London); YS:O3/1406, Ezra Haddad, testimony, 13 October 1959.

36. Mu'allim Nissim, *'Ala difaf al-Furat*, 60.

37. Letter dated 6 June 1939, reprinted with annotation and translated from the German in Moreh and Yehudah, eds., *Sin'at yehudim*, 215–16 (document 1).

38. Ibid.

39. FO 371/23203, 18 July 1939, Captain H. M. Merry, Air Ministry to Foreign Office.

40. Marmorstein, "Fritz Grobba," 376–78; Elie Kedourie estimates that Emile Marmorstein, an Ashkenazi Jew residing in Baghdad at the time, wrote the original piece in May 1941, when Grobba returned to the city under the Kaylani regime to act as a German representative. See also Arazi et al., eds., *Yehudey 'Iraq*, 24.

41. Marmorstein, "Fritz Grobba," 376–78. The German Embassy itself employed the Jewish intellectual, Salim Ishaq (1877–1948), until 1934. Ishaq had attempted to resign earlier to protest the persecution of Jews in Germany. Grobba reportedly pleaded with him to remain with the embassy, and the latter stayed on for a few more months and then tendered his resignation: Moreh, *Ha-Ilan*, 384–85; Twena, *Golim u-ge'ulim*, 6:54.

42. FO 371/24561, Basil Newton (Baghdad) to Foreign Office (Halifax), 27 May 1940.

43. Marmorstein, "Fritz Grobba," 378; FO 371/23203, 25 May 1939, Sir Basil Newton (Baghdad) to Sir Oliphant (London). Newton reported that it was Nuri al-Sa'id who prevented the German club from being opened. FO 371/23203, 18 July 1939, Captain H. M. Merry, Air Ministry to Foreign Office.

44. *Al-Misbah* no. 23 11 September 1924, pp. 1–2.

45. *Al-Hilal*, 10:31, 1 July 1921.

46. Ghanima, *Nuzhat al-mushtaq*.

47. On Jawahiri, see Jubran, *Majma' al-adad*.

48. *Al-Hatif*, 4:159, 17 March 1939, 1.

49. Landau, *Search for Tomorrow*, 226–27.

50. The Central Committee of the Iraqi Communist Party, 24 September 1940, cited in Sibahi, *'Uqud min ta'rikh*, 197. According to Batatu, an issue of *Al-Sharara* from February 1941 suggested that the Arab countries adopted neutrality of Iraq: Batatu, *Old Social Classes*, 442–49.

51. Gershoni, "Beyond Anti-Semitism."

52. FO 371/27065, 15 April 1941, Kinahan Cornwallis (Baghdad) to Foreign Office (London).

53. On Rashid 'Ali and his context, see: Tarbush, *Role of the Military*; Simon, *Iraq Between Two World Wars*, 135–55; Hamdi, *Rashid Ali al-Gailani*.

54. Testimony by Gurji Barshan, Moreh and Yehudah, eds., *Sin'at yehudim*, 239–41 (document 14).
55. Shalom Darwish, testimony given in Haifa, Israel, 29 June 1969, reprinted in Arazi et al., eds., *Yehudey Iraq*, 32; Ezra Haddad, testimony given in Tel Aviv, 18 July 1960, reprinted in Arazi et al., eds., *Yehudey Iraq*, 50.
56. FO 371/27065, Kinahan Cornwallis (Baghdad) to Anthony Eden (London); FO 371/27067, 26 April 1941, from Basil Newton (Baghdad) to Anthony Eden (London).
57. FO 371/27067, 1 May 1941, Air H.A. Iraq to H.Q. RAF, M.E.
58. The British Embassy in Amman was even concerned about the possible influence of Baghdadi radio on Jordanian children. FO 371/27068, Kinahan Cornwallis (London) to Anthony Eden (Foreign Office), 5 May 1941; FO 371/27068, Colonial Office (High Commissioner MacMichael) to Foreign Office, 6 May 1941; on the radio transmissions from Germany, see al-Bahri, *Huna Berlin!*
59. FO 371/27070, 17 May 1941, High Commissioner, H. MacMichael to Secretary of State for the colonies; 21 May 1941, Secretary of State for the colonies to High Commissioner, H. MacMichael.
60. FO 371/27063, Sir Basil Newton (Baghdad) to Anthony Eden (London); 7 February 1941; FO 371/27029, Kinahan Cornwallis (Baghdad) to Foreign Office (London), 15 July 1941. An informant "very friendly to Nuri Said" reported that the regime was indeed waging a propaganda campaign against Britain. FO 371/27068, 10 May 1941, Professor Namier (Jewish Agency for Palestine) to Mr. R. A. Butler (Foreign Office, London).
61. FO 371/27070, 16 May 1941, Kinahan Cornwallis (Baghdad) to Foreign Office (London); FO 371/27071, 21 May 1941, Kinahan Cornwallis (Baghdad) to Foreign Office (London).
62. FO 371/27072, 25 May 1941, Sir R. Bullard (Teheran) to Foreign Office (Cairo and Jerusalem).
63. FO 371/27079, 30 June 1941; FO 371/27077, Kinahan Cornwallis (Baghdad) to Anthony Eden (London), 6 June 1941; AIR 40/1420, 2 June 1941, Baghdad (via Habaniyya) to Foreign Office; War Cabinet distribution, to Kinahan Cornwallis; FO 371/27064, 14 April 1941, Government of India, External Affairs Department, to Secretary of State for India; FO 371/27067, 1 May 1941, Air H.A. Iraq to H.Q. RAF, M.E.
64. FO 371/27077, Kinahan Cornwallis (Baghdad) to Anthony Eden (London), 6 June 1941; FO 371/27068, U.S. Embassy, American Minister in Baghdad, Department of State, 7 May 1941; FO 371/27070, 19 May 1941, Herschel Jonson (U.S. Embassy) to Mr. Baxter (FO).
65. FO 371/27070 MICE (Middle East Intelligence Center, War Office) to Air Office, 17 May 1941.
66. FO 371/27068, Kinahan Cornwallis (Baghdad) to Anthony Eden (London), 4 May 1941; FO 371/27072, 23 May 1941, Cornwallis (Baghdad) to Foreign Office (London).
67. FO 371/27072, 26 May 1941, His Majesty's Charge d'Affairs, Iraq, to Foreign Office; on BBC propaganda, see also FO 371/27067, 1 May 1941, Air H.A. Iraq to H.Q. RAF, M.E.
68. Kedourie, "Sack of Basra," 283–314.
69. Barshan, *Yehudi be-tzel ha-Islam*, 104.

70. Sylvia G. Haim, "Aspects of Jewish Life in Baghdad Under the Monarchy," *MES*, 12:2 (1976), 192; testimony of Ezra Haddad, Yad Va-Shem, O3/1406, 14 October 1959.

71. FO 371/27070, MICE (Middle East Intelligence Center, War Office) to Air Office, 17 May 1941.

72. FO 371/27067, 1 May 1941, from Air H.A. Iraq to H.Q. RAF, M.E.

73. A letter written to Kaylani, 7 May 1941, Batatu, *Old Social Classes*, 442–45.

74. FO 371/27070, MICE (Middle East Intelligence Center, War Office), to Air Office, 17 May 1941.

75. Haim, "Aspects of Jewish Life," 192–93; Matilda Mazal Museiri, "A Report on Iraqi Jews," April 1942, in: *MZH*, 1:59–61; Barshan, *Yehudi be-tzel ha-Islam*, 104; testimony of Abraham Twena, recorded 7 January 1966, reprinted in Moreh and Yehudah, eds., *Sin'at yehudim*, 286–90 (document 29); S 25/5289, "Report on the *Farhud*" (document E), reprinted in *Pe'amim* 8 (1981): 70–77 (the editors believe it was probably written by Yusuf al-Kabir).

76. Document 29; document E; H. Cohen, "The Anti-Jewish Farhud"; Barshan, *Yehudi be-tzel ha-Islam*, 104.

77. Shalom Darwish, testimony given in Haifa, 29 June 1969, reprinted in Arazi et al., eds., *Yehudey 'Iraq*, 32.

78. According to testimonies of drivers, they report that Yunis gave an order to attack the Jews of Baghdad. S 25/9999, 13 July 1941, evidence of Jewish drivers in Baghdad.

79. FO 371/27072, Sir H. Knatchbull Hugessen (Angora) to Foreign Office, 25 May 1941.

80. FO 371/27074, Kinahan Cornwallis (Baghdad) to Foreign Office, 2 June 1941; FO 371/27078, letter from the Jewish Agency to British Embassy (Baghdad), 23 July 1941; FO 371/27078, Kinahan Cornwallis (Baghdad) to Anthony Eden (London), 11 July 1941; FO 371/27081, 27 October 1941, Ben Tzvi [Va'd Le'umi] to Lord Moyn (High Commissioner in Palestine); H. Cohen, "Anti-Jewish *Farhud*," 2–17; Kedourie, "Sack of Basra," 283–314; Haim, "Aspects of Jewish Life," 38–45; Arazi et al., eds., *Yehudey 'Iraq*; S 25/9999, 13 July 1941, evidence of Jewish drivers in Baghdad; S 25/5269, 12 August 1941, report by Y. Ben Tzvi based on inquiries by Moshe Yatah, S 25/5269, 20 July 1941.

81. Arazi et al., eds., *Yehudey 'Iraq*, 33–35.

82. FO 371/27070, MICE (Middle East Intelligence Center, War Office) to Air Office, 17 May 1941; FO 371/27067, 1 May 1941, Air H. A. Iraq, to H.Q. RAF, M.E.; Kedourie, "Sack of Basra," 283–314.

83. FO 371/27068, 7 May 1941, Colonial Office (Middle East) to War Office; WO 106/6107, Iraq February 1940–August 1941, report by M.O.1 (as late as October 1941 avoidance of major conflicts with Arabs was recommended).

84. FO 371/27072, 28 May 1941, His Majesty's Charge d'Affairs, Iraq, to Foreign Office.

85. WO 106/6107, Iraq, February 1940–August 1941, report by M.O.1.

86. FO 371/2730, 30 May 1941, Kinahan Cornwallis to Foreign Office; FO 371/2730, 31 May 1941, Foreign Office to Baghdad.

87. FO 371/27077, Kinahan Cornwallis (Baghdad) to Foreign Office (London); S 25/9999, 13 July 1941, evidence of Jewish drivers in Baghdad; S 25/9999, 14 July 1941, testimony of a Baghdadi eyewitness.

88. FO 371/31371, 27 April 1942.

89. Testimony of Jacob Peres, reprinted in Moreh and Yehudah, eds., *Sin'at yehudim*, 251.

90. Arazi et al., eds., *Yehudey 'Iraq*, 20; testimony of Victor Shalom Rabi', 19 July 1960, Arazi et al., eds., *Yehudey 'Iraq*, 36; FO 371/27078, letter from the Jewish Agency to British Embassy (Baghdad), 23 July 1941.

91. FO 371/27078, Kinahan Cornwallis (Baghdad) to Anthony Eden (London), 11 July 1941; S 25/5289, testimony by Moseh Yatah to B. Joseph, 20 July 1941 (document A), reprinted in *Pe'amim* 8 (1981): 60–64; document E; al-Hasani, *Al-Asrar al-khaffiyya*, 246–56.

92. S 25/10372, 25 June 1941, Eliyahu Epstein to Moshe Shertok. For Taha al-Hashimi's view of the police: Kuriyya, *Yahud al-'iraq*, 147; on Amin al-Mumayyiz's view of the police and the army, see ibid., 147–49.

93. FO 371/27078 11 July 1941, Sir K. Cornwallis (Baghdad) to Anthony Eden (London). See also FO 371/27077, From Kinahan Cornwallis (Baghdad) to Foreign Office (London).

94. Testimony by Obadiah Gurji in Moreh and Yehudah, eds., *Sin'at yehudim*, 227–29 (document 7).

95. S. Fattal, *Be Simta'ot*, 115–16.

96. Basri, *Rihlat al-'umr*, 59–60.

97. Sha'shu', *Yemey Baghdad*, 181–82.

98. Moreh, *Ha-Ilan*, 204.

99. Document A.

100. Kahila, *Hayinu ke-holmim*, 43.

101. Ya'qov-Yaron, *Shalom lakh Baghdad*, 42.

102. Recorded in the Arabic original in Moreh, *Ha-Ilan*, 189.

103. Kedourie, "Sack of Basra," 283–314.

104. Twena, *Golim u-ge'ulim*, 6:31; on Taha al-Hashimi's account of the Bedouins within the rioters, see Kuriyya, *Yahud al-'iraq*, 147.

105. On conditions in the countryside and migration to the city, see: Bashkin, *Other Iraq*, chap. 6; al-Hilali, *Nazarat fi islah al-rif*; M. Jamil, *Al-Badw wa'l-qaba'il*; Sluglett and Sluglett, "Transformation of Land Tenure"; al-Zahir, *Al-Iqta' wa'l dawawin*.

106. FO 371/27078, Kinahan Cornwallis (Baghdad) to Anthony Eden (London), 11 July 1941.

107. FO 371/27081, 11 July 1941, a letter from Kinahan Cornwallis (Baghdad) to London, reprinted in Moreh and Yehudah, eds., *Sin'at yehudim*, 273–74 (document 26); the quote is taken from the original; FO 371/27078, 29 July 1941, reprinted in *Sina't Yehudim*, 275.

108. Kedourie, "Sack of Basra," 283–314; Hasani, *Al-Asrar al-khaffiyya*, 82. The number six hundred appears also in Zionist accounts; see, for example, S 25/9999, 4 July 1941, minutes of a conversation between the representatives of the Babylonian (Jewish) community (*'adat ha-Bavlim*) and Itzhak Ben Tzvi.

109. S 25/5296, 12 August 1941, Eliyahu Epstein to Moshe Shertok.
110. S 25/5269, 20 July 1941, testimony of Yatah to B.Yossef.
111. S 25/10372, 25 June 1941, Eliyahu Epstein to Moshe Shertok.
112. Twena, *Golim u-ge'ulim*, 6:31–32.
113. Ben Porat, *Le-Baghdad ve-hazara*, 27–28.
114. Ya'qov-Yaron, *Shalom lakh Baghdad*, 43.
115. Testimony of Abraham, recorded on 7 January 1966, reprinted in Moreh and Yehudah, eds., *Sin'at yehudim*, 286–90 (document 29).
116. S 25/5289, recorded 17 July 1941, reprinted in Moreh and Yehudah, eds., *Sin'at Yehduim*, 249 (document 19).
117. OYA testimony no. 6922: Avraham Moreh, "Aunt of the 'Abduh Family."
118. *MZH*, 1:59–61.
119. Haim, "Aspects of Jewish Life," 194; other testimonies, however, critique Sa'ib for his lack of care to the Jewish patients.
120. S 25/5289, testimony given on 1 July 1941, reprinted in Moreh and Yehudah, eds., *Sin'at yehudim*, 229–30 (document 9).
121. Twena, *Golim u-ge'ulim*, 6:64.
122. S 6/4575 April 1942, report by Matilda Musseiri, *MZH*, 1:51–66.
123. Arazi et al., eds., *Yehudey 'Iraq*, 45; Twena, *Golim u-ge'ulim*, 6:31–32; S. Fattal, *Be Simta'ot Baghdad*, 115–16; Haim, "Aspects of Jewish Life," 193–94.
124. Hasani, *Al-Asrar al-khaffiyya*, 246–56.
125. Ben Porat, *Le-Baghdad ve-hazara*, 28.
126. Sagiv, *Yahadut*, 92–103; Twena, *Golim u-ge'ulim*, 6:97; Kedourie, "Sack of Basra," 283–314; WO 106/6107, Iraq, February 1940–August 1941, report by M.O.1; FO 371/27079, Kinahan Cornwallis (Baghdad), to Foreign Office, 25 July 1941; FO 371/27071, 19 May 1941, Basra Consul to Foreign Office.
127. FO 371/27065, 18 April 1941; from Kinahan Cornwallis (London) to Foreign Office; Cornwallis writes that some local people have happy memories of British and Indian soldiers from the last war.
128. FO 371/27079, 25 July 1941, Kinahan Cornwallis (Baghdad) to Anthony Eden (London).
129. FO 371/27067, 29 April 1941, Air Ministry, H.Q. Iraq, to MICE (Middle East Intelligence Center, War Office); FO 371/27067, 1 May 1941, from Air H.A. Iraq, to H.Q. RAF, M.E.
130. Testimony of Shelomo 'Azariya, 18 September 1998, in Sagiv, *Yahadut*, 105.
131. S 107/901, 2 July 1941, letter from the president of the Jewish community in Basra to the Jewish agency.
132. Testimony of Shelomo 'Azariya, 18 September 1998, in Sagiv, *Yahadut*, 105; Twena, *Golim u-ge'ulim*, 6:98.
133. Testimony of Shelomo 'Azariya, 18 September 1998, in Sagiv, *Yahadut*; testimony of David Haham, Sagiv, *Yahadut*, 111.
134. Testimony of Kenneth Qattan in Sagiv, *Yahadut*, 103–4.
135. Testimony of Abraham Ovadia, from 6 December 1998, Sagiv, *Yahadut*, 102; Sagiv, *Yahadut*, 109.

136. Izzat Mu'allim, quoted in Twena, *Golim u-ge'ulim*, 6:90–91; testimony of David Nissim, Moreh and Yehudah, eds., *Sin'at yehudim*, 302–3; Mu'allim Nissim, *'Ala difaf*, 304.

137. Moreh and Yehudah, eds., *Sin'at yehudim*, 308.

138. J. Cohen, *Hilla*, 120.

139. Ibid., 121–22; testimony of David Mu'allim, Twena, *Golim u-ge'ulim*, 6:87–89; testimony of David Mu'allim, in Moreh and Yehudah, eds., *Sin'at yehudim* 310–11 (document 36).

140. Twena, *Golim u-ge'ulim*, 6:85.

141. FO 371/27067, 29 April 1941, from Air Ministry, A. H.Q. Iraq, to MICE (Middle East Intelligence Center, War Office).

142. Twena, *Golim u-ge'ulim*, 6:84; testimony of David Semah, quoted in Moreh and Yehudah, eds., *Sin'at yehudim*, 311–13.

143. Twena, *Golim u-ge'ulim*, 6:85. Another testimony to the feeling of insecurity in the North is a murder which occurred in the Kurdish village of Sandur, where between eight to ten Jews were killed in the winter of 1941. The reason for the murders had to do with a cow stolen from a Jewish household by three members of a neighboring village, who then attacked the Jews from whom the cow was stolen; R. Gabbai, *Pera'ot Baghdad* (n.p., 1982); FO 624/23 11, February 1941, from Iraqi Ministry of Internal Affairs to Captain Holt.

144. Al-Hasani, *Al-Asrar al-khaffiyya*, 246–56.

145. FO 371/27078, Kinahan Cornwallis (Baghdad) to Anthony Eden (London), 11 July 1941.

146. Document 26; S 25/5289, Mosheh Yatah to M. Sharet (Shertok) (document F), reprinted in *Pe'amim* 8 (1981): 78–79; FO 371/27078, 29 July 1941; Hasani, *Al-Asrar al-khaffiyya*, 246–56; S 25/5269, 12 August 1941, report by Y. Ben Tzvi based on inquiries by Moshe Yatah, S 25/5269, 20 July 1941.

147. FO 371/27082, Kinahan Cornwallis (Baghdad) to Anthony Eden (London), 6 November 1941.

148. FO 371, 14 December 1941, Kinahan Cornwallis (Baghdad) to Anthony Eden (London); 24 January 1942, Cornwallis (Baghdad) to Eden (London).

149. *Sawt al-Haqq*, no. 27, 9 July 1941, 1; *Sawt al-Haqq*, no. 202, 16 February 1942, 1.

150. *Sawt al-Haqq*, no. 40, 24 July 1941, 1, 4.

151. *Sawt al-Haqq*, no. 111, 16 October 1941, 1.

152. *Sawt al-Haqq*, no. 214, 1 March 1942, 1.

153. *Sawt al-Haqq*, no. 252, 19 April 1942, 1.

154. *Sawt al-Haqq*, no. 24, 6 July 1941, 1, 4.

155. FO 371, 14 October 1942, Mr. Thompson (Baghdad) to Anthony Eden (London).

156. S 25/10372, 28 July 1941, Eliyahu Sasson to Moshe Shertok. In late June, the Zionist diplomat Eliyahu Epstein reported that the American military attaché in Istanbul, who had visited Baghdad recently, believed there would be no such riots in the future. S 25/10372, 25 June 1941, Eliyahu Epstein to Moshe Shertok.

157. FO 371/27074 Consul in Basra to Foreign Office, 1 June 1941; FO 371/27074, 3 June 1941, Kinahan Cornwallis to Foreign Office; 7 June 1941, Cornwallis to Foreign

Office; Basri, *Rihla*, 59–60; document A; Akram Zu'aytar, *Min ajli ummati* (For My Nation), 7–71, Beirut: Al-Mu'assa al-'arabiyya li'l Dirasat wa'l Nashr, Beirut: 1994.

158. S 25/5296, 13 July 1941, account of the riots (*pera'ot*) in Iraq (document F); S 25/5289, report by Enzo Sereni, reprinted in *Pe'amim* 8 (1981): 90–91 (document G). "Report on a Conversation Between Nuri al-Sa'id and the Leaders of the Jewish Community," 2 February 1943, *MZH*, 1:181–84; FO 371/27116, 10 September 1941, Mr. Motefiore to Mr. Collier; document F; Ezra Kedourie, "Report," 29 October 1942, *MZH*, 1:121–25; Enzo Sereni, "Proposal for Solving the Problem of Iraqi Jewry," 13 November 1942, *MZH*, 1:137–48; Enzo Sereni, "Report," 3 February 1943, *MZH*, 1:168–73; Me'ir-Glitzenstein, "Ha-Pera'ot bi-yehudey Baghdad"; Gabbai, *Ha-isha ha-yehudit*, 107–8.

159. S 25/5296, 12 August 1941, translation of a leaflet by Rabbi Sasun Khaduri.

160. S 25/5296, 13 July 1941, account of the riots (*pera'ot*) in Iraq.

161. FO 371/27116, 10 September 1941, Mr. Motefiore to Mr. Collier; document F; Ezra Kedourie, "Report," 29 October 1942, *MZH*, 1:121–25; Enzo Sereni, "Proposal for Solving the Problem of Iraqi Jewry," 13 November 1942, *MZH*, 1:137–48; Enzo Sereni, "Report," 3 February 1943, *MZH*, 1:168–73; Me'ir-Glitzenstein, "Ha-Pera'ot bi-yehudey Baghdad," 21–37; Gabbai, *Ha-isha ha-yehudit*, 107–8.

162. YS:O3/1406, Ezra Haddad, letter to Itzhak Ben Tzvi, President of the State of Israel (Jerusalem), 16 September 1959.

163. "Leaflets for Defense in Baghdad: Shabab al-Inqadh," 1 April 1942, *MZH*, 1:43–44.

164. "Report on Baghdad," 3 September 1949, reprinted in *Pe'amim* 8 (1981) (document D): 69; Hagana Archive, Tel Aviv, 14/19, report by Eshel, 27 October 1941 (account on buying weapons among Baghdadi Jews), *MZH*, 1:50.

165. Report by Matilda Musseiri, *MZH*, 1:51–66.

166. FO 371/40090, 15 April 1944, report by Major Wilkins, Technical Adviser to Iraq, Criminal Investigation report, report on the attitude of Jews toward Great Britain.

167. FO 371/27116, 27 August 1941, Government of India to Baghdad Embassy.

168. A cynical comment in a British account acknowledged: "Many (Jews) have made pathetic attempts to obtain visas for India for themselves or their families only to find this way of escape now closed." FO 371/27078, 11 July 1941, Kinahan Cornwallis (Baghdad) to Anthony Eden (London).

169. Letter from Eliyahu Epstein to Sharet, 28 August 1941 (document C), reprinted in *Pe'amim* 8 (1981): 66–69.

170. Ibid.

171. Enzo Sereni (17 April 1905–18 November 1944): an Italian Zionist socialist. He was sent to Iraq from April 1942 to May 1943, and wrote a few reports about his experiences. Sereni parachuted into Italy in 1944, was captured by the Germans, and was executed in Dachau concentration camp. Israeli Galili Archive, file no. 8, 2 July 1941, report by Enzo Sereni to the Histadrut, *MZH*, 1:75–92.

172. Report by Matilda Musseiri, *MZH*, 1:51–66.

173. Esther Me'ir-Glitzenstein, "Hanhagat ha-yishuv ha-yehudi be-eretz israel ve ha-pera'ot bi yehudey Baghdad," in Moreh and Yehudah, eds., *Sin'at yehudim*, 129–48; S 25/9999, 4 July 1941, minutes of a conversation between the representatives of the

Babylonian (Jewish) community (*'adat ha-bavlim*) and Itzhak Ben Tzvi; S 25/9999, 13 July 1941, evidence of Jewish drivers in Baghdad.

174. Me'ir-Glitzenstein, "Hanhagat ha-yishuv"; FO 371/27081, 27 October 1941, BenTzvi [Va'd Le'umi] to Lord Moyn (High Commissioner in Palestine).

175. S 46/61, 6 July 1941, internal information brochure.

176. S 25/5269, an undated leaflet by the Irgun.

177. Me'ir-Glitzenstein, "Hanhagat ha-yishuv"; "Report on Baghdad," 3 September 1949, reprinted in *Pe'amim* 8 (1981), 69 (document D); Hagana Archive, Tel Aviv, 14/19, report by Eshel, 27 October 1941 (account on buying weapons among Baghdadi Jews), *MZH*, 1:50; S 6/2281, protocol of a conversation about the immigration of youth from Iraq, *MZH*, 1:45.

178. J2206/1, the Department of Press and Propaganda (Hasbara) of the National Committee (Va'd le'umi), 4 July 1941.

179. J2206/1, 1 July 1941, Committee of Babylonian Rabbis, Committee of the Babylonian Community.

180. S25/5289, Jerusalem, 27 July 1941 (document 30), reprinted in Moreh and Yehudah, eds., *Sin'at yehudim*, 3.

181. Wild, "National Socialism," 139–70.

Chapter 5: Red Baghdad

1. Fattal, *Be Simta'ot*, 280.
2. Me'ir, *Be'ikar*.
3. Batatu, *Old Social Classes*, 543, 571, 651–50.
4. Barrak, *Al-Madaris al-yahudiyya*, app. 3.
5. Bashkin, *Other Iraq*, 87–125; Ismael, *Rise and Fall*; Batatu, *Old Social Classes*, 404–712; Al-Hizb al-shuyu'i al-'iraqi, *Shuhadaa' al-hizb*; Sibahi, *'Uqud min ta'rikh*; al-Khurasan, *Safahat min ta'rikh*.
6. Fahd, *Kitabat al-Rafiq Fahd*.
7. Me'ir, *Be'ikar*, 72–73, 85; on Al-Ahali, see: al-Wakil, *Jama'at al-Ahali*; al-Amin, *Jama'at al-Ahali*.
8. See 2 July 1942, report by Anzo Sereni, *MZH*, 1:80–83.
9. S 25/5289, 3 February 1943, report by Enzo Sereni, *MZH*, 1:168–73.
10. Ibid.
11. Ezra Khadduri, report (on the Iraqi Jewish community), January 1944, *MZH*, 1:247.
12. ICP member Ya'qub Cohen felt that the revolution should be carried out by the students, the intelligentsia and the petty bourgeoisie and not the workers and peasants. This was a clear deviation from the ICP line and Cohen was expelled from its ranks. Together with Dhu Nun Ayyub he founded the Congress faction in 1942. Jewish communists Ibrahim Naji Shumail, Yusuf Harun Zilkha, and Yusuf Mukmal joined another splinter group led by Abdallah al-Qarini. When these splinter groups were united into Wahdat al-Nidal, Shumail, Masri, and Zaluf played a part in its central leadership committee, composed of twelve members. In 1945, they all return to the ICP. See: Me'ir, *Be'ikar*, 88; Batatu, *Old Social Classes*, 498–99.

13. FO 371/68481A, 10 February 1948, "Report on Communist Organizations and the League of Iraqi Communists," J. G. Robertson to Foreign Office (received from Security Intelligence, Middle East, 9 February 1948).

14. FO 371/75131, March 1949, "The ICP," MI5 to Foreign Office.

15. S 25/3529, 31 March 1946, Me'ir Shilon-Shlank (Baghdad) to Eliyahu Sasson (the political division of the Jewish Agency).

16. S 25/5289, 12 July 1946, report on Iraqi Jews submitted to David Ben Gurion.

17. Report to the Jewish agency from Me'ir Shilon-Shlank, June 1946, *MZH*, 3:437–38.

18. Me'ir, *Be'ikar*, 101.

19. According to Batatu the ICP had a few hundred supporters in 1935; four hundred members in 1936, eighty members in 1940; over a thousand members in 1942 and three thousand to four thousand members in 1948: Batatu, *Old Social Classes*, 642.

20. Batatu, *Old Social Classes*, 632; Me'ir, *Be'ikar*, 101.

21. Batatu, *Old Social Classes*, 1990–93.

22. For the number of the league's members, see p. 146.

23. These were members of the anti-Zionist communist league and the communist-leaning Hizb al-Taharrur. According to Barrak, these Jews later joined the ICP: 123 joined in 1946, 10 joined in 1945, and 4 in 1947.

24. Workers were 28.8 percent of the members, students were 25 percent, clerks 16.30 percent and teachers 2.04 percent.

25. Al-Barrak, *Al-Madaris al-yahudiyya*, app. 3.

26. Masri, "Dhikrayat."

27. A report by Shemaryahu Gutman, 4 February 1943, reprinted in *MZH*, 1:174–81.

28. S. Fattal, *Be-Simta'ot*, 282.

29. *Al-Majalla*, no. 1, 1 June 1942, 1–9; *Al-Majalla*, no. 2, 16 June 1942, 26.

30. *Al-Majalla*, no. 2, 16 June 1942, 26, an essay by Na'im Salih [Tweig].

31. *Zo Hadrech*, 28 March 1984; OYA, interview with Sami Michael, no. 7169, interviewer Gidom Lve Ari, 1978 cassette 346; Salim Fattal notes that his uncle's death during Farhud in Bab al-Sheikh resulted in his decision to join the ICP: S. Fattal, *Be-Simta'ot* 275.

32. S 20/539/I, April 1949, "Secret Report on Iraq by the American-Jewish Committee."

33. See 22 May 1946, Me'ir Shilon-Shlank (Baghdad) to Eliyahu Sasson, reprinted in *MZH*, 3:397–98.

34. April 1948, letter from Yerhmiel Asa (Baghdad) to his wife, Miriam, and his daughters, *MZH*, 4:1009–12.

35. *Zo Hadrech*, 28 March 1984, 8–9; OYA, interview with Sami Michael, no. 7169, interviewer Gidom Lve Ari, 1978 cassette 346.

36. FO 371/68459, 14 June 1948, Mr. Davis (British Consulate, Basra) to Foreign Office.

37. Ibid.

38. Me'ir, *Be'ikar*, 105.

39. *Zo Hadrech*, 28 March 1984.

40. S 25/5289, 3 February 1943, "A Report by Enzo Sereni," *MZH*, 1:168–73.
41. *Zo Hadrech*, 28 March 1984.
42. *Al-Ittihad*, 24 May 1984 (a story by a "an old comrade in the Iraqi Communist Party who lives now in a European country"). Activists such as Ya'qub Cohen felt that the aims of the ICP, namely, the materialization of sovereignty by democratic elections, were consonant with his worldview. "Confession of Mir Ya'qub Cohen," *MS*, 1:122–24; see "Confession of Shlomo Sasun Dallal," *MS*, 3:560–69.
43. "Confession of Shlmo Sasun Dallal," *MS*, 3:560–69.
44. S 25/5289, 12 July 1946, "Report on Iraqi Jews to David Ben Gurion."
45. *Zo Hadrech*, 28 March 1984; Ballas, *Be-Guf rishon*, 29–30; Kahila, *Hayinu ke-holmim*, 65, S. Fattal, *Be-Simta'ot*, 293–95.
46. Sasun Dallal, "Message to the Public," 22 January 1949.
47. *Zo Hadrech*, 28 March 1984, FO 371/82403, 17 January 1950, "Iraq: Annual Review for 1949," Henry Mack to Mr. McNeil.
48. FO 371/75131, March 1949, "The ICP," MI5 to Foreign Office; Me'ir, *Be'ikar*, 92–97; "Mir Ya'qub Cohen," *MS*, 1:122–24; "Confession of Fu'ad Bahjat," 27 February 1949, *MS*, 3:603–15; "Ezra Fuad Sasun Mash'al," *MS*, 3:694–96.
49. FO 371/75131, March 1949, "The ICP," MI5 to Foreign Office; on Sayyif and Sadiq, see also al-Hajj, *Shahada*, 116–17.
50. "Confession of Malik Sayyif," 10 November 1948, *MS*, 1:27–28, 40–41; on Mir Yaq'ub Cohen's relations with Jewish merchants, see: *MS*, 2:349; Me'ir, *Be'ikar*, 92–93.
51. FO 371/75131, March 1949, "The ICP," MI5 to Foreign Office.
52. FO 371/68481A, 10 February 1948, "Report on Communist Organizations and the League of Iraqi Communists J. G. Robertson to Foreign Office" (received from Security Intelligence Middle East, 9 February 1948).
53. Batatu, *Old Social Classes*, 653.
54. "Confession of Musa Suliayman from Irbil," *MS*, 3:663–64.
55. OYA, interview with Sami Michael.
56. On the activities among the railway workers, and in Basra, see: "Entry on Ishaq Shirazi," *MS*, 2:346; "Confession of Muhammad Husayn al-Shabibi," *MS*, 2:269–70; "Confession of Malik Sayyif," 10 November 1948, *MS*, 1:31.
57. FO 371/75131, March 1949, "The ICP," MI5 to Foreign Office; the account references the 1946 activities of Salim Menashe among the shoemakers, Moshe Cohen among the tailors, and Hesqel Ibrahim among the workers and Ishaq Shirazi in factories in the south; Naji Sha'ul in the port authorities and amongst train workers. On the activities of Moshe Cohen in al-Karkh and later in Ba'quba, and Mir Ya'qub Cohen in al-Karkh, see "Confession of Fu'ad Bahjat," 27 February 1949, *MS*, 3:603–15. On the activities of Yusuf Zaluf in al-'Ashshsar, and among the workers of Basra, see: "Confession of Yusuf bin Menashe Zaluf," *MS*, 1:108; "Confession of Sabri 'Abd al-Karim," *MS*, 3:672–77. On Sami Michael's activities among the students, Naji Sha'ul activities among clerks, see Me'ir, *Be'ikar*, 99; see also *MS*, 2:255.
58. "Confession of Muhammad Husayn al-Shabibi," *MS*, 2:269–70; "Confession of Malik Sayyif," 10 November 1948, *MS*, 1:30–31.
59. *Al-Majalla*, no. 2, 16 June 1942, 51–52 (a story by Ya'qub Mir Masri).

60. Ibrahim Naji Shumail and Ya'qub Sehayek hosted Fahd and Zaki Basim many times, and made their homes available for important meetings of the ICP. Other meetings were gathered at the homes of Mir Ya'qub Cohen, Yehuda Sadiq, Yusuf Harun Zilkha. See: FO 371/75131, March 1949, "The ICP," MI5 to Foreign Office; "Confession of Husayn Muhammad al-Shabibi," *MS*, 2:269–70; "Confession of Fu'ad Bahjat," 27 February 1949, *MS*, 3:603–15; "Confession of Malik Sayyif," 10 November 1948, *MS*, 1:31; Me'ir, *Be'ikar*, 92–93, 150.

61. *Forget Baghdad*, a documentary film by Samir; Al-Sayyab, *Kuntu shuyu'iyan*.

62. "Entry on Yesqel Menahem Qujman," *MS*, 3:691–93; "Entry on Ezra Fu'ad Sasun Mash'al," *MS*, 3:694–96; on Sadiq's activities in Dar al-mu'allimin and in the agricultural school, see: FO 371/75131, March 1949, "The ICP," MI5 to Foreign Office; on the activities of Sha'ul Tuwiq in al-Madrasa al-sina'iyya, Dar al-ma'ullimin, and vocational schools in Baghdad, see "Confession of Jasim Hamudi," *MS*, 1:95–96; on the activities of Morris Sha'ul in the law school, see "Confession of Ahmad Naji," *MS*, 1:124–30; on the activities of Hesqel Qujman in the Pharmacy College, see: "Confession of Majid Ra'uf," *MS*, 3:618–20; Masri, "Dhikrayat."

63. Al-Hajj, *Shahada*, 91.

64. Me'ir, *Be'ikar*, 172–73; "Confession of Malik Sayyif," 10 November 1948, *MS*, 1:39; "Confession of Yusuf bin Menashe Zaluf," *MS*, 1:108; FO 371/75131, March 1949, "The ICP," MI5 to Foreign Office; *Zo Hadrech*, 28 March 1984; "Confession of Jasim Hamudi," *MS*, 1:95–96; "Confession of Ahmad Naji," *MS*, 1:124–30: "Confession of Malik Sayyif," *MS*, 1:39; Masri, "Dhikrayat." This system enabled *Al-Qa'ida* to sell about three thousand copies in 1949.

65. Ballas, *Be-Guf rishon*, 24–25. On Ballas, see also Bashkin, "Iraqi Arab-Jewish Identities."

66. Ibid.

67. S. Fattal, *Be-Simta'ot*, 319.

68. Ibid., 321.

69. Ibid., 322.

70. Fahd, *Kitabat*, 93–94.

71. Bashkin, "Lands, Hands, and Socio-Cultural Boundaries."

72. Letter sent by Sasun Dallal to Zaki Watban (Basra), 15 December 1948, *MS*, 3:488–95; letter from Sasun Dallal to Zaki Watban, 6 January 1949, 6, *MS*, 3:495–97; letter from Sasun Dalla to Fu'ad Bahjat (Kirkuk), 19 January 1949, *MS*, 3:547–48; "Entry on Shelmo Sasun Dallal," *MS*, 3:560–69; "Confession of Jasim Hamudi," *MS*, 1:95–96.

73. On the involvement of Jews in the publishing of *Al-Qa'ida*, see: "Confession of Husayn Muhammad al-Shabibi," *MS*, 2:269–70; FO 371/75131, March 1949, "The ICP," MI5 to Foreign Office; "Confession of Malik Sayyif," *MS*, 1:26; Masri, "Dhikrayat."

74. OYA, interview with Sami Michael; *Zo Hadrech*, 28 March 1984.

75. FO 371/75131, March 1949, "The ICP," MI5 to Foreign Office; the account references the activities of Salim Menashe among the shoemakers, Moshe Cohen among the tailors, Hesqel Ibrahim among the workers, and Ishaq Shirazi in factories in the south; Naji Sha'ul among the port authorities and among train workers. On the activities of Moshe Cohen in al-Karkh and later in Ba'quba, and Mir Ya'qub Cohen in

al-Karkh, see "Confession of Fu'ad Bahjat," 27 February 1949, *MS*, 3:603–15; on the activities of Yusuf Zaluf in al-'Ashshar, and among the workers of Basra, see "Confession of Sabri 'Abd al-Karim," *MS*, 3:672–77; on Sami Michael's activities among the students and Naji Sha'ul's activities among clerks, see Me'ir, *Be'ikar*, 99.

76. In the years 1947–49, 113 Jews, 574 Muslims, 54 Christians, and 13 Sub'is constituted the party's law-rank echelons. In 1943–49, the ICP's middle-rank members included 22 Jews, 203 Muslims, and 23 Christians. In the top party command Jewish representation was about 9.1 percent for the years 1941–49. Jews constituted 10.7 percent of the ICP's central committee in 1941–48 (Na'im Tweig and Yehuda and Hesqel Sadiq), and 16.7 percent in 1948–49 (Sasun Dallal and Ya'qub Qujman). In April–June 1949 the ICP's central committee included three members: one of whom, Ya'qub Qujman, was a Jew. Me'ir, *Be'ikar*, 90, 102–3; "Entry on Ishaq Shirazi," *MS*, 2:346; "Confession of Muhammad Husayn al-Shabibi," *MS*, 2:269–70; "Confession of Malik Sayyif," 10 November 1948, *MS*, 1:31; Batatu, *Old Social Classes*, 520–21, 700, 1990–95.

77. FO 371/75182, 12 January 1949, Henry Mack (Baghdad) to Foreign Office; FO 371/75182, 12 January 1949, Board of Deputies of British Jews, Mr. Brotman to Mr. Malcolm Malker in the Foreign Office.

78. All photos of the women that appear in this volume are of Jewish women (Daisy Hesqel, Habiba Sasun Mas'al, Simha bint Yaq'ub, Najiyya bint Menahem Qujman); the photos of the arrested men are all Jewish (Ya'qub bin Yonah, Ishaq Ilaiya Khazzum, Henri Ya'qub, Reuben Dangur, Fa'ud Salim, Ezra Shelomo Salih, Ibrahim Ezra).

79. Mu'allim, *Fi tariqi ila'l-Mu'ataqal*, 34–37, 60–61; *Zo Hadrech*, 28 March 1984, 8–9; Ballas, *Be-Guf rishon*, 8, 32–33; OYA, interview with Sami Michael; S. Fattal, *Be-Simta'ot* 309–11, 333.

80. FO 371/68481A, 10 February 1948, "Report on Communist Organizations and the League of Iraqi Communists," J. G. Robertson to Foreign Office (from Security Intelligence Middle East, to Foreign Office, Mr. A. S. Halford, 9 February 1948); FO 371/75131, March 1949, "The ICP," MI5 to Foreign Office.

81. *Al-Ittihad*, 16 April 1984; Me'ir, *Be'ikar*, 100.

82. *Al-Ittihad*, 13 April 1984; Me'ir, *Be'ikar*, 174; FO 371/91696, 8 August 1951, Troutback, Embassy Baghdad to Herbert Morrison; Me'ir, *Yehudim tahat shilton 'iraqi*, 106–9; "Confession of Ya'qub Mir Masri *MS*, 1:682.

83. Yehuda Taggar, quoted in Me'ir, *Yehudim tahat shilton 'iraqi*, 110.

84. Hesqel Qujman reports that Jewish communists in Nuqrat Salman felt responsible for the Zionist prisoners, because of their Jewish identity. Muslim communists assisted Jewish prisoners in receiving medical help after being tortured during their police investigation or abused by the jail authorities. In Kut, communist prisoners gave the Zionists permission to use their ovens so that they could bake bread and got Vitamin and Calcium shots to Zionist prisoner Abraham Barzilai, while in the central jail in Baghdad a communist Kurd saved a Zionist prisoner after the jail authorities failed to provide him with appropriate medical care. Me'ir, *Yehudim tahat shilton 'iraqi*, 11, 113–16; Atlas, *'Ad 'amud*, 274–77.

85. On a strike in Abu Ghraib, during which prisoners organized a collective strike demanding clean drinking water, and where communists, Zionists, and others collabo-

rated, see Obed Yosef, "Mizchronotav shel asir zion be-'Iraq," in Yehuda, ed., *Mi-Bavel li-Yerushalayim*, 99–102.

86. FO 371/91696, 8 August 1951, Troutback, Embassy Baghdad to Herbert Morrison; Me'ir, *Yehudim tahat shilton 'iraqi*, 106–9; Qujman, www.ahewar.org/rate/bindex.asp?yid=32.

87. Atlas, *'Ad 'amud ha-teliya*, 274–77.

88. Me'ir, *Yehudim tahat shilton 'iraqi*, 116–17.

89. Sadiq became interested in communist ideas in 1938; three years he later became a party member. His college years at the Teachers Training College cemented his communist beliefs. He wavered in his support for the ICP, becoming involved with a few splinter groups for a time. In 1944 he joined the ICP's general conference with his brother Hesqel and became a member of the party's central committee. After graduation from the Teachers Training College, he was appointed to a teaching post at the agricultural school (Madrasat al-zira'a), where he organized students, and later moved on to a position in a middle school in the Baghdadi neighborhood of al-Karkh. He joined the League for Combating Zionism when it was first organized, and the period 1943–45 saw him organizing cells, committees, and unions for students, which included both Arabs and Kurds, and setting up cells in factories. At this time he was active in Dar al-Hikma and assisted with the publication and distribution of *Al-Qa'ida*. In 1946 he was fired from his teaching position because of his political views. He served as the leader of the students' committee in Baghdad, and was responsible for maintaining connections with organizers in Irbil, Mosul, Sulaimaniya, Hilla, and 'Amara. When the Wathba broke out, he was put in charge of organizing demonstrations. FO 371/75131, March 1949, "The ICP," MI5 to Foreign Office; Me'ir, *Be'ikar*, 90–91; *MS*, 1:1–7 (general entry on the ICP): "Confession of Malik Sayyif," 10 November 1948, *MS*, 1:20–26, 56, 64–64; "Entry on Yehuda Sadiq," *MS*, 2:339–40: "Confession of Yehuda Sadiq," *MS*, 1:69–89; letter from Fahd to Yehuda Sadiq, 17 May 1948; *MS*, 1:69–89, "Confession of Jasim Hamudi," *MS*, 1:95–9–98; "Confession of Fu'ad Bahjat," 27 February 1949, *MS*, 3:603–15; al-Hajj, *Shahada*, 116.

90. Me'ir, *Be'ikar*, 92–93.

91. Al-Hajj, *Shahada*, 116–17.

92. FO 371/75131, March 1949, "The ICP," MI5 to Foreign Office.

93. Masri, "Dhikrayat," 63; al-Hajj, *Shahada*, 131–32.

94. Entry on Shelomo Sasun Dallal, *MS*, 3:560–69; *MS*, 1:17–18; FO 371/75130, 28 April 1949, Henry Mack (Baghdad) to Foreign Office.

95. Bar-Moshe, *Yetsi'at 'Iraq*, 242–43.

96. Sasun Dallal, message to the public, 22 January 1949, reprinted in *MS*, 3:466.

97. Letter from Sasun Dallal to 'Abd al-Latif al-Sa'adi, 28 December 48, *MS*, 3:466–68; letter from Sasun Dallal to 'Abd al-Latif al-Sa'adi (Irbil), 6 January 1949, *MS*, 3:480–82; letter from Sasun Dallal to 'Abd al-Latif al-Sa'adi, 16 January 1949, *MS*, 3:471–76; letter from Sasun Dallal to Fu'ad Bahjat (Kirkuk), 19 January 1949, *MS*, 3:547–48.

98. Letter from Sasun Dallal to Fu'ad Bahjat (Kirkuk), 25 January 1949, *MS*, 3:543–46; letter from Sasun Dallal to Fu'ad Bahjat (Kirkuk), 29 December 1948, *MS*, 3:514–19; letter from Sasun Dallal to Zaki Watban, 6 January 1949, *MS*, 3:495–97; letter from Sasun

Dallal to Zawki Watban (Basra), 15 December 1948, *MS*, 3:488–95; letter from Sasun Dallal to Fu'ad Bahjat (Kirkuk), 18 December 1948, *MS*, 3:508–13; letter from Sasun Dallal to Sabri 'Abd al-Karim (Basra), 20 January 1949, *MS*, 3:499–500.

99. *MS*, 3:595.

100. "Confession of Ezra Fu'ad Sasun Mash'al," *MS*, 3:694–96.

101. Letter from Sasson Dallal to Hamid 'Uthman (Sulamaniya), 16 January 1949, *MS*, 3: 476.

102. Letter from Sasun Dallal to 'Abd al-Latif al-Sa'adi, 16 January 1949, *MS*, 3:471–76; letter from Sasun Dallal to Zawki Watban (Basra), 15 December 1948, *MS*, 3:488–95; letter from Sasun Dallal to Fu'ad Bahjat (Kirkuk), 18 December 1948, *MS*, 3:508–13; "Confession of Fu'ad Bahjat," 27 February 1949, *MS*, 3: 603–15; "Confession of Sabri 'Abd al-Karim," *MS*, 3:672–77.

103. See, for example, the "Confession of Fu'ad Bahjat," 27 February 1949, *MS*, 3:603–15; "Confession of Sabri 'Abd al-Karim," *MS*, 3:672–77.

104. *Zo Hadrech*, 28 March 1984, 9–8; Ballas, *Be-Guf rishon*, 8–9.

105. FO 371/75130, 14 February 1949, Henry Mack (Baghdad) to Departmental Distribution, "Execution of ICP's Leaders, Including Yehuda Sadiq, Arrested October 1948"; FO 371/75130, 3 March 1949, from Henry Mack (Baghdad) to Bevin.

106. J. Cohen, *Hilla*, 240; S. Fattal, *Be-Simta'ot*, 308.

107. Bar-Moshe, *Yetsi'at 'Iraq*, 208–9; S. Fattal, *Be-Simta'ot*, 308.

108. FO 371/75130, 28 April 1949, Henry Mack (Baghdad) to Foreign Office; FO 371/75130, 28 April 1949, Henry Mack (Baghdad) to Foreign Office; FO 371/75130, 7 May 1949, Henry Mack (Baghdad) to Foreign Office; FO 371/75130, 4 May 1949, Mack to Foreign Office, 371/75130, 6 May 1949, Henry Mack (Baghdad) to Foreign Office; FO 371/75130, 2 June 1949, Mack to Foreign Office.

109. Bar-Moshe, *Yetsi'at 'Iraq*, 241.

110. Ibid., 241–45.

111. Zilkha, *Al-Sahayuniyya, 'aduwat al-'Arab wa'l Yahud*, 11–25.

112. Ibid., 66, 78, 82.

113. Ibid., 73.

114. Ibid., 25–35, 50–54.

115. Ibid., 42.

116. Ibid., 45–66.

117. Ibid., 20.

118. Ibid., 23.

119. Ibid., 68–74.

120. Ibid., 126–27.

121. Ibid., 118.

122. Ibid., 1–9, 132–33, 104–5.

123. Ibid., 111–12.

124. FO 371/75127, 30 September 1948, Henry Mack (Baghdad) to Foreign Office.

125. Pamphlet dated 2 November 1945, 'Usbat mukafahat al-Sahayuniyya, *Manshurat*, 22–23; FO 624/116 27, January 1947, "Air Staff Intelligence Memorandum: National and International Organizations in Iraq in Which Covert or Covert Communist Influ-

ence Predominate"; FO 371/45389, "Anti-Zionist League," 8 December 1945, report by J. Grant McDonald; "Confession of Yusuf bin Menashe Zaluf," *MS*, 1:108; see also *MS*, 2:255.

126. FO 371/75131, March 1949, "The ICP," MI5 to Foreign Office; FO 624/116, 27 January 1947, "Air Staff Intelligence Memorandum: National and International Organizations in Iraq in Which Covert or Covert Communist Influence Predominate"; Me'ir, *Be'ikar*, 109–11; Yasin, "'Usbat mukafahat al-Sahayniyya fi'l Iraq," 159–60; "Confession of Yusuf bin Menashe Zaluf," *MS*, 1:108.

127. FO 624/100, 19 November 1946, Central Intelligence Directorate (Baghdad) to Mr. Walker (British Embassy).

128. FO 371/45389, "Anti-Zionist League," 8 December 1945, J. Grant McDonald.

129. FO 371/68481A, 10 February 1948, "Report on Communist Organizations and the League of Iraqi Communists," J. G. Robertson to Foreign Office (from Security Intelligence Middle East, to Mr. A. S. Halford, 9 February 1948).

130. FO 371/45389, 20 December 1945, "Anti-Zionist League in Baghdad Memorandum," Stonehewer-Bird (Baghdad, British Embassy) to Bevin (Foreign Office).

131. FO 371/45389, "Anti-Zionist League," 8 December 1945, J. Grant McDonald.

132. Ibid.

133. "Confession of Yusuf bin Menashe Zaluf," *MS*, 1:108; see also *MS*, 2:255.

134. "Confession of Mir Ya'qub Cohen, *MS*, 1:122–24; "Confession of Yesqel Menahem Qujman, *MS*, 3:691–93; FO 371/68481A, 10 February 1948, "Report on Communist Organizations and the League of Iraqi Communists," J. G. Robertson to Foreign Office (received from Security Intelligence Middle East, to Mr. A. S. Halford, Foreign Office, 9 February 1948).

135. FO 371/45389, "Anti-Zionist League," 8 December 1945, J. Grant McDonald; FO 371/68481A, 10 February 1948, "Report on Communist Organizations and the League of Iraqi Communists," J. G. Robertson to Foreign Office (from Security Intelligence Middle East, to Foreign Office, Mr. A. S. Halford, 9 February 1948).

136. FO 371/75131, March 1949, "The ICP," MI5 to Foreign Office; "Confession of Yehuda Sadiq," *MS*, 1:69–89. On Sadiq, see also: FO 371/75131, March 1949, "The ICP," MI5 to Foreign Office; 'Abd al-Qadir Yasin argues that the idea of establishing the league was Sadiq's, a member of the central committee of the ICP. See Yasin, *'Usbat*, 158–66.

137. FO 624/116, 27 January 1947, "Air Staff Intelligence Memorandum: National and International Organizations in Iraq in Which Covert or Covert Communist Influence Predominate."

138. FO 371/45389, "Anti-Zionist League," 8 December 1945, J. Grant McDonald. Me'ir notes that Na'im Salman estimates the number of supporters at two thousand, among them 50 percent Jews, but this seems highly unlikely to Me'ir. Me'ir, *Be'ikar*, 125.

139. S 25/4039, 4 May 1946, Me'ir Shilon-Shlank to Eliyahu Sasson, reprinted *MZH*, 3:389–91; Me'ir, *Be'ikar*, 125; FO 624/116, 27 January 1947, "Air Staff Intelligence Memorandum: National and International Organizations in Iraq in Which Covert or Covert Communist Influence Predominate."

140. FO 371/45389, "Anti-Zionist League," 8 December 1945, J. Grant McDonald.

141. "Confession of Yusuf bin Menashe Zaluf, *MS*, 1:108; see also 2:255.

142. Masri, "Dhikrayat," 55–65.

143. Pamphlet dated 12 September 1945, 'Usbat mukafahat al-Sahayuniyya, *Manshurat*, 3, 2–4; pamphlet dated 22 November 1945, Twena, 'Usbat mukafahat al-Sahayuniyya, *Manshurat*, 13.

144. 'Usbat mukafahat al-Sahayuniyya, *Manshurat*, 28–29, 30–32.

145. FO 371/45389, 20 December 1945, "Anti-Zionist League in Baghdad—Memorandum," Stonehewer-Bird (Baghdad, British Embassy) to Bevin (Foreign Office).

146. FO 371/68481A, 10 February 1948, "Report on Communist Organizations and the League of Iraqi Communists," J. G. Robertson to Foreign Office (received from Security Intelligence Middle East to Foreign Office, Mr. A. S. Halford, 9 February 1948).

147. Pamphlet dated 29 May 1946, 'Usbat mukafahat al-Sahayuniyya, *Manshurat*, 50–52.

148. Pamphlet dated 7 May 1946, 'Usbat mukafahat al-Sahayuniyya, *Manshurat*, 36.

149. 'Usbat mukafahat al-Sahayuniyya, *Manshurat*, 24–25.

150. Yasin, "'Usbat mukafahat al-Sahyaniyya," 164–66.

151. S 25/5289, letter to *Kol ha-'Am* (mandatory Palestine), 5 April 1946.

152. 'Usbat mukafahat al-Sahayuniyya, *Manshurat*, 6–7, 9–10.

153. 'Usbat mukafahat al-Sahayuniyya, *Manshurat*, 10–11.

154. Me'ir, *Be'ikar*, 122; FO 371/75131, March 1949, "The ICP," MI5 to Foreign Office; "Confession of Yusuf bin Menashe Zaluf," MS, 1:108; see also 2:255; "Confession of Mir Yaq'ub Cohen, MS, 1:122–24.

155. Pamphlet dated 29 May 1946, 'Usbat mukafahat al-Sahayuniyya, *Manshurat*, 50–52; Me'ir, 121.

156. Pamphlet dated 27 May 1946, 'Usbat mukafahat al-Sahayuniyya, *Manshurat*, 43–45.

157. 'Usbat mukafahat al-Sahayuniyya, *Manshurat*, 59–60.

158. FO 371/45389, "Anti-Zionist League," 8 December 1945, J. Grant McDonald; al-Hajj, *Shahada*, 92.

159. "Confession of Mir Ya'qub Cohen," MS, 1:122–24; al-Hajj, *Shahada*, 92; *Zo Hadrech*, 28 March 1984, 8–9.

160. Al-Sayyab, *Kuntu shuyu'iyyan*, 43–44.

161. Ibid., 44–45, 48–49.

162. Me'ir, *Be'ikar*, 115.

163. S 25/8003, 1 May 1946, letter from Y.L.

164. Me'ir, *Be'ikar*, 114.

165. FO 624/100, 11 June 1946, CID Baghdad to British Embassy.

166. Batatu, *Old Social Classes*, 532.

167. FO 624/116, 27 January 1947, "Air Staff Intelligence Memorandum: National and International Organizations in Iraq in Which Covert or Covert Communist Influence Predominate"; Me'ir, *Be'ikar*, 118–19; FO 624/100, 11 June 1946, CID Baghdad to British Embassy; al-Hajj, *Shahada*, 92; *Zo Ha-Derech*, 28 March 1984.

168. 'Usbat mukafahat al-Sahayuniyya, *Manshurat*, 112.

169. *Zo Hadrech*, 28 March 1984.

170. S 25/3529, 22 May 1946, letter from Me'ir Shilon-Shlank to Eliyahu Sasson (Jewish Agency); FO 624/116, 27 January 1947, "Air Staff Intelligence Memorandum:

National and International Organizations in Iraq in Which Covert or Covert Communist Influence Predominate."

171. FO 624/116, 27 January 1947, "Air Staff Intelligence Memorandum: National and International Organizations in Iraq in Which Covert or Covert Communist Influence Predominate."

172. Al-'Usba, no. 45, 30 May 1946, 2, 3 (copy saved in S 25/8003).

173. FO 624/116, 27 January 1947, "Air Staff Intelligence Memorandum: National and International Organizations in Iraq in Which Conert or Covert Communist Influence Predominate."

174. FO 371/68481A, 10 February 1948, "Report on Communist Organizations and the League of Iraqi Communists," J. G. Robertson to Foreign Office (received from Security Intelligence Middle East, to Foreign Office Mr. A. S. Halford, 9 February 1948).

175. Al-Sayyab, *Kuntu shuyu'iyyan*, 48–49.

176. 'Usbat mukafahat al-Sahayuniyya, *Manshurat*, 67.

177. Ibid., 68.

178. Pamphlet dated 12 August 1946, 'Usbat mukafahat al-Sahayuniyya, *Manshurat*, 53–55.

179. Pamphlet dated 18 June 1946, 'Usbat mukafahat al-Sahayuniyya, *Manshurat*, 76–78.

180. 'Usbat mukafahat al-Sahayuniyya, *Manshurat*, 70–73.

181. Yasin, "'Usbat mukafahat al-Sahayuniyya," 164.

182. FO 624/100, 11 June 1946, CID Baghdad to British Embassy; Me'ir, *Be'ikar*, 124; letter from Me'ir Shilon-Shlank to Eliyahu Sasson (Jewish Agency), reprinted in *MZH*, 3:397–98; *Zo Hadrech*, 28 March 1984; *Al-Ittihad*, 24 May 1984.

183. 'Usbat mukafahat al-Sahayuniyya, *Manshurat*, 71–73.

184. Pamphlet dated 11 June 1946, 'Usbat mukafahat al-Sahayuniyya, *Manshurat*, 83–90.

185. 'Usbat mukafahat al-Sahayuniyya, *Manshurat*, 92–96.

186. Ibid., 98.

187. Ibid., 99.

188. Three other members were similarly tried: Khalil bin Nasif was sentenced for half a year with hard labor, Sami Mikha'il and Emanuel bin Butrus were sentenced for three months in jail. 'Usbat mukafahat al-Sahayuniyya, *Manshurat*, 99–100.

189. Ibid., 104–8.

190. Ibid., 109–10.

191. Bar-Moshe, *Yetsi'at 'Iraq*, 197.

192. Me'ir, *Be'ikar*, 136.

193. Al-Hajj, *Shahada*, 109–10; Masri, "Dhikrayat," 63; Khayri, *Sada al-sinnin*, 137–39; Murad al-'Umari, "Fi'l dhikra al-'ashira li wafa' Kamil al-Chardirhci" *Al-Anba'*, 3 February 1987; Batatu, *Old Social Classes*, 599–603.

194. FO 371/110992, 23 December 1953, Troutback (Baghdad) to Allen (Foreign Office).

195. Batatu, *Old social classes*, 598.

196. Ballas, *Be-Guf rishon*, 29.

197. Batatu, *Old Social Classes*, 651–50.

198. Ibid., 543.
199. Ibid., 571.

Chapter 6: An End?

1. Somekh, *Baghdad, Etmol*, 143.
2. Shiblak, *Lure of Zion*, 64–128; H. Cohen, *Ha-Pe'ilut*, Gat, *Jewish Exodus from Iraq*; Shenhav, *Arab Jews*; Me'ir-Glitzenstein, *Zionism in an Arab Country*.
3. Me'ir-Glitzenstein, *Zionism in an Arab Country*; Me'ir-Glitzenstein, *Ben Bagdad le-Ramat Gan*, 52–56.
4. Report on a conversation between Jewish representatives and Nuri Sa'id, 5 February 1943, *MZH*, 1:181–84.
5. S 25/3529, 31 March 1946, Me'ir Shlank (Baghdad) to Eliyahu Sasson (Jerusalem); S 25/8003, 5 April 1946, memorandum of Ibrahim al-Kabir's memorandum to the Anglo-American investigation committee.
6. FO 371/45334, 28 May 1945, Stonehewer-Bird (Baghdad, British Embassy) to Anthony Eden (Foreign Office).
7. Kazzaz, *Yehudim*, 264–27.
8. CO 537/3985, 15 May 1948, Henry Mack to Foreign Office; CO 537/3985, 13 April 1948, Mack to Foreign Office.
9. FO 371/75183, 12 December 1949, Henry Mack (British Embassy, Baghdad) to Clement Attlee (Foreign Office); FO 371/75183, 12 December 1949, dispatch no. 236, Government of Iraq, received by the U.S. Embassy, 18 November 1949.
10. FO 371/68459, 13 November 1948, Mr. Davis (British Consulate, Basra) to Foreign Office.
11. FO 371/68459, 13 November 1948, Mr. Davis (British Consulate, Basra) to Foreign Office.
12. FO 371/75183, 28 October 1949, "Memorandum on the Situation of the Jews in Iraq," Y. H. Bernstein (Jewish agency for Palestine, N.Y.) to MP Hector McNeil (N.Y.); FO 371/68459, 13 November 1948, Mr. Davis (British Consulate, Basra) to Foreign Office; FO 371/75183, 15 December 1949, "Copy of CID File: Arrests of Zionist Leaders," MI5 (Mr. D. L. Portman), to A. M. Williams (Foreign Office); FO 371/75183, 12 December 1949, Henry Mack (Baghdad) to Foreign Office; Kazzaz, *Yehudim*, 274.
13. FO 371/75183, 12 December 1949, Henry Mack (Baghdad) to Foreign Office.
14. FO 371/75183, 28 October 1949, "Memorandum on the Situation of the Jews in Iraq," Y. H. Bernstein (Jewish Agency for Palestine, N.Y.) to MP Hector McNeil.
15. Somekh, *Baghdad, Etmol*; Murad, *Mi-Bavel ba-mahteret*, 32–33; J. Cohen, *Hilla*, 224–25, 235.
16. FO 371/75183, 14 November 1949, Henry Mack to Foreign Office.
17. FO 371/75183, 12 December 1949, Henry Mack (Baghdad) to Foreign Office; FO 371/75183, 15 December 1949, "Copy of CID's report: Arrests of Zionist Leaders," MI5 (Mr. D. L. Portman) to A. M. Williams (Foreign Office).
18. Haim, "Aspects of Jewish Life," 195–96. See also: FO 371/68459, 13 November 1948, Mr. Davis (British Consulate, Basra) to Foreign Office; FO 371/75183, 12 December 1949, Henry Mack (Baghdad) to Foreign Office.

19. Kazzaz, *Yehudim*, 275–79; Sagiv, *Yahadut be-mifgash*, 126–43; Shahrabany, *Ha-Berikha mi-Basra*, 139.
20. FO 371/68459, September 1948, Consul General, Basra, to Baghdad.
21. Haddad, *Avney Derech*, 78.
22. Shahrabany, *Ha-Berikha mi-Basra*, 139.
23. Ozer Benjamin, http://iraqijews.awardspace.com/iran.doc (accessed January 15, 2012).
24. Kazzaz, *Yehudim*, 286.
25. Simhoni, "Ha-Reka' ha-medini," 105–6.
26. Ibid., 101–2; Gat, *Kehila yehudit be-mashber*, 27–57.
27. Haim, "Aspects of Jewish Life," 197; CO 323/910/4, 21 May 1950, Henry Mack to Bevin (Foreign Office).
28. Hillel, *Ruh qadim*, 282–89.
29. Hillel, "Ha-mahalachim sheholidu et ha-'aliya ha-hamonit me-'Iraq," in Yehuda, ed., *Mi-Bavel li-Yerushalayim*, 35; Simhoni, "Ha-Reka' ha-medini," 110.
30. FO 371/82405, 3 March 1950, Information Section-Supplement to Decree no. 62, British Embassy, Baghdad; Gat, *Kehila yehudit be-mashber*, 57–66; Shina, El'azar, and Nahtomi, *Perakim*, 27.
31. Shina, El'azar, and Nahtomi, *Perakim*, 27–28.
32. Me'ir-Glitzenstein, *Ben Bagdad le-rRamat Gan*, 34–37; on the rates of Jews leaving, see Gat, *Kehila Yehudit be-mashber*, 175–75.
33. J. Cohen, *Hilla*, 237.
34. Hillel, "Ha-mahalachim sheholidu," 35.
35. Me'ir-Glitzenstein, *Ben Bagdad le-Ramat Gan*, 44–47; *Al-Hawadith*, no. 2214, 22 May 1950, 2.
36. Me'ir-Glitzenstein, *Ben Bagdad le-Ramat Gan*, 49; Haim, "Aspects of Jewish Life," 200–201; FO 371/91635, 15 January 1951, from Sir A. Kirkbride (Amman) to Foreign Office (a report on Nuri Sa'id's visit to Jordan).
37. FO 371/75126, 21 July 1949, Consul General Basra to His Majesty's Secretary of State for Foreign Affairs; FO 371/75126, 15 November 1949, Consul General in Basra to His Majesty's Secretary of State for Foreign Affairs (London).
38. FO 371/82404, 16 February 1950, His Majesty's Consul General Basra to Secretary of State for Foreign Affairs; FO 371/82404, 24 March 1950, Consul General Basra to Secretary of State for Foreign Affairs (London).
39. FO 371/82404, 29 October 1950, Consul General Basra to Secretary of State for Foreign Affairs (London).
40. FO 624/220, December 1952, Consul General Basra to British Ambassador (Baghdad).
41. FO 371/82404, 24 March 1950, Consul General Basra to Secretary of State for Foreign Affairs (London).
42. FO 371/82404, 13 April 1950, Consul General Basra to Secretary of State for Foreign Affairs (London).
43. FO 371/82404, 17 May 1950, Consul General Basra to Secretary of State for

Foreign Affairs (London); on the rate of migration from Basra and 'Amara, see also *Al-Hawadith*, no. 2185, 17 April 1950, 2.

44. In June, no Jews registered. See FO 371/82404, 15 June 1950, Consul General Basra to Secretary of State for Foreign Affairs (London). In August, only three thousand were allowed to leave: FO 371/82404, 9 August 1950, Consul General Basra to Secretary of State for Foreign Affairs (London). Similar accounts of persecutions are found also in Shahrabany, *Ha-brikha mi-basra*, 143–49.

45. FO 371/75182, 8 March 1949, U.S. Embassy (Baghdad) to Secretary of State (Washington, D.C.).

46. FO 371/75127, 3 January 1949, Henry Mack (Baghdad) to Foreign Office.

47. Semah, "Sasson Semah: Tzir ha-parlament ha-'iraqi, perakim be-itzug yehudey mosul," in Avisur, ed., *Mehkarim*, 85–86.

48. Haddad, *Avney Derech*, 77; Shina, El'azar, and Nahtomi, *Perakim*, 15–16.

49. *Zo Hadrech*, 28 March 1984, 8–9; OYA, interview with Sami Michael, no. 7169, interviewer Gidom Lve Ari, 1978 cassette 346.

50. See also parallel articles in *Al-Nahda*, no. 116, 27 October 1949, 1; *Al-Nahda*, no. 110, 20 October 1949, 1.

51. *Al-Yaqdha*, no. 813, 30 April 1950, 2.

52. *Al-Yaqdha*, no. 795, 9 April 1950, 2; *Al-Yaqdha*, 14 September 1950, 922, 2; *Al-Yaqdha*, no. 971, 16 November 1950, 2; *Al-Yaqdha*, no. 822, 11 May 1950, 2.

53. *Al-Yaqdha*, no. 800, 14 April 1950, 2.

54. Ibid.

55. *Al-Yaqdha*, no. 950, 22 October 1950, 2.

56. *Al-Yaqdha*, no. 803, 16 April 1950, 2.

57. *Al-Yaqdha*, no. 925, 18 September 1950, 2.

58. *Al-Yaqdha*, no. 859, 25 June 1950, 2.

59. *Al-Yaqdha*, no. 943, 13 October 1950, 2.

60. *Al-Yaqdha*, no. 818, 7 May 1950, 1.

61. *Al-Yaqdha*, no. 949, 20 October 1950, 2.

62. *Al-Yaqdha*, no. 927, 22 September 1950, 2; *Al-Yaqdha*, no. 801, 16 April 1950, 2.

63. *Al-Yaqdha*, no. 964, 8 November 1950, 1, 2; *Al-Yaqdha*, no. 927, 22 September 1950, 2; *Al-Yaqdha*, no. 958, 1 November 1950, 2; *Al-Yaqdha*, no. 977, 23 November 1950, 2; *Al-Yaqdha*, no. 951, 23 November 1950, 2; for a similar story, see *Al-Yaqdha*, no. 951, 23 October 1950, 2.

64. *Al-Yaqdha*, no. 926, 19 September 1950, 2; on the need to hire Palestinian teachers instead of Jews, see also *Al-Yaqdha*, no. 916, 1 September 1950, 2.

65. *Al-Yaqdha*, no. 918, 10 September 1950, 2.

66. *Al-Yaqdha*, no. 848, 12 June 1950, 2; *Al-Yaqdha*, no. 857, 20 June 1950, 2. *Al-Yaqdha* went so far as to propose that Iraqi Jews should not travel to Israel via Turkey or Iran but rather via Arab states in order to expedite their departure from Iraq. *Al-Yaqdha*, no. 966, 2 November 1950, 2.

67. *Al-Yaqdha*, no. 788, 30 March 1950, 2.

68. *Al-Yaqdha*, no. 832, 12 May 1950, 2. See also CO 323/910/4, 21 May 1950, Henry Mack to Bevin (Foreign Office).

69. *Al-Yaqdha*, no. 862, 28 June 1950, 2.
70. FO 371/75183, 14 November 1949, Henry Mack to Foreign Office.
71. CO 323/910/4, 21 May 1950, Henry Mack to Bevin (Foreign Office).
72. Kazzaz, *Yehudim*, 268–71.
73. Al-Suwaydi, *Mudhakkarati*, 473–74.
74. *Al-Zaman*, no. 3483, 11 February 1949, 1.
75. *Al-Hawadith*, no. 2154, 19 April 1950, 1, 4. See also the story in *Al-Hawadith*, no. 2255, 25 July 1950, 2, that connected the claims of Jewish persecution in Iraq to political Zionism which was linked to communism; and the story about America fighting against the Zionist-communist elements that threaten world peace: *Al-Hawadith*, no. 2282, 28 December 1950, 1, 4.
76. FO 371/110992, 23 December 1953, Troutback (Baghdad) to Allen (Foreign Office).
77. FO 371/75182, 19 February 1949, Foreign Office to Baghdad.
78. FO 371/75182, 12 February 1949, Hugh Dow (Jerusalem) to Baghdad.
79. FO 371/75182, 17 February 1949, Henry Mack (Baghdad) to Foreign Office.
80. FO 371/75182, 24 February 1949, Henry Mack (Baghdad) to Foreign Office and Jerusalem.
81. FO 371/75182, 18 October 1949, Sir K. Helm (Tel Aviv) to Baghdad, Cairo, Foreign Office.
82. Simhoni, "Ha-Reka' ha-medini," 94–95.
83. FO 371/75182, 8 March 1949, U.S. Embassy (Baghdad) to Secretary of State (Washington, D.C.); see also FO 371/82422, 21 March 1950, Commercial Counselor (Baghdad) to Board of Trade (London).
84. By 1951 Sa'id realized that the Jews were about to leave Iraq, and wanted to see them depart immediately regardless of the Palestinian question. The British report that he asked the Jordanians to stop deceiving refugees on the possibility of their being admitted to Israel and for all Arab countries to take steps to resettle them. FO 371/91635, 15 January 1951, from Sir A. Kirkbride (Amman) to Foreign Office (London) (a report on Nuri Sa'id's visit to Jordan).
85. Schechtman, *Population Transfers*.
86. Samuel, "Government of Israel and Its Problems," 1–16.
87. Simhoni, "Ha-Reka' ha-medini," 112.
88. *Al-Hawadith*, 9 July 1949, no. 1953, 1, 4; *Al-Hawadith*, no. 2025, 10 October 1949, 2, 4; *Al-Hawadith*, no. 2035, 21 October 1949, 2, 4; *Al-Hawadith*, no. 2149, 4 March 1950, 1, 4; Kazzaz, *Yehudim*, 295; *Al-Sha'b*, no. 1290, 10 April 1949, 1.
89. Me'ir-Glitzenstein, *Ben Bagdad le-Ramat Gan*, 48, Me'ir-Glitzenstein, *Zionism in an Arab Country*, 160–213.
90. FO 371/75183, 10 November 1949, Henry Mack to Foreign Office. Zionist emissary Shelomo Hillel recalls that in 1949 the international press in Israel was very interested in stories about Iraqi Jewry, and Hillel and others provided journalists with information about the situation in Iraq. Hillel, "Ha-mahalachim sheholidu," 40.
91. Simhoni, "Ha-Reka' ha-medini," 96–100; FO 371/75183 12 December 1949, Henry Mack (Baghdad) to Clement Attlee, Foreign Office.

92. Shenhav, "The Jews of Iraq."

93. Me'ir-Glitzenstein, *Ben Bagdad le-Ramat Gan*, 60–61; on the efforts to save Zionist activists from execution, see Gat, *Kehila yehudit be-mashber*, 162–64.

94. Me'ir-Glitzenstein, *Ben Bagdhad le-Ramat Gan*, 52.

95. Yehuda, ed., "Ha-'Alaiya me-'Iraq be-re'shit shenot he-'esrim u-be'ayoteha," in *Mi-Bavel li-Yerushalayim*, 3–17; Masliyah, "Zionism in Iraq," 217–19; Haddad, *Avney Derech*, 74; Sehayek, "Ha-'aliya ha-halutzit ha-rishona me-'irak, kevutzat Ra'anana, in Yehuda, ed. *Mi-Bavel li-Yerushalayim*, 17–28; *Al-Misbah*, no. 99, 27 May 1926, 4; *Al-Misbah*, no. 100, 3 June 1926, 1; *Al-Misbah*, no. 113, 22 September 1926, 1; *Al-Misbah*, no. 5, 8 May 1924, 5; *Al-Misbah*, no. 23, 1 September 1924, 5; *Al-Misbah*, 28 January 1926, 86:2; *Al-Misbah*, no. 125, 11 December 1927, 3; *Al-Misbah*, no. 110, 29 September 1926, 4; *Al-Misbah*, no. 118, 7 March 1927, 4; *Al-Misbah*, no. 113, 23 October 1927, 8; *Al-Misbah*, no. 51, 14 May 1925, 1; H. Cohen, *Ha-Pe'ilut*, 88–105; OYA, Moshe Sofer, "Jewish Education and the Zionist Movement in Baghdad in 1924–1929," an interview conducted (in Hebrew) by Haim Cohen, 3 May 1963.

96. Shina, El'azar, and Nahtomi, *Perakim*, 3.

97. "Leaflets for Defense in Baghdad: Shabab al-Inqadh," 1 April 1942, *MZH*, 1:43–44; J. Cohen, *Hilla*, 186–90.

98. Shina, El'azar, and Nahtomi, *Perakim*, 4–5.

99. Report by Enzo Sereni, 2 July 1942, *MZH*, 1:80–82; S 25/5289, 3 February 1943, report by Enzo Sereni, *MZH*, 1:168–71. Report by Shalom Rashba from Kirkuk and Mosul, 15 August 1942, reprinted in *MZH*, 1:96–102.

100. Report by Shemaryahu Gutman, 4 February 1943, *MZH*, 1:174–81; S 25/5289, 3 February 1943, report by Enzo Sereni, *MZH*, 1:168–73.

101. Rina Dalomi, "Ha-Halutz ha-tza'ir ve hishtatfut ha-havera ba-pe'ilut ha-halutzit-mahtartit be-'Iraq," in Yehuda, ed., *Mi-Bavel li-Yerushalayim*, 95–96; Masliyah, "Zionism in Iraq," 222–23; Shina, El'azar, and Nahtomi, *Perakim*, 10–14.

102. Simhoni, "Ha-Reka' ha-medini," 102–4.

103. FO 371/75182, 12 January 1949, Henry Mack (Baghdad) to Foreign Office; Board of Deputies of British Jews, Mr. Brotman to Mr. Malcolm Malker (Foreign Office); FO 371/75182, 16 March 1949, Anglo-Jewish Association (London, Stein) to Under-Secretary of State, Foreign Office; FO 371/75182, 8 March 1949, U.S. Embassy (Baghdad) to Secretary of State (Washington, D.C.); FO 371/75182, 18 October 1949, Sir K. Helm (Tel Aviv) to Baghdad, Cairo, Foreign Office; FO 371/75182, 21 October 1949, Henry Mack to Foreign Office, Tel Aviv, Cairo; FO 371/75183, 15 December 1949, MI5 (Mr. D. L. Portman) to A. M. Williams (Foreign Office) (report given by the CID on arrests of Zionist leaders); FO 371/75182, 24 October 1949, Sir K. Helm (Tel Aviv) to Foreign Office; Shina, El'azar, and Nahtomi, *Perakim*, 20.

104. Shalom Darwish, "Ha-Yahasim ben mosadot ha-kehila leven ha-mahteret ha-halutzit," in Yehuda, ed. *Mi-Bavel li-Yerushalayim*, 83–85; Masliyah, "Zionism in Iraq," 223.

105. Shina, El'azar, and Nahtomi, *Perakim*, 20; see also Kazzaz, *Yehudim*, 284.

106. Murad, *Mi-Bavel ba-mahteret*, 37.

107. Dalomi, "Ha-Halutz ha-tza'ir," *Mi-Bavel*, 97.

108. FO 371/75182, 24 October 1949, Henry Mack to Foreign Office; Shina, El'azar, and Nahtomi, *Perakim*, 20–21.

109. Shina, El'azar, and Nahtomi, *Perakim*, 21–22; Hillel, *Ruh qadim*, 259–61.

110. Mordechai Ben Porat, "Mivtza Ezra u Nechemia" (Operation Ezra and Nehemiah), in Yehuda, ed., *Mi-Bavel li-Yerushalayim*, 48.

111. Shina, El'azar, and Nahtomi, *Perakim*, 24–25, Bibi, *Me-Araba'*, 39–140; Sagiv, *Yahadut be-mifgash*, 215–52; Me'ir-Glitzenstein, *Zionism in an Arab Country*, 131–60.

112. FO 371/91689, 3 February 1951, T. E. Baron (British Embassy, Baghdad) to Foreign Office; FO 371/91693, 26 June 51, BBC Baghdad.

113. FO 371/91689, 3 February 1951, T. E. Baron (British Embassy, Baghdad) to Foreign Office.

114. FO 371/91689, 27 June 1951, H. Beeley (British Embassy, Baghdad) to G. W. Fulonge (Foreign Office).

115. FO 371/91693, 26 June 1951, BBC Baghdad.

116. FO 371/91689, 27 June 1951, H. Beeley (British Embassy, Baghdad) to G. W. Fulonge (Foreign Office).

117. FO 371/91689, 27 June 1951, H. Beeley (British Embassy, Baghdad) to G. W. Fulonge (Foreign Office): FO 371/91689, 8 November 1951, H. Beeley (British Embassy, Baghdad) to Eastern Department (Foreign Office); FO 371/91689, 17 December 1951, H. Beeley (British Embassy, Baghdad) to Eastern Department (Foreign Office).

118. Me'ir, *Be'ikar*, 231–32; the full account of the Mosad investigation committee is given in: Ben Porat, *Le-Bagdad ve-hazara*, appendix.

119. Simhoni, "Ha-Reka' ha-medini," 105; on the enormous amount of Jews waiting to immigrate, see Gat, *Kehila yehudit be-mashber*, 174–75.

120. FO 371/82422, 21 March 1950, Commercial Counselor (Baghdad) to Board of Trade (London); FO 371/91635, 15 January 1951, Sir A. Kirkbride (Amman) to Foreign Office (London) (a report on Nuri Sa'id's visit to Jordan, in which he tried, with no success, to convince the Jordanians to let Iraqi Jews pass through their territory); Gat, *Kehila yehudit be-mashber*, 153–65.

121. *Derech Ha-Halutz* (The Pioneer's Way), 1 May–June 1945, 6–8, reprinted in Sehayek, *Haluzot ba-mahteret*, 79; Nahtomi, "Ha-hinuch be-misgeret ha-mahteret ha-halutzit be-'Iraq," in Yehuda, ed., *Mi-Bavel li-Yerushalayim*, 87; Salim Aloni, "May 1st," *Derech Ha-Halutz*, May 1945, *MZH*, 2:558–59; Sehayek, *Haluzot ba-mahteret*, 81; Yoav from Sulaimaniya, *'Am ha-seminarim, 'alon ten'utat ha-halutz bi-Yerushalayim*, April 1948, 19, reprinted in Sehayek, *Haluzot ba-mahteret*, 95; Berta Sofer, "Our Movement in Iraq," 2 December 1944, *MZH*, 2:397.

122. Esther Darwish Tzorani, speech in Second Zionist Conference, 2 December 1944, reprinted in Sehayek, *Haluzot ba-mahteret*, 78–79; Evelyn Salton-Zlikha, "Until When Shall We Wait?" *Derech Ha-Halutz*, May 1945, *MZH*, 2:564–65.

123. A survey conducted with thirty Zionist members showed that most were young girls in their teens or twenties. Half came from upper-middle-class and affluent families, fourteen came from middle-class families, and one was poor. Twenty-nine defined themselves as either traditional or religious. Eleven studied in governmental schools, five in foreign schools, and the rest in Alliance and in Jewish schools. Six

women emphasized they were willing to rebel against their parents to come to Israel. Sehayek, *Halutzot ba-mahteret*, 121; Dalomi, "Ha-Halutz ha-tza'ir," *Mi-Bavel*, 97; Me'ir-Glitzenstein, *Zionism in an Arab Country*, 90–104.

124. On the negative image of exile as positioned vis-à-vis the generation of Israeli born Jews, see Almog, *Sabra*.

125. *Derech Ha-Halutz*, no. 2, June–July 1945, *MZH*, 2:647.

126. Herzeliya [Violet ben Porat], "Travelling in the City," *Derech Ha-Halutz*, no. 3, August 1945, *MZH*, 2:719–20.

127. Carmela [Berta Sofer], "Our Movement in Iraq," *Derech Ha-Halutz* 2 December 1944, *MZH*, 2:397; Ahuva Me'ir characterized the Iraqi Jewish community as enslaved and living a humble life, full of shame and self-contempt. Zionism, she asserted, aimed at creating a working nation, rather than "people who only wish to find pleasure in parties and trips, spoiled people who disrespect labor." *Derech Ha-Halutz*, July 1946, reprinted in Sehayek, *Halutzot ba-mahteret*, 95.

128. 'Imanuel Nahtumi, "Ha-hinuch be-misgeret," *Mi-Bavel li-Yerushalayim*, 86.

129. Yizkor, *Derech Ha-Halutz*, no. 1, May 1945, *MZH*, 2:555; a similar Yizkor was published in *Derech Ha-Halutz*, no. 6, May–June 1946, *MZH*, 3:420.

130. *Derech Ha-Halutz*, no. 4, 6 November–4 December 1945, *MZH*, 3:187; see also Yosef Me'ir, "Let Us Learn Our Lesson!" *Derech Ha-Halutz*, no. 4, 6 November–4 December 1945, *MZH*, 3:188–89.

131. Aliza Qattan, "The Lessons from These Days," *Derech Ha-Halutz*, May 1945, *MZH*, 2:555–56.

132. Tenu'at ha-Halutz, *Hagg ha-'atzma'ut be-Bavel*, 5–7; reprinted and annotated in Baruch, ed., *'Atzma'ut ba-mahteret*.

133. Tenu'at ha-Halutz, *Hagg ha-'atzma'ut be-Bavel*, 8.

134. Anonymous, "El lokhamey ha-hofesh," in *Hagg ha-'atzma'ut be-Bavel*, 10–11. The edition printed in Israel identified the writer as Ezra Haddad.

135. Shina, El'azar, and Nahtomi, *Perakim*, 18.

136. Ilana (Baghdad), "Speech in a Holiday's Celebration," in Tenu'at ha-Halutz, *Hagg ha-'atzma'ut be-Bavel*, 22; the reference here is to a famous saying of a Zionist hero, Yosef Trumpeldor.

137. Ilan Lev (Baghdad), "Lo nerata'," Tenu'at ha-Halutz, *Hagg ha-'atzma'ut be-Bavel*, 26–27.

138. J. Cohen, *Hilla*, 237; Somekh, *Baghdad, Etmol*, 144–45.

139. *Al-Sha'b*, no. 1286, 4 April 1949, 2.

140. *Al-Sha'b*, no. 1298, 19 April 1949, 1.

141. *Al-Sha'b*, no. 1324, 20 May 1949, 2; *Al-Sha'b*, no. 1340, 9 June 1949, 1.

142. *Al-Zaman*, no. 3841, 31 May 1950, 1; *Al-Zaman*, no. 3483, 11 February 1949, 1; *Al-Zaman*, no. 3547, 13 June 1949, 1; *Al-Hawadith*, no. 2154, 1 March 1950, 2; *Al-Hawadith*, no. 2159, 16 May 1950, 2; *Al-Hawadith*, no. 2388, 3 January 1951, 2.

143. *Al-Zaman*, no. 3656, 24 November 1949, 1; *Al-Zaman*, no. 3656, 24 October 1949, 1; *Al-Zaman*, no. 3657, 25 October 1949, 1; *Al-Zaman*, no. 3658, 26 October 1949, 1; *Al-Zaman*, no. 3661, 30 October 1949, 1; *Al-Zaman*, no. 3667, 6 November 1949, 1; *Al-Zaman*, no. 3668, 7 November 1949, 1; *Al-Zaman*, no. 3681, 22 November 1949, 1.

144. *Al-Hawadith*, no. 2040, 27 October 1949, 1.
145. *Al-Zaman*, no. 3838, 27 May 1950, 1, 4; *Al-Zaman*, no. 3845, 5 June 1950, 1.
146. *Al-Hawadith*, no. 1953, 9 July 1949, 1, 4; *Al-Hawadith*, no. 2025, 10 October 1949, 1, 4; *Al-Hawadith*, no. 2039, 26 October 1949, 1; *Al-Hawadith*, no. 2052, 11 November 1949, 1, 4; *Al-Hawadith*, no. 2054, 14 November 1949, 1; *Al-Hawadith*, no. 2060, 21 November 1949, 1; *Al-Hawadith*, no. 2172, 31 March 1950, 1; *Al-Hawadith*, no. 2174, 3 April 1950, 1; *Al-Hawadith*, no. 2180, 11 April 1950, 1; *Al-Hawadith*, no. 2182, 13 April 1950, 1, 4; *Al-Hawadith*, no. 2187, 19 April 1950, 1, 4; *Al-Hawadith*, no. 2269, 10 August 1950, 1, 4.
147. *Al-Hawadith*, no. 2056, 16 November 1950, 1, 4.
148. *Al-Hawadith*, no. 2269, 10 August 1950, 1; *Al-Hawadith*, no. 2361, 1 December 1950, 1; *Al-Hawadith*, no. 2387, 1 January 1951, 1.
149. *Al-Hawadith*, no. 2415, 3 February 1951, 1.
150. *Al-Hawadith*, no. 2206, 12 May 1950, 2; *Al-Hawadith*, no. 2169, 1 March 1950, 2.
151. *Al-Zaman*, 20 September 1950, 1.
152. *Al-Zaman*, no. 3662, 31 October 1949, 1, 4; *Al-Zaman*, no. 3666, 5 November 1949.
153. *Al-Zaman*, no. 3643, 9 October 1949, 1.
154. *Al-Hawadith*, no. 2025, 10 October 1949, 2.
155. *Al-Zaman*, no. 3651, 18 November 1949, 1.
156. *Al-Zaman*, no. 3860, 22 June 1950, 1.
157. *Al-Zaman*, no. 3587, 20 July 1949, 1; *Al-Zaman*, no. 4038, 28 January 1951, 1; *Al-Zaman*, no. 3651, 18 November 1949, 1.
158. *Al-Zaman*, no. 3845, 20 June 1950, 1.
159. *Al-Hawadith*, no. 1953, 9 July 1949, 1, 4.
160. Kazzaz, *Yehudim*, 278–97.
161. Simhoni, "Ha-Reka' ha-medini," 111–12; Kuriyya, *Yahud al-'Iraq*, 151–54.
162. Semah, "Sasson Semah," 85–86.
163. Kuriyya, *Yahud al-'Iraq*, 152–53; Me'ir, *Be'ikar*, 65–66; S 20/539, 1 April 1949, "Secret Report on Iraq: The American-Jewish Committee"; Ballas, *Be-Guf rishon*, 13.
164. FO 371/75183, 5 October 1949, Sir A. Gadogan (N.Y.) to Baghdad.
165. Kazzaz, *Yehudim*, 282–83.
166. FO 371/75183, 25 October 1949, Henry Mack (Baghdad) to Foreign Office; FO 371/75183, 4 November 1949, Mack to Foreign Office.
167. Haim, "Monarchy," 206.
168. Kazzaz, *Yehudim*, 301–4.
169. Although some critics refer to the text as a novel, it depicts actual historical events which are renarrated as dramatized dialogues and monologues.
170. Bar-Moshe, *Yetsi'at 'Iraq*, 227.
171. Ibid., 140–42.
172. Ibid., 101, 203.
173. Bar-Moshe, *Yetsi'at 'Iraq*, 105–6.
174. Ibid., 158.
175. Ibid., 239–40.

176. Ballas, "Iya," in *Otot setav*, 11.
177. Ibid., 17.
178. Ibid., 33.
179. Ibid., 50.
180. Bashkin, "Representations of Women."
181. Somekh, *Baghdad, Etmol*, 144.
182. Kazzaz, *Yehudim*, 238–45, 294–305; Moreh and Yehuda, eds., *Sin'at yehudim*.

Conclusions

1. Kazzaz, *Yehudim*, 305–8; Kazzaz, *Sofah shel golah*; Shohet, *Beney 'adat Mosheh*.

Bibliography

Archives

Colonial Office. National Archives, London.
Commonwealth and Foreign and Commonwealth Offices. National Archives, London.
Empire Marketing Board. National Archives, London.
Foreign Office Records. National Archives, London.
Government Communications Headquarters Records. National Archives, London.
Jewish Agency Records. Central Zionist Archive, Jerusalem.
Jewish National Fund Records. Central Zionist Archive, Jerusalem.
Or Yehuda Archive. Museum for the History of Babylonian Jewry, Or Yehuda.
Yad Va-Shem, Oriental Collection. Holocaust Museum, Jerusalem.

Newspapers and Journals

Al-Adab (Beirut)
Al-Anba (Jerusalem)
Al-Burhan (Baghdad)
Al-Hasid (Baghdad)
Al-Hatif (Najaf and later Baghdad)
Al-Hawadith (Baghdad)
Al-Hilal (Cairo)
Al-Ittihad (Haifa)
Al-Majalla (Baghdad)
Al-Misbah (Baghdad)
Sawt al-Haqq (Baghdad)
Al-Yaqdha (Baghdad)
Al-Zaman (Baghdad)
Zo Ha-Derech (Tel Aviv)

Official Reports

Great Britain. *Iraq Administration Reports, 1914–1932*. 10 vols. Slough, England: Archive Editions, 1992.
Al-Majlis al-jismani al-isra'ili, Baghdad. *Al-Nizam al-dakhili li-madaris al-ta'ifa al-isra'iliyya bi-Baghdad, 1930*. Baghdad: n.p., 1930.

———. *Rapport du comité des écoles israélites sur les écoles israélites de Baghdad, 1930*. Baghdad: n.p., 1930.

———. *Taqrir 'an al-madaris al-isra'iliyya fi Baghdad li sanat, 1929–1930*. Baghdad: n.p., 1930.

———. *Taqrir 'an al-madaris al-ahliyya al-isra'iliyya, sanat 1950*. Baghdad: n.p., 1950.

Al-Shurta al-'amma. *Mawsu'a siriyya khassa bi'l hizb al-shuyu'i al-'iraqi*. 3 vols. Baghdad: Matba'at mudiriyyat al-tahqiqat al-jina'iyya, 1949.

Other Sources

'Abd al-Ilah, Ahmad. *Nash'at al-qissa wa tatawwuruha fi'l 'Iraq, 1908–1939*. Baghdad: Matba'at Shafiq, 1989.

Abdul-Jabar, Faleh, ed. *Ayatollahs, Sufis, and Ideologues: State, Religion and Social Movement in Iraq*. London: Saqi, 2002.

———. *The Shi'ite Movement in Iraq*. London: Saqi, 2003.

Abdul-Jabar, Faleh, and Hosham Dawod, eds. *Tribes and Power: Nationalism and Ethnicity in the Middle East*. London: Saqi, 2003.

Abdullah, Thabit A. J. *A Short History of Iraq: From 636 to the Present*. London: Pearson, 2003.

Adang, Camilla. *Muslim Writers on Judaism and the Hebrew Bible: From Ibn Rabban to Ibn Hazm*. New York: Brill, 1996.

Agasi, Tikva. *Mi-Baghdad le-Israel*. Ramat Gan, Israel: Kolgraph, 2004.

Alcalay, Ammiel. *After Jews and Arabs: Remaking Levantine Culture*. Minneapolis: University of Minnesota Press, 1993.

Almog, Oz. *The Sabra*. Berkeley: University of California Press, 2000.

Almozlino, Shoshana Arbeli. *Me-ha-Mahteret be-Bavel le-memshelt Israel*. Tel Aviv: Ha-Kibbutz ha-me'uhad, 1998.

al-'Alwaji, 'Abd al-Hamid. *Al-Intaj al-nisawi fi'l 'Iraq*. Baghdad: Wizarat al-i'lam, 1975.

al-Amin, Muzaffar 'Abd Allah. *Jama'at al-Ahali: Munshu'ha, 'aqidatuha, wa-dawruha fi'l siyasa al-'iraqiyya, 1932–1946*. Beirut: Al-Mu'assasa al-'arabiyya li'l dirasat wa'l nashr; Amman: Dar al-faris, 2001.

Anidjar, Gil. *Our Place in al-Andalus: Kabbalah, Philosophy, Literature in Arab Jewish Letters*. Stanford, Calif.: Stanford University Press, 2002.

———. "Secularism." *Critical Inquiry* 33:1 (2006): 52–77.

———. *Semites: Race, Religion, Literature*. Stanford, Calif.: Stanford University Press, 2008.

'Aqabiya, Ya'qub Eliyahu, ed. *Al-Ta'ifa al-isra'iliyya fi mawakib shuhada' al-huriyya*. Baghdad: Matab'at al-Rashid, 1948.

Arazi, Tuvia, Mordechai Bibi, Shalom Darwish, Rahamim Gabbai, Ezra Haddad, David Fattal, and Ethan Shemesh, eds. *Yehudey 'Iraq tahat ha-shilton ha-'aravi: Parashat me'oraot Baghdad ba-rishon u-ba-sheni be-Juni 1941*. Jerusalem: Yad va-Shem, 1960.

Asad, Talal. *Formations of the Secular: Christianity, Islam, Modernity*. Stanford, Calif.: Stanford University Press, 2003.

Asia, Judah. *Ha-Gesharim shel hayay*. Tel Aviv: Dahlia Asia Pelled, 2005.

Atlas, Yehuda. *'Ad 'amud ha-teliya*. Tel Aviv: Ma'arakhot, 1978.

Aviezar, Shemu'l. *Mey ha-veradim.* Tel Aviv: Gevanim, 1996.
Avisur, Yitzhak, ed. *Mehkarim be-toldot yehudey 'Iraq u-betarbutam.* Or Yehuda: Merkaz moreshet yahadut Bavel, 1991.
Ayalon, Ami. *The Press in the Arab Middle East.* New York: Oxford University Press, 1995.
Ayyub, Dhu al-Nun. *Al-Athar al-kamila li-athar Dhi al-Nun Ayyub.* Baghdad: Wizarat al-i'lam, 1978.
al-Bahri, Yunus. *Huna Berlin!* N.p., 1960.
Balbul, Ya'qub. *Mukhtarat min al-jamra al-ula wa mihnat al-'aql.* Reprinted, edited, and translated into Hebrew by Shemu'el Moreh. Jerusalem: Agudat ha-akedema'im yotz'ey 'Iraq be-Israel, 2006.
Ballas, Shim'on. *Be-Guf rishon.* Tel Aviv: Ha-Kibbutz ha-me'uhad, 2009.
———. *Otot setav.* Tel Aviv: Zemora bitan, 1992.
———. *Ve hu aher.* Tel Aviv: Ha-Kibbutz ha-me'uhad, 1991.
Baram, Amatzia. "A Case of an Imported Identity: The Modernizing Secular Ruling Elites of Iraq and the Conception of Mesopotamian-Inspired Territorial Nationalism, 1922–1992." *Poetics Today* 15:2 (1994): 279–319.
Baram, Amatzia, Ronen Zeidel, and Achim Rohde, eds. *Iraq Between Occupations: Perspectives from 1920 to the Present.* New York: Palgrave-Macmillan, 2010.
Bar-Moshe, Ishaq. *Bayt fi Baghdad: Riwaya.* Jerusalem: Manshurat rabitat al-jami'iyin al-yahud al-nazihin min al-'Iraq fi Isra'il, 1983. In Hebrew: *Bayit be-Baghdad.* Jerusalem: Moreshet, 1982.
———. *Al-Khuruj min al-'Iraq: Dhikrayat, 1945–1950.* Jerusalem: Manshurat majlis al-ta'ifa al-safaradiyya, 1975. In Hebrew: *Yetsi'at 'Iraq: zikhronot mi-shenot 1945–1950.* Jerusalem: Va'ad 'adat ha-sefaradim bi-Yerushalayim be-hishtatfut ha-mahlaka li-kehilot sefaradiyot shel ha-histadrut ha-ziyonit ha-'olamit, 1977.
al-Barrak, Fadhil. *Al-Madaris al-yahudiyya wa'l iraniyya fi'l 'Iraq: dirasa muqarana.* Baghdad: n.p., 1985.
Barshan, Yehuda (Gurji). *Yehudi be-tzel ha-Islam.* Ramat Gan, Israel: Havazelet, 1997.
Baruch, Ezra, ed. *'Atzma'ut ba-mahteret: Kakh hagegu yehudim be-'Iraq et yom ha-'atzma'ut ha-rishon shel Israel.* Jerusalem: Research Institute of the Zionist-Pioneer Underground Movement in Iraq / Amos Foundation, 2001.
Bashkin, Orit. "Un arabe juif dans l'Irak de l'entre-deux-guerres: La carrière d'Anwar Shā'ul." *Vingtième Siècle: Revue d'Histoire* 103:3 (2009): 120–31.
———. "To Educate an Iraqi-Jew: Or What Can We Learn from Hebrew Autobiographies About Arab Nationalism and the Iraqi Education System (1921-1952)." In *World Yearbook of Education 2010: Education and the Arab "World": Political Projects, Struggles, and Geometries of Power,* ed. André E. Mazawi and Ronald G. Sultana, 163–81. New York: Routledge 2010.
———. "The Iraqi Afghanis and 'Abduhs: Debates over Reform Among Shi'ite and Sunni 'Ulama' in Interwar Iraq." In *Guardians of Faith in Modern Times: "Ulama" in the Middle East,* ed. Meir Hatina, 141–70. Leiden: Brill, 2008.
———. "Iraqi Arab-Jewish Identities: First Body Singular." *AJS Perspectives: The Magazine of the Association for Jewish Studies.* Association of Jewish Studies. Fall 2010: 18–19.

———. "Iraqi Women, Jewish Men, and Global Noises in Two Texts by Ya'qub Balbul." In *Transnational Borderlands in Women's Global Networks: The Making of Cultural Resistance*, ed. Clara Román-Odio and Marta Sierra, 119–40. New York: Palgrave, 2011.

———. "Lands, Hands, and Socio-Cultural Boundaries: A Reading in Dhu Nun Ayyub's *The Hand, the Land, and the Water* (1948)." *Middle Eastern Studies* 46:3 (2010): 401–15.

———. "Looking Forward to the Past: *Nahda*, Revolution, and the Early *Ba'th* in Iraq." In *Other Renaissances: New Approaches to World Literature*, ed. Brenda Deen Schildgen, Gang Zhou, and Sander L. Gilman, 59–86. New York: Palgrave, 2006.

———. "*Al-Misbah* (1924–1929): 'Iton Yehudi 'iraqi." Master's thesis, Tel Aviv University, 1998.

———. *The Other Iraq: Pluralism and Culture in Hashemite Iraq*. Stanford, Calif.: Stanford University Press, 2009.

———. "'Religious Hatred Shall Disappear from the Land': Iraqi Jews as Ottoman Subjects, 1864–1913." *International Journal of Contemporary Iraqi Studies* 4:3: 305–23.

———. "Representations of Women in the Writings of the Iraqi Intelligentsia in Hashemite Iraq, 1921–1958." *Journal of Middle East Women's Studies* 4:1 (2008): 52–78.

———. "Why Did Baghdadi Jews Stop Writing to Their Brethren in Mainz? Some Comments about the Reading Practices of Iraqi Jews in the 19th Century." *Journal of Semitic Studies* (2005): 95–110.

———. "When Dwelling Becomes Impossible: Arab-Jews in America and in Israel in the Writings of Ahmad Susa and Shimon Ballas." In *The Arab Diaspora: Voices of Anguished Scream*, ed. Zahia Salhi, 83–107. London: Routledge, 2005.

Basri, Mir. *A'lam al-yahud fi'i 'Iraq al-hadith*. Jerusalem: Manshurat rabitat al-yahud al-nazihin min al-'Iraq, 1986.

———. *Rihlat al-'umr: Min difaf Dijla ila wadi al-Tims*. Jerusalem: Rabitat al-jami'iyin al-yahud al-nazihin min al-'Iraq fi Isra'il, 1991.

———. *Rijal wa zilal: qisas wa-suwar qalamiyya*. Baghdad: Sharikat al-tijara wa'l tiba'a al-mahduda, 1955.

———. *Mabahith fi'l iqtisad al-'iraqi: 20 maqala mukhtara fi'l iqtisad wa'l tijara wa'l zira'a wa'l sina'a wa'l mal wa'l naqd wa'l 'umran*. Baghdad: Sharikat al-tijara, 1948.

Bat, Ye'or. *Juifs et chrétiens sous l'Islam: Les dhimmis face au défi intégriste*. Paris: Berg, 1994.

Batatu, Hanna. *The Old Social Classes and the Revolutionary Movements of Iraq*. Princeton, N.J.: Princeton University Press, 1978.

Beinin, Joel. *The Dispersion of Egyptian Jewry: Culture, Politics, and the Formation of a Modern Diaspora*. Berkeley: University of California Press, 1998.

Ben Porat, Mordechai. *Le-Baghdad ve-hazara*. Tel Aviv: Ma'ariv, 1996.

Ben Ya'qov, Avraham. *Yehudey Bavel mi-sof tekufat ha-ge'onim ve-'ad yemeynu*. Jerusalem: Yad Ben-Tzvi, 1965.

Benjamin, Sandra, ed. *The World of Benjamin of Tudela: A Medieval Mediterranean Travelogue*. Madison: Fairleigh Dickinson University Press; Cranbury, N.J.: Associated University Presses, 1995.

Berg, Nancy E. *Exile from Exile: Israeli Writers from Iraq*. Albany: State University of New York Press, 1996.

———. *More and More Equal: The Literary Works of Sami Michael*. Lanham, Md.: Lexington Books, 2005.

Bibi, Mordechai. *Me-Araba' kenafot ha-naharayim*. Tel Aviv: Ha-Kibbutz ha-me'uhad, 1983.

Bozdogan, Sibel, and Resat Kasaba, eds. *Rethinking Modernity and National Identity in Turkey*. Seattle: University of Washington Press, 1997.

Brubaker, Rogers. "Ethnicity Without Groups." *Archives Européenes de Sociologie* 43:2 (2002): 163–89.

Butti, Rafa'il. *Dhakira 'iraqiyya, 1900–1956*. Damascus: Al-Mada, 2000.

Çetinsaya, Gökhan. *Ottoman Administration of Iraq, 1890–1908*. London: Routledge, 2006.

Chakrabarty, Dipesh. *Provincializing Europe*. Princeton, N.J.: Princeton University Press, 2000.

Chatterjee, Partha. *The Nation and Its Fragments: Colonial and Postcolonial Histories*. Princeton, N.J.: Princeton University Press, 1993.

———. "Secularism and Toleration." *Economic and Political Weekly* 29:28 (1994): 1768–77.

Cleveland, William L. *The Making of an Arab Nationalist: Ottomanism and Arabism in the Life and Thought of Sati' al-Husri*. Princeton, N.J.: Princeton University Press, 1971.

Cohen, Haim. "The Anti-Jewish *Farhud* in Baghdad, 1941." *Middle Eastern Studies* 3:1 (1966): 2–17.

———. *Ha-Pe'ilut ha-tzionit be-'Iraq*. Jerusalem: Ha-sifriya ha-tzionit, 1969.

———. "Teosofim yehudim be-Basra." *Ha-Mizrah ha-Hadash* 15 (1965): 401–6.

Cohen, Jonah. *Hilla 'al gedot ha-Perat*. Carmiel, Israel: Jonah Cohen, 2004.

Cohen, Mark. *Under Crescent and Cross: The Jews in the Middle Ages*. Princeton, N.J.: Princeton University Press, 1994.

Commins, David Dean. *Islamic Reform: Politics and Social Change in Late Ottoman Syria*. New York: Oxford University Press, 1990.

Darwish, Salman, *Kull shay hadi fi'l 'iyada*. Jerusalem: Manshurat rabitat al-jami'iyin al-yahud al-nazihin min al-'Iraq fi Isra'il, 1981.

Darwish, Shalom. *Ahrar wa 'abid*. Baghdad: Al-Rashid, 1941.

———. *Ba'd al-nas*. Baghdad: Sharikat al-tijara wa'l tiba'a al-mahduda, 1948.

Dawn, Ernest C. "The Formation of Pan-Arab Ideology in the Inter-War Years." *International Journal of Middle East Studies* 20:1 (1988), 67–91.

Davis, Eric. *Memories of the State: Politics, History, and Collective Identity in Modern Iraq*. Berkeley: University of California Press, 2005.

DeYoung, Terri. *Placing the Poet: Badr Shakir al-Sayyab and Postcolonial Iraq*. Albany: State University of New York Press, 1998.

Drori, Ezra. *Mi-Bavel la-Carmel*. Haifa: Carmel, 2005.

Dodge, Toby. *Inventing Iraq: The Failure of Nation Building and a History Denied*. New York: Columbia University Press, 2003.

al-Dujayli, Hasan. *Taqaddum al-ta'lim al-'ali fi'l 'Iraq*. Baghdad: Matba'at al-Irshad, 1963.

Efrati, Noga. "Competing Narratives: Histories of the Women's Movement in Iraq, 1910–1958." *International Journal of Middle East Studies* 40:3 (2008): 445–66.

———. "The Other 'Awakening' in Iraq: The Women's Movement in the First Half of the Twentieth Century." *British Journal of Middle Eastern Studies* 31:2 (2004): 153–73.

———. "Women in Elite's Discourses: Iraq, 1932–1958." Ph.D. diss., Haifa University, 2001.

Ende, Werner. "Ehe auf Zeit in der innerislamischen Diskussion der Gegenwart." *Die Welt des Islams* 20:1–2 (1980): 1–43.

Eppel, Michael. "The Elite, the Effendiyya, and the Growth of Nationalism and Pan-Arabism in Hashemite Iraq, 1921–1958." *International Journal of Middle East Studies* 30:2 (1998): 227–50.

———. *The Palestine Conflict in the History of Modern Iraq: the Dynamics of Involvement, 1928–1948.* London: Cass, 1994.

Elshakry, Marwa. "Darwin's Legacy in the Arab East: Science, Religion, and Politics, 1870–1914." Ph.D. diss., Princeton University, 2003.

El Shakry, Omnia. *The Great Social Laboratory: Subjects of Knowledge in Colonial and Postcolonial Egypt.* Stanford, Calif.: Stanford University Press, 2007.

Farouk-Sluglett, Marion, and Peter Sluglett. "Some Reflections on the Sunni/Shi'i Question in Iraq." *Bulletin (British Society for Middle Eastern Studies)* 5:2 (1978): 79–87.

———. "Transformation of Land Tenure and Rural and Social Structures in Central and Southern Iraq, c. 1870–1958." *International Journal of Middle East Studies* 15:4 (1983): 491–505.

Fattah, Hala, *The Politics of Regional Trade in Iraq, Arabia, and the Gulf, 1745–1900,* Albany: State University of New York Press, 1997.

Fattal, Badri. *Halomot be-Tatran, Baghdad.* Jerusalem: Carmel, 2005.

Fattal, Salim. *Be-Simta'ot Baghdad.* Jerusalem: Carmel, 2003.

Fawzi 'Abd al-'Aziz, Hisham. "Al-Nashat al-sahayuni fi'l 'Iraq fi dhill al-intidab al-baritani." *Shu'un Falastiniyya* 180 (1988): 41–60.

Forget Baghdad. Documentary film by Samir. Seattle: Arab Film Distribution, 2000.

Gabbai, Nili. *Ha-Isha ha-yehudit be-Baghdad.* Jerusalem: Agudat ha-akadema'im yotze'y 'Iraq be-Israel, 2006.

Gabbai, Rahamin. *Pera'ot Baghdad, Juni 1941.* Jerusalem: n.p., 1982.

Gabbay, Rony. *Communism and Agrarian Reform in Iraq.* London: Croom Helm, 1978.

Gelvin, James L. *Divided Loyalties: Nationalism and Mass Politics in Syria at the Close of Empire.* Berkeley: University of California Press, 1998.

Ghanima, Yusuf Rizkallah. *Nuzhat al-mushtaq fi ta'rikh yahud al-'Iraq.* Baghdad: Al-Maktaba al-'arabiyya, 1924. English version: *Nostalgic Trip into the History of the Jews of Iraq.* Trans. with introduction and update by A. Dallal. Lanham, Md.: University Press of America, 1998.

Gat, Moshe. *Kehila yehudit be-mashber.* Jerusalem: Zalman Shazar, 1989. English version: *The Jewish Exodus from Iraq, 1948–1951.* Portland, Oreg.: Cass, 1997.

Gershoni, Israel. *Beyond Anti-Semitism: Egyptian Responses to German Nazism and Italian Fascism in the 1930s.* San Domenico di Fiesole and Florence: Robert Schuman Center for Advanced Studies, European University Institute Working Papers, Mediterranean Programme Series 32, 2001.

———. "Egyptian Liberalism in an Age of 'Crisis of Orientation': *Al-Risala*'s Reaction to Fascism and Nazism, 1933–39." *International Journal of Middle East Studies* 31:4 (1999): 551–76.

———. *Or ba-tsel: Mitsrayim ve-ha-fashizm, 1922–1937.* Tel Aviv: 'Am 'oved, 1999.
Gershoni, Israel, and James Jankowski. *Confronting Fascism in Egypt: Dictatorship Versus Democracy in the 1930s.* Stanford, Calif.: Stanford University Press, 2009.
———. *Egypt, Islam, and the Arabs: The Search for Egyptian Nationhood, 1900–1930.* New York: Oxford University Press, 1986.
———. *Redefining Egyptian Nation.* Cambridge: Cambridge University Press, 1995.
Goitein, S. D. *A Mediterranean Society: The Jewish Communities of the Arab World as Portrayed in the Documents of the Cairo Geniza.* Berkeley: University of California Press, 1967–93.
Grunebaum, G. E. von. S.v. "I'djāz." *Encyclopaedia of Islam.* 2nd ed. Ed. P. Bearman, Th. Bianquis, C. E. Bosworth, E. van Donzel, and W. P. Heinrichs. Leiden: Brill, 2009. Brill online: www.brillonline.nl.proxy.uchicago.edu/subscriber/entry?entry=islam_SIM-3484 (accessed January 4, 2012).
Haddad, Ezra. *Avney Derech.* Tel-Aviv: Irgun yotzey 'Iraq be-Israel, 1970.
———. *Rihlat Binyamin.* Baghdad: Al-Matba'a al-sharqiyya, 1945.
Haim, Sylvia G. *Arab Nationalism: An Anthology.* Berkeley: University of California Press, 1976.
———. "Arabic Antisemitic Literature: Some Preliminary Notes." *Jewish Social Studies* 17:4 (1955): 307–12.
———. "Aspects of Jewish Life in Baghdad Under the Monarchy." *Middle Eastern Studies* 12:2 (1976): 188–208.
al-Hajj, Aziz. *Shahadat al-ta'rikh: Awrak fi'l sira al-dhatiyya al-siyasiyya.* London: Mu'assasat al-Rafid, 2001.
Hamdi, Walid M. S. *Rashid Ali al-Gailani and the Nationalist Movement in Iraq, 1939–1941: A Political and Military Study of the British Campaign in Iraq and the National Revolution of May 1941.* London: Darf, 1987.
Haqqaq, Lev. *Igrot ha-rav Shelomo Bekhor Hotzin.* Tel Aviv: Hillel ben-Haim / Ha-Kibbutz ha-me'uhad, 2005.
———. *Nitzaney ha-yetzira ha-'ivrit ha-hadasha be-Bevel.* Or Yehuda: Merkaz moreshet yahadut Bavel, ha-Makhon le-heker yahadut Bavel, 2003.
Har'el, Yaron. *Ben Tekhakhim le-mahapekha: Minuy rabanim rashiyim ve-hadahatam bi-kehilot Baghdad, Damesek ve-Haleb, 1744–1914.* Jerusalem: Yad Ben-Tzvi, 2007.
al-Hasani, 'Abd al-Razzaq. *Al-Asrar al-khaffiyya fi harakat 1941 al-taharruriyya.* Sayda, Lebanon: Matba'at al-'irfan, 1964.
Hever, Hanan. *Ha-Sipur ve-ha-le'om: Keri'a bikortit be-kanon ha-siporet ha-'ivrit.* Tel Aviv: Resling, 2007.
al-Hilali, 'Abd al-Razzaq. *Nazarat fi islah al-rif.* Beirut: Dar al-kashshaf, 1950.
Hillel, Shelomo. *Ruh qadim.* Jerusalem: 'Idanim, 1985.
Al-Hizb al-shuyu'i al-'iraqi. *Shuhada' al-hizb, shuhada' al-watan: Shuhada' al-hizb al-shuyu'i al-'iraqi.* Beirut: Dar al-kunuz al-adabiyya, 2001.
Hobsbawm, Eric. *Nations and Nationalism Since 1780: Programme, Myth, Reality.* Cambridge: Cambridge University Press, 1992.
Hobsbawm, Eric, and Terence Ranger, eds. *The Invention of Tradition.* Cambridge: Cambridge University Press, 1983.

Hochberg, Gil Z. *In Spite of Partition: Jews, Arabs, and the Limits of Separatist Imagination.* Princeton, N.J.: Princeton University Press, 2007.
Hooper, Charles Arthur. *The Constitutional Law of Iraq.* Baghdad: Mackenzie and Mackenzie, 1928.
Hourani, Albert. *Arabic Thought in the Liberal Age.* London: Oxford University Press, 1962.
Husayn, Taha. *Al-Ayyam.* Cairo: Matba'at al-ma'arif, 1944–45.
al-Husri, Sati'. *Abhath mukhtara fi'l qawmiyya al-'arabiyya.* Beirut: Dar al-Quds, 1974.
Ibrahim, 'Abd al-Fattah. *Muqaddima fi'l ijtima'.* Baghdad: Matba'at al-Ahali, 1939.
Ibn al-Husayn, Faysal. *Faysal ibn al-Husayn: Fi khutubihi wa aqwalihi.* Baghdad: Mudiriyat al-di'ayat al-'amma, 1946.
Ingrams, Doreen, ed. *The Awakened: Women in Iraq.* London: Third World Centre, 1983.
Ireland, Philip. *Iraq: A Study in Political Development.* London: Cape, 1937.
Ismael, Tareq Y. *The Rise and Fall of the Communist Party of Iraq.* New York: Cambridge University Press, 2007.
Jabra, Jabra I. "Modern Arabic Literature and the West." In *Critical Perspectives on Modern Arabic Literature*, ed. Issa J. Boullata, 7–22. Washington, D.C.: Three Continents Press, 1980.
———. *Princesses' Street: Baghdad Memories.* Fayetteville: University of Arkansas Press, 2005.
Jubran, Sulayman. *Majma' al-addad: Dirasa fi sirat al-Jawahiri wa-shi'rihi.* Beirut: Al-Mu'assasa al-'arabiyya li'l-dirasat wa'l-nashr, 2003.
Jamil, Husayn. *Al-Hayat al-niyabiyya fi'l 'Iraq, 1925–1946: Mawaqif jama'at al-Ahali minha.* Baghdad: Maktabat al-Muthanna, 1983.
Jamil, Makki. *Al-Badw wa'l-qaba'il al-rahhala fi'l 'Iraq.* Baghdad: Matba'at al-Rabita, 1956.
al-Jawahiri, 'Imad Ahmad. *Nadi al-Muthanna wa-wajihat al-tajammu' al-qawmi fi'l 'Iraq, 1934–1942.* Baghdad: Matba'at Dar al-Jahiz li'l tiba'a wa'l nashr, 1984.
Kahila, Avraham. *Hayinu ke-holmim.* Jerusalem: Research Institute of the Zionist-Pioneer Underground in Iraq, 2007.
Kattan, Naïm. *Adieu, Babylone: Roman.* Montreal: La Presse, 1975.
Kazzaz, Nissim. *Ha-Yehudim be-'Iraq ba-ma'a he-'esrim.* Jerusalem: Yad Ben-Tzvi, 1991.
———. "'Itona'im yehudiyim be-'Iraq." *Kesher* 7 (1990): 36–40.
———. "'Itonim ve 'itona'im yehudiyim be-'Iraq." *Kesher* 6 (1989): 68–74.
———. "Ha-Pe'ilut ha-politit shel yehudey 'Iraq be-shalhey ha-shilton ha-ottomani." *Pe'amim* 36 (1988): 35–40.
———. *Sofah shel golah: Ha-Yehudim be-'Iraq aharey ha-'aliya ha-hamonit, 1951–2000.* Or Yehuda: Merkaz moreshet yahadut Bavel, ha-Makhon le-heker yahadut Bavel, 2002.
Kedourie, Elie, and Aharon David Shohet. "The Jews of Baghdad in 1910." *Middle Eastern Studies* 7:3 (1971): 355–61.
———. "The Sack of Basra and the Farhud in Baghdad." In *Arabic Political Memoirs and Other Studies*, 283–314. London: Cass, 1974.
Kerr, Malcolm. *Islamic Reform.* Berkeley: California University Press, 1966.
Khaduri, Sha'ul Sasun. *Ra'i wa-ra'iya: Sirat hayat al-hakham Sasun Khaduri.* Jerusalem: Rabitat al-jami'iyin al-yahud al-nazihin min al-'Iraq, 1999.
al-Khalili, Ja'far. *Al-Qissa al-'iraqiyya, qadiman wa-hadithan.* Baghdad: Matba'at al-ma'arif, 1957.

Khadduri, Majid. *Independent Iraq, 1932–1958: A Study in Iraqi Politics*. London: Oxford University Press, 1960.
Khattat, Qasim, Mustafa 'Abd al-Latif Saharti, and Muhammad 'Abd al-Mun'im Khafaji. *Ma'ruf al-Rusafi: Sha'ir al-'Arab al-kabir, hayatuhu wa-shi'ruhu.* Cairo: Al-Ha'ya al-misriyya al-'amma li'l-ta'lif wa'l nashr, 1971.
Khayri, Zaki. *Sada al-sinnin fi dhakirat shuyu'i 'iraqi mukhadrim.* Al-mu'allif, 1995.
Khazzoom, Aziza. "The Great Chain of Orientalism: Jewish Identity, Stigma Management, and Ethnic Exclusion in Israel." *American Sociological Review* 68:4 (2003): 481–510.
al-Khurasan, Salah. *Safahat min ta'rikh al-haraka al-shuyu'iyya fi'l 'Iraq.* Beirut: Dar al-Furat, 1993.
von Kugelgen, Anke. "A Call for Rationalism: 'Arab Averroists' in the Twentieth Century." *Alif: Journal of Comparative Poetics* 16 (1996): 97–132.
Kuriyya, Ya'qub Yusuf. *Yahud al-'Iraq: Ta'rikhuhum, ahwaluhum, hijratuhum.* Amman: Al-Ahliyya, 1998.
Lajnat Ta'awun al-tullab fi Madrasat al-Alliance (Albert Da'ud Sassun). *Ma'asi al-hayah bi qalam al-shab al-adib al-marhum Eliyahu Khaduri Mu'allim: Sudira bi-munasabat murur 'amm 'ala wafatihi.* Baghdad: Matba'at al-Rashid, 1941–42.
Landau, Rom. *Search for Tomorrow.* London: Nicholson and Watson, 1938.
Lazarus-Yafeh, Hava. *Intertwined Worlds: Medieval Islam and Bible Criticism.* Princeton, N.J.: Princeton University Press, 1992.
Levi, Shoshana. *'Al Em ha-derekh.* Tel Aviv: Levi, 2001.
Levy, Lital. "Historicizing the Concept of Arab Jews in the *Mashriq*." *Jewish Quarterly Review* 98:4 (2008): 452–69.
———. "Jewish Writers in the Arab East: Literature, History, and the Politics of Enlightenment, 1863-1914." Ph.D. diss., University of California, Berkeley, 2007.
Lewis, Bernard. *The Jews of Islam.* Princeton, N.J.: Princeton University Press, 1984.
Longringg, Stephan. *Iraq, 1900 to 1950.* London: Oxford University Press, 1953.
Luizard, Pierre-Jean. *La formation de l'Irak contemporain: Le rôle politique des ulémas chiites à la fin de la domination ottomane et au moment de la construction de l'état irakien.* Paris: Editions du Centre national de la recherche scientifique, 1991.
al-Ma'adidi, 'Isam Jum'a Ahmad. *Al-Sahafa al-yahudiyya fi'l 'Iraq.* Cairo: Al-Dar al-dawliyya li'l istithmarat al-thaqafiyya, 2001.
MacDonald, D. B., P. N. Boratav, K. A. Nizami, and P. Voorhoeve. S.v. "Djinn." *Encyclopaedia of Islam.* 2nd ed. Ed. P. Bearman, Th. Bianquis, C. E. Bosworth, E. van Donzel, and W. P. Heinrichs. Leiden: Brill, 2009. Brill online: www.brillonline.nl.proxy.uchicago.edu/subscriber/entry?entry=islam_COM-0191 (accessed January 4, 2012).
Madrasat Shammash. *Minhaj al-hafla al-riyadiyya al-sanawiyya li-madrasat Shammash al-thanawiyya.* Baghdad: Al-Matba'a al-sharqiyya, 1945.
———. *Minhaj al-hafla al-riyadiyya al-sanawiyya li-madrasat Shammash al-thanawiyya.* Baghdad: Al-Matba'a al-sharqiyya, 1947.
al-Majlis al-jismani al-'isra'ili bi-Baghdad. *Na'im Zilkha, ba'd ma qal 'anhu al-kuttab wa'l khutaba' wa-arbab al-shuhuf bi-munasabat wafatihi.* Baghdad: Matba'at dar al-salam, 1929.

Makdisi, Saree. "Postcolonial Literature in a Neocolonial World: Modern Arabic Culture and the End of Modernity." *Boundary* 22:1 (1995): 85–115.

Makiya, Kanan. *Republic of Fear: The Politics of Modern Iraq*. Berkeley: University of California Press, 1989.

Marmorstein, Emile. "Fritz Grobba." *Middle Eastern Studies* 23:3 (1987): 376–78.

———. "Hahkam Sasson in 1949." *Middle Eastern Studies* 24:3 (1988): 364–68.

Marr, Phoebe. "The Development of Nationalist Ideology in Iraq, 1921–1941." *Muslim World* 75:2 (1985): 95–97.

Ma'ruf, Khaldun Naji. *Al-Aqaliyya al-yahudiyya fi'l 'Iraq bayn sanat 1921 wa 1952*. Baghdad: Markaz al-dirasat al-filastiniyya, jami'at Baghdad; Wizarat al-ta'lim al-'ali wa'l-bahth al-'ilmi, 1975–76.

Masliyah, Sadok H. "Zionism in Iraq." *Middle Eastern Studies* 25:2 (1989): 216–37.

Masri, Ya'qub Mir. "Dhikrayat." *Al-Thaqafa al-Jadida* 5 (March 1985): 55–65.

Matthews, Roderic D., and Matta Akrawi. *Education in Arab Countries of the Near East: Egypt, Iraq, Palestine, Transjordan, Syria, Lebanon*. Washington, D.C.: American Council on Education, 1949.

Me'ir, Yosef. *Be'ikar ba-mahteret, yehudim u-politika be-'Iraq*. Tel Aviv: Naharayim, 1993.

———. *Hitpathut tarbutit hevratit shel yehudey 'Iraq me'az 1830 ve 'ad yemenu*. Tel Aviv: Naharayim, 1989.

———. *Yehudim tahat shilton 'iraqi ba-me'a ha-'esrim: Asirey tziyon ve-harugey malkhut be-'Iraq*. Tel Aviv: Irgun yotzey ha-mahteret ha-halutzit be-'Iraq; Makhon le-heker tenu'at ha-mahteret ha-tziyonit-halutzit be-'Iraq, 2008.

Me'ir-Glitzenstein, Esther. *Ben Bagdad le-Ramat Gan: Yotz'ey 'Iraq be-Yisra'el*. Jerusalem: Yad Ben-Tzvi, 2008.

———. "Ha-Pera'ot bi-yehudey Baghdad." *Pe'amim* 8 (1981): 21–37.

———. *Zionism in an Arab Country: Jews in Iraq in the 1940s*. London: Routledge, 2004.

Michael, Sami. *Victoria*. Tel Aviv: 'Am 'oved, 1993.

Mikha'il, Murad. *Al-A'mal al-shi'riyya al-kamila*. Shifa 'Amr, Israel: Dar al-sharq, 1988.

Monroe, Paul. *Report of the Education Inquiry Commission*. Baghdad: Government Press, 1932.

Moreh, Shemu'el. "Anwar Sha'ul Zal—rishon ha-meshorerim ha-yehudim be-'Iraq ba-safa ha-'aravit." *Pe'amim* 22 (1985): 129–31.

———. *Ha-Ilan ve-ha-'anaf: Ha-safrut ha-'aravit ha-hadasha ve-yetziratam shel yehudey 'Iraq*. Jerusalem: Magnes, 1997.

———. "Ha-Te'atron ha-yehudi be-'Iraq ba-mahatzit ha-risho'na shel ha-me'a ha-'eshrim." *Pe'amim* 23 (1985): 64–98.

———. "'Al ha-Shira ve ha-safrut ha-yafa hel yehudey 'Iraq." In *Iraq*, ed. Haim Sa'dun, 101–7. Jerusalem: Israeli Ministry of Education/Yad Ben-Tzvi, 2002.

———. *Al-Qissa al-qasira 'inda yahud al-'Iraq, 1924–1978*. Jerusalem: Hebrew University Press, 1981.

Moreh, Shemu'el, and Tzvi Yehuda, eds. *Sin'at yehudim u-fera'ot be-'Iraq*. Or Yehuda: Merkaz moreshet yahadut Bavel, 1992.

Mu'allim, Me'ir. *Fi tariqi ila'l mu'ataqal*. Jerusalem: n.p., 1983.

Mu'allim Nissim, 'Izzat. *'Ala difaf al-Furat: Dhikrayat ayyam maddat wa-inqadat*. Shifa 'Amr, Israel: Dar al-mashriq, 1980.
Mubarak, Zaki. *Layla al-marida fi'l 'Iraq: Ta'rikh yufassil waqa'i Layla bayna al-Qahira wa-Baghdad min sanat 1926 ila sanat 1938*. Cairo, 1938–39. Repr., Beirut: Al-Maktaba al-'asriyya, 1976.
———. *Wahi Baghdad*. Baghdad: Al-Maktaba al-'asriyya, 1938.
al-Musawi, Muhsin J. *Reading Iraq*. London: Tauris, 2006.
Murad, Emile. *Mi-Bavel ba-mahteret*. Tel Aviv: 'Am 'oved, 1972.
Naggar, David. *Bab al-Sheikh*. Tel Aviv: Kobbi Ran, 2007.
Nakash, Yitzhak. *Shi'is of Iraq*. Princeton, N.J.: Princeton University Press, 1994.
Needham, Anuradha Dingwaney, and Rajeswari Sunder Rajan, eds. *The Crisis of Secularism in India*. Durham, N.C.: Duke University Press, 2007.
Nordbruch, Götz. *Nazism in Syria and Lebanon: The Ambivalence of the German Option, 1933–1945*. New York: Routledge, 2009.
Obadiah, Ibrahim. *Sittin 'amman: Ana wa'l shi'r*. Jerusalem: Rabitat al-jam'iyin al-yahud al-nazihin min al-'Iraq, 2006.
Obermeyer, Jacob. *Modernes Judentum in Morgen und Abendland*. Vienna: Fromme, 1907.
al-Rawi, 'Abd al-Latif. *'Usbat mukafahat al-Sahayuniyya fi'l 'Iraq, 1945–1946: Dirasa wa watha'iq al-yasar al-'iraqi wa'l mas'ala al-falastiniyya*. Damascus: Dar al-Jalil, 1986.
Rejwan, Nissim. *The Jews of Iraq: 3000 Years of History and Culture*. Boulder, Colo.: Westview Press, 1985.
———. *The Last Jews in Baghdad: Remembering a Lost Homeland*. Austin: University of Texas Press, 2004.
Rizk Khoury, Dina. *State and Provincial Society in the Ottoman Empire: Mosul, 1540–1834*. Cambridge: Cambridge University Press, 1999.
Sabar, Ariel. *My Father's Paradise: A Son's Search for His Jewish Past in Kurdish Iraq*. Chapel Hill, N.C.: Algonquin Books of Chapel Hill, 2008.
Sagiv, David. *Yahadut be-mifgash ha-Nahariyim: Kehilat yehudey Basra*. Jerusalem: Merkaz moreshet yahadut Bavel, 2004.
Samuel, Edwin. "The Government of Israel and Its Problems." *Middle Eastern Journal* 3:1 (1949): 1–16.
Sassoon, David, ed. *Masa' Bavel*. Jerusalem: Defus 'Azriel, 1955
Sayf, Malik. *Li'l ta'rikh lisan: Dhikrayat wa-qadaya khassa bi'l hizb al-shuyu'i al-'Iraqi mundhu ta'sisihi hatta al-yawm*. Baghdad: Al-Dar al-wataniyya, 1983.
Sehayek, Sha'ul. "Changes in the Social Status of Urban Jewish Women in Iraq as the Nineteenth Century Turned." *Women in Judaism: A Multidisciplinary Journal* 3:2 (2003): 51–68.
———. "Demut ha-yehudi be-re'i ha-'itonut ha-'aravit ben ha-shanim, 1858–1908." Ph.D. diss., Hebrew University, Jerusalem, 1991.
———. *Haluzot ba-mahteret: Hishtalvut bahurot bi-tenu'at he-haluz ha-mahtartit be-'Iraq*. Or Yehuda: Merkaz moreshet yahadut Bavel, 2000.
———. *Parasha 'aluma: Korot mifgasham shel alfey hayalim yehudim polanim 'im yehudim be-'Iraq u-ve-Iran ba-shanim, 1942–1943*. Tel Aviv: Sha'ul Sehayek, 2003.
Selim, Samah. "The People's Entertainments: Translation, Popular Fiction and the *Nahdah*

in Egypt." In *Other Renaissances*, ed. Brenda Deen Schildgen, Gang Zhou, Sander L. Gilman, 71–107. New York: Palgrave, 2006.
Shahrabany, Ahser. *Ha-Brikha mi-Basra*. Modi'in, Israel: Ahser Shahrabany, 2008.
al-Sayyab, Badr Shakir. *Kuntu shuyu'iyyan*. Cologne: Matba'at al-jamal, 2007.
Sha'shu', Avner. *Yemey Baghdad—me-eretz ha-naharayim le-eretz Israel—sippur ma'vakah le-'aliya shel mishpaha mi-Bavel*. Tel Aviv: n.p., 1999.
Sha'ul, Anwar. *Fi Ziham al-Madina*. Baghdad: Sharikat al-tijara wa'al tiba'ah al-mahduda, 1955.
———. *Al-Hisad al-awwal*. Baghdad: Al-Mu'llif, 1930.
———. *Qisas min al-gharb*. Baghdad: Matba'at al-Ma'arif, 1937.
———. *Qissa hayati fi wadi al-Rafidayn*. Jerusalem: Manshurat rabitat al-jami'iyin al-yahud al-nazihin min al-'Iraq fi Isra'il, 1980.
———. *Wa-baza'a fajr jadid*. Jerusalem: Manshurat rabitat al-jama'iyin al-yahud al-nazihin min al-'Iraq fi Isra'il, 1983.
———. *Wilhelm Tell*. Baghdad: n.p., 1932.
Shawkat, Sami. *Hadhihi ahdafuna*. Baghdad: Majjalat al-mu'allim al-jadid, 1939.
al-Sheikh Da'ud, Sabiha. *Awwal al-tariq ila'l nahda al-nisawiyya fi'l 'Iraq*. Baghdad: Matba'at al-Rabita, 1959.
Schechtman, Joseph. *Population Transfers in Asia*. New York: Hallsby Press, 1949.
Shenhav, Yehouda. *The Arab Jews: A Postcolonial Reading of Nationalism, Religion, and Ethnicity*. Stanford, Calif.: Stanford University Press, 2006.
———. "The Jews of Iraq, Zionist Ideology, and the Property of the Palestinian Refugees of 1948: An Anomaly of National Accounting." *International Journal of Middle East Studies* 31:4 (1999): 605–30.
Shiblak, Abbas. *The Lure of Zion: The Case of Iraqi Jews*. London: Saqi, 1986.
Shina, Shelomo, Ya'qov El'azar, and Emanuel Nahtomi. *Perakim be-toldon ha-mahteret: Yotsi'im la'or bimel'ot 'esrim shana le-hisul golat Bavel*. Tel Aviv: Irgun yotzey ha-mahteret ha-halutzit be-'Iraq, 1970.
Shohat, Ella. "The Invention of the Mizrahim." *Journal of Palestine Studies* 29:1 (1999): 5–20.
———. "Sephardim in Israel: Zionism from the Standpoint of Its Jewish Victims." *Social Text* 19:20 (1988): 1–35.
———. *Taboo Memories, Diasporic Voices*. Durham, N.C.: Duke University Press, 2006.
Shohet, Maurice. *Beney 'adat Mosheh: Mi-toldot Yehudey Bavel me-az kinun ha-mishtar ha-republikani, 1958–1975*. Tel Aviv: Ha-Kongres ha-yehudi ha-'olami, 1979.
Shtahl, Neta. *Tselem yehudi: Yitsugav shel Yeshu ba-sifrut ha-'ivrit shel ha-me'ah ha-'esrim*. Tel Aviv: Resling, 2008.
Sibahi, Aziz. *'Uqud min ta'rikh al-hizb al-shuyu'i al-'Iraqi*. Damascus: Al-Thaqafa al-jadida, 2002.
Simhoni, Dafna. "Kavim le-re'shit ha-modernizatzia shel yehudey Bavel ba me'a ha-tesha' esreh 'ad shenat 1949." *Pe'amim* 36 (1988): 7–16.
———. "Ha-Reka' ha-medini le-mivtza' 'aliyat yehudey 'Iraq, 1950–1951." In *Mehkarim be-toldot yehudey 'Iraq u-betarbutam*, ed. Yitzhak Avisur, 6: 89–112. Or Yehuda: Merkaz moreshet yahadut Bavel, 1991.

Simon, Reeva. "Ha-Hinukh ba-kehila ha-yehudit be-Baghdad 'ad shenat 1914." *Pe'amim* 36 (1988): 52–56.

———. *Iraq Between Two World Wars: The Creation and Implementation of a Nationalist Ideology*. New York: Columbia University Press, 1986.

Sluglett, Peter. *Britain in Iraq, 1914–1932*. London: Ithaca Press for the Middle East Centre, St Antony's College, Oxford, 1976.

Smith, Charles D. *Islam and the Search for Social Order in Modern Egypt: A Biography of Muhammad Husayn Haykal*. Albany: State University of New York Press, 1983.

Snir, Reuven. *'Arviyut, yahadut, tzionut: Ma'vak zehuyot bi-yetziratam shel yehudei 'Iraq*. Jerusalem: Yad Ben-Tzvi, 2005.

Somekh, Sasson. *Baghdad, Etmol*. Tel Aviv: Ha-Kibbutz ha-me'uhad, 2004. 3rd ed., March 2004. 1st ed. appeared in December 2003. English version: Sasson Somekh, *Baghdad, Yesterday: The Making of an Arab Jew*. Jerusalem: Ibis, 2007.

———. "Lost Voices: Jewish Authors in Modern Arabic Literature." In *Jews and Arabs: Contacts and Boundaries*, ed. Mark Cohen and Abraham L. Udovitch, 9–21. Princeton, N.J.: Princeton University Press, 1989.

Spivak, Gayatri Chakravorty. "Nationalism and the Imagination." *Lectura* 15: 75–98.

Starkey, Paul. S.v. "Nahda." *Encyclopedia of Arabic Literature*. Ed. Julie Scott Meisami and Paul Starkey. London: Routledge, 1998.

Stillman, Norman A. *The Jews of Arab Lands in Modern Times*. Philadelphia: Jewish Publication Society, 1991.

al-Suwaydi, Tawfiq. *Mudhakarati: Nisf qarn min ta'rikh al-'Iraq wa'l qadiyya al-'arabiyya*. London: Dar al-Hikma, 1999.

Susa, Ahmad. *Fi tariqi ila'l islam*. Cairo: Al-Matba'a al-salafiyya, 1936. Repr., Beirut: Al-Mu'assasa al-'arabiyya li'l dirasat wa'l nashr, 2006.

———. *Hayati fi nisf qarn*. Baghdad: Dar al-shu'un al-thaqafiyya al-'amma, 1986.

Tamari, Salim. *Mountain Against the Sea: Essays on Palestinian Society and Culture*. Berkeley: University of California Press, 2009.

Tarbush, Mohammad A. *The Role of the Military in Politics: A Case Study of Iraq to 1941*. London: Kegan Paul International, 1982.

Tenu'at ha-Halutz. *Hagg ha-'atzma'ut be-Bavel*. Baghdad: Central Secretariat, 1949. The book in its entirety was reprinted and annotated in: Ezra Baruch, ed., *'Atzma'ut ba-mahteret: Kakh hagegu yehudim be-'Iraq et yom ha-'atzma'ut ha-rishon shel Israel*. Jerusalem: Research Institute of the Zionist-Pioneer Underground Movement in Iraq / Amos Foundation, 2001.

Thompson, Elizabeth. *Colonial Citizens: Republican Rights, Paternal Privilege, and Gender in French Syria and Lebanon*. New York: Columbia University Press, 2000.

Tibi, Bassam. *Arab Nationalism: Between Islam and the Nation-State*. New York: St. Martin's Press, 1997.

Twena, Avraham. *Golim u-ge'ulim*. Vol. 5, *Ha-Hinukh ha-yehudi be-Baghdad, 1832–1951*. Ramla: Bet ha-keneset ge'ula, 1975.

———. *Golim u-ge'ulim*. Vol. 6, *Me'ora'ot hagg ha-Shavu'ot, Juni 1941*. Ramla: Bet ha-keneset ge'ula, 1979.

'Usbat mukafahat al-Sahayuniyya. *Manshurat 'usbat mukafahat al-Sahayuniyya.* Baghdad: Matba'at dar al-Hikma, 1946.

al-Wakil, Fu'ad Husayn. *Jama'at al-Ahali fi'l 'Iraq, 1932–1937.* Baghdad: Al-Jumhuriyya al-'iraqiyya; Wizarat al-thaqafa wa'l i'lam, 1980.

Watenpaugh, Keith. *Being Modern in the Middle East: Revolution, Nationalism, Colonialism, and the Arab Middle Class.* Princeton, N.J.: Princeton University Press, 2006.

Wiebke, Walther. "From Women's Problems to Women as Images in Modern Iraqi Poetry." *Die Welt des Islams* 36:2 (1996): 219–41.

Wien, Peter. *Iraqi Arab Nationalism: Authoritarian, Totalitarian, and Pro-Fascist Inclinations, 1932–1941.* New York: Routledge, 2006.

———. "Who Is 'Liberal' in 1930s Iraq? Education as a Contested Terrain in a Nascent Public Sphere." In *Nationalism and Liberal Thought in the Arab East: Ideology and Practice*, ed. Christoph Schumann, 31–47. London: Routledge, 2010.

Wild, Stefan. "National Socialism in the Arab Near East Between 1933 and 1939." *Die Welt des Islams* 1:4 (1985): 136–37.

Wilson, Arnold. *Loyalties: Mesopotamia, 1914–1917*, London: Oxford University Press, H. Milford, 1930.

———. *Mesopotamia, 1917–1920: A Clash of Loyalties; A Personal and Historical Record.* London: Oxford University Press, H. Milford, 1931.

Wistrich, Robert S. *Anti-Zionism and Anti-Semitism in the Contemporary World.* New York: New York University Press, 1990.

Woodsmall, Ruth F. *Study of the Role of Women: Their Activities and Organizations, in Lebanon, Egypt, Iraq, Jordan, and Syria, October 1954–August 1955.* New York: International Federation of Business and Professional Women, 1956.

Ya'qov-Yaron, Avner. *Shalom lakh Baghdad.* Jerusalem: Ha-Makhon le-heker ha-mahteret ha-tzionit, 2004.

Yasin, Abd al-Qadir. "'Usbat mukafahat al-Sahayniyya fi'l 'Iraq." *Shu'un Falastiniyya* (November 1963): 158–66.

Yehuda, Tzvi, ed. *Mi-Bavel li-Yerushalayim: Kovetz mehakrim u-te'udut 'al ha-ziyonut ve-ha-'aliya me-'Iraq.* Tel Aviv: Merkaz moreshet yahadut Bavel, 1980.

Yusuf, Salman Yusuf [Fahd]. *Kitabat al-Rafiq Fahd.* Baghdad: Al-Tariq al-jadid, 1976.

al-Zahir, 'Abd al-Razzaq. *Al-Iqta' wa'l dawawin fi'l 'Iraq.* Cairo: Matba'at al-sa'ada, 1946.

Zilkha, Yusuf Harun. *Al-Sahayuniyya 'aduwat al-'Arab wa'l Yahud.* Baghdad: Matba'at dar al-Hikma, 1946.

Zohar, Tzvi. "Yahaso shel ha-rav 'Abdallah Somekh le-tmurot ha-me'a ha-yod tet, ka-mishtakef bi-yetzirato ha-hilchatit." *Pe'amim* 36 (1988): 89–107.

Zu'aytar, Akram. *Bawakir al-nidal, min mudhakkirat Akram Zu'aytar, 1909–1935.* Beirut: Al-Mu'assasa al-'arabiyya li'l-Dirasat wa'l nashr, 1994.

———. *Min ajli Ummati.* Beirut: Al-Mu'assasa al-'arabiyya li'l-Dirasat wa'l nashr, 1994.

Zubaida, Sami. "Being Iraqi and a Jew." In *A Time to Speak Out: Independent Jewish Voices on Israel, Zionism, and Jewish Identity*, ed. Anne Karpf, Brian Klug, Jacqueline Rose, and Barbara Rosenbaum, 267–77. London: Verso, 2008.

———. "The Fragments Imagine the Nation: The Case of Iraq." *International Journal of Middle East Studies* 32:2 (2002): 205–15.

Index

Abbasid empire, 28
'Abd al-Ilah (Regent), 19, 39
'Abduh, Muhammad, 28
'Abdulhamid II, 164
Abi Talib, 'Ali Ibn, 53
Abu Hanifa, 56
Achcar, Gilbert, 8
Acre, 50, 55
'Adas, Shafiq, 188–90, 214
Al-Adib (journal), 25
Agasi, Rabbi Shim'on, 85
Al-Ahali (political party), 18, 19, 45, 85, 111, 144
Al-Ahali (school), 78
Al-'Ahd (newspaper), 205
Ahl al-dhimma (protected minority), 139–40
Al-Ahrar (newspaper), 35
Algeria, 232
'Al Ha-Mishmar (newspaper), 216
Al-'Alim al-'Arabi (newspaper), 106, 107, 173, 205
Alliance schools, 39, 60, 61, 64, 68, 73, 74, 77, 80–81, 85–86, 110
'Amara, 128, 193
American Embassy, Baghdad, 114
Amin, Qasim, 28, 90, 99
'Anan bin Da'ud, 54, 56
Anders, Władyław, 107
Anglo-American Investigation Committee, 168, 173, 186

Animals, slaughter of, 66
Anti-Semitism: class struggle and, 163–64, 173–74; in German propaganda, 105–6, 108–10, 114, 130; Hitler and, 139; Kaylani coup and, 113–15; nationalism and, 102–11, 147–48; and persecution in Iraq, 185–202; persistence of, 163; published material on, 62–63, 105–8; responses to, 106–11; state-sponsored, 155; violence stemming from, 100–105, 112–25; Zionist opposition to, 13, 102
Arab Democratic Committee, 178
Arabic language, 20–21, 23–24, 46, 49–56, 72–74, 81, 150, 231
Arab intellectuals: and fascism, 8–9; Jews supported by, 10–11; and women, 84; writings by, 24–25
Arabization: of Benjamin of Tudela's travels, 47–56; through education, 72–78, 83; impact of, 99; secularization in relation to, 98
Arab Jews, 14, 28, 37, 47, 182, 197; and communism, 142; defined, 2; demise of concept of, 214, 223; European Jews' attitudes toward, 166; identity formation of, 2–4, 68, 71–72, 225, 234; in Israel, 216–17; League for Combating Zionism and, 4, 162, 164, 169; self-identification as, 2, 6; as teachers, 78; and travel, 48–49

Arab League, 171
Arab nationalism: anti-Jewish sentiment in, 6–7; education and, 78; Jews and, 3, 8, 10, 22, 25–26, 234; and Nazism/fascism, 8–9; and Ottoman empire, 10; secularization of history by, 27–28; and Semitic culture, 11–12. *See also* Iraqi nationalism; Patriotism
Arab Revolt, 13, 17–18, 26, 38
Arab revolt in Palestine, 14, 35–36, 103–5
Al-Arazi, Mahdi, 175
'Arif, Tahir Muhammad, 122–23
Aryanism, 12
Asad, Talal, 5
Ashkenazi Jews, 49, 204, 235. *See also* European Jews
Al-'Askrai, Ja'far, 39
Assa, Yerahmiel, 148
Assyrians, massacre of, 137
'Ayni, Khaduri, 67
Ayyub, Dhu Nun, 147, 264n12
'Azariya, Shelomo, 127
Al-'Azzawi, 'Abbas, 25, 77, 111, 247n109

Baban, Ahmad, 171
Babylon, 4, 44, 53–54, 76, 77, 163
Al-Badri, 'Abd al-Ghafur, 36
Baghdad: Benjamin of Tudela's travels and, 52–53; Farhud in, 101, 112–25; and formation of Iraq, 17; ICP in, 145–46; Jews in, 19, 20, 22, 193; leisure activities in, 61; schools in, 68, 70, 73
Balbul, Ya'qub, 24, 26, 30, 40–41, 64, 70, 93, 96, 111; "The Revolt of Ignorance," 30–32
Balfour Declaration, 165, 167
Balkans, 11
Ballas, Shim'on, 152, 178, 231, 232; "Iya," 223–25
Banks, 151
Bar-Moshe, Ishaq, 39, 71, 108, 159, 161, 176–77, 232; *The Exodus from Iraq*, 220–23
Al-Barrak, Fadhil, 141–42, 145, 146

Barshan, Gurji, 78–79, 115
Bash-A'yan, Ahmad, 126
Basim, Zaki, 143, 151, 156, 161, 267n60
Basra: Farhud in, 100–101; and formation of Iraq, 17; Jews in, 19, 192–93; schools in, 70; violence against Jews in, 125–28
Basri, Mir, 23, 24, 39, 44, 80, 108, 196, 217–18, 220, 230
Basri, Yusuf, 207
Al-Bassam, Sadiq, 187, 198, 218
Al-Basun, Salim, 36, 144, 244n22
Bata Shoe Store, 120, 151
Batatu, Hanna, 141, 145, 146, 151, 158, 178–80
Al-Ba'th (newspaper), 173
Ba'th Party, 220, 230
Battat, Reuben, 61, 190
Bechor, Ya'qub, 154
Bedouins, 30–31, 120
Begin, Menachem, 216
Bell, Gertrude, 37–38
Beney Berith, 62
Ben Gurion, David, 145, 192, 201, 216
Benjamin, Marcel, 190
Benjamin, 'Ozer, 190
Benjamin of Tudela, 47–56
Berg, Nancy, 241n12
Bergson, Henry, 64, 248n20
Bible, 52, 222
Bombings of Jewish centers (1950–1951), 206–8
Bonaparte, Napoleon, 50, 55
Boy Scouts, 73, 79–80
Britain: anti-Nazi actions of, 110; anti-Semitism in, 165; and Arab Revolt, 17; attitudes toward, 14, 21, 108, 113–15, 128; and Farhud, 117; ICP and, 143–44, 149, 168; involvement of, in Iraq, 2, 17–19, 36, 43–44, 80, 97–98, 112–15, 125–26; Iraqi Jews protected by, 104–5; Iraqi Jews' relations with, 135; League for Combating Zionism and, 170; and Palestine, 34–36, 103–4, 172, 185; and Zionism, 164–66

British Broadcasting Corporation (BBC), 9, 110, 114
Brotman, Adolph, 80–81, 82, 97–98
Brotman, Mrs. (teacher), 86
Brubaker, Rogers, 2
Al-Burhan (newspaper), 26, 43–44, 62–66, 90–92
Al-Bustani, Butrus, 73
Butrus, Emanuel bin, 273n188
Butti, Rafa'il, 25, 60

Capitalism, 163
Carroll, Lewis, 81
Cells, communist party, 152
Chadirchi, Kamil, 105
Chakrabarty, Dipesh, 6
Chatterjee, Partha, 5
Children's literature, 23
Christian intellectuals, 11
Christianity, 51
Class struggle, Jewish role in, 163–64, 173–74
Cohen, Haim, 184
Cohen, Jonah, 45, 75–77, 81, 83, 191
Cohen, Ya'qub, 45, 162, 171, 264n12, 266n42, 267n60
Colonialism, 34, 36
Committee for the Defense of Palestine, 103, 104
Communism. See Iraqi Communist Party
Comte, Auguste, 59
Congress faction, 264n12
Constitution, Iraqi, 38, 59
Constitutional revolution (1908), 17, 81, 21
Conversions, 35, 63, 73, 94
Cornwallis, Kinahan, 102, 131
Corruption, 66, 206
Cultural Jewish Society, 61

Dallal, Da'ud, 150
Dallal, Shelomo Sasun [Sassoon], 94, 141, 149, 150, 154, 158–61, 179

Al-Damir (newspaper), 170
Dangur, Reene, 229
Daniel, Ezra Menahem, 21, 55, 61, 185, 195, 202, 205, 207, 219, 220, 227
Daniel, Menahem Salih, 21, 86–87
Dar al-hikma, 154, 169
Darwish, Allen Yusuf Ya'qub, 94–95
Darwish, Esther, 209
Darwish, Mahmud, 231
Darwish, Salman, 23, 36
Darwish, Shalom, 24, 30, 39, 40, 45–46, 70, 79, 92, 107, 116, 144; "In the Year 2541," 95–96; "The Liberation of a Slave," 32–33
Davar (newspaper), 216
Davis, Eric, 7
Denationalization law, 191, 194, 200, 207, 215, 218, 219, 228
Denominational schools, 69, 71
Department of Civil Aviation, 188
Devash, Isaac, 82
Dickens, Charles, 81
Al-Dik, Shafiq Hasan, 197
Directorate General of Ports, 188
Directorate General of Posts, 188
Dir Yasin massacre, 186
Diwaniyya, 128
Dulaimi, Naziha, 94

Eastern Jews/Jews of the East, 25, 48–49, 216, 171, 234
Economic Class (library), 61
Economy, Jewish role in, 20, 60, 107, 138, 163, 186, 193, 195–96, 199–200, 208
Edmonds, C. J., 104
Effendia (middle class), 58–99; education, 67–84; leisure of, 60–61; and national ideology, 7–8; political involvement of, 18; secularism debates, 62–67; women, 84–97
Egypt, 62, 111
Einstein, Albert, 63
Elisar, Eliyahu ben, 202

Elites, Iraqi: anti-democratic stance of, 22, 139; anti-Jewish sentiment of, 13, 227, 228; Britain and, 144, 227; communism and, 14, 142, 143, 147, 167; fascist and Nazi sympathies of, 8; Jewish sympathizers among, 214; liberal views of, 105; and Zionism, 235
Employment: in government service, 20, 21, 38, 43–44, 60, 187–88, 196, 215, 219–20; women and, 88
English language, 67, 68, 71, 73, 72, 80–81, 83, 85, 86, 87, 91, 164, 171, 250–51n89
Enlightenment, 80
Epstein, Eliyahu, 105, 118, 121, 136
Equality, 28, 39, 148–49
Ethiopia, 9, 63, 106, 107
Ethnic cleansing, 228
Ethnicization, 2, 3
Eugenics, 90
Europe, criticisms of, 11
European Jews: Eastern Jews denigrated by, 166; emigration to Israel of, 204; Iraqi Jews compared to, 4–5, 25, 56, 62, 180, 211–12; persecution of, 48–49, 56, 107, 163; travels of, 48; vocabulary of, 210
Exile, 209–13
Ezekiel, 44
Ezer, Eliyahu, 148
Ezra, Me'ir, 82
Ezra-Ezer, Madeline Mir, 94

Fahd. *See* Yusuf, Yusuf Salman "Fahd"
Fahmi, Mahmud, 112
Al-Fajr al-Jadid (journal), 170
Faluja, 114
Family, ICP membership within, 150
Farhud, 112–25; context of, 112–15; deaths of rioters during, 121; defensive tactics during, 124; events of, 116–25; impact of, 138–39, 211–12; individuals behind, 115–16, 177, 200; looting during, 101, 117–21; Muslim protectors during, 101–2, 122–25; Pan-Arabism and, 45, 57; perpetrators of, 117–21; personal account of, 100–101; police actions during, 117–19; responses to, 22, 130–38, 203; women's response to, 89; and Zionism, 7, 12, 121, 136–38, 184
Fascism, 8–9, 45, 107–8. *See also* Nazism
Al-Fatat (journal), 88
Fattal, Salim, 141, 152–53, 178, 265n31
Faysal I, king of Iraq, 2, 17–18, 37–40, 84, 103
Faysal II, king of Iraq, 18–19
Field trips, 75–76
Films, pro-German, 106, 108
Ford, Henry, 165
Ford Motor Company, 188
Foreign language instruction, 80–81, 85
France, 17
Frank 'Ayni (school), 87–88
Freedom of religion, 59
Free verse, 23–24
French language, 68, 80–81
French Revolution, 163
Friendship, 4, 84, 102, 122, 133, 152, 157, 190, 221, 227, 237
Al-Futuwwa, 79–80, 106, 113, 128, 130

Gat, Moshe, 184
Germany: Iraq and, 8–9, 105–6; modernization of, 106; opposition to, 110–11; propaganda of, 105–6, 108–10, 114, 130
Gershoni, Israel, 8
Ghanima, Yusuf, 110, 218, 221
Ghazi, king of Iraq, 18, 70
Ghazi, Prince, 39
Ghettos, 210
God, 33
Golani, Gideon, 209
Goldberg, Reuben, 82
Greece, 132
Grobba, Fritz, 106, 108–10, 130, 139
Gurji, Obadiah, 119
Gutman, Shemaryahu, 203

Ha-Aretz (newspaper), 136, 216
Habibi, Emile, 231
Hadassa, 62
Haddad, Ezra, 35–36, 46, 47–56, 65, 68, 72–73, 82, 105, 107, 134, 189, 194, 225, 234, 247n99; "To the Freedom Fighters," 212
Haddad, Sha'ul, 26, 79
Hadyarkhana Mosque, 46
Haim, Abraham (Ibrahim), 61, 87, 190, 219
Haim, Amal, 87–88
Haim, Rabbi Yosef, 20
Haim, Sylvia, 115, 189, 220
Al-Hajj, 'Aziz, 152, 158
Hakham, Moshe, 232
Hakham, Rachel, 89
Hakham-bashi, 65, 127
Al-Hamawi, Yaqut, 53
Hammurabi, 76
Al-Hanafi, Jalal, 133
Haqqaq, Naji, 119
Hashemite monarchy, 25, 26, 38, 39, 69, 79, 96, 236
Hashim, house of, 17–18
Al-Hashimi, Muhammad, 29
Al-Hasid (journal), 24–29, 42–43, 64–66, 74, 88, 107–8, 111
Al-Hatif (journal), 24, 111, 205
Al-Hawadith (newspaper), 200, 205, 215–18
Haydarkhane Mosque, Baghdad, 34
Ha-Zofeh (newspaper), 216
Hebrew language, 20, 81, 202, 231
Hebrew Literary Society, 202
Herut (newspaper), 216
Herut Party, 216
Herzl, Theodor, 164
Hesqel, Sasun, 21
Al-Hilal (journal), 11, 110
Hilla, 19, 128, 203
Hillel, Shelomo, 191–92
Al-Hilli, Safi al-Din, 39
Histadrut, 145

Historiography: about Iraqi Jews, 6–9; Iraqi, 101; recent approaches to, 230, 233; Zionist, 6, 49, 51, 56, 102, 241n12
History: Haddad's edition of Benjamin of Tudela's travels and, 47–56, 247n99; Iraqi Jews' sense of, 25–27, 44–45; Jewish sense of, 49, 211–12; pedagogy for, 251n73
Hitler, Adolf, 116; *Mein Kampf*, 106, 139
Hizb al-taharrur (Liberation Party), 169, 172, 173, 174
Holidays, 211, 212
Holocaust, 56, 102, 165, 184, 204, 212
Honor killings, 33, 93
Hotzin, Rabbi Shelomo Bekhor, 20, 21
Hugo, Victor, 80
Human rights, 174
Hungary, 204
Hunger strikes, 157
Huri, Eliyahu, 150
Huri, Moshe, 148, 150
Husayn, Sherif, 26
Husayn, Taha, 23, 25, 59; *Al-Ayyam*, 244n18
Al-Husayni, 'Abd al-Qadir, 186
Al-Husayni, Hajj Amin, 103–6, 113, 129, 130, 132, 139–40, 177
Al-Husayni, Jamal, 171
Al-Husri, Sati', 25, 43, 72, 234
Hussein (Muhammad's grandson), 75

'Ibn Abd Rabbihi, 53
Ibn Hawqal, 48
Ibn Jubayr, 48
Ibn al-Muqaffa', 24
Ibrahim, 'Abd al-Fattah, 222
Ibrahim, Estherina, 40, 88, 92–93
Ibrahim, Hafiz, 23
Ibrahim, Suhil, 244n22
ICP. *See* Iraqi Communist Party
'Inbar, Sulayman, 21
Intellectuals. *See* Arab intellectuals; Christian intellectuals; Iraqi intellectuals; Jewish intellectuals
Iran, 62, 190–91, 206

Iraq: Benjamin of Tudela's travels and, 52–53; colonialism and, 2, 17–19, 34; constitution of, 38, 59; demographics of, 16; government employment in, 20, 21, 38, 43–44, 60, 187–88, 196, 215, 219–20; history of, 2; and ICP, 143, 155, 160; identities in, 7, 16; Iraqi Jews in relation to, 6, 19–22, 37–47, 56–57, 83, 124–25, 155, 161, 183–228, 230; Islam as official religion of, 59; Israel's war with (1948), 184, 186, 212–13, 218; and League for Combating Zionism, 167, 168, 174–77, 182; parliament of, 218; response of, to Farhud, 130–34; revival of, 26–27; rise of state in, 17–22; senate of, 218; social critique of, 208–9, 213–14; women's role in, 92–93; and Zionism, 184–85, 187–90, 204–5, 207, 235

Iraqi Communist Party (ICP), 141–82; anti-British stance of, 143–44, 149, 168; anti-fascism of, 9; anti-Nazism of, 111, 143, 147; anti-Semitism opposed by, 147–48; attitudes toward, 13–14; formation of, 18; and Iraqi nationalism, 45; Jews and, 8, 13–14, 141–42, 144–61, 178–82; and Kaylani coup, 115; and League for Combating Zionism, 167–79; membership of, 45, 144, 146, 265n19, 265n23, 265n24, 268n76; message of, 143; motivations for joining, 146–49; origins of, 142–43; power of, 19; prison activities concerning, 156–57; publications of, 154, 158, 159; significance of, 142, 231–32; splinter groups of, 145, 264n12; the state's relations with, 143, 155–56, 160; students/youth and, 83, 94, 145, 146, 151–52, 155, 180; and the Wathba, 149; and women, 85, 93–95, 156, 157; and Zionism, 144–46, 156–57, 162, 177–78, 198

Iraqi intellectuals: anti-Nazi, 111; attitudes of, toward the Jews, 110–11, 221–22; and Ottoman Empire, 17; Palestine supported by, 184. *See also* Jewish intellectuals

Iraqi Jews: acceptance of, in Iraqi society, 7; anti-colonialism of, 36; Arab affiliation of, 2–4, 6, 22–37, 56–57; attitudes toward, 8, 13–14, 214–25; British relations with, 135; conflicts or divisions among, 6, 22; critique of, 208–11, 226; and culture, 15–16; discrimination against, 83; Eastern affiliation of, 4–5; economic status of, 20, 136; education of, 67–84; emigration of, 13, 136–37, 148, 182, 183–84, 187, 190–93, 199–201, 203–4, 206–8, 219, 220, 228, 277n84; European Jews compared to, 4–5, 25, 56, 62, 180, 211–12; as exiles, 209–13; and the Farhud, 116–25, 134–36; geographical divisions of, 19–20; government service of, 20, 21, 38, 60, 187–88, 196, 215, 219–20; historiography of, 6–9; identity formation of, 2–6, 16–17, 56–57, 225, 234–35; Iraq as homeland of, 4–5; and Israel, 136, 201, 204–5, 217, 230–31; and Kaylani coup, 112–16; leadership of, 61, 65–66, 205–6, 219; Muslim protectors of, 101–2, 122–29, 139–40; and the nation-state, 6, 14, 19–22, 37–47, 56–57, 83, 124–25, 155, 161, 183–228, 230; persecution and difficulties of, 14, 185–202, 204–5; political involvement of, 45–46; population exchange involving, 199–200, 202, 217; population of, 22; recent history of, 229–37; religious identity of, 97–98; responses of, to anti-Semitism, 106–7; and secularism, 5; violence against, 100–105, 116–28; women's issues among, 84–97; and Zionism, 5–7, 12–13, 34–36, 102–3, 185–86, 201–14, 235

Iraqi law number 51, 155
Iraqi nationalism: and anti-Semitism, 102–11, 147–48, 194, 214; character of, 79; diversity within, 7, 16, 140; and Farhud, 101–2; Faysal I and, 38; Jewish role in, 15–16; Kaylani coup and, 112–16; tribal and religious values vs., 129; and Zionism, 13. *See also* Arab nationalism; Patriotism; Right-wing political groups
Iraqi Petroleum Company, 174
Iraqi State Railways, 188, 193, 196
Iraq Times (newspaper), 215
Al-'Irfan (journal), 25
Irgun, 137. *See also* Zionism: underground of
Al-'Is, Muhammad Husayn Abu, 168
Ishaq, Salim, 257n41
Islam: critiques of, 30–33; in educational curriculum, 72; Jews in relation to, 28–33, 46, 48, 54, 56; reform within, 28–29; as state religion, 59; tolerance within, 132, 139–40
Israel: Eastern Jews in, 216–17; economy of, 215; emigration to, 13, 136, 182, 183, 192; and Iraqi Jews, 136, 201, 204–5, 217, 230–31; Iraqi portrayals of, 198; in Iraqi press, 216–17; Iraq's war with (1948), 184, 186, 212–13, 218; living conditions in, 216–17; and separation of Arabs and Jews, 183; statehood of, 83, 148, 159, 178, 186; treatment of Palestinians by, 196–97; Zionism and, 184
Israel's Independence Day, 212
Al-Istiqlal (political party), 19, 148, 157, 177, 181, 194, 227, 234
Al-Istiqlal (newspaper), 35, 36
Italy, 8–9, 106, 107, 112, 163

Jabotinsky, Ze'ev, 104
Jabr, Salih, 190–91, 206, 218, 228
Al-Jahiz, 24
Jalak, Rafiq, 160

Al-Jamali, Fadhil, 219
Jankowski, James, 8
Japan, 8
Al-Jawahiri, Muhammad Mahdi, 77, 110–11, 147
Jawwad, Mustafa, 247n109
Jerusalem, 51
Jewish Clarion (newspaper), 171
Jewish intellectuals: Arab identification of, 2–3, 23–37, 57; and Aryan-Semitic dichotomy, 12; and modernity, 4–5; Palestine supported by, 12–13, 104–5; and secularism, 5, 58–62; and Wathba demonstrations, 47; and women, 89–90
Jewish mysticism, 50–51
Jewish National Fund, 190, 202
Jewish question/problem, 12–13, 162–63, 165, 167, 194
Jews. *See* Arab Jews; Ashkenazi Jews; European Jews; Iraqi Jews; Sephardic Jews
Jonah, 44
Jori Drug Store, 150
Jubrān, Jubran Khalil, 24
Judaism: criticisms of, 65–66; and education, 67–70; Iraqi Jews and, 97–98; Iraq's significance for, 44; leadership of, 61, 65–66, 82, 205–6, 219; skepticism about, 58; and women, 89–90; Zionism conflated with, 102–3, 155, 162, 165–66, 195, 201, 228
Judeo-Arabic language, 20, 21

Al-Kabir, Ibrahim, 21, 38, 89, 186
Al-Kabir, Rina, 89
Al-Kabir, Yusuf, 61, 205, 220
Kahila, Abraham, 120
Kalachi, Menashe, 128
Kalthum, Umm, 39
Karaites, 54, 235
Kashrut laws, 97
Kata'ib al-shabab, 113, 130
Al-Katib al-Misri (journal), 25

Kattan, Na'im, 44
Al-Kaylani, Rashid 'Ali, 19, 22, 101, 110, 112–16, 125–26, 129, 131, 134, 200
Kaylani coup, 79, 101, 112–16, 133
Kazzaz, Nissim, 6–7
Kedourie, Elie, 114, 117, 120, 121
Kedourie, Ezra, 203
Kedourie, Laura, 85
Kemalist movement, 27
Khaduri, Chief Rabbi Sasun, 35, 46, 65–66, 82, 116, 185, 186, 188, 197, 205–6, 219–20
Khalifa, Menashe, 148
Al-Khalili, Ja'far, 111
Al-Khalisi, Muhammad Mahdi, 197
Al-Khattab, 'Umar ibn, 53
Khayri, Zaki, 168
Khouri, Iliyas, *Bab al-Shams*, 232
Al-Khuri, Bishara, 25
Khusraw, Nasir, 48
Kilani, Kamil, 23, 251n59
Kol ha-'Am (newspaper), 170
Kosher meat, 66, 206
Kufa, 53
Ku Klux Klan, 62
Kurdish Jews, 217, 218–19
Kurdish language, 70
Kurdistan, 19–20
Kurds: attitudes toward, 13; in Iraq, 16–17; Palestinian exiles and, 105; Pan-Arabism and, 45
Kut jail, 156
Kuttabs, 68
Al-Kuwaiti, Da'ud, 229
Al-Kuwaiti, Salih, 229

Language(s): Arabic, 20–21, 23–24, 46, 49–56, 72–74, 81, 150, 231; in educational curriculum, 80–81, 85; English, 80–81; French, 68, 80–81; Hebrew, 20, 81, 202, 231; of Iraqi Jews, 20; Judeo-Arabic, 20, 21; Kurdish, 70; nationalism and, 4, 16; Turkish, 20–21, 81; Yiddish, 231

Lasky, Harold, 154
Laura Kedourie School, 85–87
League for Combating Illiteracy, 176
League for Combating Zionism: activities of, 171–74, 177; formation of, 161–62, 167; ICP and, 13, 167–79; Iraq's persecution of, 167, 168, 174–77, 182; Jews in, 13, 142, 146, 150, 169; membership of, 146, 169; opposition to, 172–73; and Palestine, 162, 173; popularity of, 13, 169; publications of, 151; self-presentation of, 169–71
League of Nations, 2, 18, 35
Leblanc, Maurice, *Arsène Lupin*, 244n18
Left, the, 19, 45, 180, 213–14
Leisure activities, 60–61
Lenin, Vladimir, 154, 160
Lev, Ilan, 213
Levy, Gurji, 108, 185
Liberation Party. *See* Hizb al-taharrur
Libraries, 61, 73, 250n58
Literacy, 154
Literary activities, 24–25
Literary salons, 93
Looting, 101, 117–21, 125–26
Lot, 51–52
Lughtat al-'Arab (journal), 73
Lulu (female student), 87–88

Al-Ma'arri, Abu al-'Ala, 23
Al-Mabda' (newspaper), 45
Mack, Henry, 199
Al-Madfa'i, Jamil, 130, 133
Madi, Iliya Abu, 24
Magnes, Judah Leon, 185
Mahfuz, Nagib, 232
Al-Majalla (journal), 147, 151
Al-Mallah, Mahmud, 77
Al-Mansur, Abu Ja'far, 54
Mao Zedong, 160
MAPAI (Mifleget po'aley eretz Israel; political party), 137
Maqsud, Qasim, 128–29

Marriage, 89–91
Marx, Karl, 59, 160
Mash'al, Menashe, 195
Mash'al, Sa'ida, 94
Al-Masrhiq (journal), 73
Masri, 'Amuma, 94, 95
Masri, Ya'qub Mir, 146, 147, 151, 154, 158, 162, 168, 169, 175–76
Mas'uda Shemtove Synagogue, 207
Matba'at al-Rashid, 74
Maude, Frederick Stanley, 173
Al-Mazini, 'Abd al-Qadir, 25
Meccans, 31
Media, on Nazism/fascism, 9. *See also* Newspapers; Radio
Me'ir-Glitzenstein, Esther, 136, 184, 201, 243n32, 245n132, 263n158, 263n173, 264n174, 264n177, 274n2
Meir, Golda, 216
Me'ir, Yosef, 141, 145, 158, 169
Menashe, Albertine, 94
Menashe, Salim, 161, 168
Menashe, Sha'ul, 100–101
Michael, Sami, 151, 231
Midhat Pasha, 17
Middle class. *See* Effendia
Middle East Journal, 200
Midrash Talmud Torah (school), 68, 73
Mikha'il, Murad, 24, 30, 110
Mikha'il, Sami, 273n188
Ministry of Defense, 188
Ministry of Economics, 188
Ministry of Education, 69, 72, 77, 78, 80, 86, 188, 196–97
Ministry of Finance, 188
Ministry of Foreign Affairs, 188
Ministry of Interior, 188
Miqdadi, Darwish, 132
Al-Misbah (newspaper), 24, 26, 28, 34, 38, 39, 42, 61–63, 73, 90–91, 107, 110, 202
Mizrahi Jews, 49
Modernism, free verse movement in, 23–24
Modernity: attitudes toward, 3, 10; education and, 71–72, 80; middle class and, 7–8
Modernization, 17, 28, 106
Molière, 61
Molotov, Vyacheslav, 147
Montessori method, 86
Moreh, Shemu'el, 40, 232
Mosley, Oswald, 163
Mosul: British bombing of, 114; and formation of Iraq, 17; Jews in, 19, 128–29, 193–94; schools in, 70
Movement for Jewish Resistance, 203
Mu'allim, Eliyahu Khaduri, 74
Mu'allim, 'Izzat Sasun, 108
Mu'allim, Salman, 78
Mu'allim, Victor, 78
Mubarak, Zaki, 15, 25
Al-Mufti, Khalil Amin, 176
Al-Mufti, Ra'uf, 129
Muhammad (prophet), 31, 46
Mukhlis, Mawlud, 171
Mukmal, Salih Sasun, 109
Mukmal, Yusuf, 45, 244n22, 264n12
Al-Mulla, Miriam, 88, 92–93
Al-Muqtataf (journal), 11
Murad, Emile, 205
Murad, Hesqel, 108
Murad, Salima, 229
Musa, Salama, 59
Al-Musawwar (journal), 88
Muslim Young Men's Association, 106
Al-Mustaqbal (newspaper), 35
Al-Mutanabbi, Abu al-Tayyib, 23
Al-Mutawasita al-ahliyya li'l banat (school), 86
Al-Muthanna, 103, 104, 106, 111
Mysticism. *See* Jewish mysticism

Nadhami, 'Umar, 220
Nahda: characteristics of, 10; in Iraq, 26–27; Jews and, 10–11, 25–27
Al-Nahda (newspaper), 194, 215
Nakkash, Samir, 232
Nasif, Khalil bin, 273n188

National Democratic Party (NDP; al-Hizb al-watani al-dimukrati), 19, 45, 144, 148, 157
Nationalism: language and, 4, 16; Pan-Arab, 7, 16; and sectarianism, 63; territorial-patriotic, 16; tribal and religious values vs., 129. *See also* Arab nationalism; Iraqi nationalism; Right-wing political groups
Nazism: Arab nationalism and, 8–9; opposition to, 107–11, 131–32, 143, 147; Palestinian support for, 104; and persecution of Jews, 107, 163
NDP. *See* National Democratic Party
Newspapers, 24–25, 214–18. *See also specific titles*
Newton, Basil, 110
Nietzsche, Friedrich, 64
Night schools, 78
Nissim, Fahima Mu'allim, 78, 88
Nissim, Shim'on Mu'allim, 71, 90; *Letters Before Marriage*, 90
No'am school, 86, 87
Nonsectarianism, 60, 78, 94, 96, 149, 151, 181–82. *See also* Sectarianism
Nordbruch, Götz, 8
Nuqrat al-Salman prison, 156, 157
Nur'el, No'am, 86
Nur'el, Tova, 86

Obadiah, Ibrahim, 25, 30, 41–42, 232; "In the Memory of the Great Arab Revival," 26; "My Country," 41; "Palestine and Colonialism," 36
Ottoman empire, 4, 10, 11, 17, 28, 65

Al-Pachachi, Hamdi, 171
Al-Pachachi, Muzahim, 187, 200, 218
Palestine: Arab revolt in, 14, 35–36, 103–5; Benjamin of Tudela's travels and, 51; Britain and, 34–36, 103–4, 172, 185; independence for, 166; Iraqi intellectuals' support for, 184; Iraqi Jews and, 12–13, 34–36, 47, 103–5, 136–38, 147–48, 186, 199–200; labor market in, 145; League for Combating Zionism and, 162, 173; Pan-Arabism and, 34; partition of, 178, 186; population exchange involving, 199–200, 202, 217; refugees from, 193, 197, 199–202; Zionism and, 164–65
Pan-Arabism: defined, 16; education and, 79; Faysal and, 103; ICP criticisms of, 181; Iraqi Jews and, 36; Iraqi left and, 45; Jewish resistance to, 45, 57; and Palestine, 34; and political opposition, 19; pro-German sentiment and, 147; Wathba demonstrations and, 46
Pan-Islamism, 11
Paramilitary youth organizations, 79, 106, 113, 116, 128, 130
Parliament, Iraqi, 218
Patriotism, 41–43, 45–47, 56–57. *See also* Arab nationalism; Iraqi nationalism
People, the (political party). *See* Al-Ahali (political party)
Philanthropy, 89, 253n117
Physical education, 79
Pluralism, 236–37
Poland, 204
Population exchange, 199–200, 202, 217
Porat, Mordechi Ben, 122–23, 125
Porat, Violet Ben, 210
Port Authority, 196
Portsmouth Treaty, 198
Press, the. *See* Newspapers
Progress Library, 61
Proletariat, 13
Public schools, 75
Public sphere, 18, 40, 142, 181, 193, 197, 199
Public Works Department, 188

Al-Qadiri, Rasul, 107
Al-Qa'ida (newspaper), 151, 154, 158, 159, 169
Al-Qarini, Abdallah, 264n12

Qasim, 'Abd al-Karim, 230
Qasim, Yahya, 215
Qattan, 'Aliza, 212
Qattan, Masur, 162, 167, 175–76
Qattan family, 127
Al-Qazwini, Mirza al-Sayyid, 76, 77, 128
Qishtanyni, Naji, 174
Qujman, Hesqel, 150
Qujman, Ya'qub, 150
Qur'an, 29, 31–32, 46, 50, 52, 72–73, 222, 225, 234
Al-Quwatli, Shukri, 171

Rabbis: criticisms of, 29; leadership of, 61, 65–66, 82, 205–6; progressive, 65; and women's issues, 85, 90
Rachel Shahmon (school), 39, 71, 77, 78, 81, 252n97
Al-Radini, Sayyid Muhammad Salih, 127
Radio, 113–14
Radio Baghdad, 113–14
Al-Rawi, Jamil, 133
Red Crescent, 113, 115
Reform, 3, 17, 19, 20, 28–29, 37, 60, 62, 63–64, 66, 67, 85, 98, 110; under Bakr Sidqi, 105; of Germany under Nazi rule, 106; of Jewish education, 70; of Jewish women's status, 3, 90–91
Religion: criticisms of, 29, 63–66; education and, 59, 69, 71; freedom of, 59; as private, 63. *See also* Islam; Judaism
Al-Rida Sadiq, 'Abd, 77
Right-wing political groups, 147–49, 180–81, 183–84, 192–94, 208. *See also* Iraqi nationalism
Al-Risala (journal), 25, 111
Romania, 204
Rosenthal (Jewish doctor), 109
Rousseau, Jean-Jacques, 80
Al-Rumi, Ibrahim, 129
Al-Rusafi, Ma'ruf, 23, 24, 25, 29, 43, 84, 110
Rushdie, Salman, 32

Al-Sab'awi, Yunis, 106, 113, 115–16, 130, 131, 139
Al-Sabbagh, Salah al-Din, 112
Sabbath laws, 65, 68, 82, 97–98
Sadiq, Hesqel, 158
Sadiq, Yehuda, 141, 150, 154, 158, 160–61, 169, 171, 179, 182, 267n60, 269n89
Al-Sadr, Muhammad, 186–87
Al-Safwani, Salman, 194, 196
Sa'id, Fahmi, 112
Al-Sa'id, Nuri, 14, 112, 115, 133, 161, 171, 185, 187, 190, 192, 198, 199, 208, 218, 219, 227, 277n84
Saladin (Salah al-Din al-Ayyubi), 50, 61
Salih, Menashe, 86
Salman, Na'im, 154
Salman, Sa'ida, 94
Salton-Zilkha, Evelyn, 209
Al-Sam'ani, Tawfiq, 217
Samara, Da'ud, 38
Al-Samara'i, Fa'iq, 195
Samaritans, 54
Al-Samaw'al ibn 'Adiya, 1
Samuel, Edwin, 200
Samuel, Herbert, 200
Al-Sanhuri, 'Abd al-Razzak, 25
Sarraf family, 127
Sasson (Sasun), Eliyahu, 133, 169
Sasun Dallal. *See* Dallal, Shelomo Sasun [Sassoon]
Sasun-Mu'allim family, 128
Sausman (Jewish doctor), 109
Sawt al-Ahali (newspaper), 205, 214–15
Sawt al-Haqq (newspaper), 131–32
Al-Sayyab, Badr Shakir, 172, 174
Sayyab family, 151
Al-Sayyid, Mahmud Ahmad, 25, 43
Sayyif, Malik, 150, 158, 182
Schechtman, Joseph, 200
Secret Encyclopedia Concerning the Iraqi Communist Party, A, 145
Sectarianism, 63, 78–79, 139, 236. *See also* Nonsectarianism
Secularism: Arabization in relation to, 98;

Arab nationalism and, 27–28; debates over, 62–67; education and, 68, 81–83; Jewish intellectuals and, 5, 58–62; significance of, 236; women and, 93
Sehayek, Maliha, 24, 25, 88–89, 93
Sehayek, Ya'qub Ephraim, 150, 156, 162, 267n60
Semah, David, *Until Spring Comes*, 232
Semah, Sasson, 218–19
Semitic culture and languages, 11–12, 139
Senate, Iraqi, 218
Sephardic Jews, 204. *See also* Arab Jews
Sepphoris, 52
Sereni, Enzo, 136, 144, 148, 203, 263n171
Sha'ar ha-'aliya camp, 217
Al-Sha'b (newspaper), 151, 162, 167, 200, 205, 214–15, 217
Shabib, Kamal, 112
Al-Shabibi, Muhammad Husayn, 143, 151, 156, 161
Al-Shabibi, Muhammad Rida, 25
Al-Shahrastani, Hibat al-Din, 111
Shakespeare, William, 61, 74; *The Merchant of Venice*, 107
Shalom, Salih, 207
Shammash (high school), 77, 80–81, 84, 86, 87, 202, 254n135
Al-Sharara (newspaper), 144, 154
Sharara, Muhammad, 77
Sharet, Moshe, 136–37, 201
Sharif, 'Abd al-Rahim, 221–22
Sharif, 'Aziz, 175
Sha'ul, Anwar, 1, 24, 25, 26, 28–29, 30, 34, 40, 43, 44, 63, 65–67, 80, 87–88, 92, 107, 110, 220, 230, 232, 234; "The National Sentiment," 42
Sha'ul, Ya'qub, 244n22
Shawkat, Sa'ib, 104, 106, 109, 124
Shawkat, Sami, 91, 106, 139
Shawqi, Ahmad, 23
Al-Sheikh Da'ud, Sabiha, 78
Al-Sheikh Da'ud, Salman, 66
Shemtov, Hesqel, 190, 206, 215
Shenhav, Yehouda, 184, 201, 241n12

Sheridan, Richard, *Wilhelm Tell*, 34
Sherifians, 13, 18, 19
Shiblak, Abbas, 184
Shi'is: attitudes toward, 13; and Kufa, 53; as majority in Iraq, 16
Shilon-Shlank, Me'ir, 169
Shina, Salamn, 34
Shina, Shelomo, 212
Shohat, Ella, 241n12
Shohet, Moshe, 190
Shrine of Ezekiel, 52
Shukr, Khaduri, 185
Shumail, Ibrahim Naji, 94–95, 150, 156, 162, 169, 264n12, 267n60
Sibawahi, 177
Sidqi, Bakr, 105, 112
Simhoni, Dafna, 204
Al-Siyasa (journal), 88
Smuggling, 206
Snir, Reuven, 7, 30
Social democrats: anti-fascism of, 9; anti-Nazism of, 111; Jews and, 8; and Palestine, 105
Socialism, 143, 144, 145, 164, 203, 209
Societies, cultural, 42–43, 61, 89
Society for the Protection of the Child, 42
Society for the Revival of Art, 43
Society of Exiled Academic Jews, 232
Society of Jewish Youth, 61
Sodom, 52
Sofer, Berta, 210
Sofer, Moshe, 78, 81–82, 202
Sofer family, 127
Somekh, 'Abdallah, 65
Somekh, Menashe, 144, 214–15, 244n22
Somekh, Rabbi 'Abdallah, 20
Somekh, Sasson, 24, 58, 81, 183, 225, 231, 232
Soviet Union (USSR): Jews' admiration of, 144, 146–47, 149, 180; Jews in, 157, 165; and Palestine, 178
Spencer, Herbert, 59
Spivak, Gayatri, 3–4
Stalin, Joseph, 147, 160, 170, 172, 178

Stonehewer-Bird (British ambassador), 168
Sufism, 30
Sulaimaniya, 70, 129
Sulayman, Hikmat, 105
Sunnis: and Kufa, 53; as minority in Iraq, 16; political dominance of, 18; and secularism, 5
Supreme Arab Committee (Palestine), 171
Al-Suri, Muhammad Hasan, 83
Susa, Nissim, 35, 63
Al-Suwaydi, Naji, 206
Al-Suwaydi, Tawfiq, 171, 190–91, 192, 198, 228
Swift, Jonathan, *Gulliver's Travels*, 81
Syria, 7, 79, 111, 152–53, 171

Al-Tafakkur (journal), 21
Talmud, 38, 44, 53, 213
Teacher instruction, 72
Teachers: Arab Iraqi nationalism imparted by, 77–78; ethnicity of, 70–71, 77–78; politics involving, 83–84, 130, 131, 133, 186, 196, 202; quality of, 72; women as, 88
Teachers Club, 42
Teachers Training College, 15, 25, 78, 152, 196
Temple Mount, 48
Territorial-patriotic identity, 16
Terrorism, 104, 159, 160
Al-Thaqaqfa (journal), 25
Al-Tharaya (journal), 25
Theosophy, 67, 248n30
Timman, Ja'far Abu, 45, 105
Tolerance, 28, 48–49, 54, 56, 132, 236–37
Torah, 48, 50, 52
Tribal peoples, 30–31, 128–30
Turkey, 27, 62
Turkish language, 20–21, 81
Turkmen: in Iraq, 16–17; Pan-Arabism and, 45
Tweig, Na'im, 45, 144, 147, 244n22
Tweig, Rina, 88

Tweig, Sha'ul, 173
Twena, Avraham, 67–68, 120, 122

Uganda, 165
Al-'Umar, Ibrahim Hilmi, 66
Al-'Umari, Arshad, 112, 115–16, 198
Al-'Umari, Murad, 45, 144, 244n22
Um Durman (newspaper), 170
Al-Umma (newspaper), 205
United Nations, 172, 178, 186, 201
United States: anti-Semitism in, 165; and Israel, 215; and Palestine, 172
Al-'Usba (newspaper), 168, 171–72, 174–75
USSR. *See* Soviet Union
Ustaz, 68

Vocational education, 86–87
Voltaire, 80

Wahdat al-nidal (communist group), 162, 264n12
Al-Wahhab, 'Abd, 39
Wahhabis, 54
Wandering Jew, 48, 49, 56
Al-Wardi, 'Ali, 60
Al-Watan (newspaper), 151, 222
Al-Wataniyya (school), 39, 71, 73, 82
Wathba, 14, 19, 45–46, 142, 143, 149, 154, 155, 158, 160, 198, 226, 232
Weizmann, Chaim, 165, 185
Western culture, 81
Al-Witri, Akram, 183, 225
Women: clothing of, 89; conferences on, 93; education of, 85–88, 91; employment of, 88; ICP and, 85, 93–95, 156, 157; issues for Jewish and Iraqi, 84–97; Jewish middle-class, 209; liberation of, 84, 91, 209; and marriage, 89–91; and philanthropy, 89, 253n117; and politics, 93–97; in prison, 156, 157; rights of, 84, 91, 95–96, 209; role of, in nation-state, 92–93; and secularism, 93; and Zionism, 205, 209, 279n123

World War I, 17
World War II, 111, 112
Writers, 24–25

Yad Va-Shem, Jerusalem, 102
Al-Yaqdha (newspaper), 173, 194–97, 205, 214–15, 218, 221, 227
Ya'qub, Moshe, 162
Al-Ya'qubi, 48, 53
Yaron, Avner Ya'qov, 120, 123
Yatah, Moshe, 137
Yazan, Sayif bin, 88
Yehuda, Nisim Hesqel, 162
Yiddish, 231
Yishuv, 136, 202
Yizkor, 211
Young Jews Association, 34
Young Pioneer, 203
Young Turks, 81
Youth: and communism, 83, 94, 145, 146, 151–52, 155–56, 180; leisure activities of, 27, 61; Pan-Arabism among, 105; patriotism of, 42; pro-German sentiment among, 105; responses of, to the Farhud, 135, 138, 203; and Zionism, 12, 22, 180, 183, 203, 205, 208–11, 213. *See also* Education; Paramilitary youth organizations
Youth to the Rescue, 134–35
Yusuf, Yusuf Salman "Fahd," 143, 151, 153–54, 156, 158–61, 171, 173, 178, 267n60

Zachariah, Me'ir, 79
Al-Zahawi, Jamil Sidqi, 23, 25, 84
Za'im, Husni, 152
Zaluf, Menashe, 169, 171
Zaluf, Yusuf, 154

Al-Zaman (newspaper), 200, 205, 215–18
Zangwill, Israel, 165
Za'rur, Menashe, 36, 244n22
Zaydan, Jurji, 73
Al-Zayyat, Ahmad Hasan, 25
Zilkha, Na'im, 66–67
Zilkha, Rachel, 94
Zilkha, Yusuf Harun, 147, 168, 171–72, 174, 177, 264n12, 267n60; *Zionism: The Enemy of Arabs and Jews*, 156, 162–67
Zionism: anti-Arab sentiments of, 137; Britain and, 164–66; critiques of, 164; education and, 78; and the Farhud, 7, 12, 121, 136–38; historiography of, 6, 49, 51, 56, 102, 241n12; ICP and, 144–46, 156–57, 162, 177–78, 198; impact of, 12–13, 102–3, 202–14, 226–27, 241n12; Iraq and, 184–85, 187–90, 204–5, 207, 235; Iraqi Jews and, 5–7, 12–13, 34–36, 102–3, 185–86, 201–14, 235; Iraqis' opposition to, 103; Jewish opposition to, 165–66; Judaism conflated with, 102–3, 155, 162, 165–66, 195, 201, 228; *Al-Misbah* and, 34; and Palestine, 164–65; pre-1947 role of, 5–7, 34–36, 202–4, 226; principles of, 184; and renaming, 211; self-defense organization of, 203, 204; underground of, 6, 137, 142, 184, 187, 204, 206, 207, 231; women and, 205, 209, 279n123; youth and, 12, 22, 180, 183, 203, 205, 208–11, 213. *See also* League for Combating Zionism
Zionist Foundation of Aram Naharyarim, 202
Ziyad, Tawfiq, 232
Zu'aytar, Akram, 132
Zubaida, Sami, 7, 83–84

The authorized representative in the EU for product safety and compliance is:
Mare Nostrum Group
B.V Doelen 72
4831 GR Breda
The Netherlands

www.ingramcontent.com/pod-product-compliance
Lightning Source LLC
Chambersburg PA
CBHW031757220426
43662CB00007B/437